LINCOLN IN THE WORLD

LINCOLN IN THE WORLD

The Making of a Statesman

AND THE

Dawn of American Power

KEVIN PERAINO

CROWN PUBLISHERS   NEW YORK

Library of Congress Cataloging-in-Publication Data
Peraino, Kevin.
    Lincoln in the world : the making of a statesman and the
dawn of American power / Kevin Peraino.—First edition.
        pages   cm
    Includes bibliographical references.
    1. United States—Foreign relations—1861–1865. 2. Lincoln,
Abraham, 1809–1865. I. Title.
    E469.P47   2013
    973.7092—dc23   2013022550

ISBN 978-0-307-88720-7
eISBN 978-0-307-88722-1

Printed in the United States of America

Jacket design by Christopher Brand
Jacket images: John Parrot/Stocktrec Images/Getty Images

CREDITS FOR PHOTO INSERT
Library of Congress: pages 1, 2 (bottom), 3, 4, 7, 8 (top right and bottom).
Abraham Lincoln Presidential Library and Museum: page 2 (top).
Massachusetts Historical Society: page 5 (top).
International Institute of Social History: page 5 (bottom).
Getty Images: page 6.
Brown University Library: page 8 (top left).

10 9 8 7 6 5 4 3 2 1

First Edition

To my parents,

Sam and Donna Peraino

If we remain one people, under an efficient government, the period is not far off when we may defy material injury from external annoyance; when we may take such an attitude as will cause the neutrality we may at any time resolve upon to be scrupulously respected; when belligerent nations, under the impossibility of making acquisitions upon us, will not lightly hazard the giving us provocation; when we may choose peace or war, as our interest guided by justice shall counsel.

—GEORGE WASHINGTON, *1796*

Westward the star of empire takes its way;
The girls link-on to Lincoln, as their mothers did to Clay.

—LINCOLN CAMPAIGN BANNER, *1858*

Contents

LINCOLN IN THE WORLD

Prologue

IN THE COLD, DIM BALCONY OF FORD'S THEATRE, MARY LINCOLN
RESTED A HAND ON HER HUSBAND'S KNEE, THEN HUDDLED
CLOSER TO HIS SIDE. SHE WAS NOT ALWAYS SUCH A TENDER WIFE.
During spells of anger, she had been known to batter her husband
with broomsticks, books, timber, and "very poorly pitched pota-
toes"—at least once drawing blood from his nose. Mary, whom a
White House secretary had nicknamed Hellcat, was at her worst
when she felt trapped. The sight of transatlantic steamers preparing
to cross the ocean could touch off a storm of self-pity. "How I long
to go to Europe," she would complain. Mary mercilessly taunted her
husband that for her next marriage, she would make sure to choose a
man who could afford the price of passage.[1]

Mary might not have considered her husband wealthy, but tonight—finally—she could not deny that he was powerful. When
the couple had entered the theater, a half hour late, the entire performance came to a halt. The orchestra brayed "Hail to the Chief"
over the unyielding roar of the crowd. The First Lady, battling a
headache, had not wanted to go out at all. The president, too, appeared stooped, exhausted, and sad. Actually, though, Lincoln had
good news for his wife. They would finally travel to Europe. When
his term was over, he told Mary, he wanted to do some exploring, to

go "abroad among strangers." The couple would spend time "moving and travelling," he promised.[2]

Mary had always been the more cosmopolitan of the two. As a girl in Lexington, Kentucky, she had attended a boarding school where students spoke French, run by Parisian aristocrats who had fled the Reign of Terror. The great American diplomat Henry Clay was a neighbor and close family friend; a young Mary once stopped by his estate to parade her new pony. As an adult, there was something slightly pathetic about her pining. A White House staff member complained that the First Lady put on "the airs of an Empress." Her affectations grated on Lincoln's diplomats. She overused the word *sir*—"as if you were a royal personage," one of them griped. When asked if she spoke French, the First Lady replied: "Très poo."[3]

Mary was like a "toothache," Lincoln's law partner once remarked, keeping her husband "awake night and day" to political opportunities. When it came to foreign affairs, however, Lincoln had become his own man. The Illinoisan had been telling friends for years that he wanted to visit Britain, the land of his forebears and his favorite writers, Shakespeare, Byron, and Burns. As the Civil War erupted and intensified, the president repeatedly underlined the conflict's global importance, arguing that "the central idea" behind the Union effort was to prove to the world "that popular government is not an absurdity." He had long since come to terms with America's rise to power. "We are a great empire," he told a Michigan crowd as early as 1856. "We stand at once the wonder and admiration of the whole world."[4]

Now America's army had grown to the largest on the planet, and its massive new navy threatened the Continent's outdated fleets. Hyperventilating European newspaper correspondents worried that the American president might send "a fleet of gunboats sailing up the Seine" or his million-man army marching through Hyde Park. At the start of the Civil War, cartoons in Britain's popular *Punch* magazine had portrayed Lincoln as a "silly-faced" buffoon. By the end, the magazine's depictions of the American president "bore the stamp of despotic ferocity."[5]

As Lincoln sat in the dark of the theater, his ambitious wife gripping his hand, the night's entertainment must have seemed somehow appropriate. The play, a lighthearted tale of an American trying to collect his inheritance in Europe, had the audience in hysterics. And then, in an instant, the laughter ended and the screaming began. Mary Lincoln saw the sickening flash accompanied by the report of a pistol. She felt a body dash past, brushing against her shawl, and watched her husband's head slump onto his chest. In another moment a distant voice cried out, "Thus ever to tyrants!" in a foreign tongue from ages past.[6]

Abraham Lincoln is not often remembered as a great foreign-policy president.[7] He had never traveled overseas and had no personal friends in Europe. His upbringing in rural Kentucky and Indiana was so provincial that, when a stranger came to town who could speak a few words of Latin, he "was looked upon as a wizzard." As a rising politician he had studied just enough German to charm immigrant voters. As for French, the nineteenth-century language of diplomacy, he did not understand enough to read a menu. ("Hold on there," the Railsplitter once told a waiter in a New York French restaurant. "Beans. I know beans.") The Illinoisan's only pre-presidential brush with the diplomatic service came in 1841, when a friend tried to get him appointed chargé d'affaires in Colombia. Lincoln had been struggling with a bout of depression—he had gone "crazy as a *loon*," one acquaintance recalled—and his allies thought a change of scenery would do him good. The secretary of state, Daniel Webster, not surprisingly passed him over.[8]

In the White House, Lincoln's attempts at diplomatic finesse could seem comically inept. His efforts to bow elegantly to visiting diplomats were so "prodigiously violent" that they had "almost the effect of a smack" in their "rapidity and abruptness." On one occasion, receiving a delegation of Potawatomi Indians, Lincoln greeted his guests in broken English. "Where live now?" he asked, as his aides chortled. "When go back Iowa?" Foreign envoys accustomed to the refined rituals of European chancelleries were repelled. "His conversation consists of vulgar anecdotes at which he himself laughs uproariously," the Dutch minister complained. Even Lincoln's young son Tad noted that his father looked "pretty plain" compared to the European diplomats at one state dinner, who were "all tied up with gold cords" and "glittered grand." The president recognized his shortcomings. "I don't know anything about diplomacy," he told one foreign envoy. "I will be very apt to make blunders."[9]

Nor, at least at first glance, did the American president's foreign-policy team seem very promising. The tiny diplomatic corps in the midnineteenth century was still a dumping ground for political enemies and inconvenient radicals. "There is hardly a court in Europe which has not had some specimen of the American character in its worst form—a sot, or rake, or swindler," the *New York World* warned as Lincoln took office. Lincoln's choice for secretary of state, William Henry Seward, was actually a capable diplomat who had traveled widely. Yet he could also be vain and impetuous. He tended to drink heavily at dinner parties and issue idle threats of war from behind a cloud of cigar smoke. "When he was loaded," recalled the son of Lincoln's minister to Britain, "his tongue wagged."[10]

Lincoln's men in the field could be just as volatile. The president's personal secretary John Hay noted that while Lincoln's envoys were "generally men of ability," they were "not always of that particular style of education which fits men for diplomacy." At the American legation in Paris, "French is a language as unknown as Hottentot," Hay observed, adding acidly that the post's secretary "will have to postpone his French studies till he acquires enough English to enable him to make a decent appearance in society." Lincoln's minister in the French capital—"a gentleman not remarkable for his alertness or undeviating attention to the public business," in the words of one historian—ended up dying in the Paris apartment of "a woman not his wife," and his body had to be smuggled back to his home. Cassius Marcellus Clay, the president's fiery minister in Russia, was fond of walking around with three pistols and a dagger he called an "Arkansas toothpick" dangling from his waistband. Hay judged Clay to be "the most wonderful ass of the age." Lincoln acknowledged that his man in St. Petersburg possessed "a great deal of conceit and very little sense."[11]

And yet somehow Lincoln and his team managed to pull off one of the most breathtaking feats in the annals of American foreign policy: they avoided European intervention on behalf of the Confederacy, which could well have led to a Southern victory. European opinion about the conflict was diverse and nuanced, but plenty of aristocrats were content to watch the young republic founder. Even cold-eyed observers like the *Economist*'s Walter Bagehot, who ultimately expected the North to win, crowed that the war would leave the United States "less aggressive, less insolent, and less irritable." Amid such tension, even a small indignity could have sparked a devastating transatlantic conflict. "A single major mistake," notes one modern diplomatic scholar, "could have changed the course of the Civil War."[12]

The iconoclast H. L. Mencken once described Lincoln as "the American solar myth, the chief butt of American credulity and sentimentality . . . a mere moral apparition, a sort of amalgam of John Wesley and the Holy Ghost." This "plaster saint," Mencken insisted, was suited only "for adoration in the chautauquas and the Y.M.C.A.s." Many Americans share that view. All we really need to know about Lincoln, the thinking goes, we learned in kindergarten. "There can be no new 'Lincoln stories,'" one of the president's former secretaries wrote 115 years ago. "The stories are all told."[13]

And yet for all that has been written, Lincoln's life is only rarely examined against the backdrop of his own world. "We all need a course in Lincoln," observed former secretary of state Charles Evans Hughes. In the age of Lincoln, we see shadows of our modern global arena. The midnineteenth century was an era of brutal realism, the world stage dominated by powerful, self-interested warriors. Britain's foreign policy was directed by Lord Palmerston, its shrewd, ruthless prime minister. Dubbed Lord Pumicestone by the British press, Palmerston was perhaps best known for declaring that Britain had no eternal friends—only national interests. The continent's other leaders were no more charming. In Prussia, Otto von Bismarck saw Europe's future emerging from the interplay of "blood and iron." Foreign policy, he said, was "the art of the possible, the science of the relative." France's Napoleon III was less competent, but certainly not warm and fuzzy. Victor Hugo described the emperor as "a man of middle height, cold, pale, slow, who looks as if he were not quite awake . . . esteemed by women who want to become prostitutes and by men who want to become prefects."[14]

Lincoln, too, could be cold and ruthless. He was better suited to the age of great-power politics than might be assumed. A skilled chess player, he was steeped in the rational philosophy and political economy of Enlightenment thinkers, and as a young politician, he glorified "reason, cold, calculating, unimpassioned reason" as the only road to peace. Lincoln, said his former law partner, Billy Herndon, was "a realist as opposed to an idealist." He was temperamentally suited to view the world without illusion. The future president's mind "crushed the unreal, the inexact, the hollow, and the sham," Herndon recalled. "Everything came to him in its precise shape and color." Lincoln's whole life, said another old colleague, "was a calculation of the law of forces."[15]

Modern realists see strong similarities to our own times in the nineteenth-century age of the great powers. They argue that the post–Cold War notion that America is now the world's sole superpower is fundamentally flawed. Even before the recent credit crunch and stock market crash, Third World nations like China and India had been slowly eroding the relative power of the United States. In reality we will soon be, if we are not already, living in a multipolar world of competing nations with vastly divergent interests.

Such a world demands reasoned calculation, not self-righteous crusades. "For most of its history, the United States was in fact a nation among others, not a preponderant superpower," notes Henry Kissinger, a dean of the realist school. The era before the "American Century," he has argued, may well be a more accurate predictor of what is to come.[16]

And yet, like ours, the nineteenth century was also an information age, an era of rapid liberalization and globalization.[17] Steamships had cut the Atlantic passage to a little over a week, and telegraph workers feverishly strung copper lines across the continent and below the oceans. Fueled by the popularity of the recently invented steam press, the number of American periodicals exploded from 850 in 1828 to more than 4,000 by the eve of the Civil War. "There has never been an age so completely enthralled by newspapers as this," observed John Hay in the fall of 1861. Karl Marx, himself a journalist and contemporary of Lincoln's, marveled at "the sheet lightning of the daily press" and the other "immensely facilitated means of communication." National differences, Marx believed, were "daily more and more vanishing."

The new technologies revolutionized the practice of foreign affairs. "Diplomacy has so few secrets nowadays," lamented the French empress, Eugénie, as she tried to stay ahead of events. The advances in nineteenth-century communications, historian Daniel Walker Howe notes, "certainly rivaled, and probably exceeded in importance, those of the revolutionary 'information highway' of our own lifetimes." The same proliferating media empowered all types of preachers and reformers, filling the globe with a cacophony of moral (and too often self-righteous) appeals.[18]

In the changing world, Lincoln lifted a global megaphone. By exploiting the newspaper culture and innovations like the daguerreotype, the president anticipated Theodore Roosevelt's bully pulpit by a generation.[19] Secretary of State Seward also seized the new tools of diplomacy, publishing his official dispatches for their public-relations value. The Lincoln administration, the president's man in Paris explained in 1864, "is the first that has deliberately conducted its diplomacy *à découvert* and with direct and constant accountability to the public. . . . How differently would the last fifty years of European history read if every minister of foreign affairs had thus gone to the public confessional at the commencement of every year!"[20]

Lincolnian diplomacy was not quite so artless as that. The president, while "not a trickster," as his law partner once put it, could be "thoroughly and deeply secretive." Lincoln, like many a successor in the White House, was aggravated by the invasions of the chirping classes. When a visitor showed Lincoln a newly designed weapon, the president shot back: "Now have any of you heard of any machine, or invention, for preventing the escape of gas from newspaper offices?" Still, Lincoln understood intuitively how any glut of information makes power "less tangible and less coercive." Public opinion, Lincoln declared in 1858, was "everything in this country." In the realm of international affairs, it could also prove to be a flighty mistress.[21]

F oreign affairs has long been considered treacherous ground in the field of Lincoln studies. It occupies one of the few sparsely stocked corners of an otherwise massive library. Part of the reason is that books that try to place Lincoln at the center of his own foreign policy tend to end up as hagiographies, because the president often delegated day-to-day policy to his secretary of state. At the other extreme, in comprehensive diplomatic histories and specialized monographs, Lincoln the man gets lost amid a flurry of detail and bit players. This book makes no attempt to serve as a complete history of Union and Confederate foreign relations.[22] I have ignored, or mentioned only in passing, many important diplomatic events and topics in which Lincoln did not play a central role—the Confederate shipbuilding programs in Europe, for example, or the minutiae of the debates in Paris and London about whether to intervene.

Instead, I have included only those episodes in which Lincoln was deeply involved or which tell us something important about the character of a Lincolnian foreign policy. "In comparison with Woodrow Wilson, or Theodore Roosevelt, or Franklin Roosevelt, Lincoln's activity in the realm of diplomacy was slight," writes James Randall, the distinguished Lincoln biographer. "Yet if one subtracts from American international dealings those touches that were peculiarly Lincoln's own, the difference becomes so significant that his contribution must be regarded as a sizeable factor."[23] A successful study of Lincoln's role in U.S. foreign relations, therefore, demands a fresh approach that is impressionistic and selective—while at the same time remaining a holistic human story.

To that end, I have tightly focused my narrative around six distinct episodes that helped to define the character of a Lincolnian foreign policy: his debate, as a young congressman, with law partner Billy Herndon over the conduct of the Mexican War; his conflict with Secretary of State William Seward over the control of foreign policy; his standoff with Britain's Lord Palmerston during the *Trent* crisis of 1861; his race with Karl Marx to master the new art of molding public opinion; and his deadlock with Napoleon III over the French occupation of Mexico. An epilogue examines John Hay's postassassination battle to define the soul and legacy of a Lincolnian foreign policy. True character, it is said, is revealed when a human being makes choices under pressure. Watching Lincoln choose, under the tremendous pressure of a war, is the best way to closely examine that character.[24]

Studying foreign policy through the eyes of the personalities who practice it is not a particularly modern approach. Actual power, realists insist, is the function of impersonal factors like access to capital, levels of industrialization, tons of steel produced. "To understand the course of world politics," argues historian Paul Kennedy, author of *The Rise and Fall of the Great Powers*, "it is necessary to focus attention upon the material and long-term elements rather than the vagaries of personality." Kennedy's observation has much merit. Lincoln lived through—and ultimately helped to manage—a process of seismic economic change. By the start of the Civil War the United

States had become an economic colossus, with a greater relative share of manufacturing output than Russia, Germany, or the Hapsburg Empire.[25]

The commercial surge left a deep imprint on midcentury diplomacy. Scholars now view this period as the seed bed for America's later imperial growth. Seward, a man of his times, loudly and repeatedly evangelized commercial expansion. Lincoln more often preferred to stress the moral perils of human bondage in his public remarks; he relentlessly defied expansionists when they aimed to spread the peculiar institution. Still, these were largely differences of rhetorical emphasis. Lincoln's and Seward's core views on expansion were actually not all that different. As long as it would not strengthen the position of slaveholders, Lincoln insisted that he was "not generally opposed to honest acquisition of territory." In the White House he steadfastly backed expansionist measures like the Pacific Railroad and the Homestead Act.

Like many in the Whig party, Lincoln viewed westward expansion as a safety valve to relieve urban poverty. "In the filling up of countries, it turns out after a while that we get so thick that we have not quite room enough . . . and we desire to go somewhere else," Lincoln told a Cincinnati audience in the fall of 1859. "Where shall you go to escape from over-population and competition? To those new territories which belong to us, which are God-given for that purpose." He considered it a short leap between promoting commerce at home and protecting it with gunboats on the high seas: "The driving [of] a pirate from the track of commerce on the broad ocean, and the removing [of] a snag from its more narrow path in the Mississippi river, can not, I think, be distinguished in principle. Each is done to save life and property, and for nothing else."[26]

In the corridors of the White House, the rise to power could be dizzying. As the Civil War ground on, John Hay had come to see Lincoln as a kind of "backwoods Jupiter," wielding the "bolts of war and the machinery of government" with a firm and steady hand.

He referred to the president in his diary and letters by the nickname Tycoon, after the shoguns that effectively ruled Japan. And yet, even as Lincoln's power grew, he had become "in mind, body and nerves a very different man" by the start of his second term, his secretary noted. "The boisterous laughter became less frequent year by year; the eye grew veiled. . . . He aged with great rapidity."[27]

Lincoln's guilt seemed to grow with his power. As the war neared its climax, the president would sometimes read aloud to Hay late at night from Shakespeare's tragedies, as his young secretary drifted off to sleep. Lincoln's favorite soliloquy in *Hamlet* was King Claudius's failed attempt at prayer: "O my offense is rank! It smells to heaven." The president was fascinated, Hay recalled, by Richard II's third-act speech about the "sad stories of the death of kings." In *Macbeth*, Lincoln was struck by "how true a description of the murderer that one was; when, the dark deed achieved, its tortured perpetrator came to envy the sleep of his victim."[28]

Lincoln lived in a romantic era, an age obsessed by guilt and sin. Throughout his life he admired Lord Byron's poetry, with its melancholy, remorseful protagonists. He would read it aloud to anyone who would listen, kicking his feet up onto his office table. He particularly liked the poet's *Fugitive Pieces*, with their tales of crusading knights who come to ugly ends abroad. Another favorite was Byron's *Childe Harold's Pilgrimage*, the story of a young man with a "thirst for travel" who sets out across Europe looking for adventure and redemption.[29]

There is no greater drama, Lincoln and his team intuitively recognized, than the intersection of power and personality.[30] "Power is poison," Henry Adams, the son of Lincoln's minister in London, observed in the years following the Civil War. Its effect, Adams concluded, "is the aggravation of self, a sort of tumor that ends by killing the victim's sympathies." Adams, like modern realists, believed that foreign affairs had become "a struggle not of men but of forces." And yet the young diplomat was also fascinated by the human element— "the whole unutterable fury of human nature beating itself against the walls of its prison-house," desperately seeking a "door of escape." At the least, Adams believed, the intersection of power and character are worth studying in presidents like Lincoln, because the effects are the same on society at large.[31]

F oreign affairs, at least in some quarters, have often been considered best left to a brotherhood of well-bred and well-connected "wise men." The rough-and-tumble of American popular government is frequently seen as a hindrance to the long-term planning, efficient decision making, and patient state building that a sturdy foreign policy demands. "I do not hesitate to say that it is especially in their conduct of foreign relations that democracies appear to be decidedly inferior to other governments," Alexis de Tocqueville observes in *Democracy in America.* "Foreign politics demand scarcely any of those qualities which are peculiar to a democracy; they require, on the contrary, the perfect use of almost all those in which it is deficient."[32]

Lincoln was certainly neither well bred nor well connected internationally. And yet, as I hope to show in the following pages, he should be considered one of America's seminal foreign-policy presidents—a worthy model for students of global affairs. My argument is not simply that the plain-talking Railsplitter, through his common sense and good judgment, was somehow more adept at the arts of diplomacy than the polished and gold-braided envoys of Europe—although that was sometimes the case. "Where men bred in courts, accustomed to the world, or versed in diplomacy, would use some subterfuge, or would make a polite speech, or give a shrug of the shoulders as the means of getting out of an embarrassing position," observed one British journalist, "Mr. Lincoln raises a laugh by some bold west-country anecdote, and moves off in the cloud of merriment produced by his joke." Lincoln's warm chuckle—which one observer compared to "the neigh of a wild horse"—served him well in the high-stakes game of transatlantic brinksmanship.[33]

Yet the more important point is that Lincoln during the Civil

War boldly tested the versatility of American democracy itself—Tocqueville's original foreign-affairs bugbear. The Founding Fathers, eager to avoid the pitfalls of Old World monarchies, had wisely—but also somewhat schizophrenically—divided the power to conduct foreign policy between the executive and legislative branches of government. Lincoln, a former Whig congressman, possessed a deep reverence for America's national lawmaking bodies. Yet he also discovered over the course of his presidency that acute international crises often demanded the firm hand of a chief executive and the steady keel of his State Department. "Necessity," he once remarked, "knows no law." Although Lincoln considered many of his innovations temporary war measures, historians of the twentieth century's "imperial presidency" have identified lasting precedents in his handling of foreign affairs. All the while, Lincoln and his party worked assiduously to build a centralized American state—a critical prerequisite to America's later rise to power.[34]

It would be flat wrong, of course, to label Lincoln an imperialist. He wore his power well, and had a keen sense of international justice and the limits of American influence. He displayed many of the characteristics of great diplomats.[35] He was comfortable with the give-and-take of negotiation. He was cool and courteous as he pursued the national interest. Britain's Lord Palmerston once observed that the practice of foreign affairs is not "an occult science." It simply demands "plain dealing" and "a regard to justice." Lincoln had read and reread George Washington's farewell address—one of America's bedrock international-relations texts. A wise foreign policy, according to Washington, demands the pursuit of "our interest guided by justice." Lincoln adopted that sound advice as his virtual motto, once suggesting that Americans should celebrate the first president's birthday by rereading the "immortal" document.[36]

Even Lincoln's antislavery position was colored by his vision of America's place in the wider world. The sixteenth president was born only thirty-three years after the Declaration of Independence. The rights of black Americans, Lincoln believed, were guaranteed by the same principle that justified the nation's freedom from British domination. "When we were the political slaves of King George, and wanted to be free, we called the maxim that 'all men are created equal' a self-evident truth," Lincoln wrote one correspondent in 1855. "But now when we have grown fat, and have lost all dread of being slaves ourselves, we have become so greedy to be masters that we call the same maxim 'a self-evident lie.' The fourth of July has not quite dwindled away; it is still a great day—for burning fire-crackers!!!"[37]

Viewed against the backdrop of the global arena, then, our grade-school portrait of the sixteenth president morphs into something pleasantly exotic. One of the unexpected joys of studying Lincoln in the twenty-first century is how much astonishing new material about him has come to light. In recent years, scholars led by Lincoln biographer Michael Burlingame have sifted through not just the traditional letters, diaries, and other primary sources in an effort to uncover fresh material about Lincoln, but they have also combed through the archived papers of past biographers and historians, searching for valuable and revealing snippets that have somehow ended up on the cutting-room floor. Their efforts have revealed countless examples of previously uncovered details that have helped to draw a more accurate picture of Lincoln and his presidency.[38]

For this book I have taken a similar approach, revisiting not only the memoirs and dispatches of Lincoln's diplomats, but also searching the unpublished archives of previous Lincoln biographers for clues to his foreign policy. The papers of the imperialist senator and Lincoln biographer Albert J. Beveridge, housed at the Library of Congress, include stacks of transcripts of useful Mexican War–era newspaper clippings. In the personal collection of Mary Lincoln biographer Ruth Randall, we learn that a disgruntled former State Department employee liked to refer to the First Lady as "that 'Springfield bitch' "—a small but revealing detail omitted from Randall's own sympathetic treatment of her subject.[39] The uncataloged files of Lincoln biographer William H. Townsend—stored in a dark corner of a labyrinthine basement in Lexington, Kentucky—include fascinating photographs, newspaper clippings, and other material about Lincoln's colorful minister to Russia, Cassius Marcellus Clay.

Even the archives of minor diplomatic clerks can shed light on Lincoln and his foreign-policy team. A contemporary account in the papers of Edward Lee Plumb, a businessman and State Department aide, describes a glittering White House reception at which an exhausted but cheery Lincoln mingles with the diplomatic corps in the wake of the *Trent* affair—a valuable fly-on-the-wall perspective. In another collection, the personal correspondence of Lincoln's minister in the Netherlands, we find a missive to a friend in the Senate deriding the "pusillanimity" of the administration's Mexico policy—a telling peek at just how difficult it could be to keep America's strong-willed foreign envoys on the same song sheet. Taken together with the shelves of diplomatic memoirs and letter books of official dispatches, a textured and surprising portrait emerges of a diplomat in chief whose presidency helped point the way to America's rise to power.[40]

It would be folly, of course, to turn Lincoln into a plaster Richelieu. His foreign policies also included some turkeys. Lincoln clung relentlessly to the misguided idea of colonizing freed slaves to Africa or Latin America. He persistently urged his military commanders to fortify the Mexican border to deter the French army to its south— a fateful decision that led to a military fiasco. (General William Tecumseh Sherman famously derided that campaign as "one damn blunder from beginning to end.") Even the U.S. consul in Paris, who was an admirer of the president, later recalled that Lincoln had made some "great blunders" in international affairs in addition to his inspired choices. "No one," the diplomat concluded, "is wise and cool enough to make no blunders" in a conflict as unpredictable and unprecedented as the American Civil War.

Still, it is well worth studying Lincoln's lapses in judgment along with his masterstrokes. Our cardinal sin in international relations, as Walter Lippmann once chided American utopians, is the "error of forgetting that we are men and of thinking that we are gods. We are

not gods. . . . We are mere mortals with limited power and little universal wisdom." As Lincoln pursues his diplomacy, we are reminded
of perhaps the most important lesson in modern foreign affairs: that
we are human after all.[41]

L incoln's foreign-affairs education began in the fall of 1847, as
columns of American soldiers were hurtling into Mexico City.
The Mexican War, which had been raging for more than a year, was
America's first full-scale foreign conflict. Haggard-looking veterans
had been flooding back to Springfield for months, parading through
the streets waving captured flags and drawing huge crowds. The
newspapers were plastered with the army's exploits. Americans were
thrilled by the excitement. The country, a young Herman Melville
marveled, had been thrown into "a state of delirium" by the war.[42]

As triumphant American troops patrolled the Mexican capital,
Lincoln and his family clambered into a stagecoach and set out from
muddy Springfield on their first trip to Washington. The Illinoisan,
who had just been elected to his first term in Congress, was full of
anticipation. For years he had been relentlessly lobbying for this post,
sending a flurry of letters to anyone who would listen. Mary, one of
Lincoln's friends observed, wanted "to loom largely" in the capital.
Lincoln's neighbors were skeptical. It would be impossible to turn
the disheveled, six-foot-four giant into a gentleman, they sniped.[43]

It is easy to imagine the Illinois lawyer and his young family
as they traveled east through the blazing fall foliage of the Indiana
woods, into the crisp, cold Kentucky hills—and then on to Washington. By the fall of 1847, Lincoln had come to question the wisdom
of the Mexican War, but he was not immune to ambition or flights
of fancy. Foreign affairs, for better or worse, are a spectacle of power
and romance—a relentlessly human endeavor. A week or so after he
arrived in the nation's capital, the young congressman scratched out
a letter to his Springfield law partner, Billy Herndon. "As you are
all so anxious for me to distinguish myself," Lincoln wrote, "I have
concluded to do so, before long."[44]

———◆———

CHAPTER ONE

Lincoln vs. Herndon

A BRAHAM LINCOLN WAS NERVOUS. THE FLOOR OF THE U.S. HOUSE OF REPRESENTATIVES IN THE 1840S WAS NOT A PARTICULARLY PLEASANT PLACE TO GIVE A SPEECH—ESPECIALLY THE FIRST major effort of a freshman congressman's career. The chamber was designed to resemble the Roman Pantheon, framed by marble pillars and crimson drapes, but it reminded more than one visitor of an unruly schoolhouse. Members kicked their heels up on the mahogany desks, hollered at the speaker, rustled newspapers, puffed on cigars, and spat tobacco juice on the filthy carpet. The noise, amplified by a cavernous, sixty-foot ceiling, reminded one visitor of "a hundred swarms of bees." One of Lincoln's fellow Illinoisans complained that he "would prefer speaking in a pig pen with 500 hogs squealing" or talking "to a mob when a fight is going on" than trying to keep the attention of his colleagues. It was, he recalled, "the most stupid place generally I was ever in."[1]

Lincoln was accustomed to speaking before juries, but he could never completely suppress the butterflies. Thirty-eight years old, a "rail in broadcloth," the gentleman from Illinois presented an arresting figure. His suits, more often than not, were rumpled, and his pants tended to hover above his ankles. His law partner at the time, William Herndon, described Lincoln as a "sinewy, grisly" character, with a wild shock of hair that "lay floating where the fingers or the winds left it, piled up at random." Regardless of his appearance, Lincoln knew on this day that he was likely to get the House's attention. He had decided to pick a fight over the origins of the Mexican War, the two-year-old conflict that promised—or threatened—to remake the American West.[2]

Lincoln had been laying the groundwork for his speech for weeks. He had voted for fellow representative George Ashmun's resolution condemning the 1846 American invasion of Mexico as unnecessary and unconstitutional. President James K. Polk claimed that the conflict was a war of self-defense, retaliation for attacks by Mexican guerrillas. Lincoln wasn't buying. He demanded to know "the particular spot of soil" where American blood had been shed, insisting that U.S. troops had provoked the war by aggressively pushing into contested land.[3]

In the red-and-gold House chamber, with its plaster statue of *Liberty* and its large portraits of Washington and Lafayette, Lincoln went on the attack. He insisted in his high-pitched tenor that his "first impulse" regarding Mexico had been to "remain silent on that point, at least till the war should be ended." Yet he finally determined that "I can not be silent, if I would." Lincoln compared Polk to a shifty lawyer trying to defend a hopeless case. The president "is deeply conscious of being in the wrong," Lincoln told the chamber. He "feels the blood of this war, like the blood of Abel, is crying to Heaven against him." Young Hickory, as Polk was known, had been deluded by dreams of military glory: "that attractive rainbow, that rises in showers of blood—that serpent's eye, that charms to destroy." The freshman congressman's attacks quickly grew uncomfortably personal. The president, he boomed, was "a bewildered, confounded, and miserably perplexed man," whose "mind, tasked beyond its power, is running hither and thither, like some tortured creature, on a burning surface." Polk's justifications were nothing more than "the half-insane mumbling of a fever dream."[4]

Lincoln spoke quickly as he made his case against Polk, emphasizing his points with an "abundance of gesture." As a young legislator, Lincoln could be an uneven speaker, shifting on his feet and ranging up and down the chamber's aisles. His colleagues back in Illinois had once joked about creating a committee to hold him in place. In later years, Lincoln would eventually learn to control his flailing arms, locking them behind his back and instead gesturing mostly with his head. Only occasionally would he shoot out "that long bony forefinger of his to dot an idea or express a thought." Today, still green and anxious, Lincoln rushed through the address in about forty-five minutes, fearing that he would be cut off by the speaker if he went on too long.[5]

Lincoln's broadside attracted little attention—at least at first. Polk, who had once counseled treating political enemies with "silent contempt," did not bother to respond. He didn't even mention Lincoln in his otherwise lengthy diary. Lincoln seemed pleased with his effort, spending a substantial amount of his own money sending copies of the address home to constituents. A week after his appearance, he dropped a note in the mail to his old friend and law partner, Billy Herndon. "I have made a speech," Lincoln wrote, "a copy of which I will send you by next mail."[6]

Lincoln's criticism of Polk had merit. By attempting to fortify the Rio Grande, the president had acted provocatively. Friendly newspapers cheered Lincoln's volley. "Evidently there is music in that very tall Mr. Lincoln," the *Baltimore Patriot* exulted. The congressman, reported the *Missouri Republican*, "commanded the attention of the House, which none but a strong man can do." Still, in the nineteenth century, periodicals usually acted as party organs. In hawkish Illinois, Democratic-controlled papers pounced. The *Illinois State Register* called Lincoln's resolutions "trash," and complained that the "littleness of the pettifogging lawyer" had "disgraced" the state. It attacked the congressman with headlines like: "Out damned SPOT!" and dubbed Lincoln the "Benedict Arnold of our district." The nickname that ultimately stuck, coming back to haunt Lincoln in his later political career, was simply Spotty.[7]

The congressman suffered another stroke of bad luck a little over a month later: the war ended. Polk's envoy had secured excellent terms from the defeated Mexicans. In exchange for $15 million and the withdrawal of U.S. troops, the United States would take control of a vast tranche of territory that comprises modern-day New Mexico, California, and other western states. Americans, in general, were elated. But Lincoln's hobbyhorse had been shot out from under him.[8]

Far more troubling were the letters that began pouring in from an unlikely critic: Billy Herndon. Lincoln's law partner believed that Polk had the right to deter enemy troops by sending U.S. forces "into the very heart of Mexico" if necessary. Moreover, in expansionist Illinois, Lincoln was destroying his career by challenging Polk on the war, Herndon believed. Lincoln's partner would later boast about his "mud instinct"—his ability to read the political mood. Herndon contended that no politician could survive a vote in which he appeared to oppose his own country in wartime. Lincoln's law partner wrote to his friend again and again to press his case.[9]

Lincoln quickly responded to Herndon, hoping to set his partner straight. The congressman regretted the disagreement, he told the younger man—"not because of any fear we shall remain disagreed, after you shall have read this letter, but because, if *you* misunderstand, I fear other good friends will also." Lincoln made a distinction between challenging the war's origins, by voting for the Ashmun amendment, and agreeing to send supplies to the troops. "I will stake my life, that if you had been in my place, you would have voted just as I did," he insisted. "Would you have voted what you felt you knew to be a lie? I know you would not." Skipping the vote was not an option. "No man can be silent if he would," the congressman wrote. "You are compelled to speak; and your only alternative is to tell the *truth* or tell a *lie*. I can not doubt which you would do." Lincoln could not have been happy with his partner's challenge, but he did his best to maintain the relationship. Although he addressed his Mexican War letters using the formal "William," rather than the more familiar "Billy," Lincoln closed them with his usual affectionate signoff.[10]

The Mexican War did no lasting damage to Lincoln's relationship with his law partner. It did, however, mark a turning point in Lincoln's maturity as a foreign-policy thinker—and, in a larger sense, in Americans' conception of their country's place in the world. The early nineteenth century was a romantic era. It was also a period of intense religious revival. Traveling evangelists helped to infuse the country with a crusading spirit. For decades Americans had justified westward expansion with appeals to natural right. In the 1840s, however, a new dynamic emerged. Hawks, especially in the northeastern and northwestern states, began advocating the moral reform of distant societies. The Mexican War was "the best kind of conquest," Walt Whitman wrote in 1847. "What has miserable, inefficient Mexico—with her superstition, her burlesque upon freedom, her actual tyranny by the few over the many—what has she to do with the great mission of peopling the new world with a noble race? Be it ours, to achieve that mission!"[11]

Neither Herndon nor Lincoln was conventionally devout, but Lincoln's law partner did absorb much of the reform-minded ethos of the time. Herndon, notes his biographer, David Donald, represented an increasingly common American type. He was "a child of that universally optimistic age when everyone had the cure for the world's ills," Donald observes. "It was the day of the crank, the crusader, and the crackpot. . . . Everybody believed in immediate perfectibility through reform." Herndon was always pushing a cause, and tended to see issues in Manichaean terms. Lincoln was cooler and more cerebral; he did not want to rashly overturn the existing sectional balance. The story of the congressman and his law partner is a fitting prelude to the story of Lincoln's Civil War diplomacy— and a vivid illustration of a debate that continues to shape American foreign policy to the present day.[12]

The Insidious Wiles of Foreign Influence

N othing in Lincoln's early life had prepared him for the foreign-policy donnybrook that accompanied the Mexican War. Yet his childhood was less isolated than is often depicted. Lincoln spent his formative years in a new nation still raw from its war of independence. His earliest memories reflect the instability of the era. In the Kentucky cabin where Lincoln was raised, his parents cared for companies of volunteers returning home from the War of 1812—"strings of them," one of Lincoln's cousins remembered. His parents coached him to always treat the soldiers with respect. As a young boy, Lincoln revered the heroes of the American Revolution. He believed that there was "something more than common that those men struggled for," he later recalled, "something that held out a great promise to all the people of the world to all time to come." He read more than one biography of George Washington, who counseled would-be statesmen to remain "constantly awake" to "the insidious wiles of foreign influence." A successful foreign policy, Washington advised, should both promote American interests and display a regard for international justice.[13]

For the young Lincoln, foreigners were still exotic, the subject of romantic adventures and dangerous liaisons. With his friends, the boy sang ribald "field songs" about erotic escapades abroad. One old standby was titled "None Can Love like an Irishman." ("The turban'd Turk, who scorns the world, / May strut about with his whiskers curled, . . . / Yet long may he pray with his Alcoran / Before he can love like an Irishman.") Lincoln—whom one neighbor described as "a tall spider of a boy"—read *The Arabian Nights*, the classic Middle Eastern yarns. He particularly liked "Sinbad the Sailor," the story of a man from modern-day Iraq who is obsessed with "traveling about the world of men and seeing their cities and islands."[14]

Lincoln increasingly shared Sinbad's obsession. As a teenager, he found ways to see the world outside his tiny Indiana community. He built a small skiff and took it floating out onto the Ohio River. One day a couple of steamboat passengers asked for the young man's help to haul their trunks aboard their boat. When they were done, each man tossed Lincoln a silver half-dollar. "I could scarcely believe my eyes as I picked up the money," he later recalled. "The world seemed wider and fairer before me."[15]

The following year a local store owner hired Lincoln to take a shipment of meats and grains on his flatboat down the river to New Orleans. Lincoln's father, Thomas, had visited the city more than two decades earlier and may have told his son stories about his own adventures there. Now the younger Lincoln poled his way down the Mississippi River, drifting across the thirty-first parallel at the Louisiana state line, which not so long ago had marked the international boundary. As historian Richard Campanella notes, entering New Orleans was the closest Lincoln "ever came to immersing himself in a foreign culture."

In the Crescent City, steamships bobbed along the mouth of the Mississippi, carrying goods destined for Europe. Locals, including large communities of refugees from Haiti, Nova Scotia, and Latin America, streamed down the cobblestone streets chattering in French, Spanish, and Portuguese. Diplomats from Brazil to Sicily to Sardinia dined on turtle steaks and other exotic fare at the Globe Coffee House on Chartres Street. The city's women were notoriously lovely. During the War of 1812, British troops had egged themselves on toward the city with promises of "beauty and booty." Alexis de Tocqueville, who visited around the same time as Lincoln, remembered seeing "faces with every shade of color."

Lincoln returned to New Orleans in 1831, this time passing St. Louis—a city founded by French fur traders that retained much of its Old World character. The region, observed one visitor, was now home to "foreigners of every description—Germans, Spaniards, Italians, Irish, &c." The leafy hills along the riverbank were dotted with Catholic chapels and Spanish-style homes. The roots of Lincoln's ethnic and religious tolerance, some historians argue, can be found in these early journeys. In later life, writes Campanella,

"Lincoln explicitly embraced the sort of pluralism he first witnessed in the large Catholic and foreign-born population of New Orleans."[16]

Lincoln's encounters with the wider world seemed to shape his early writing. His first major political statement, a March 1832 hand-bill, argues that local schools should make more of an effort to teach students about foreign cultures. The goal, he writes, should be to assure that every man is capable of reading "the histories of his own and other countries, by which he may duly appreciate the value of our free institutions." The document also makes the case for improving local roads and building canals—vital links to the outside world. Such developments, he insists, would make it easier to export local crops and bring in "necessary articles from abroad." And yet, Lincoln often seemed conflicted about the benefits of foreign trade. He frequently mocked Americans who felt the need to ape European fashions.[17]

This is the Lincoln—the flatboatman coming to terms with America's place in the world—whom Billy Herndon first spotted one day in 1832 by the banks of the Sangamon River. Lincoln had volunteered to help pilot a steamboat called the *Talisman* down the slender waterway. Then a teenager a decade younger than Lincoln, Herndon and a clutch of other boys had cantered alongside on horseback as the boat chugged up the river. Local townsmen helped the craft along, hacking away with axes at the thick brush blocking the route. The technology was primitive. Whenever the steam whistle wailed, the boat lurched to a stop. Still, Herndon was enthralled. When the *Talisman* finally reached its destination, near a local mill, Herndon and the other teens jumped off their horses and spilled onto the boat, "lost in boyish wonder."[18]

Steam power promised to shrink the world. It seemed, at least at first, certain to inspire greater harmony with distant peoples. Yet old-fashioned grudges remained a reality on the frontier. In the spring of 1832, battles erupted with the "British Band" of Indian warriors led by Black Hawk, who had sided with the redcoats during the War of 1812. A unit of volunteers elected Lincoln captain, and he shipped off to the front. Lincoln later mocked his own war experience, insisting that he had killed only mosquitoes. "The whole thing was a sort of frolic," remembered one of Lincoln's friends.[19]

Still, moments of peril interrupted their romp. On one occasion Lincoln and his unit stumbled upon the scene of a massacre. Scalps were impaled on ram rods and the bodies of dead children hung upside down. Another time, Lincoln and his men discovered and had to bury the dead bodies of fellow troops. "The red light of the morning sun was streaming upon them as they lay, heads toward us, on the ground, and every man had a round red spot on the top of his head, about as big as a dollar, where the redskins had taken his scalp," Lincoln recalled. "It was frightful, but it was grotesque, and the red sunlight seemed to paint everything all over."[20]

Because of—or in spite of—his early war experience, Lincoln was generally reluctant to challenge foreign powers during this period. A series of articles in his local newspaper in the late 1830s, likely written by Lincoln, taunted Democrats who wanted to gin up a war with Britain or France. In an 1838 address before the Young Men's Lyceum in Springfield, Lincoln jeered at Democratic hawks. "At what point shall we expect the approach of danger?" he asked his audience. "By what means shall we fortify against it? Shall we expect some transatlantic military giant, to step the Ocean, and crush us at a blow? Never! All the armies of Europe, Asia and Africa combined, with all the treasure of the earth (our own excepted) in their military chest; with a Buonaparte for a commander, could not by force, take a drink from the Ohio, or make a track on the Blue Ridge, in a trial of a thousand years."[21]

The real peril, Lincoln argued, "cannot come from abroad." Instead, he feared "an Alexander, a Caesar, or a Napoleon" would spring up at home. The American population had been doubling every two decades—expanding six times faster than most other countries'. The economy was growing by almost 4 percent each year. And yet for the young lawyer beginning his career, personal wealth and power remained elusive. Money was so tight and housing so scarce that

Lincoln was forced to share a bedroom with several other bachelors above a Springfield dry-goods store.[22]

Lincoln's roommates included Billy Herndon, then a nineteen-year-old clerk at the shop downstairs. Kinetic and sloe-eyed, with a wide smile and a mop of blue-black hair, Herndon had until recently been studying at a nearby college. Yet political developments had ultimately changed his plans. After an abolitionist newspaperman, Elijah Lovejoy, was murdered by a proslavery mob, Herndon had been swept up in the antislavery backlash on campus. Herndon's father, a stalwart Democrat, had somehow learned of his son's agitation. He halted the boy's tuition payments, dismissing his son as "a damned abolitionist pup." Herndon was on his own.[23]

The dry-goods store quickly turned into a meeting place for the capital's young wits. The men gathered in the back around a wood-burning stove, discussing politics and reading poetry. Lincoln honed his debating and storytelling skills before a small audience that included some of the capital's rising figures. Herndon, still a junior member, would sit on a keg, taking it all in. The philosophical discussions may have fired both men's imaginations, but they still did not pay the bills. "Poverty," Herndon wrote in 1842, "is staring us all in the face."[24]

Priests, Dogs, and Servants

In Springfield, it was known as Aristocracy Hill. On top sat the mansion of Ninian W. Edwards, one of the wealthiest men in town. Edwards was Springfield royalty. His father had been the state's governor, and had been named the first U.S. minister to Mexico. (After being caught up in a political controversy, however, he never actually made it to Mexico City.) In his gold-lace cloak and elegant broadcloth suit, the father would have looked at home in most of the world's chancelleries. A Springfield resident remembered how the local patriarch flew around town in "a magnificent carriage drawn by very spirited horses." John Hay recalled the politician as "a magnificent old gentleman in fair top-boots and ruffled wristbands" who projected *the grand Seigneur airs of the Old School*." At his son's two-story brick mansion on Aristocracy Hill, the hosts chattered in French as distinguished guests arrived for regular weekend salons.[25]

For a muddy backwater of twenty thousand, Sangamon County— dubbed Empire County by its optimistic early residents—could be surprisingly cosmopolitan. The local schools taught Latin and Greek, Spanish and French. After the state capital was moved to Springfield in the late 1830s, the public square sprouted new shops, taverns, and hotels. When the legislature was in session, pretty young women flooded into the city to attend the balls and "hops." At private salons draped in velvet and damask, local hostesses poured blackberry cordials and homemade wine, and served pound cake on china and silver place settings. With no streetlamps, and only lard oil and candles to light the affairs, the whole town could be plunged into virtual blackness on a moonless night. Still, there was something decidedly European about the capital's pretensions. Springfield society, according to one acquaintance of Lincoln and Herndon, came complete with "priests, dogs, and servants."[26]

Lincoln was not immediately charmed by the capital. The whole place was "rather a dull business," he told a friend shortly after arriving. The young bachelor was lonely. "I have been spoken to by but one woman since I've been here, and should not have been by her, if she could have avoided it," he complained. He eventually began showing up at the Edwards mansion on Aristocracy Hill each Sunday, relaxing in the shade of the thick canopy of trees on the grounds, and getting to know members of the powerful political family. Gangly, with a shock of unkempt black hair and enormous hands, he initially struck his host as "a mighty rough man." Lincoln must have known he was out of place. But he was ambitious, a young politician on the rise, and Edwards was a leading patron of the aristocratic "silk-stocking" faction of the Whig party. Lincoln was impressed—if slightly intimidated—by the scene. There was, he wrote a friend, "a great deal of flourishing about in carriages" in Springfield.[27]

It was in the Edwards circle that Lincoln first met Mary Todd, the daughter of a Lexington banker who was staying at her brother-in-law's mansion. Pretty but portly, with "clear blue eyes, long lashes, light brown hair with a glint of bronze, and a lovely complexion," she was nearly as ambitious as Lincoln. Mary had grown up on a slaveholding estate in Kentucky, in a household full of French mahogany furniture and expensive Belgian rugs. She had studied her dance steps at Mentelle's, a Lexington boarding school run by Parisian aristocrats. The schoolmistress, Madame Mentelle, could be slightly intimidating. As a girl in France, her father was said to have once locked her in a room with the corpse of an acquaintance to toughen her up. The young women were schooled as if the whole world were their salon. Mary, her cousin recalled, learned to speak "the purest Parisian." Madame Mentelle's husband, Augustus, would play the violin while the girls practiced steps that included "Spanish, Scottish, Polish, [and] Tyrolienne dances and the beautiful Circassian Circle." In Springfield, Herndon later recalled, the urbane Mary "soon became one of the belles, leading the young men of the town [in] a merry dance."[28]

Lincoln seemed like an odd match for the worldly-wise debutante. Mary was lively and outgoing. Lincoln was antisocial, a "cold man" who had "no affection," Mary's sister recalled. In the Edwards salon, Mary would do most of the talking, while Lincoln "would listen and gaze on her as if drawn by some superior power, irresistibly so." Mary's family was put off by Lincoln's poor breeding. (The young woman's stepmother liked to say that "it took seven generations to make a lady," according to one historian.) But Mary was intrigued by the driven young lawyer. She told friends her ideal beau was a man destined for "position, fame, and power." She was, her sister later recalled, "the most ambitious woman I ever saw." More than a decade before the Civil War, Mary told a friend that she believed

Lincoln would one day become president. "If I had not thought so," she added, "I never would have married him, for you can see he is not pretty."[29]

Lincoln and Mary wed in November 1842. Herndon considered the bride "a polished girl, well educated, a good linguist, a fine conversationalist." Still, Mary could also be "haughty." Lincoln, Herndon recalled, had been attracted at least partly by Mary's "family power." Another old friend believed the marriage was "a policy match all around." Mary provided Lincoln with an entrée not just to the party, but also to the wider world. The Whig ethos, the scholar Allen Guelzo has written, represented a promise of escape from "the restraints of locality and community"—an opportunity for young Americans "to refashion themselves on the basis of new economic identities in a larger world of trade." The Edwards family, with their French conversationalists and worldly statesmen, seemed certain to widen Lincoln's horizons. As a gift, Ninian W. Edwards once presented Lincoln with a copy of Gibbon's *Decline and Fall of the Roman Empire*. Whatever Lincoln's motives in courting Mary, he later told a friend that he considered his marriage a "matter of profound wonder."[30]

Still, despite his new family's influence in the party, Lincoln began noticing that his popularity with the city's younger, working-class Whigs had dropped off after his marriage into Springfield's aristocracy. In 1843 he wrote to a local politician complaining that he had been pigeonholed as "the candidate of pride, wealth, and aristocratic family distinction." Even Lincoln sometimes mocked his in-laws' pretensions. ("One 'd' was good enough for God," he joked, "but not for the Todds.") To succeed in Springfield politics, Lincoln would need a liaison to the city's "young, rowdy set." The energetic, likable Herndon had always carried weight with the "shrewd, wild boys about town" who resented the influence of the aristocrats. Shortly after his marriage to Mary, Lincoln asked the much less accomplished Herndon to be his law partner. "Billy," Lincoln told the twenty-six-year-old, "I can trust you, if you can trust me."[31]

The two men rented a spare, uninspiring office on Springfield's central square. The place was usually a mess, and had windows that looked out over "stable-roofs, ash-heaps, and dingy back yards." Lincoln stored some papers tucked into his stovepipe hat. He kept others among a bundle in a corner of the office with a note that read WHEN YOU CAN'T FIND *IT* ANYWHERE ELSE, LOOK INTO THIS. "The furniture, somewhat dilapidated, consisted of one small desk and a table, a sofa or lounge with a raised head at one end, and a half-dozen plain wooden chairs," recalled a student who worked in the office. "The floor was never scrubbed." Shelves above the desk bulged with law books. Lincoln liked to sprawl across the sofa and read aloud from the newspaper. Herndon found himself annoyed "almost beyond the point of endurance." Lincoln neglected the office finances and shirked his legal research. Some days Herndon simply fled the office.[32]

Perhaps as escape from the drudgery of the law, both Lincoln and Herndon plunged into the national political swirl. As the 1844 presidential election approached, the debate over American expansion—specifically the annexation of Oregon and Texas—monopolized the national conversation. International affairs had long seeped into the American political dialogue; it had played a major role in both the 1796 and 1812 presidential elections. The 1844 contest, however, marks "the first presidential campaign fought primarily over foreign policy." Though Lincoln considered annexation an "evil," he later recalled that "individually I was never much interested in the Texas question." He could not believe that absorbing the territory would make much of a difference either way. Lincoln soon discovered how wrong he was. In 1844, international relations would make for potent politics. For the young lawyer, the campaign proved to be a kind of foreign-affairs awakening.

For years American settlers had been flooding west and south. The slang GTT—"Gone to Texas"—was quickly taking its place in the national lexicon. The clamor for territory drowned out all other campaign issues. The Whig nominee, Henry Clay, made the case that taking Texas would shatter the sectional balance, touching off "an insatiable and unquenchable thirst for foreign conquest." During a speech at the Illinois statehouse one night in May, Lincoln agreed that annexation would be "altogether inexpedient." He complained that Democrats were obsessed with the issue, and mockingly suggested that their campaign slogan be changed to "nothing but Texas." Unfortunately for the Whigs, Americans were also captivated by annexation. In November 1844 the expansionist Democratic candidate, a relative unknown named James K. Polk, defeated Clay for the White House. A little over a year later, Congress voted to absorb Texas.[33]

American Blood upon American Soil

Polk moved swiftly to shore up his new acquisition. "The world has nothing to fear from military ambition in our government," he declared during his inaugural address on a rainy March day. "Foreign powers should therefore look on the annexation of Texas to the United States not as the conquest of a nation seeking to extend her dominions by arms and violence, but as the peaceful acquisition of a territory once her own." Still, Polk had designs on territory far beyond Texas. The president particularly coveted the land owned by Mexico that makes up modern-day California, with its Pacific ports and promises of trade far beyond the continental United States. Polk dispatched an envoy to Mexico City with an offer of $15 million to $20 million for the western regions. In case the Mexicans were inclined to waver, he also ordered a unit of two thousand troops under General Zachary Taylor to march deep into Texas, almost to the Rio Grande.[34]

The land between the Nueces River and the Rio Grande was cowboy country, a dusty, sun-bleached stretch of territory that had long been populated mostly by longhorn cattle and the Mexican *rancheros* and *vaqueros* that tended to them. Texans claimed the Rio Grande as the legitimate border, but Mexicans—and even many Americans—considered the area disputed territory. Now Polk's men ordered Taylor to push as close to the Rio Grande "as prudence will dictate." The general was instructed not to fire on the Mexicans unless they crossed the river or "an actual state of war should exist." Yet when Polk's envoy was rejected by Mexican officials in December, tensions increased decidedly. In January 1846, Polk ordered Taylor's men still closer to the border. The general's force, which had swelled to 3,550 men, marched to the river just across from the Mexican town of Matamoros. Before aiming their cannon at the town, the soldiers hoisted the American flag and obnoxiously blared "The Star-Spangled Banner."[35]

By March, the American troops were eager for a fight. They had spent a long winter enduring torrential rains in leaking tents. Brawls broke out among the troops. Wary Mexicans carefully watched the gringos from their rooftops in Matamoros. To the Americans, Mexico seemed to beckon from across the river. The young men were desperate for female companionship. (One lieutenant, Ulysses S. Grant, was nearly drafted by his fellow soldiers to play a woman in a performance of *The Moor of Venice*.) American soldiers watched in amazement as pretty young Mexican women crept down to the Rio Grande, stripped off their clothes, and then leaped nude into the water.[36]

In mid-April, Mexican forces quickened their calls for an American retreat. The Mexican commander demanded that the U.S. troops withdraw, or else "arms, and arms alone, must decide the question." Taylor then blockaded the Rio Grande, virtually guaranteeing that the Mexicans would be forced to attack. On April 26, 1846, a unit of Mexican solders crossed the Rio Grande into disputed territory and ambushed the Americans, killing eleven soldiers and capturing many more. "Hostilities may now be considered as commenced," Taylor declared.[37]

Polk seized his opportunity. He hastily put together a message to Congress asking for a declaration of war. "Mexico has passed the boundary of the United States, has invaded our territory and shed American blood upon the American soil," Polk insisted. (Many of his countrymen—including Lincoln—would ultimately dispute that claim.) "As war exists, and, notwithstanding all our efforts to avoid it, exists by the act of Mexico herself, we are called upon by every consideration of duty and patriotism to vindicate with decision the honor, the rights, and the interests of our country."[38]

The war in Mexico coincided with a period of rising ambition in Lincoln. Herndon later remarked that his law partner's drive was like "a little engine that knew no rest." For years Lincoln had been angling for a spot in Congress. As tensions rose along the Mexican border, Lincoln flooded the region with letters making the case for his candidacy. "I wish you would let nothing appear in your paper which may operate against me," he wrote to one editor in November 1845. "I now wish to say to you that if it be consistent with your feelings, you would set a few stakes for me," he implored another acquaintance. The young lawyer insisted that after years of patiently supporting other Whig candidates for the congressional seat, he was now entitled to his own shot. "Turn about is fair play," he implored potential allies. Lincoln's main competition was John J. Hardin, a talented politician who had once helped to avert a duel between Lincoln and a man the young lawyer had insulted. Hardin shrewdly tried to tap into the increasingly bellicose mood over Mexico. He insisted to one correspondent in early 1846 that it was "the duty of all true patriots to strengthen the hands of the government by all means against all aggression and insult from foreign nations." Ultimately Lincoln managed to secure the nomination, but only after severely straining his relationship with Hardin.[39]

Ten days after Lincoln's nomination, Polk asked Congress for his declaration of war on Mexico. Americans immediately rallied around the flag. When Congress asked for fifty thousand volunteers, three hundred thousand answered the call. The prairie "blazed with martial spirit." Illinois had long been one of the most hawkish states in the union. More young men asked to enlist than there were spaces in the state's three regiments. Hardin quickly shipped off to the front lines. The new recruits, Herndon later recalled, included "some of the bravest men and the best legal talent in Springfield." Missouri ended up being the only state that sent more volunteers to Mexico than Illinois.[40]

Lincoln remained behind, plugging along with his campaign amid the tumult. He seems, at first, to have tried to avoid the issue of expansionism. The Democratic *Illinois State Register* hammered Lincoln, attempting to force him to define his positions on foreign policy. The paper particularly needled him about Oregon, which Illinoisans coveted even more than Texas. Hawkish Midwesterners had been insisting on a territorial concession from Britain reaching all the way up to the 54'40" line of latitude—a demand that many Whigs considered unnecessarily provocative. Was Lincoln for " 'compromising' away our Oregon territory to England" like "his brother Whigs in Congress?" the *State Register* asked. "No shuffling, Mr. Lincoln! Come out square!"[41]

On Mexico, at least at first, Lincoln seemed to share the country's sense of outrage. In late May he spoke at a war rally in Springfield, delivering what the local newspaper reported as a "warm, thrilling, and effective" appeal to support the troops. Herndon later recalled that his partner had "urged a vigorous prosecution" of the war and "admonished us all to permit our government to suffer no dishonor, and to stand by the flag till peace came and came honorably to us."[42]

Regenerating the World

The war dominated news coverage throughout the summer. New technologies like the telegraph and the steam-powered printing press had revolutionized the American media during the 1840s. The first telegraph line was built two years before the war, and the Hoe rotary press, which used steam power to spin a series of cylinders, was patented in 1847. Both inventions spawned a new "penny press"—cheap newspapers that printed lurid war reports and egged on the public and Congress. The Mexican War also heralded the birth of the modern war correspondent. The ink-stained adventurers sent their dispatches back from the front lines via telegraph. The whole apparatus worked to encourage the American thrust west and south. The new technology, notes historian Daniel Walker Howe, "proved a major facilitator of American nationalism and continental ambition."[43]

A new national spirit of reform grew hand in hand with the telegraph and the penny press. The technology seemed to reinforce beliefs—particularly among evangelical Christians and many romantic transcendentalists—that the millennium was at hand. A Boston magazine declared it "a great blessing" for Mexico to be conquered, and looked forward to the day when America would "regenerate the world." Supercilious volunteers wrote home from Mexico about the nation's "national indolence" and "air of decay." When a country "keeps a 'disorderly house,'" the *Democratic Review* declared, "it is the duty of neighbors to interfere."[44]

Although the war fervor was particularly intense in New York and the Midwest, enthusiasm cut across party and geographic lines.[45] "We are now all Whigs and all Democrats," declared one newspaper reporter, echoing Thomas Jefferson's inaugural address. The whole war effort was draped in a kind of romantic gauze. Soldiers wrote home about the beauty of Mexican women. "Nearly all of them have well-developed, magnificent figures," wrote one captain, and they "dress with as little clothing as you can well fancy." American factory girls shamelessly flirted with young soldiers. Vigilant parents had to keep a tight leash on teenage boys, many of whom were eager to run off and join the fighting. Hacks churned out novelettes lauding the mission. In the books, notes historian Robert W. Johannsen, U.S. troops were "cast as redeemers, striving to free the people from the bondage imposed by government and Church, to regenerate the nation, and bring it to a state of true republicanism."[46]

Lincoln was a cautious pragmatist and not given to swooning. Still, the young candidate found himself in a political quandary. On

the one hand, he remained wary of overthrowing the sectional balance. Still, it would have been impossible for Lincoln to completely
ignore the popular enthusiasm at home. In July, Lincoln's old friend
(and sometime political foe), the British-born Edward D. Baker, received special permission to take a leave of absence from Congress
and recruit an Illinois unit to follow him to Mexico. Thousands of
Springfieldians poured into the streets, hoisting American flags and
howling their approval. Baker marched his unit through the throng
amid whistling fifes and pounding drums.[47]

Mary also watched her friends depart for Mexico. One childhood pal from Kentucky, Cassius Marcellus Clay, took command of
a company of cavalry and set off for the Rio Grande. Clay—whom
Lincoln would one day appoint minister to Russia—cut a dashing
figure. With his strong features and thick black hair, Clay displayed,
as one admirer put it, "the glory of a perfect physical manhood." Still,
detractors saw only a vainglorious buffoon. The *Boston Liberator* predicted that he would be "the first to perish on the Mexican soil, an
ignoble death." Lincoln's allies, however, defended the Kentuckian.
"Foreign nations," declared the *Sangamo Journal*, to which Lincoln
was closely tied, "will find Americans acting as one man, with one
soul."[48]

In the early days of the war, that statement was accurate enough.
Both Lincoln and his opponent, a Methodist revival preacher named
Peter Cartwright, appear to have supported the conflict, largely neutralizing it as a campaign issue. Throughout the summer of 1846, Lincoln spoke at least occasionally on the Mexico and Oregon questions.
Yet Lincoln avoided making major news on the topic. The strategy
seems to have worked. Lincoln trounced Cartwright in the August 3
election, winning the poll by a wide margin.[49]

The year that followed must have been maddening for Lincoln.
Because the Thirtieth Congress was not due to convene for another
sixteen months, the newly elected legislator could do little more than
sit on the sidelines as the Mexican War unfolded. "Being elected to
Congress," he wrote to a friend in October 1846, "though I am very

grateful to our friends, for having done it, has not pleased me as much as I expected."[50]

An inveterate news junkie, Lincoln carefully followed developments as American forces pushed deeper into Mexico. (Newspapers, Herndon once reported, were Lincoln's "food.")[51] In February 1847, the Mexican general Santa Anna launched a major offensive targeting the forces of U.S. General Zachary Taylor at Buena Vista in northern Mexico. Rain poured down on the clashing armies as Taylor's men met the advance. The death tolls, for the time, were huge. More than 270 Americans fell on the battlefield, along with twice as many Mexicans. But Taylor and his men ultimately held their ground, and the Battle of Buena Vista entered the annals of great American military victories. Taylor's laconic request during the fighting—"A little more grape, please, Captain Bragg"—was turned into a slogan. Americans thrilled at the news. Shows about the victory at Buena Vista played to sold-out crowds on the Bowery in New York.[52]

For Springfield, the victory turned out to be bittersweet. Among the dead: John Hardin, Lincoln's old friend and recent competitor. Hardin had fought heroically, leading a force of Illinois troops into the fray and snatching a Mexican battle flag before he was killed.[53] The news of Hardin's death reached the Illinois capital in March. Even the politician's Democratic rivals lauded the local martyr. "Beloved by all who knew him, and without a personal enemy on earth, his fate will cast a gloom, not only over this whole state but throughout the nation," wrote the *Illinois State Register.* At a memorial a few days later, Lincoln graciously offered a resolution celebrating the victory and praising Hardin.[54]

Hardin's funeral later that summer reignited Illinois's martial flame. A friend of Lincoln's remembered the ceremony as a "gala day." Still, it also somehow lacked dignity. Jacksonville, the Illinois town where the funeral was held, was a dry town, but revelers managed to smuggle in plenty of liquor. Noisy, drunken teenagers caroused, and soldiers paraded through the town to Hardin's house. The central square, observed Lincoln's friend, "is overrun with mounted marshals, dressed with enormous white sashes, who are curvetting and galloping about in every direction, apparently with no other object in view than to show themselves off." At the burial, buglers from Hardin's regiment played taps, and local legislators wore black crepe armbands in his memory.[55]

The war euphoria began to take on a circus atmosphere in Springfield. At the Battle of Cerro Gordo, troops from the Fourth Illinois captured Santa Anna's wooden leg, and hauled the prosthesis back to the state capitol. The American forces sometimes seemed intoxicated by their victories. Volunteers returned home from the battles amid "a veritable frenzy of robberies, murders, and rapes." At least one mother of a Mexican girl begged for help recovering her missing daughter, who had run off with an American soldier. In Springfield, a local Presbyterian preacher complained that returning veterans had become "a moral pest to society." Still, the clergyman's views were by no means universal. During one appearance he was threatened and shouted down by local politicians.[56]

American troops finally punched through to Mexico City in September 1847. Earlier that year, General Winfield Scott had landed a force of American troops in the Gulf Coast city of Vera Cruz. Scott steadily pushed west toward the capital while Taylor's men surged south. Now, under the scorching September sun, columns of Scott's men poured into Mexico City's central square through clouds of still-dissipating gunpowder fumes. Mexicans, perhaps impressed by the gold-braided figure of General Scott on horseback, found themselves bursting into applause. At Chapultepec, the hilltop Mexican palace, ecstatic soldiers plunged an American flag into the ramparts, and then swarmed around their victorious commander. The Duke of Wellington ultimately praised Scott as the "greatest living soldier."[57]

The United States was still vibrating with enthusiasm in the fall of 1847, as Abraham and Mary Lincoln prepared to leave Springfield for Washington. Lincoln, by his thirty-eighth birthday, had achieved an admirable degree of success in his home state. A reporter who traveled with Lincoln throughout the district found himself amazed at how the gangly lawyer seemed to know everyone he met. He had clearly charmed his local Whig newspaper. "Mr. Lincoln, the member of Congress-elect from this district, has just set out on his way to the city of Washington," reported the *Illinois Weekly Journal* in late October. "His family is with him; they intend to visit their friends and relatives in Kentucky before they take up the line of march for the seat of government. Success to our talented member of Congress. He will find many men in Congress who possess twice the good looks, and not half the good sense, of our own representative."[58]

A Spirit of Wild Adventure

The Lincolns stopped at Mary's family home in Kentucky on their way to Washington, arriving in Lexington on a bitterly cold November day. The entire Todd family crowded into their chilly front hallway as the visitors stepped inside. Mary, then a twenty-nine-year-old beauty, entered first. "To my mind," recalled her half-sister, Emilie, "she was lovely," with "clear, sparkling blue eyes . . . smooth white skin with a fresh, faint wild-rose color in her cheeks; and glossy light brown hair, which fell in soft, short curls behind each ear." Lincoln, clutching his son Robert, followed behind his wife. As the congressman-elect placed the boy on the floor, Emilie, then just a small girl, could not help but think of the story of "Jack and the Beanstalk." She feared, she later recalled, that Lincoln "might be the hungry giant of the story." Lincoln wore a black cloak draped over his shoulders and a fur cap with ear straps that covered most of his face. "Expecting to hear the, 'Fee, fi, fo, fum!,' " Emilie remembered, "I shrank closer to my mother and tried to hide behind her voluminous skirts."[59]

Lexington was nearly deserted. Many of the city's young men were still away fighting in Mexico. The national euphoria was tempered by a deep sense of sorrow for some of the city's most prominent citizens who had been killed in the war. Henry Clay Jr., the son of the Todds' illustrious neighbor, was one casualty. Like Hardin, the young man had been killed at the Battle of Buena Vista, speared multiple times by enemy lances. By the time Lincoln arrived in Lexington, the Sage of Ashland was complaining that he had been "tortured" by the stories of his son's death and "the possible outrages committed upon his body." Clay, Lincoln was soon to find out, had turned bitterly against the Mexican War by the fall of 1847.[60]

In the stately Todd home, Lincoln spent most of his time upstairs in a back parlor and a narrow passageway filled with bookshelves. The Todd library included copies of Gibbon's *Decline and Fall of the Roman Empire*, and lives of Cromwell and Napoleon. Still, for Lincoln, the highlight of the Lexington stop must have been the opportunity to see his idol Henry Clay in person. Lincoln once remarked that he "almost worshipped" the Whig elder. Clay, Lincoln said, was his "beau ideal of a statesman." At one point the Railsplitter even began dressing like his hero, sporting a denim suit instead of English broadcloth, to support local manufactures. In early November, the local newspaper reported that the famed orator would deliver an address on the Mexican War at the Lexington courthouse. Lincoln would not have missed the performance.[61]

Clay, like Lincoln, had at first mildly rallied behind the Mexican War effort. "I felt half inclined to ask for some little nook or corner in the army in which I might serve in avenging the wrongs to my country," Clay told a banquet audience in New Orleans in late 1846, perhaps attempting to make a joke. "I have thought that I might yet be able to capture or to slay a Mexican." Yet when his own son decided to join the U.S. troops, Clay balked. Though he ultimately gave his son a couple of pistols to take with him to Mexico, the father complained that he wished the war were "more reconcilable with the dictates of conscience." If he had any remaining sympathies for the war effort, they evaporated after his boy was killed at Buena Vista. By April 1847 the Sage of Ashland was deriding the war as "calamitous, as well as unjust and unnecessary."[62]

By Lincoln's visit, Clay was past his prime. At seventy-one, he had failed in several bids for the presidency. The Great Compromiser acknowledged that he was "in the autumn of life" and felt "the frost of age." Yet when he spoke, the old man could still draw a crowd. His voice, one contemporary recalled, could sound "soft as a lute or full as a trumpet." On the Friday night before his remarks, supporters flooded into Lexington, filling the local taverns. The audience grew so large that the event's organizers, which included Lincoln's father-in-law, moved it from the courthouse to a large brick building that could accommodate the throng. Clay took his place at the head of a makeshift platform organizers had thrown up at the front of the room. Rain had been pouring down on the city when the statesman began to speak.[63]

As Clay began his remarks, he noted that the weather was "dark and gloomy, unsettled and uncertain, like the condition of our country, in regard to the unnatural war with Mexico." He insisted that the war should be brought to "a satisfactory close." The conflict, he told the crowd, "is no war of defense, but one unnecessary and of offensive aggression. It is Mexico that is defending her fire-sides, her castles and her altars, not we."

The war threatened to shatter the union's delicate sectional balance, and was slowly eroding the American character. "War unhinges society, disturbs its peaceful and regular industry, and scatters poisonous seeds of disease and immorality, which continue to germinate and diffuse their baneful influence long after it has ceased," he said. "Dazzling by its glitter, pomp and pageantry, it begets a spirit of wild adventure and romantic enterprise, and often disqualifies those who embark in it, after their return from the bloody fields of battle, from engaging in the industrious and peaceful vocations of life."

Clay subtly criticized his own party. Whigs, he said, had "lent too ready a facility" to the prosecution of the conflict, "without careful examination into the objects of the war." Congress had an obligation to exert its constitutional authority and force President Polk to more clearly define the war's aims. "Such a vast and tremendous power ought not to be confided to the perilous exercise of one single man," he said. If Polk had the power to start a war alone, he asked, "where is the difference between our free government and that of any other nation which may be governed by an absolute czar, emperor, or king?" Clay insisted that he was particularly "shocked and alarmed" by the increasingly loud talk of annexing the entire country of Mexico. "Of all the dangers and misfortunes which could befall this nation," he said, "I should regard that of its becoming a warlike and conquering power the most direful and fatal."[64]

Clay spoke for two and a half hours, reviewing the history of the Mexican War and offering his prescriptions for ending it. Soon after he concluded his remarks, news of the speech flashed throughout the country. James Gordon Bennett, editor of the *New York Herald*, paid $500 to charter a train to take the text of Clay's speech from Lexington to Cincinnati. From there telegraph operators beamed it to the newspaper's offices in Manhattan. Britain's foreign minister, Lord Palmerston, praised the speech for rejecting Polk's "aggressive policy." At least some Illinois Whigs, however, worried that Clay's bold anti-war stance could hurt the party in the next year's presidential election. "That speech of Mr. Clay," an Illinois friend wrote Lincoln, "will beat us as a party for years to come, unless we can unite upon 'Old Zac' [Zachary Taylor]."[65]

Lincoln may have had the opportunity to continue the dialogue over a dinner with Clay that November. An acquaintance of Lincoln's later insisted that the two men had shared a meal at Ashland during this visit. Historians find this difficult to believe, since Lincoln never mentioned the encounter and there is no corroborating evidence to support the claim. In any case, Lincoln later told friends that he was slightly disappointed with his first impression of the statesman. Clay had read from a prepared text rather than speaking extemporaneously. His delivery, one of Lincoln's acquaintances later recalled, "did not come up to Mr. Lincoln's expectations." Still, the remarks clearly made a deep impression on the congressman-elect. In just two months, he would heed Clay's call and bring the fight to President Polk on the floor of the U.S. House of Representatives.[66]

The So-Called City of Washington

T he nation's capital in the fall of 1847 was still "an ill-contrived, ill-arranged, rambling, scrambling village." Farm animals, including pigs and geese, wandered through the city's muddy streets. Only Pennsylvania Avenue, with its rows of shops selling "French wines, Parisian millinery, and fine English woolens" held much charm for worldly visitors. One French diplomat complained that the whole place amounted to "neither city nor village" and said it displayed "a miserable, desolate look." The diplomat derided the capital as "the so-called city of Washington."[67]

The Lincolns arrived at the central station late on the night of December 2, 1847. At the depot, the usual throng of bums and pushy hackney-cab drivers likely provided an unpleasant welcome. The congressman-elect and his family made their way to Brown's "Indian Queen" Hotel, a local flophouse with an image of Pocahontas on the sign out front. In the reservation book, someone scrawled a terse record of their visit: "A. Lincoln & Lady 2 children, Illinois." The family soon moved to Mrs. Sprigg's, a pleasant boardinghouse on the current location of the Library of Congress, with windows overlooking the "shade trees and shrubbery" of Capitol Park.[68]

From Mrs. Sprigg's, it was only a short walk for Lincoln to the House chamber in the Capitol building. The hall resembled a Greek amphitheater, with rows of mahogany desks arranged in a semicircle around a "richly draped" speaker's platform. Lincoln drew seat number 191—a dismal spot in the last row. In front of Lincoln sat Alexander Stephens, a slight, wiry figure who would one day become the vice president of the Confederacy. Stephens thought his new colleague was "careless as to his manners and awkward in his speech," but Lincoln also possessed a peculiar brand of magnetism. "Socially," recalled Stephens, "he always kept his company in a roar of laughter."[69]

Lincoln's fellow Whig congressmen included former president John Quincy Adams, who had eschewed retirement in exchange for a chance to settle some old Washington grudges. Adams could be eccentric and ornery, especially in later life. He liked to skinny-dip in the Potomac and described himself as "an unsocial savage." Yet even in the late 1840s, he remained one of the nation's most thoughtful and accomplished foreign-policy thinkers. As a young man, Adams had served as a U.S. envoy in Russia. With Henry Clay, he had helped to negotiate an end to the War of 1812 with British diplomats in Belgium. Adams could be a vigorous, self-righteous expansionist. He believed that God had anointed Americans to spread across the entire continent. Still, his moralistic worldview also came with a powerful sense of justice. "Your conscience," his father, John Adams, had once written to his son at his post in St. Petersburg, "is the minister plenipotentiary of God Almighty in your breast. See to it that this minister never negotiates in vain. Attend to him in opposition to all the courts in the world."[70]

Adams's conscience (and perhaps his political instincts) told him that the Mexican War was all wrong. The United States, the former president once declared in another context, "goes not abroad, in search of monsters to destroy." Adams now counted himself among fourteen "irreconcilables" in the House who had voted against the declaration of war. The curmudgeonly former president had little patience for the rowdy new brand of expansionism embodied in "Mr. Polk's War." In the House chamber one day, legislators cheerfully debated among themselves about the correct pronunciation of the word "Illinois." Overhearing the conversation, Adams snapped that judging "from the character of the representatives in this congress from that state, I should decide unhesitatingly that the proper pronunciation was 'All noise.' "[71]

The House swore in Lincoln and the other freshman representatives on December 6. The following day the war over the war began. On December 7, President Polk sent his annual message—a forerunner of the modern State of the Union—to Congress. A clerk read it before the assembled chamber. The president shrewdly sought to capitalize on the national elation over the capture of Mexico City. He lauded the "rapid and brilliant success of our arms and the vast extent of the enemy's territory, which [has] been overrun and con-quered." Polk faulted Mexican troops for "striking the first blow, and shedding the blood of our citizens on our own soil." The United States, the president claimed, was "the aggrieved nation" and was "compelled in self-defense to repel the invader and to vindicate the national honor and interests by prosecuting [the war] with vigor until we could obtain a just and honorable peace."

Now, Polk asserted, the U.S. was entitled to seize a large swath of Mexican territory as an indemnity. He did not want to annex the entire country. "It has never been contemplated by me, as an object of the war, to make a permanent conquest of the Republic of Mexico or to annihilate her separate existence as an independent nation," Polk said. Still, the regions that comprise modern-day New Mexico and California presented an alluring prize. The mineral wealth of the great Southwest beckoned, and the port of San Francisco promised a critical gateway to Pacific trade. The California harbors, Polk sug-gested, "would afford shelter for our Navy, for our numerous whale ships, and other merchant vessels employed in the Pacific Ocean, and would in a short period become the marts of an extensive and profit-able commerce with China and other countries of the East." Now that the West was won, Polk warned, it "should never be surren-dered to Mexico."[72]

Polk's message ignited a firestorm over what to do with the con-quered Mexican land. Some Democrats, particularly in the north-east and northwest, wanted Polk to annex the entire country. Polk preferred to hang on to some strategic Mexican territory, including the land that would become California, New Mexico, Arizona, and other Western states—but give Mexico City and other areas back to the Mexicans. Still, the All Mexico movement, fueled by breathless editorials in the penny press, had begun gaining momentum after the military victories at Buena Vista and Vera Cruz. For months Democratic newspapers in New York and the Midwest had been ringing the annexation bell. "It is a gorgeous prospect, this annexa-tion of all Mexico," declared the *New York Herald*. "Like the Sabine virgins, she will soon learn to love her ravishers." The *Illinois State Register* took a higher-toned approach, but the policy prescription was the same. The conflict had become a "war of philanthropy and benevolence," the paper claimed. Only a sustained American effort to bring backward Mexico into the nineteenth century would satisfy the country's new sense of national mission.[73]

Some modern historians have dismissed the All Mexico movement as little more than "sensationalism selling newspapers." Yet the debate over the fate of America's neighbor to the south dominated Lincoln's first months in Congress. Influential Democratic figures, like historian George Bancroft, supported the annexation proposals, as did some other politicians, like Michigan's Lewis Cass, who declared that "to attempt to prevent the American people from taking possession of Mexico, if they demand it, would be as futile in effect as to undertake to stop the rushing of the cataract of Niagara."[74]

The All Mexico movement actually represents a critical shift in the American rationale for expansion—from "an almost Nietzschean self-realizationism," according to one historian, to a new "quasi-altruism." Expansionists now saw their role as "a religious duty to regenerate the unfortunate people of the enemy country by bringing them into the life-giving shrine of American democracy." As with the agitation over Texas annexation, the enthusiasm sometimes resembled the wild euphoria of an evangelical revival. At other times, as with the Texas debate, it carried romantic overtones. At a mass meeting in January 1848, the Texas statesman Sam Houston advised doubters to make a trip to Mexico. "Look out for the beautiful *señoritas*, or pretty girls," he told his audience, "and if you choose to annex them, no doubt the result of this annexation will be a most powerful and delightful evidence of civilization."[75]

Aside from the opposition to Polk's proposals, most Whigs, like Lincoln, shared little in common with the All Mexico crowd. The Whig delegation in Congress had long since grown wary of the war. Polk noticed that as early as December 1846 many Whigs had stopped showing up at White House receptions. "This is probably to be attributed to the excitement growing out of the party debate . . . on the subject of the Mexican War and my course in conducting it," the president wrote in his diary. The following year, Whig senator Thomas Corwin of Ohio—Lincoln's future minister to Mexico— delivered a blistering indictment of the war. "If I were a Mexican I would tell you, 'Have you not room in your own country to bury your dead men? If you come into mine, we will greet you with bloody hands, and welcome you to hospitable graves.' " Whig representative Joshua Giddings, one of Lincoln's fellow boarders at Mrs. Sprigg's, complained about the bad behavior of U.S. troops and threatened to cut their supplies.[76]

Lincoln had never been as strident an opponent of the war as either Corwin or Giddings. And yet, perhaps convinced by his idol Henry Clay's address in Lexington, Lincoln plunged himself into opposition politics almost as soon as he entered the House. Lincoln's rationale for taking on Polk was twofold. First, he considered the war "*unnecessary*, inasmuch as Mexico was in no way molesting, or menacing the U.S. or the people thereof." Second, he thought the conflict was "*unconstitutional*, because the power of levying war is vested in Congress, and not in the President." Lincoln did not con- tend, as some Whigs did, that the war revealed a deliberate plot of slaveholders to extend their territory. Instead, he thought Polk was simply a demagogue. The American invasion, Lincoln explained, amounted to little more than "a war of conquest brought into exis- tence to catch votes."[77]

A few days before Christmas 1847, Lincoln submitted his "spot resolutions" to the House. The document closely followed Clay's prescription for challenging Polk. The goal, Lincoln stated, was to "establish whether the particular spot of soil on which the blood of our *citizens* was so shed, was, or was not, *our own soil*, at that time." The Illinois congressman asked a series of rhetorical questions of the president, suggesting that the outbreak of hostilities had been the re- sult of American provocation, not Mexican belligerence.[78]

On January 8, 1848, Lincoln sat down and wrote a letter to his law partner back in Springfield. The congressman reported that he had begun "getting the hang of the House," and had made a short speech on a minor issue. "I find speaking here and elsewhere about the same thing," Lincoln said. "I was about as badly scared, and no worse, as I am when I speak in court." He added that he was about to make another, more important, speech soon. "I hope," Lincoln told Herndon, "to succeed well enough to wish you to see it."[79]

No One Man

Herndon's violent reaction to Lincoln's Mexican War speech caught the congressman off guard. Once "you get over your scare," Lincoln told his partner, "read [the speech] over again, sentence by sentence, and tell me honestly what you think of it." A second reading apparently did nothing to placate the younger man. Herndon wrote back, arguing that Polk's invasion was perfectly justified.[80]

Lincoln fired off another tart response. "Allow the President to invade a neighboring nation, whenever *he* shall deem it necessary to repel an invasion, and you allow him to do so, whenever he may choose to say he deems it necessary for such purpose—and you allow him to make war at pleasure," the congressman complained. "Study to see if you can fix *any limit* to his power in this respect, after you have given him so much as you propose. If, to-day, he should choose to say he thinks it necessary to invade Canada, to prevent the British from invading us, how could you stop him?" The Constitution was designed explicitly to guarantee that *"no one man"* could launch a war, Lincoln declared. Herndon's argument, the congressman scolded his friend, "destroys the whole matter, and places our President where kings have always stood."[81]

Herndon made his case on narrow grounds, offering "exclusively a constitutional argument" in support of Polk. Because the letters of Lincoln's law partner have been lost, it is left to historians to speculate about his precise thinking. In later years, as Herndon recalled the exchange, he said he was trying to save Lincoln from a political blunder. Yet there is no evidence beyond Herndon's word to support this claim. It seems more plausible that Herndon was simply caught up in the excitement of a victorious war. He devoured newspapers and could easily have been swept away by the crusades of the penny press. Lincoln's law partner was still only in his late twenties and highly susceptible to the lure of romantic adventures. Herndon's correspondence with Lincoln alternated between policy critiques and personal gossip. In one letter later that year, Herndon bragged to his law partner about "kissing a pretty girl." Lincoln good-naturedly replied: "Go it while you're young!"[82]

Herndon once described himself as "a young, undisciplined, un-educated, wild man." He acknowledged that he could be "somewhat of a radical." Lincoln's law partner would eventually develop something of a track record for advocating foreign policies that were both expansionist and reformist. Herndon once wrote an editorial recommending the annexation of Cuba—on the "rather advanced ground" that the abolition of slavery on the island would follow. Lincoln's law partner believed events in nineteenth-century North America held consequences that were "world wide and world effecting." They represented, he later insisted, "a motion and a rush of the race Godward."[83]

Lincoln also held a progressive vision of America's world role. Yet Herndon's breathless enthusiasm often grated on his sober law partner. The older man complained about the "glittering generalities" that emerged from Herndon's mouth. Lincoln liked to make his arguments carefully and logically, assembling a preponderance of irrefutable facts. Herndon preferred emotional appeals. When a lawyer gets "tears on the jury," the younger man noted, then he knows he has won the case. Herndon would sometimes make an argument to his partner by maintaining that he simply "felt it *in my bones*." Lincoln would needle Herndon, asking him how his "bones philosophy" was working out.[84]

Herndon concluded that Lincoln had committed "political sui-cide" by his opposition to the war. "When I listened to the com-ments of his friends everywhere after the delivery of his speech," he later recalled, "I felt that he had made a mistake." Lincoln's law part-ner believed that the spot resolutions and subsequent speech "sealed Lincoln's doom as a Congressman." Yet there is little evidence to support this assertion. Lincoln ultimately developed a remarkably refined position on the Mexican War—one that satisfied both the expansionists among his hawkish western constituents and his dov-ish Whig patrons back east.[85]

Lincoln and other members of Congress scrambled to try to bridge the divide as the All Mexico agitation gathered momentum. In early February 1847, Democrat John C. Calhoun laid out a pro-gram he called the defensive-line strategy. Calhoun's plan called for the United States to absorb a vast swath of land in northern Mexico while at the same time withdrawing American forces from the heart of the country. The goal was to satisfy Americans who demanded an indemnity from the Mexicans, without taking so much land that it would aggravate the divide over slavery. Lincoln, notes the historian Mark E. Neely Jr., ultimately "compromised easily with expansion-ism" and adopted Calhoun's strategy "in all its guises."[86]

The Illinois congressman recognized that it would be politi-cally impossible to end a victorious war with a total retreat. "In a final treaty of peace, we shall probably be under a sort of necessity of taking some territory," Lincoln explained. Still, he added, "it is my desire that we shall not acquire any extending so far South, as to en-large and agrivate the distracting question of slavery." When Whig newspapers like Horace Greeley's *New York Tribune* seemed to ad-vocate withdrawing U.S. troops all the way to the Nueces River, Lincoln tried to set them straight. "By putting us in the position of insisting on the line of the Nueces," Lincoln wrote, "you put us in a position which, in my opinion, we cannot maintain." The "true posi-tion," the Illinois congressman argued, should be "that the boundary of Texas extended just so far as American settlements taking part in her revolution extended." Such an argument would require defending territory south of the Nueces River.[87]

The wrangling over All Mexico came to an abrupt end on February 19, 1848, when news arrived in Washington that the president's man in Mexico City, Nicholas Trist, had secretly signed a treaty ending the war. Polk's envoy had disobeyed his instructions to return to the capital. Yet the president concluded that the treaty—which ceded territory including both the mineral-rich deserts and the Pacific ports—ultimately served the national interest. At first, expansionists balked. Both Illinois senators actually voted against the treaty, hoping to win even more territory. But the penny press finally swung behind the peace initiative, and Americans in general supported Polk. By the summer, the U.S. Army's Third Infantry Division was on its way home. As the troops marched out of Mexico City, the band played "The Girl I Left Behind Me."[88]

A Stargazing Thinking Look

At some point after the Lincolns arrived in Washington, the congressman apparently sent his wife away. The circumstances remain somewhat mysterious, and what we know of the incident comes from a letter Lincoln wrote to Mary in April. "When you were here," he explained, "I thought you hindered me." And yet, "in this troublesome world, we are never quite satisfied." Now Lincoln felt lonely. "I hate to stay in this old room by myself," he wrote. Lincoln playfully teased his wife. At the boardinghouse, "all with whom you were on decided good terms . . . send their love," he reported. "The others," Lincoln added mischievously, "say nothing." In another letter, he acknowledged Mary's desire to return to Washington. "Will you be a good girl in all things?" he asked.[89]

As spring turned to summer, Lincoln increasingly devoted his attention to the upcoming presidential election. The congressman continued to defend the Whig record of challenging the war's origins.

"It is a fact, that the United States Army, in marching to the Rio Grande, marched into a peaceful Mexican settlement, and frightened the inhabitants away from their homes and their growing crops," Lincoln wrote to one Baptist preacher in May. "Possibly you consider those acts too small for notice. Would you venture to so consider them, had they been committed by any nation on earth, against the humblest of our people? I know you would not. Then I ask, is the precept 'Whatsoever ye would that men should do to you, do ye even so to them' obsolete?—of no force?—of no application?"[90]

And yet, even as Lincoln appealed to the Golden Rule to support his Mexican War policy, he threw his support behind one of the war's heroes for the Whig presidential nomination. Henry Clay would have been the obvious choice, but the Sage of Ashland was now in his early seventies. "Mr. Clay's chance for an election is just no chance at all," Lincoln explained to one ally. A smarter choice, Lincoln insisted, would be Zachary Taylor, the victorious Mexican War general. Taylor was a sloppily attired army officer—"a thick-set man with stubby legs and heavy brows contracted into a perpetual frown." Ordinarily he would not make an ideal political poster boy. Yet, in this case, Taylor's candidacy combined the glow of a victorious warrior with the complete lack of any political record to attack. "In my judgment, we can elect nobody but Gen. Taylor," Lincoln concluded.[91]

The Illinois congressman and his pro-Taylor clique referred to themselves as the Young Indians. Lincoln wrote to Herndon in Springfield urging his partner to "gather up all the shrewd wild boys about town" and organize them into Taylor clubs. He explained that by choosing a military hero, the Whigs would turn "the war thunder" against the Democrats. Herndon did as he was told, but he was not particularly enthusiastic about the choice. The whole thing reeked of hypocrisy. "I was disposed to take a dispirited view of the situation," Herndon later recalled, "and therefore was not easily warmed up." According to one report in a Democratic newspaper, Herndon was prohibited from speaking at a Taylor rally in Springfield because of his tepid support for the candidate.[92]

Lincoln, for his part, went on the attack. The following month, in one of his most cutting and effective speeches in the House, the Illinois congressman hammered the Democratic presidential nominee, Lewis Cass. The Michigan senator had been lauded for his military record in the Black Hawk War a decade and a half before. Now Lincoln mocked the senator, claiming that Cass had "invaded Canada without resistance, and outvaded it without pursuit." The Illinois congressman walked up and down the House aisles as he made his case, flailing his arms and keeping the chamber in "a continuous roar of merriment." Lincoln reiterated his opposition to Polk's provocative maneuvers along the Rio Grande. "The marching [of] an army into the midst of a peaceful Mexican settlement, frightening the inhabitants away, leaving their growing crops, and other property to destruction, to *you* may appear a perfectly amiable, peaceful, unprovoking procedure," Lincoln said, "but it does not appear so to *us*." Cass's election, he declared, would lead "to new wars, new acquisitions of territory and still further extensions of slavery."[93]

Lincoln also tempered his expansionism when he spoke before dovish audiences. In the fall of 1848, the Illinois congressman traveled to New England to campaign for Taylor. A radical group of former northeastern Whigs, objecting to Taylor's candidacy, had created its own new Free Soil Party and nominated Martin Van Buren for the presidency. Lincoln tried to persuade his listeners to back the Whigs and Taylor instead. At one stop, in Worcester, Massachusetts, Lincoln addressed an audience in the town's cavernous Mechanics Hall. He tried to appeal to the sympathies of the Northeasterners, who traditionally had been much less comfortable with territorial expansion than Westerners. The Whig Party, Lincoln declared, "did not believe in enlarging our field, but in keeping our fences where they are and cultivating our present possession, making it a garden." By the end of the speech the Illinois congressman "brought down the house," one witness recalled, and had his audience shouting, "Go on! Go on!"[94]

The pro-Taylor assault of Lincoln and the other Young Indians ultimately paid off. The general defeated both Cass and Van Buren for the presidency, although Taylor's margin in the popular vote amounted to only three percentage points. At the general's inauguration, on a "cold, gusty day, filled with flurries of rain and snow," Lincoln shared in the revelry with mixed feelings. Although thrilled at the Whig victory, Lincoln appeared a little sad at the prospect of leaving Washington as the end of his term approached. He had campaigned for his office on the principle that "turn about is fair play." Now, honoring his promise, he was obliged to eschew a second term in order to give his former law partner Stephen Logan his own opportunity. With his return to Springfield looming, Lincoln tried to enjoy himself, remaining at Taylor's inaugural ball until after four a.m. When he finally left, the staff had already gone home, leaving the hats and coats in a heap on the floor. Drunken revelers began throwing punches as they scrambled to recover their possessions. Lincoln ultimately left the ball without finding his hat. He walked home to his boardinghouse in the cold.[95]

Lincoln's opposition to Polk's conduct of the Mexican War is often viewed as an early political failure. Herndon (and many of Lincoln's other early biographers) certainly saw it that way. There is some evidence that Lincoln himself regretted his uncompromising stance. John Hay later reported Lincoln as president quoting his fellow Illinois Whig Justin Butterfield about the wisdom of enthusiastically supporting one's country in wartime. "I opposed one war," Lincoln recalled Butterfield saying. "That was enough for me. I am now perpetually in favor of war, pestilence and famine."[96]

Modern historians, however, have questioned whether Lincoln's opposition was really such a political disaster. His stance, after all, was not so different from his other Midwestern Whig colleagues in Congress.[97] A larger but related question is whether Lincoln's position was a principled stance against American foreign-policy excess or a cynical attempt to get ahead in party politics. The answer is neither and both. Lincoln—and this was a large part of his brilliance and originality as a statesman—was somehow able to remain both a principled idealist and a pragmatic realist throughout his career. That combination would serve the sixteenth president well in his relations with the great powers of Europe, whose leaders were often masters of that same mysterious art.[98]

In any event, there is no denying that by the end of his term in Congress, Lincoln had evolved considerably as a foreign-policy thinker. As a young man he had viewed foreign affairs simply as a source of adventure and a means of escape from Midwestern drudgery. Until the debate over Texas annexation and the subsequent Mexican War, he had given the topic little serious thought. Yet over the course of Lincoln's time in Congress, he had begun to develop what would later become a sound and nuanced approach to foreign affairs. He understood that some territorial expansion was inevitable in a young and growing country. Yet he worked ceaselessly to keep it from upsetting the sectional balance and violating the principles of international justice that many Americans held dear.[99]

In the winter of 1848, however, Lincoln still remained a long way from the paragon of executive power that he would later become. His opposition to Polk's conduct had been based on the principle that "no one man" could launch a war—a stark challenge to the office of the presidency. He was determined, as he told Herndon, to keep presidents from occupying the space "where kings have always stood." Lincoln's moral sense and political instincts during the Mexican War had proved sound. Yet it would take the brutal necessities of the Civil War to convince him that the exigencies of foreign affairs would often demand the strong hand of a determined executive—sometimes, as Polk had demonstrated, even in defiance of Congress.

Lincoln returned to Springfield in early 1849. His friends noticed that he brought a considerable new trove of off-color stories home with him from Washington. (The young politician, a friend once remarked, had a lifelong "insane love in telling dirty and smutty stories.") Yet Lincoln had also acquired a renewed "soberness of thought." Lincoln had witnessed his young country in the throes of its first major growing pains. He had also seen the White House up close—a tantalizing prize. As Lincoln returned to his law practice, friends noticed a peculiar vacant stare that would sometimes flash across their former congressman's face. It resembled, one of them later recalled to Billy Herndon, a "stargazing thinking look."[100]

Ghosts of the Mexican War

To residents of Ottawa, Illinois, the columns of pilgrims streaming into town—cantering on horseback, drifting on boats, bouncing along in carriages—looked like a vast army preparing for battle. Rows of campfires blinked along the approaches into the village, warming travelers who could find no room in local hotels. The following morning, August 21, 1858, so many visitors stomped through Ottawa's dirt roads that the whole place "resembled a vast smokehouse." The unforgiving late summer sun and oppressive heat offered no quarter to the standing-room-only crowd that had assembled to watch Abraham Lincoln and Stephen Douglas debate.[101]

A decade had elapsed since Lincoln's term in Congress. Now he wanted to return to Washington. He had spent the interval building up his law practice, traveling the frontier circuit, and dabbling in the increasingly acrimonious debate over slavery—a battle that the Mexican War had helped to touch off. Now Lincoln was seeking a seat in the U.S. Senate as a candidate from the newly formed Republican Party. As Lincoln took his place on the platform in Ottawa, the ghosts of the Mexican War almost immediately came back to haunt him.

Stephen Douglas was a short, fat man whose body was topped by a "disproportionately huge head." Cheeks punched with dimples flanked his "pug nose." But when he spoke, he put his entire body into the effort, often to great effect. Today, as he hammered Lincoln on his Mexican War stance, the Little Giant "threw himself into contortions, shook his head, shook his fists." Douglas's entire body quivered "as with a palsy; his eyes protruded from their sockets; he raved like a mad bull." The voice of Lincoln's opponent sounded to one local reporter like "a demonized howl."[102]

In his opening remarks, Douglas sketched out his vision for America—an increasingly powerful young nation beginning to assert itself on the world stage. The United States had grown "from a feeble nation," he boomed, to "the most powerful on the face of the earth." If the country followed Douglas's policy proposals, it was destined to "go forward increasing in territory, in power, in strength and in glory until the republic of America shall be the North Star that shall guide the friends of freedom throughout the civilized world." Douglas tore into Lincoln over his old Mexican War speeches. "Whilst in Congress," the Little Giant began, Lincoln "distinguished himself by his opposition to the Mexican War, taking the side of the common enemy against his own country. And when he returned home, he found that the indignation of the people followed him everywhere, and he was again submerged or obliged to retire into private life, forgotten by his former friends." The overheated audience whooped and groaned at Douglas's opening volley.[103]

Lincoln, when it came time for his rejoinder, defended himself from Douglas's assault. He reminded that while he opposed the way Polk had begun the conflict, he had always voted supplies to the troops. Yet Lincoln and Douglas were not simply bickering over an old war. The classic debates, which stretched out over two months during the fall of 1858, really amounted to a profound conversation over the nature of American power itself.[104]

By the fall of 1858, Douglas had amassed a lengthy record of encouraging U.S. expansion. He had long lobbied for a transcontinental railroad, and he had supported the annexation of Texas and Oregon. In a subsequent debate, Douglas compared antiexpansionists to fathers who wanted to place their twelve-year-old sons in hoops to keep them from growing up. "Either the hoop must burst and be rent asunder," Douglas insisted, "or the child must die. So it would be with this great nation."[105]

Lincoln, for his part, argued that he was "not generally opposed to honest acquisition of territory." The real test, he said, would be whether expansion "would or would not aggravate the slavery question." Yet Douglas was relentless. By late October the Democrat was still hounding Lincoln about his Mexican War votes. Douglas maintained that Lincoln's statements on the war "were all sent to Mexico and printed in the Mexican language, and read at the head of the Mexican army." Lincoln's opposition, Douglas claimed, "induced the Mexicans to hold out the longer, and the guerrillas to keep up their warfare on the roadside, and to poison our men, and to take the lives of our soldiers wherever and whenever they could."[106]

Billy Herndon did his best to defend his law partner. He threw himself into the campaign, stumping through the state visiting out-of-the-way schoolhouses and small-town churches. For the debates with Douglas, Herndon helped Lincoln compile scrapbooks stuffed with newspaper clippings to bolster the candidate's arguments. Lincoln and Herndon must have known that American power and expansion would factor heavily into the debates. The pocket-size, leather-bound notebooks, currently archived at the Library of Congress, overflow with statistics about America's rising material strength and tables comparing the United States to European and other foreign countries. The United States boasted "the longest railroad on the globe," produced $15 million worth of nonagricultural products each year, and possessed 33,000 miles of overland telegraph wires—nearly as many as all of Europe—according to the clips. America's gold, copper, lead, and iron mines, according to another clipping, were "among the richest in the world."[107]

Herndon had always displayed an ambivalent attitude toward power. On the one hand, he sometimes seemed to embrace a muscular foreign policy—as his Mexican War stance and his at least occasional advocacy for Cuban annexation demonstrate. Although he always remained firmly in Lincoln's corner, Herndon admired Douglas's nerve and once acknowledged that he had "a kind of undeveloped feeling" for the Little Giant. And yet, even as he sometimes supported expansion, Herndon's crusading temperament never allowed him to feel comfortable with the unprincipled pursuit of the national interest. For Herndon, power was a dirty word—something to cleanse or expel. "I hate power," he once told an Illinois acquaintance.[108]

Lincoln, on the other hand, had long since made his peace with the gritty realities of power. He had put in his time on Aristocracy Hill, married one of their own. When it was politically necessary, he embraced convenient hypocrisies. He accepted power and sin as facts of life, things that could be managed but never completely eliminated. Understanding Lincoln's attitude toward power is critical to making sense of Lincoln's Mexican War policy—and later his approach to foreign affairs during the Civil War.

"The true rule, in determining to embrace, or reject anything, is not whether it have *any* evil in it; but whether it have more of evil, than of good," Lincoln once told an audience as a young congressman. "There are few things *wholly* evil, or *wholly* good. Almost everything, especially of governmental policy, is an inseparable compound of the two; so that our best judgment of the preponderance between them is continually demanded."[109]

Lincoln applied his mixed assessment of human nature to personal relationships as well as foreign affairs.[110] When Lincoln finally lost his 1858 Senate race to Douglas, he assumed he would be abandoned by the leaders of his party. After so many years in politics, he had little faith in the unconditional goodwill of powerful men. Lincoln appeared resentful and heartbroken when an acquaintance visited him at his Springfield law office on the day Douglas was reelected. "I expect everyone to desert me," Lincoln said, "except Billy."[111]

CHAPTER TWO

Lincoln vs. Seward

L INCOLN'S WORST FEARS ABOUT HIS POLITICAL FATE WERE OVERBLOWN. ONLY TWO YEARS AFTER LOSING HIS SENATE RACE, HE FOUND HIMSELF IN A SMALL, CROWDED OFFICE ON the second floor of the state house in Springfield, surrounded by supplicants of "as many nationalities as could easily be brought together [in] the West." Visitors filed past the "heaps and hills" of newspapers that were piled on the tables. A relaxed Lincoln, growing the beginnings of a wispy beard, pumped hands and warmly slapped backs. Outside, an icy wind howled over the prairie. The crush of uncouth visitors repulsed some witnesses. One newspaperman marveled at the "disagreeably intense" odor that filled the room. Lincoln was not complaining. After nearly thirty years climbing Illinois's political ladder, he was finally president-elect.[1]

The American political landscape had evolved dramatically since Lincoln's time in Congress more than a decade earlier. He had spent the first phase of his career as a loyal Whig, focusing primarily on economic issues like improving roads and canals.[2] Yet in the wake of the Mexican War, and particularly the Kansas-Nebraska Act of 1854—which reopened the possibility that slavery might be established in newly acquired territories under the doctrine of "popular sovereignty"—the old Whig Party had splintered. New battle lines emerged around the issue of human bondage. "Conscience Whigs" embraced the reinvigorated movement to abolish slavery, while more conservative "Cotton Whigs" feared a dramatic shift in the sectional balance. Lincoln attempted to bridge the divide by helping to found the new Republican Party in the mid-1850s. The Railsplitter's old antagonist Stephen Douglas, for his part, sought to take up the Democratic standard as the 1860 election approached.[3]

Lincoln's opponents, too, were badly divided along regional and ideological lines in 1860. Southern fire-eaters had nominated their own candidate, John C. Breckinridge of Kentucky, and another new group made up partly of disaffected southern Whigs—dubbed the Constitutional Union Party—siphoned off additional votes. Lincoln ultimately defeated Douglas and his other rivals by a huge margin in 1860. New Jersey was the only northern state he failed to win in the Electoral College.

Still, just weeks after the polls closed, the president-elect was forced to watch his prize dissolve. Angered by Lincoln's election and the rise of the Republicans to power, South Carolina voted to secede in December, followed by an avalanche of other states—first Mississippi, then Florida, Alabama, Georgia. Advisers urged the president-elect to hurry to Washington and take charge of the government as soon as possible. Lincoln, already looking worn and pale, was in no rush. "I expect they will drive me insane after I get there," he told reporters, "and I want to keep tolerably sane, at least until after the inauguration."[4]

Lincoln managed to keep his head almost until Inauguration Day, which in the midnineteenth century did not take place until well into the New Year. Yet by early March, as expected, the president-elect was losing it. His young secretary, John Hay, thought his boss was beginning to show the symptoms of a man under "a good deal of hydraulic pressure." On top of the secession crisis, rumors poured in from abroad about the malign intentions of the European powers. John McClintock, a Methodist pastor in Paris, wrote to caution the president that the chaos across the Atlantic looked like weakness to

Europeans. "The public mind both of France and England is be-fogged on the American question," McClintock warned Lincoln. It was "of the utmost importance," the clergyman insisted, that the president should quickly fill the consular slots in Paris and London with "*competent* men."[5]

Lincoln began by choosing William Henry Seward as his chief diplomat. Short and pompous, with a husky voice and small, dart-ing blue eyes, Seward had been the president's main competition for the Republican nomination.[6] The former New York governor could be irascible. His dinner-table conversation reminded one guest of "a man soliloquizing aloud." Yet he was also well connected and well traveled. "Governor Seward, there is one part of my work that I shall have to leave largely to you," the president told his nominee for sec-retary of state shortly after he arrived in the capital. "I shall have to depend upon you for taking care of these matters of foreign affairs, of which I know so little, and with which I reckon you are famil-iar." Lincoln ordered Seward to make sure the American legations in England, France, Spain, and Mexico were "guarded as strongly and quickly as possible."[7]

Seward was never a man to underestimate his own importance. When Lincoln offered him the post, the New Yorker dashed off a terse letter to his wife: "I have advised Mr. L. that I will not decline. It is inevitable. I will try to save freedom and my country." As the se-cession crisis worsened, Seward reported home that he had "assumed a sort of dictatorship for defense," in the capital. A couple of weeks later he told his wife that the whole government "would fall into con-sternation and despair" if he left Washington for even a few days. "I am the only *hopeful, calm, conciliatory* person here," he boasted.[8]

Lincoln may have been elected president, but Seward intended to carve out his own power center. There "exists no great difference between an elected president of the United States and a hereditary monarch," Seward explained to one European diplomat in Washing-ton. "The latter is called to the throne through the accident of birth, the former through the chances which make his election possible.

The actual direction of public affairs belongs to the leader of the ruling party here just as in a hereditary principality." Lincoln's allies wrote to warn him that Seward considered the president-elect his subordinate, "just as the queen or king of England is subject to the policy of the ministry."[9]

Indeed, at least at first, Lincoln did not seem up to the task. When he finally reached Washington, the stress physically overwhelmed him. On bad days the president threatened to storm out onto the south lawn of the Executive Mansion and hang himself from a tree. Lincoln had trouble sleeping, and he rarely found time to eat. Some afternoons he simply went to bed after lunch. "If to be the head of Hell is as hard as what I have to undergo here," the president complained, "I could find it in my heart to pity Satan himself." Lincoln had always been sensitive to changes in the climate. Harsh weather aggravated his "defective nerves," he once told a friend. The unsteady Washington elements—alternating between a crisp, cool spring, and a clammy Indian summer—may have made matters worse. By late March, high winds had enveloped the entire city in a suffocating cloud of yellow dust. Mary Lincoln told friends that the president had "keeled over" with a migraine.[10]

The Days of Principles Are Gone

A quick glance at the global chessboard in the spring of 1861 would have given any U.S. president a headache. For decades America's core foreign-policy principle had been the maintenance of its independence from Europe. The Founding Fathers had been so obsessed with this point that they derided the art of diplomacy itself. American statesmen considered European efforts to maintain a balance of power through secret treaties and cynical compromises the epitome of corruption. In the New World, which its founders had proclaimed a virtuous "city on a hill," there was no place for half-measures when it came to republican principles. George Washington, in his farewell address, had warned against being drawn into European affairs. Thomas Jefferson derided Old World diplomacy as "the pest of the peace of the world."[11]

North American geography had guaranteed the new nation a measure of natural independence. Yet complete isolation, U.S. statesmen soon learned, was impossible. Without the massive British navy to protect shipping lanes, Jefferson himself was forced to dispatch troops to the Mediterranean to confront pirates who had been preying on American vessels. In the second decade of the nineteenth century, livid over the British practice of the impressment of U.S. sailors, Americans took up arms again—a conflict that resulted in the burning of Washington. The War of 1812 ultimately ended in a stalemate, but Americans were finally beginning to feel their oats in the international arena. They largely viewed the conflict as a triumph.

In the years that followed, American adventurers repeatedly tested the national limits. Frontiersmen skirmished with British colonists along the Canadian boundary. Merchants in search of export markets nurtured U.S. commercial ties with Latin America. With expansionist nationalism on the rise, Americans displayed little patience for the continuing encroachment by foreign powers. By the winter of 1823, president James Monroe and his secretary of state, John Quincy Adams, forcefully rejected European interference in the Western Hemisphere in the text of Monroe's annual message to Congress. Monroe and Adams announced that the United States would oppose any further attempts by Europe to establish colonies in the New World.

Statesmen on the Continent—who generally considered Americans "a bumptious and absurdly self-confident folk, aggressively preaching their national faith of democracy without much regard for good manners"—were unimpressed. In succeeding decades they openly disdained and repeatedly violated the principles that Monroe and Adams had set forth. Still, the proclamation that later came to be known as the Monroe Doctrine, notes one modern diplomatic scholar, amounted to one more "ringing affirmation of America's independence from Europe."[12]

Even as the young United States was reasserting its freedom from the Old World, the classic traditions of European diplomacy were themselves in flux. After Britain defeated France in the Napoleonic Wars ending in 1815, the European powers had established a surprisingly sturdy peace agreement at the Congress of Vienna. European monarchs concluded a pact to join forces to suppress revolutionary movements wherever they might spring up in Europe—a system designed to prevent the emergence of a new Napoleon. The conservative arrangement worked well for several decades. Yet by 1848, liberal revolts—fueled by the tremendous advances in communications and the economic imbalances touched off by the industrial and market revolutions—were erupting across the Continent, threatening the old regimes. Karl Marx, then a young radical in Belgium, issued his famous manifesto, declaring that a revolutionary "spectre" was "haunting" Europe.

Communism was not the only new force that threatened to challenge the diplomatic received wisdom. A cauldron of new ideas bubbled on the Continent in the midnineteenth century. Advances in science and mathematics were changing how Europeans viewed the concepts of order and progress. Charles Darwin and Herbert Spencer began to propound their ideas about how the mightiest survive—a notion that had profound consequences for international relations. In the early 1850s, the Crimean War erupted between Russia on one side and Ottoman Turkey, Britain, France, and Sardinia on the other. It was a conflict that finally destroyed the once-sturdy peace of the post–Napoleonic War era. Principled agreement between the major powers became a rarity. Instead, the old order was replaced with an unforgiving competition for territory, natural resources, and raw power. As one Austrian diplomat put it as the Crimean War approached: "The days of principles are gone."[13]

All this—rising American nationalism on one side of the ocean and growing European realism on the other—combined to present

Lincoln with a perfect storm in the diplomatic arena in the first months of his presidency. Already Southern states had been seceding by the day, and a serious crisis loomed over how the European powers would respond to the newly proclaimed Confederate States of America. Now Lincoln was also about to be confronted by a major new challenge to America's influence in its own hemisphere.

Lincoln's first foreign-policy crisis as president actually came from one of Europe's waning powers: Spain. For years the United States and Spain had been maneuvering for influence in the Caribbean. American filibusters (freebooters) hoped to establish outposts and naval bases in the former Spanish colony of Santo Domingo (in the Dominican Republic), from which they might one day launch an invasion of Cuba. Spanish authorities, for their part, sought to restore a measure of influence after the nation had declared its independence from Spanish rule in 1821. In the months before Lincoln took office, Spanish leaders had been quietly dispatching soldiers and weapons to the mountainous, sun-splashed territory of mahogany forests and sugarcane fields. Then, just weeks into Lincoln's term, the Dominican president, faced with a plunging currency and the prospect of social unrest, officially invited Spanish forces to return to the country. A fleet of ships arrived at the Dominican port shortly after Lincoln took his oath of office. The provocative move seemed designed to take advantage of the North American chaos. For Lincoln and Seward, it also struck at what one historian has described as "the heart of our creed with regard to foreign policy."[14]

Lincoln was still ill on the morning of April 1, 1861, just days after the Spanish invasion, when Seward presented Lincoln with a striking memo. Titled "Some thoughts for the President's consideration," the secretary of state used the crisis to protest to the president that after a full month in office Lincoln was still "without a policy either foreign or domestic." Seward suggested that the United States immediately take Madrid to task and "demand explanations." The secretary of state also counseled sending American agents into Canada, Mexico, and Central America, "to rouse a vigorous continental *spirit*

of independence on this continent against European intervention."
If the Spanish failed to offer acceptable explanations for the Santo
Domingo maneuver, Seward said he would advise Lincoln to con-
vene Congress and declare war on the invaders.[15]

Seward saw his opportunity to wrest control from the ailing and
overwhelmed commander in chief. Whichever "policy we adopt,
there must be an energetic prosecution of it," the secretary of state
wrote. "For this purpose it must be somebody's business to pursue and direct it incessantly." If Lincoln could not lead the effort,
he should assign it to a member of the cabinet. "It is not in my especial province," Seward concluded, but "I neither seek to evade nor
assume responsibility." The secretary of state ordered his son Frederick to copy over the hastily written, "hardly legible" document, and
deliver it directly to Lincoln. Seward, his son later recalled, would
trust the sensitive missive to "no other hand."[16]

Lincoln must have been stunned by the document. Yet he could
not deny that his administration had found itself under a cataract of
miserable foreign-affairs news. Rumors flew in Washington that the
French might seize Haiti now that the Spanish had made their move
on Santo Domingo. On the same day Seward submitted his memo,
the *New York Times*, which maintained close ties to the secretary
of state, complained that "contemptible schemers" abroad promised
to tear the republic apart if it remained "guided by pusillanimity."
The paper warned that if the United States failed to quickly resolve
the conflict, European powers would step in. "If the weak man do
not govern his household," the *Times* cautioned, "the strong man will
govern it for him."[17]

Still, picking another fight now—even with a weak power like
Spain—would be madness. The ailing president, who for years had
fought periodic battles with a mysterious depressive illness he referred to as the hypo, summoned the strength to write out a reply to
his secretary of state in an unusually choppy, uneven hand. Lincoln
acknowledged that the seizure of Santo Domingo "certainly brings
a new item within the range of our foreign policy." Yet he assured

Seward that all was "in perfect harmony, without ever a suggestion that we had no foreign policy." Finally, Lincoln rejected his secretary of state's suggestion that a member of the cabinet take charge. "I remark that if this must be done," the president wrote, "*I* must do it."[18]

In the end, Lincoln apparently never sent his reply. The president frequently composed sharply worded letters that he ultimately tore up once his anger subsided. In this case, because no copy of Lincoln's response has been found in the Seward papers, scholars believe the president likely delivered his message orally. However he handled his impulsive secretary of state, Lincoln decided not to publicize the exchange. Seward's memo remained hidden for decades—and with it one of the most fascinating and baffling episodes in the history of American foreign policy.[19]

Beyond the Pacific Ocean

What was Seward thinking? The debate over Seward's "foreign war panacea" has been raging now for more than a century. Charles Sumner, the radical Massachusetts senator and a rival of Seward's, complained that the secretary of state simply "lost his head." Others saw the move as the culmination of a decades-long drive to extend American influence. Challenging European imperialism in the Western Hemisphere was nothing new for Seward. He had long advertised his desire to acquire Canada, and he once declared that Mexico City should be the capital of the United States. Seward, said Lincoln's secretary of the navy, Gideon Welles, was "almost crazy on the subject of territorial expansion." Lincoln's own personal secretaries shared Welles's assessment. John Hay and John Nicolay, in their ten-volume, nearly five-thousand-page biography of Lincoln, speculate that Seward aimed to ignite "a continental crusade"—"a war of conquest" that would heal America's internecine rift by rallying both North and South to the same cause. "Who," Lincoln's secretaries ask, "shall say that these imperial dreams did not contemplate the possibility of changing a threatened dismemberment of the Union into the triumphant annexation of Canada, Mexico, and the West Indies?"[20]

In this case, however, Seward was probably just bluffing, attempting to project a useful "madman image" in an effort to deter the great powers.[21] Lincoln's secretary of state, to be sure, was a vigorous expansionist. "There is no debating," writes historian George Herring, that Seward "was the key figure in mid-nineteenth-century expansion, the link between the manifest destiny movement of the 1840s and the overseas expansionism of the 1890s." In the years following the Civil War, Seward would campaign strongly for the purchase of Alaska. (His enemies derided the acquisition as "Seward's Folly.") Yet Seward recognized that America's rise to power was first contingent on healing the bitter divisions at home. Only by staring down the European powers, Seward believed, could the United States fulfill its expansionist destiny.[22]

Lincoln is not usually remembered as an expansionist at all. Yet Lincoln's and Seward's core foreign-affairs philosophies were more similar than is commonly understood.[23] The market revolution, beginning in the early nineteenth century, had produced a sea change in the way some statesmen viewed international relations. For millennia, national strength had been measured in terms of military capabilities—by the size of armies, the quantity of frigates, the courage of generals, the morale of troops. By Lincoln's presidency, at least some world leaders—particularly in the United States and Britain—had come to view power primarily in economic terms. Access to banks, capital, and international markets was a better predictor of future strength than the quantity of guns and soldiers, the thinking went. Lincoln and Seward were both students of this Hamiltonian school of foreign policy, as historian Walter Russell Mead has labeled it. Economic forces—not simply cavalry and cannon—would ultimately boost the United States to world power. Such thinking, Mead observes, amounted to "a radical innovation in the world of great-power diplomacy."[24]

Lincoln and Seward's former Whig Party had served as the vanguard of the antebellum Hamiltonians. John Quincy Adams, one of the party's founders, had hoped that Whiggery would provide a bulwark against the popularity of Andrew Jackson, whom the Whigs derided as a "military chieftain." The Whig foreign-affairs program was simple and straightforward. If the federal government directed its energies toward encouraging commercial enterprise and internal improvements, bolstering the whole system with a tariff to protect industry, the country would inevitably emerge as a world power. Lincoln was a true believer. "I have always been an old-line Henry-Clay Whig," the president remarked in 1861. The fact that Lincoln had long since joined the Republicans did not alter his core Whig principles.[25]

When asked about his platform during his first political campaign in the 1830s, Lincoln is said to have replied: "My politics are short and sweet, like the old woman's dance. I am in favor of a national bank. I am in favor of the internal improvement system and a high protective tariff." The story is perhaps apocryphal, but the message is true enough. Lincoln, for much of his political career, was actually focused primarily on issues of economic development.[26] Military conquest would contribute little to America's standing in the world if it undermined economic stability. Real predominance would require patient anticipation of what one Lincoln biographer has called "the eventual triumph of the market."[27]

Seward, despite his caricature as a land-hungry ogre, also believed that economic development was the key to achieving great-power status. The future secretary of state insisted that it would be folly to "seize with haste, and force the fruit, which ripening in time, will fall of itself into our hands." The real prize, Seward noted, was "the commerce of the world, which is the empire of the world." Seward was motivated more by the quest for foreign markets and overseas investment capital. Even when he sought territory, he was most interested in regions that could double as trade entrepôts or coaling bases. "The nation that draws the most materials from the earth," he declared, "and fabricates the most, and sells the most of productions and fabrics to foreign nations, must be, and will be, the great power of the earth." Commerce, he remarked, was the new "god of boundaries."[28]

Lincoln, in his public remarks, tended to focus on the moral perils of slavery more often than he lauded economic expansion. Still, he largely shared Seward's economic vision. Lincoln was listening as Seward refined his approach to foreign affairs over the course of the 1850s. In the winter of 1854, Seward took the floor of the U.S. Senate and mocked what he derided as "aggrandizing, conquering" warmongers. Only by healing the sectional divide, Seward insisted, would the United States succeed in its drive to achieve world power. In his gruff, monotone voice, he told the chamber that he longed to restore the days when Americans could daydream "with almost rapturous enthusiasm" about "the enlargement of our commerce in the east, and of our political sway throughout the world." In as little as thirty years, the senator declared, the United States may well find itself occupying a world in which the formidable powers of Britain and China were receding in strength. America, he insisted, needed to be prepared to fill the vacuum—even if that meant extending its influence into lands "beyond the Pacific Ocean."[29]

Six weeks after Seward's speech, a letter arrived on the senator's desk with a return address from Springfield, Illinois. According to the correspondent, a young man named Billy Herndon, Seward had "a fast and growing popularity out West." Among the senator's admirers, Herndon reported, was the lanky, rawboned lawyer who shared his office. "Mr. Lincoln," Herndon wrote Seward, "my partner and your friend, and formerly member of Congress from our district, thinks your speech most excellent."[30]

A Fondness for Foreign Travel

In the early 1830s, while Lincoln was using his flatboat to discover the world outside the Midwest, Seward was ranging even farther afield. As a boy in his hometown of Florida, New York, Seward had grown up small and shy, with a wild shock of flame-red hair. His father, Samuel, was a wealthy local businessman, but he could also be a martinet. The young Seward sometimes protested against his dad's iron rule. While in college in upstate New York, he ran away to Georgia after his old man failed to pay his tailor's bills. Eventually, however, father and son reconciled and Seward returned to New York and settled down to a career in law and politics. By 1833, when the future secretary of state was in his early thirties, Seward's sixty-five-year-old father offered to take the young lawyer on a voyage across the Atlantic.[31]

"What a romance was this journey that I was making!" Seward later wrote in his autobiography, as he recalled his first trip to Europe. Like Lincoln, the New Yorker had devoured Byron's *Childe Harold's Pilgrimage*, about a young man seeking escape and redemption abroad. Seward later recalled the trip with a kind of gauzy nostalgia. Railroads were still rare, and steamships had not yet shrunk the oceans. Seward's voyage, on a packet stuffed with letters addressed to the King of England, took more than two weeks. For a small-town lawyer from upstate New York, the whole experience was the stuff of dreams. On calm days, the young man would dive off the side of the boat for a swim in the Atlantic.[32]

The cold reality of power politics intruded, however, when Seward finally landed in Liverpool. The contrast between the young republic and the massive British Empire was staggering. To the American traveler, even "the magnificent stone docks" of the English coastline seemed far superior to "the mean, rickety, wooden slips and quays of New York." Seward roamed around London, visiting Westminster Abbey, climbing to the top of St. Paul's Cathedral, and gazing out over the sprawling industrial metropolis, smothered in "a dense cloud of fog and coal-smoke." He found himself impressed as he watched a debate from the galleries of the House of Commons. The British chamber was far more orderly and its members more energetic than the chaotic U.S. House, with its "listless" representatives.

Even the American diplomats in London seemed second-rate. The U.S. legation, Seward noted, was tucked away above a tailor's shop in the West End.[33]

And yet despite the obvious disparities in power, the Britons Seward met seemed curiously insecure. The English, he recalled, were "continually disturbed" by fears that they were becoming Americanized. Americans, the future of secretary of state noted, were perfectly justified to be jealous of their more powerful cousins across the Atlantic. But why were the British, securely wrapped in the trappings of empire, so defensive? "It seemed to me then," Seward observed, "that, little as we loved the English nation, they loved us still less." The past provided one explanation. The young traveler came across an old issue of a British magazine that referred to the U.S. legislature as the "rebel Congress" and its leaders as "most destitute of principle." The future offered another answer. With their rapidly growing economy and population, Britain's former colonies would inevitably soon eclipse their motherland.[34]

When Seward crossed the English Channel to France, he was struck by the contrast. The French country landscapes, speckled with apple, pear, and plum orchards, enchanted him. Still, poverty plagued the countryside. Paris seemed lively, he thought, but it was also full of beggars and vagrants who streamed through the narrow, unlighted, badly paved streets. The scars of revolution "disfigured" the whole place, Seward observed. "Everything," he noted, "reminded me of the frequency and violence of political changes." One day Seward and his father paid an executioner 15 francs to watch the guillotine—that iconic weapon of the French Revolution—demonstrated on a sheep.[35]

The highlight of the French leg came when father and son visited the aging and ailing Marquis de Lafayette at his Paris home and later at his country château, La Grange. As a young man in his early twenties, Seward had once shepherded the tall, dignified general around upstate New York on one of his visits to the United States. Recalling—or pretending to recall—their last meeting, Lafayette exclaimed: "I am happy to see you again!" Seward was inspired by his encounter with the last of the great Revolutionary War heroes. On the wall of Lafayette's bedroom, he noticed, the general had hung a copy of the Declaration of Independence. In his anteroom, Lafayette displayed a bust of himself.[36]

Back in the United States, Seward soon returned to the boredom of his law practice. But the travel bug refused to abandon him. He had never particularly enjoyed his work at the bar. He considered himself "little better than a galley slave," he told his father in 1835. In later years Seward would compare his job to a treadmill. Global affairs held a stubborn allure for the frustrated lawyer. Seward once joked to a friend that he had visited a phrenologist—a charlatan who measured the circumference of his brain—and was told that the lumps on his head betrayed a "fondness for foreign travel." The diagnosis, in this case, was accurate enough. "When I travel, I banish care," he wrote one acquaintance. Seward was hooked.[37]

Even when he could not travel abroad, Seward made an effort to mingle with great American diplomats at home. During a visit to Quincy, Massachusetts, in the early 1830s, Seward dropped in at the home of John Quincy Adams, the former foreign envoy, secretary of state, and president. Adams received his young visitor in the parlor of his plainly furnished home—a spare space that included a few mahogany chairs and old portraits of the Founding Fathers. To the younger man, Old Man Eloquent, now over sixty, appeared slight, balding, and overweight, and wore a melancholy expression. "He was dressed," Seward recalled, "in an olive frock-coat, a cravat carelessly tied, and old-fashioned, light-colored vest and pantaloons." The former president's eyes were "weak and inflamed" from reading.

The two men chatted for several hours about politics, public men, and mutual friends. The former president was polite but betrayed "hardly a ray of animation or feeling in the whole of it," Seward later recalled. "In short, he was exactly what I before supposed he was, a man to be respected for his talents, admired for his learning, honored for his integrity and simplicity, but hardly possessing traits of character to inspire a stranger with affection." The aging statesman ultimately grew on the future chief diplomat. Seward would one day author a biography of Adams. Much later, Seward declared that he had derived "every resolution" and "every sentiment" from the example of the former president. Modern diplomatic scholars view Seward as Adams's "logical successor."[38]

Both men were expansionists. Adams dreamed of an American empire that would stretch across the North American continent. Seward imagined it spanning the oceans. Their prescriptions for achieving those goals proved to be remarkably similar. The growth of American power first demanded independence from the avaricious and corrupt Old World. "Above all," the young Adams once told his father, "I wish that we may never have occasion for any political connections in Europe." Adams and his allies imagined an "American System" of economic development and political strategy that would oppose the Old World order. The key would be to build national institutions like banks, and foster trade and communications links throughout the New World. "The American [System]," Adams had remarked in 1795, "will infallibly triumph over the European system eventually, provided it can be pursued with as much perseverance."[39]

In practice, however, building a hemispheric system to oppose Europe's demanded a delicate balancing act. Statesmen needed to develop trade agreements with North and South American countries based on reciprocity—the notion that the United States and key partners would mutually lower tariffs to encourage commerce. At the same time, the Whigs maintained tariffs for many European nations, aiming to promote American industry. Finally, Whig statesmen recognized that American independence from Europe was a long-term goal—not always an immediate reality. In order to finance development projects like roads and canals, American policymakers needed access to British capital. That meant statesmen often preached independence while subtly refraining from policies that would antagonize the Old World.[40]

Seward came to typify this "double game." On the one hand, he declared, the long-term goal of American foreign policy should be "our own complete emancipation from what remains of European influence and prejudice." He derided Britain as "the greatest, the most grasping, and the most rapacious in the world." Seward believed the trend lines suggested that British power would vanish from the Western Hemisphere within twenty-five years—or "at least within half a century." And yet, those predictions depended on the maintenance of peace. Seward often challenged belligerent Democrats and other hawks who championed foreign wars to boost their political status. "Peaceful activity is safer," the New Yorker insisted. "It is cheaper; it is surer; it saves all the elements of national strength and national power, and increases them."[41]

An Absorbing Desire for Power

New Yorkers elected Seward governor in 1838. The young politician had won his office partly by appealing to Irish immigrants who nursed grudges against Britain. The first years of Seward's tenure in Albany vividly demonstrated the Whigs' love-hate attitude toward the European powers. A revolt against British rule in Canada was raging just north of the New York State border. The fighting occasionally spilled across the national boundary. In late 1837, Canadians loyal to Britain attacked a steamer called the *Caroline*, which the rebels had used in their insurgency, burning it into the water. The assault, which took place within New York territory, killed one American. Three years later, when a British subject named Alexander McLeod visited the state, New Yorkers arrested the man and charged him with murder and arson in connection with the *Caroline* incident.[42]

Governor Seward found himself boxed into a corner. On the one hand, he was determined to try McLeod in his own state's courts. The attack had inflamed popular passions among his constituents. After McLeod was arrested, supporters of the Canadian insurgents swarmed around the prison where he was being held, firing cannon and pounding drums. And yet the episode also infuriated British statesmen. The affair should be treated as an international incident to be resolved by the two national governments, they insisted. Lord Palmerston, the British foreign minister, threatened "immediate and frightful" war. "With such cunning fellows as these Yankees it never answers to give way," Palmerston wrote to a colleague in January 1841, at the height of the McLeod drama. The Americans, he insisted, "keep pushing on their encroachments as far as they are permitted to do so; and what we dignify by the names of moderation and conciliation, they naturally enough call fear; on the other hand as their system of encroachments is founded very much upon bully, they will give way when in the wrong, if they are firmly and perseveringly pressed."[43]

The whole episode alarmed Daniel Webster, the U.S. secretary of state. A pillar of the Whig party, Webster had long cultivated close ties to Britain. For a time he actually worked as the U.S. representative of one of England's largest banks. The secretary of state and his allies considered Seward's stance "savage as a meat axe." Webster dispatched envoys to New York in an effort to bring the governor around. Seward claimed the secretary of state was trying to "smother" him. In the end, a New York court tried and quickly acquitted McLeod—a verdict that largely defused the crisis. Yet the incident tested transatlantic relationships and offered a crisp picture of the Whig conundrum.[44]

Seward survived the crisis. By the outbreak of the Mexican War in 1846, New Yorkers had elected their popular governor to the U.S. Senate. Like Lincoln, Seward tried to walk a line—questioning the wisdom of the war without setting himself wholly in opposition to expansion. "I want no war," Seward wrote in 1846. "I want no enlargement of territory, sooner than it would come if we were content with 'a masterly inactivity.'" Seward derided the conflict as a "bastard war," but like Lincoln he was careful to make sure the troops were well supplied. The New York senator believed a full-throated opposition to the conflict would be bad politics at the least. He did "not expect," he wrote, "to see the Whig party successful in overthrowing an Administration carrying on a war . . . in which the Whig party and its statesmen are found apologizing for our national adversaries."[45]

Seward first crossed paths with Lincoln in the last days of the 1848 presidential contest, when the Illinois congressman campaigned through New England for Taylor. Whigs in Boston invited both men to address a rally at the city's Tremont Temple. Lincoln, one local newspaper reported, made a "powerful and convincing" speech that was "cheered to the echo." Seward was less impressed. Lincoln's effort, he later recalled, consisted of a "rambling, story-telling speech, putting the audience in a good humor but avoiding any extended discussion of the slavery question." Seward focused his own remarks primarily on the issue of slavery, a topic that was gaining prominence in the wake of the Mexican War. According to Seward's recollection, at a hotel after the event, Lincoln went out of his way to praise the New York senator. "Governor Seward," the younger man began, "I have been thinking about what you said in your speech. I reckon you are right. We have got to deal with this slavery question, and got to give much more attention to it hereafter than we have been doing."[46]

As the 1850s unfolded, Seward increasingly spoke out on world issues that captured American hearts and headlines. When Austrian and Russian forces attempted to crush a rebellion of Hungarians led by Louis Kossuth, Americans expressed their outrage. In 1851 Congress passed a resolution inviting Kossuth to the United States. A regal-looking figure with drooping eyelids and a bushy beard, the Hungarian leader arrived to the cheers of enormous crowds of sympathizers. Still, some Americans felt that the pro-Hungarian enthusiasm undermined America's traditional independence in foreign affairs. Seward was not convinced. "If we are never to speak out," he asked, "for what are our national lungs given us?"

The senator invited Kossuth to spend a weekend at his home. Thousands of New Yorkers crowded into the streets to watch the arrival of the Hungarian hero, whose carriage was drawn by four black horses. Supporters fired cannons, rang church bells, and waved Hungarian flags as the procession wound its way to the town's American Hotel for a reception. Seward's thirteen-year-old son, Willie, and his friends paraded loudly through the streets carrying wooden spears and wearing silk badges, claiming to represent the "Kossuth Cadets."[47]

Lincoln, too, expressed sympathy for the Hungarian cause—though he carefully qualified his support. At a meeting at the Springfield courthouse in early 1852, Lincoln offered resolutions lauding the insurgents. America's sympathy, he argued, "and the benefits of its position, should be exerted in favor of the people of every nation struggling to be free." Still, Lincoln drew a clear line between friendly solidarity and intervention. Any nation, he insisted, had the right to "throw off, to revolutionize, their existing form of government, and to establish such other in its stead as they may choose." And yet nonintervention remained a "sacred principle of the international law," he cautioned. The United States, Lincoln argued, should not ignite or materially aid such revolutions.[48]

The United States, however, was beginning to exert a measure of influence beyond its own borders. Only decades before, American statesmen had worried that they were considered merely "a cockboat in the wake of the British man-of-war," as John Quincy Adams once put it. Now Lincoln felt comfortable challenging Britain's role as international arbiter. "There is nothing in the past history of the British government," Lincoln proclaimed at the Springfield courthouse, "to encourage the belief that she will aid . . . in the delivery of continental Europe from the yoke of despotism." That responsibility, he implied, ultimately belonged to America.[49]

The United States finally possessed the power to support its friends abroad. Yet America's rising strength also carried risks—not least to its own national soul. Lincoln and Seward had both come to prominence on a wave of vast, impersonal economic forces—as had America.[50] Yet even as the country adjusted to its new world role, it was forced to reevaluate its relationships with old friends around the globe. "Worldly wisdom," Seward's wife, Frances, once wrote her husband in another context, "certainly does impel a person to 'swim with the tide'—and if they can judge unerringly which way the tide runs, may bring them to port. A magnanimous friendship might suggest a more elevated course and even reconcile one to struggling against the current if necessary." Still, she concluded, "magnanimous friendships are rare—incompatible I think with an absorbing desire for power."[51]

Rich Wines, Golden Chains, and Diamond Rings

Friendship and power, commerce and war—Europe presented a continent of contrasts when Seward finally returned in 1859, twenty-six years after his first voyage with his father. This time Seward found that all strata of British society were eager to meet him—from the royal family to the London bankers to the working classes of the country's industrial heartland. Seward's reputation had grown significantly over the course of the 1850s. Britons believed they were likely meeting the next president of the United States. In letters home, Seward boasted of the "great and titled visitors" who eagerly called on him. He was introduced, one after another, to quarters that he had once "regarded as forever inaccessible to me." The world, Seward wrote home, seemed smaller than ever.[52]

Britain's orderly elegance impressed Seward. At a concert one night at Buckingham Palace, he marveled at the massive concert hall filled with tiers of crimson-cushioned chairs. The room, he wrote home, appeared "larger than our church." As Queen Victoria entered, the crowd fluttered with graceful bows. After the performance, Victoria stopped by the diplomatic section and greeted Seward. She mentioned that Britain must have changed a great deal since his last visit. "All is changed, Madam," he replied. "It is improved?" the queen asked. "Vastly improved," Seward said. The two discussed the profound changes wrought in both Britain and the United States by the railroads, steamships, and the telegraph. "Do you think the improvement will go on?" the queen asked. "I trust so," Seward replied, "if we can preserve peace between the two branches of one great family."[53]

Still, as Seward traveled throughout Europe, he was struck by the powerful—and unpredictable—forces reshaping the continent. The source of Britain's strength, Seward recognized, was not simply in its military but in the economic underpinnings of its society. As Seward traveled north from London, into industrial Lancashire and then up to Scotland, he passed a wilderness of chimneys belching flame and thick, black coal smoke. In Glasgow, Seward observed, "for a distance of fifteen or twenty miles around it, forges, furnaces, and other huge structures fill up the scene, not merely crowding the valleys, but climbing the hills on all sides. There seemed to be no green earth. But everywhere multitudes of men and engines were tearing up the ground to its very foundations, and melting them, or dissipating them into ashes, in ten thousand fires that climbed to the sky, amid wreaths of heavy and impenetrable smoke, which blackened the earth below." Seward credited the growth to the forty years of peace that Europe had enjoyed in the wake of the Napoleonic Wars. Now, he concluded, Britain had succeeded in making the whole world "tributary to her work-shops."[54]

And yet Seward believed he saw a key irony in the outward symbols of British strength. Britain was becoming more and more like the United States, which he viewed as the prototype of middle-class society. Even as Seward strolled through the massive English country estates—with their wafting scents of honeysuckle and jasmine, their arching fountains, and their deer and pheasant wandering the grounds—he recognized that the common people would ultimately gain control of the nobility's old treasures. "How distinctly I see the transition of society indicated in these massive, modern industrial structures, towering over the dilapidated walls of baronial castles," he wrote home. "These immense estates must ultimately become prizes to the active and industrious classes." The transition may be a "slow process," but the "plebians wax stronger every day." The overall dynamic, he observed, amounted to a "revolution" that would "assimilate them to us." The "younger members of the family," Seward declared, were "really its leaders."[55]

When he crossed the English Channel to France, Seward found that nation also vastly changed—but not in the same ways. The tiny, winding streets that he had observed in 1833 had been transformed into magnificent boulevards and sprawling gardens under the leadership of Napoleon III. And yet the same grand avenues were infused with a martial spirit he had not observed in Britain. The army, Seward noted, "is everywhere" in Paris. He was struck by the "egotism" of French nationalism. Still, the future secretary of state was ultimately impressed by the emperor when the two men met at Napoleon's retreat in Compiègne. "It seemed difficult to find a subject on which we could differ, or which he did not discuss wisely," Seward later recalled. The empress struck Lincoln's future secretary of state as "graceful and pensively beautiful."

The contrasts among France, Britain, and the United States presented themselves even more sharply when he toured the Belgian battlefield at Waterloo, where the Duke of Wellington's armies had ultimately defeated Napoleon Bonaparte. As he stood on the same ground as the renowned generals, Seward found himself slightly conflicted. On the one hand, he admired Napoleon's efforts to improve "the material and moral conditions" of his country. In retrospect, however, the French emperor's reckless daring doomed him to defeat at the hands of his British adversary—that patient "nation of shopkeepers."[56]

The intersection of trade, commerce, and nationalism—all rising forces in the midnineteenth century—presented Seward with a fascinating puzzle. On the one hand, the industrial and market revolutions were clearly reshaping the world. At times, they seemed to promise closer ties among nations and growing harmony among men. At other moments, however, the same economic forces seemed to reinforce nationalism, adding fuel to new and ancient enmities. On board his steamer across the Atlantic, Seward listened as American residents boasted about "seizing and annexing Cuba." On another occasion, a fight broke out among passengers—"coats stripped, knives drawn"— in the steerage compartment. It would be folly, Seward observed, to assume that economic progress necessarily marched hand in hand with peace. "When will war-making kings and emperors lack for armies to fight?" Seward asked. "Not in our day, I ween."[57]

Seward tried to find a middle path through this thicket. He worked ceaselessly to improve American trade and commerce. But he wanted to make sure that the fruits of economic development benefitted Americans—not "some foreign monopoly," as he put it. "I can understand the proposition of free-trade," Seward once acknowledged. "It is an intelligible theory, and at some future period down the vista of years, it is probable that the world will come to understand that universal free-trade is the wisest and most beneficent system of fiscal administration for any government and for all governments." In his own time, Seward embraced selected reciprocal trade agreements. In the mid 1850s he voted for a major treaty that would lower tariffs with Canada. Yet Seward also believed that if the U.S. government did not intervene to protect American industries, young domestic manufacturers would find themselves overwhelmed by more powerful foreign competitors like Britain and France.[58]

Lincoln shared Seward's approach to trade. Like the New Yorker, Lincoln had long advocated material improvements—roads, canals, railroads—that would help get American products to world markets. Yet the New World would not win its independence from Europe simply by aping the Old World's fashions and institutions. Lincoln liked to mock fellow citizens obsessed with "foreign luxuries—fine cloths, fine silks, rich wines, golden chains, and diamond rings." He ridiculed those who felt the need to "strut in British cloaks."[59] Like Seward, Lincoln thought untrammeled free trade premature. America, Lincoln believed, would need to blaze its own path.

The Terror of the World

I n the midnineteenth century, it was still considered poor form
to actively seek the presidential nomination. So in the spring of
1860, when an acquaintance asked Lincoln about his thoughts on the
upcoming race, the Illinoisan hesitated a little. Seward, the odds-on
favorite for the Republican nomination, could not win in a contest
against Democrat Stephen Douglas, Lincoln told his correspondent.
Then again, Lincoln admitted, his opinions were colored by his own
ambitions. "The taste *is* in my mouth a little," Lincoln confided, adding: "Let no eye but your own see this—not that there is anything
wrong, or even ungenerous, in it; but it would be misconstrued."[60]

Like Lincoln's past campaign against Douglas, in 1858, the current race was certain to address the central foreign-policy question
of the day—namely, American expansion. The 1850s had witnessed
the growth of a movement spearheaded by Douglas that sought to
assert American power abroad. Calling itself Young America, it represented the latest evolution of the Manifest Destiny phenomenon
of the Mexican War era. Young Americans shared the romantic
spirit of the previous decade. They crowed about supporting fellow
republicans abroad—and converting any autocratic holdouts. They
believed that the United States was destined to become, as Douglas
once put it, "the admiration and terror of the world." They meant it
in a good way.

As Lincoln contemplated a presidential run, he took direct aim
at the Democratic foreign-policy platform. At a speaking engagement in Springfield, he trotted out an old lecture, "Discoveries and
Inventions," in which he mocked Democrats, Douglas, and Young
America.[61] The speech, which Lincoln delivered on several occasions throughout the late 1850s, was not one of his most compelling
efforts. Billy Herndon derided it as "a cold flat thing," and it seemed
to bore audiences. And yet, as a window onto Lincoln's thinking
about the intersection of commerce and foreign policy, it is a critical
document. On this day, in April 1860, Lincoln's audience included

John Hay—the young Illinois native who, as secretary of state to presidents McKinley and Roosevelt, would ultimately carry a Hamiltonian approach to foreign policy into the Gilded Age.[62]

The speech is actually one of Lincoln's more thoughtful meditations on the relationship between power and character. In the opening of his address, he surveyed the technological progress of the past decades. Lincoln gushed about the growth of the railroads—the "iron horse" that was "panting" impatiently across the country. He marveled at the communications revolution led by the telegraph—"the lightening" that "stands ready harnessed" to carry the news across the globe "in a trifle less than no time." The modern world had showered Americans with material gifts: "cotton fabrics from Manchester and Lowell; flax-linen from Ireland; wool-cloth from [Spain;] silk from France; furs from the Arctic regions." American dinner tables, Lincoln declared, were covered with "coffee and fruit from the tropics; salt from Turk's Island; fish from New-foundland; tea from China, and spices from the Indies."

And yet, Lincoln believed, unchecked expansion threatened to undermine the American character. Lincoln mocked the hypocrisy of "conceited," "arrogant," land-hungry Democrats. They own "a large part of the world, by right of possessing it; and all the rest by right of *wanting* it, and *intending* to have it," Lincoln said. Young America, he continued, displayed an unseemly " 'longing after' territory," sarcastically adding that its "desire for land is not selfish, but merely an impulse to extend the area of freedom." Douglas and the Democrats, he said, his words dripping with irony, were "very anxious to fight for the liberation of enslaved nations and colonies, provided, always, they have land." Lincoln did his best to highlight the perils of untrammeled territorial expansion. Economic growth, Lincoln believed, should be channeled toward assuring American freedom from the Old World. Instead, Lincoln worried, the Democrats' hunger for land would reduce Americans to slaves of their own appetites.[63]

On the most immediate foreign-policy issue in the 1860

campaign—the proposed annexation of Cuba—both Lincoln and Seward essentially walked in lockstep with their party. In 1859 the U.S. Senate had issued a report advocating the purchase of the Caribbean island. Seward had long coveted Cuba, and once argued that the island represented a natural extension of American territory. "Every rock and every grain of sand in that island," he had declared, was "drifted and washed out from American soil by the floods of the Mississippi, and the other estuaries of the Gulf of Mexico." Still, by the late 1850s, Seward opposed annexation. Lincoln, too, apparently counseled against absorbing the island. A September 1860 editorial in the Whig *Illinois State Journal*, which scholars believe may have been written by Lincoln, argues against annexation and needles Douglas and the Democrats for their designs on Cuba.[64]

Foreign policy, however, was largely a sideshow to the overriding issue of the 1860 campaign: slavery and the possibility of Southern secession. Seward was experienced and well traveled, and his high profile made him an apparent shoo-in for the Republican nomination. Lincoln recognized his long odds. "Everybody knows them," Lincoln remarked of Seward and his other competition. "Nobody, scarcely, outside of Illinois, knows me." Seward could also boast the backing of Thurlow Weed, one of the country's shrewdest and most ruthless political operatives. Lincoln boosters counseled the Illinois lawyer to imitate his opponent. "Do like Seward does," Chicago mayor John Wentworth advised Lincoln in the spring of 1860. "Get someone to *run* you."[65]

In late May, Republicans gathered in Chicago at the "Wigwam"—a makeshift hall on the corner of Lake and Market streets that had been built for the 1860 convention. It was, one reporter recalled, "a gorgeous pavilion aflame with color and all aflutter with pennants and streamers." Delegates debated the prospective GOP platform, ultimately approving expansionist planks like support for a transcontinental railroad and laws that would encourage western migration. Meanwhile, Weed—whom Republicans referred to as Lord Thurlow or the Dictator—had arrived in Chicago on a thirteen-car train from New York, carrying $100,000 cash, accompanied by a posse of whisky-swilling pro-Seward operatives. He worked the delegations, amid the flags and red-white-and-blue bunting, with motions "as rapid as a rope-dancer's."[66]

Weed tried to create an aura of inevitability around his man. But Seward had serious flaws as a candidate. As the debate over slavery had intensified, Seward predicted that the regional differences would erupt into an "irrepressible conflict"—a statement that unnerved some dovish voters. Lincoln's campaign staff shrewdly used his opponent's words against him. The Lincoln men whispered that Seward's hard-line stance had rendered him unelectable. Lincoln's team knew that Seward and Weed would be formidable opponents. They cleverly asked delegates to make Lincoln their "second choice."

Seward, meanwhile, ensconced himself at his vast estate in Auburn, New York—a twenty-room mansion set amid five acres of spectacular gardens and fruit trees. Huge crowds gathered on the lawn and spilled out into the street. "All right," Seward's men at the convention site had telegraphed their boss the day of the balloting, "everything indicates your nomination today sure." Now, as voting began, a rider stationed at the local telegraph office galloped to the Seward estate and announced his enormous lead to the crowd. Seward, now fifty-nine, with a shaggy mop of gray hair, beamed confidently at his supporters. "I shall be nominated on the next ballot," he declared, to a chorus of huzzahs.[67]

As the voting began, Seward easily won the first ballot, with 173½ votes to Lincoln's 102. Wild cheering broke out in Auburn when the horseman arrived with the tally. Seward, according to one witness, processed the news "without the movement of a muscle of his countenance." Yet as the polling continued, ballots shifted away from marginal candidates with no chance of victory and into Lincoln's column. Delegates seemed to be buying the line that Seward's radical rhetoric would fatally hinder him in the border states during a general election. The pleas to convention-goers to make Lincoln their "second choice" was proving to be sound strategy.

At the Wigwam, trying to maintain the momentum, Lincoln's advance men whipped the crowd into a fury. "Imagine all the hogs ever slaughtered in Cincinnati giving their death squeals together," wrote one newspaperman. "I thought the Seward yell could not be surpassed; but the Lincoln boys . . . made every plank and pillar in the building quiver." Moments later, Seward's team was forced to dictate a curt telegram and dispatch it to Auburn: "Lincoln nominated third ballot." The color drained from Seward's face. On the Wigwam floor, a reporter saw Thurlow Weed "press his fingers *hard* upon his eyelids to keep back the tears." Seward himself later mused that it was lucky he had not kept a diary at the time of the vote, or his entries would have been full of "cursing and swearing."[68]

In Chicago, jubilant Lincoln supporters streamed out of the Wigwam, burning tar barrels, pounding drums, and firing cannon. Lincoln got the news at the local newspaper office in Springfield, where he had gone to wait for the results. "Well, gentlemen," he said when his nomination was confirmed, "there is a little woman at our house who is probably more interested in this dispatch than I am." At the state capitol building in Springfield, cheering Lincoln supporters packed into a raucous rally in the rotunda. Church bells clanged, and a Mexican War–era cannon thundered. The Lincoln men eventually marched to the nominee's house amid blaring music and fluttering banners. Late into the night, revelers burned bonfires and filled the sky with fireworks.[69]

Seward was devastated. Months after the balloting, the New Yorker was still smarting from the defeat. "Disappointment!" he cried. "You speak to me of disappointment. To me, who was justly entitled to the Republican nomination for the presidency, and who had to stand aside and see it given to a little Illinois lawyer!" Seward, when he cooled down, eventually agreed to campaign for Lincoln, speaking at whistle stops around the country. The New Yorker cut his usual melodramatic figure, dressing in "a strange and indescribable Syrian cashmere cloak," according to Charles Francis Adams Jr., son of Lincoln's future man in London. As the train rumbled across the country, Seward fortified himself with brandy and chain-smoked cigars. At one stop, in Toledo, Ohio, an inebriated Stephen Douglas stumbled into Seward's car in the dead of night. Waving a whisky bottle, he demanded that Seward come out and make a speech. Seward refused and went back to bed.[70]

Toward the end of the campaign, in October 1860, Seward's train made a quick stop in Springfield. Lincoln briefly boarded Seward's car, but the former opponents treated each other coolly. One newspaperman reported that the two men acted "as if each was afraid of his own virtue in the presence of the other." Another observer wrote that Lincoln's demeanor "was marked rather by deference and respect than cordiality." Lincoln, recalled a third witness to the meeting, appeared shy and stiff, "as if he felt out of place." Seward seemed no more comfortable. The entire whistle stop took all of fifteen minutes. Then the wounded New Yorker was gone again.[71]

Lincoln's opponents, meanwhile, did their best to remind voters of his stance on the Mexican War. "Mr. Speaker!" went one Democratic chant. "Where's the spot? Is it in Spain or is it not? Mr. Speaker! Spot! Spot! Spot!" The heckling seemed to have some effect. "Will you be kind enough," a New York iron importer wrote Lincoln in October 1860, "to say if you *did* or *did not* while you were in Congress vote against supplies to the American army while on the battlefields of Mexico?" Lincoln swiftly wrote back to refute the accusation, adding that it would be "a matter of record in the Journals and Congressional Globe" if he had. "No man making that, or any such charge, should be listened to," Lincoln scolded his correspondent.[72]

The 1860 campaign also featured a fierce battle for the loyalty of foreign-born voters. For years, refugees from Europe—a handful of whom had fled the tumult of the liberal revolutions and conservative counterrevolts of 1848—had been streaming into the American Northwest, where voting laws made it relatively easy for newcomers to gain the franchise. German immigrants, in particular, tended to be intensely politically active. They flocked to crowded rallies to hear native speakers like Carl Schurz, a Lincoln supporter from

Wisconsin who loudly advocated for voting rights and western land grants. Schurz boasted that his acolytes consisted of a "solid column of German and Scandinavian anti-slavery men, who know how to handle a gun and who will fight, too." Actually, German voters were far less homogeneous than Schurz claimed; many Catholic Germans, for example, remained wary of the xenophobic nativism of some Republicans. Nevertheless, Schurz founded a "foreign department" of the Republican national committee and sent speakers fanning out across the heartland.[73]

Lincoln, a long-standing supporter of immigrant rights, did his best to court the increasingly powerful constituency. He forcefully rejected the nativism of many of his fellow former Whigs. (Billy Herndon, for example, had been known to exclaim, "God damn the Irish!" Even Mary Lincoln had once written of "the *necessity* of keeping foreigners within bounds," complaining of the "wild Irish.")

Lincoln worried that if anti-immigrant sentiment got much worse, Americans would soon have to change the Declaration of Independence to read, "all men are created equal, except negroes, *and foreigners, and catholics.*" In that event, Lincoln lamented, "I should prefer emigrating to some country where they make no pretence of loving liberty—to Russia, for instance, where despotism can be taken pure, and without the base alloy of hypocracy." As the 1860 campaign approached, he wrote a letter to a German-American supporter observing that "I have some little notoriety for commiserating [with] the oppressed condition of the negro; and I should be strangely inconsistent if I could favor any project for curtailing the existing rights of *white men*, even though born in different lands, and speaking different languages from myself."[74]

Democrats traditionally had better luck wooing foreign-born voters. Yet with the Democratic field hopelessly divided in 1860, the Republican ticket was virtually assured of victory in November. As the fall unfolded, the reality of Lincoln's impending election began to set in. "It now really looks as if the Government is about to fall into our hands," Lincoln wrote Seward in mid-October. On election night,

Lincoln ended up winning more than twice as many electoral votes as his closest Democratic challenger. "I guess there's a little lady at home who would like to hear this news," he told supporters at the telegraph office after the returns were finalized. When he reached his house, Lincoln exclaimed, "Mary, Mary, we are elected."[75]

High Road to a Slave Empire

Meditating on his election, Lincoln once mused that it was "very strange that I, a boy brought up in the woods, and seeing, as it were, but little of the world, should be drifted into the very apex of this great event." The men who would become Lincoln's future diplomats shared the president-elect's sense of wonder. John Bigelow, whom Lincoln would eventually appoint as his consul in Paris, wrote to a correspondent in England that the Illinoisan was "not precisely the sort of man who would be regarded as one entirely *a la mode* at your splendid European courts. . . . He is essentially a self made man and of a type to which Europe is as much a stranger as it is to the Mastodon."[76]

And yet a perilous world almost immediately confronted the president-elect. Charles Sumner thought the 1860 election would "cause a reverberation that will be heard throughout the globe."[77] As the winter deepened, Northerners and Southerners staked out increasingly firm positions on American expansion—the same issue that Lincoln had been debating since the Mexican War. By November 1860, the president-elect had developed exceptionally nuanced arguments on the subject. Like many in his party, Lincoln supported westward expansion and commercial development. That social mobility, he believed, was the very thing that differentiated the United States from Old Europe.[78] Yet he opposed most compromises that would avert the secession crisis at the cost of extending slavery.

In his makeshift office in the capitol building in Springfield, Lincoln tried to make sense of the crisis. The city had become "one grand mud hole," observed a journalist. "It has been raining, snow-ing, sleeting, blowing, and freezing for eight days." Lincoln sur-rounded himself with a surprisingly cosmopolitan crowd. Advice poured in from Europeans—many of them hawkish German émi-grés who had experienced the revolutions of 1848 firsthand. Gustave Koerner, a German immigrant and one of Lincoln's Illinois allies, presented Lincoln with the recent example of Switzerland, whose government called up 100,000 troops and managed to intimidate a few breakaway cantons into abandoning their rebellion.[79]

The coaching may have had some effect. The president-elect dis-patched a barrage of letters to political allies in Washington and else-where making his position on expansion southward abundantly clear. "Let there be no compromise on the question of *extending* slavery," Lincoln wrote to Illinois senator Lyman Trumbull. "Stand firm. The tug has to come, & better now, than any time hereafter." Lin-coln cautioned another friend to prevent "compromise of any sort" on the extension of slavery. Any deal, the president-elect believed, would provide a signal for Southern filibusters to pour into the new territory and begin claiming the land for future slave states. "On that point hold firm," Lincoln wrote, "as with a chain of steel." To Penn-sylvania congressman James Hale, Lincoln insisted that if his ad-ministration struck a deal, one "year will not pass" before the United States will "have to take Cuba" in order to satisfy the slave states. Only "one compromise," Lincoln concluded, "would really settle the slavery question, and that would be a prohibition against acquiring any more territory."[80]

At the same time, Lincoln began attempting to woo Seward. On December 8, he sent his one-time opponent a letter asking him to join the cabinet as secretary of state. Lincoln then penned a sec-ond, longer letter—marked *"Private & Confidential"*—that he dis-patched along with the first. The second missive assured Seward that he genuinely wanted him to take the job. The president-elect made reference to rumors in the newspapers that he would offer Seward the post simply "as a compliment, and with the expectation that you would decline it." Lincoln insisted that he had intended Seward for the position since the day of his nomination. He concluded by praising his former opponent's "integrity, ability, learning, and great experience." Seward responded a few days later, asking for "a little time to consider whether I possess the qualifications and temper of a minister and whether it is in such a capacity that my friends would prefer that I should act if I am to continue in the public service."[81]

Still, the two men were once again drifting apart—this time over a matter of policy. Seward and Thurlow Weed began pushing for a deal to avert the secession crisis. Both men favored a plan that would extend the line of the Missouri Compromise all the way to the Pacific Ocean. In such a package, slavery would be protected south of the line, and prohibited north of it. Many Northeastern businessmen—including a significant number of Seward's constituents—favored such a deal if it would prevent a disruptive war. In late December, Kentucky senator John J. Crittenden introduced a series of constitutional amendments based on a similar plan. Seward, at first, joined the chorus of politicians lobbying to approve the Crittenden Compromise. But Lincoln feared that any deal that allowed the extension of slavery southward would lead to war in the long run.[82]

Seward's secession-winter maneuvering, the scholar Eric Foner has noted, "has proved to be something of a puzzle for historians." Seward had long been considered a firm antislavery man. His radical reputation contributed to his defeat for the Republican nomination in 1860. Yet there was a great deal of subtlety in his position. The New Yorker had opposed the peculiar institution because he believed it hindered America's rise to world power. A free-labor economic system would achieve that goal far more efficiently, he believed. And yet if Northern statesmen refused to compromise with slaveholders, the Union would be torn apart—almost certainly halting its imperial drive.[83]

As the New Year approached, Weed traveled to Springfield—at least partly to try to impress upon Lincoln the wisdom of the Crittenden Compromise. But Weed's was a hopeless mission. The president-elect believed the Crittenden measure would likely defuse the crisis in the short term. Still, Lincoln was sure that the debate would ultimately flare up again in the near future, when Southern sympathizers attempted to seize Mexico. Lincoln responded to the Dictator's pleas with "undisguised hostility," the *New York Herald* reported. "I will be inflexible on the territorial question," Lincoln explained, adding that he believed any compromise would offer an invitation to filibusters. Weed found the president-elect "at ease and undisturbed" during their all-day meeting at Lincoln's home. Ultimately, though, the political operative's mission failed. Lincoln sent Weed back east with his own set of compromise resolutions that would prevent the extension of slavery. The president-elect suggested that Seward should introduce the resolutions himself.[84]

While Weed worked on Lincoln in Springfield, Seward brazenly tested new ideas. During one trip from his home in upstate New York to Washington, Seward stopped at the Astor House Hotel in Manhattan and gave an impromptu speech to a boisterous dinner of the New England Society. The future secretary of state arrived late in the night, and cracked jokes to the liquor- and cigar-fueled audience. Seward may have gotten carried away. At one point he seemed to intimate that a war with a foreign power could help to unify the United States. "I am very sure," Seward said, "that if anybody was to make a descent upon New York tomorrow—whether Louis Napoleon, or the Prince of Wales, or his mother, or the Emperor of Russia or Austria—if either of them were to make a descent upon the City of New York tomorrow, I believe all the hills of South Carolina would pour forth their population to the rescue of New York." The crowd, according to a newspaper reporter who was present, responded with loud cheering and "every demonstrable evidence of delight." Historians have long pointed to this speech as confirmation that Seward advocated picking a fight with Europe to head off the domestic crisis. Yet, when read in context, it seems unlikely that he genuinely desired a war with a distant foe.[85]

Seward eventually fell in line, voting against the Crittenden

Compromise and accepting Lincoln's invitation to join the cabinet. But the New Yorker refused to stop angling for a deal. On January 12, 1861, Seward appeared in the Senate chamber and delivered one of his most memorable addresses, urging concessions to avert the crisis. "Hours before the Senate met," the *Chicago Tribune* reported, "the galleries were full to crushing and fainting. The lobbies and cloakrooms were literally packed with an anxious throng." Spectators included the "whole diplomatic corps," which "gave the deepest attention to every word."

Seward enumerated a list of potential compromises designed to placate the South. Yet the speech is most notable as a window onto Seward's approach to politics and foreign affairs. Lincoln's future secretary of state struck his favorite theme about the importance of maintaining U.S. prestige in the wider world. "The American man-of-war is a noble spectacle," Seward told the Senate in his husky monotone. "I have seen it enter an ancient port in the Mediterranean. All the world wondered at it, and talked of it. Salvos of artillery, from forts and shipping in the harbor, saluted its flag. Princes and princesses and merchants paid it homage, and all the people blessed it as a harbinger of hope for their own ultimate freedom. I imagine now the same noble vessel again entering the same haven. The flag of thirty-three stars and thirteen stripes has been hauled down, and in its place a signal is run up, which flaunts the device of a lone star or a palmetto tree. Men ask, 'Who is the stranger that thus steals into our waters?' The answer contemptuously given is, 'She comes from one of the obscure republics of North America. Let her pass on.'"

Avoiding such an ignoble fate, Seward believed, would demand a flexible and pragmatic approach to the secession crisis. "I learned early from Jefferson that, in political affairs, we cannot always do what seems to us absolutely best," Seward told the packed chamber. "We must be content to lead when we can; and to follow when we cannot lead; and if we cannot at any time do for our country all the good that we would wish, we must be satisfied with doing for her all the good that we can." After Seward finished, the assembled diplomats eagerly quizzed U.S. senators about whether the New Yorker's counsel would be followed.[86]

Lincoln was also a pragmatist who reined in the most radical elements of his party. But Seward's freelancing aggravated him. The president-elect was "not overpleased with Seward's speech," one acquaintance reported. Lincoln complained that his secretary of state designate was making his remarks without getting his input. Lincoln's most strident allies in Illinois marveled at the compromises of the man they once viewed as a leading antislavery agitator. "What do you think of Seward?" one of Lincoln's supporters asked his wife. "The mighty is fallen. He bows before the slave power." Seward felt that he was doing the right thing in difficult circumstances. "Distraction rules the hour," he wrote home to his family. "I hope what I have done will bring some good fruits." Yet even Seward's outspoken wife replied by complaining of her husband's "concessions."[87]

For weeks Seward had been urging Lincoln to leave Springfield and come to Washington early. The capital, he explained, was full of "a feverish excitement" that "awakens all kind of apprehensions of popular disturbance and disorders." Seward suggested that Lincoln plan to arrive in Washington by early February. The president-elect's presence would be "reassuring and soothing," he explained. The following day Seward reiterated his plea for Lincoln to arrive "earlier than you otherwise would" and come in "by surprise." Yet Lincoln took his time, instead holding court in Springfield.[88]

In the meantime President James Buchanan and his secretary of state, Jeremiah S. Black, fumblingly tried to salvage America's reputation abroad. Buchanan, who had served overseas as the U.S. minister in London, declared secession unconstitutional, but he also maintained that the federal government could not prevent it. Eventually, however, Black issued a circular urging his diplomats to guard against European overtures to the Confederacy. "If the independence of the 'Confederated States' should be acknowledged by the great powers of Europe," Black wrote, "it would tend to disturb the friendly relations, diplomatic and commercial, now existing between those powers and the United States."[89]

Lincoln's allies, however, complained that Buchanan's diplomatic corps was dangerously subversive. Missouri congressman Francis P. Blair Jr. wrote to the president-elect cautioning that the existing foreign envoys were as "traitorous" as Buchanan's cabinet. Blair worried that the American emissaries were using "all their art and power to persuade the Courts to which they are accredited that the *separation* of the states was a fixed fact." Blair urged Lincoln to swiftly appoint "men of tact and ability" with "some European reputation" to "counteract the impressions made by those now in Europe."[90]

In Springfield, meanwhile, the president-elect received a visit in late January from Matías Romero, the twenty-three-year-old Mexican envoy to Washington. The two men discussed Mexican affairs, and Lincoln asked about the dismal conditions of the peons—the involuntary servants who worked as planters in Mexican fields. Romero reported home to his government that the president-elect "did not appear to be well-informed on Mexican affairs." Still, Romero was impressed with Lincoln's sincerity—a welcome change from the cynical envoys he was used to dealing with. The Mexican representative praised the president-elect as a "simple and honest man." His conversation with Lincoln, Romero told his superiors, was refreshingly free of the "pompous and empty phrases used by persons educated in the school of false pretenses who have the habit of promising much but doing nothing."[91]

By early February, the president-elect was more convinced than ever that caving in on expansion would place Mexico at the mercy of Southern filibusters. He wrote to Seward emphasizing that he remained "inflexible" on the "territorial question." Lincoln explained that he would reject any "compromise which *assists* or *permits* the extension of the institution on soil owned by the nation." Furthermore, he added, "any trick by which the nation is to acquire territory, and then allow some local authority to spread slavery over it, is as obnoxious as any other." Such schemes, Lincoln insisted, would only place the United States on "the high road to a slave empire."[92]

Seward recognized that Lincoln's inflexible stance would likely lead to war with the South. With his attempts at conciliation failing, the future secretary of state apparently began looking for another way out of the crisis. In late January, Seward warned a foreign diplomat that the only solution may be to pick a fight with Europe. "If the Lord would only give the United States an excuse for a war with England, France, or Spain," he told Rudolf Schleiden, Bremen's envoy to Washington, "that would be the best means of reestablishing internal peace." Two weeks later Seward complained again to Schleiden that he could find no excuse for a foreign war.[93]

While Seward blustered in Washington, Lincoln holed himself up in the back room of a general store in Springfield, and began writing his first inaugural. For inspiration, Lincoln asked Herndon to fetch Henry Clay's address on the sectional crisis of 1850, the text of the U.S. Constitution, and Andrew Jackson's proclamation against nullification. Herndon brought the requested materials to the "dingy, dusty, and neglected back room" where his partner was working. Lincoln also wanted a copy of Washington's farewell address—the seminal foreign-policy statement that Lincoln had read as a boy. When Lincoln was finished, he sent a draft to Seward, who was stunned by the uncompromising document. On February 24, Seward wrote Lincoln warning that if he delivered his bold address as it was, "the dismemberment of the republic would date from the inauguration."[94] He urged the president-elect to tone down the most strident passages.

By the time he left for Washington, Lincoln was already weary. A friend observed in January that the president-elect appeared "care worn and more haggard and more stooped than I ever saw him." Shortly before his departure, Lincoln asked to meet his law partner at their office. Lincoln told Herndon to leave the sign hanging out front. They would resume their practice when his term was up. The pressure of the office already seemed to be weighing on Lincoln. The president-elect, Herndon recalled, "threw himself down on the old office sofa," and spent several moments silently staring at the ceiling. Later, as the two men walked out of the office together, Lincoln confided to his partner that he was "sick of office-holding already." He told Herndon that he shuddered to "think of the tasks that are still ahead."[95]

In the days before their departure, the Lincolns threw a huge party at their Springfield home. Hundreds of revelers packed into the house. "Such a crowd," one guest reported, "I seldom, or ever saw at a private house." Guests waited for twenty minutes just to get into the front hall. Finding the exits at the end of the night was no easier. The Lincolns navigated the crowd good-naturedly. Mary wore a dress made of "white moiré antique silk, with a small French lace collar." At one point, a guest recalled seeing Lincoln's son Robert approach his father, playfully extend his hand, and exclaim, "Good evening, *Mr. Lincoln!*" The president-elect gave his son "a gentle slap in the face."[96]

After twelve years, the Lincoln family was finally returning to the capital. After the president-elect packed up his belongings, he labeled his baggage with a succinct tag. It read simply: A. LINCOLN, WHITE HOUSE, WASHINGTON, D.C.[97]

The First Trick

The tensions of the secession winter obscured the fundamental similarities in the worldviews of Lincoln and his chief diplomat. Both men wanted to preserve a united nation that guaranteed all its citizens upward mobility and the freedom to expand into new territory. Both men remained eager to promote American commerce with the wider world. Lincoln and Seward simply held a difference of opinion about the best way to pursue that goal. Seward believed the best strategy was to punt—striking a bargain with Southerners while maintaining a fragile unity. Lincoln did not see the virtue in postponing what he considered the inevitable. If a war was the only remedy, then it was better to face it now than later.[98]

The two men did, however, possess radically different temperaments. Lincoln was a humble man who maintained a healthy appreciation of the limits of his own power. Seward, on the other hand, almost maniacally attempted to shape the world around him. Wiry and diminutive—at five foot six, he was an inch shorter than his wife—Seward was endlessly seeking opportunities to enhance his stature. As governor of New York, the ceremonial head of the state militia, he spent the modern equivalent of $5,300 of his own money on a bespoke uniform including an ostentatious sash and epaulets. He was so vain that he would sometimes tip his hat to strangers on the street "who looked as though they might recognize him." After he eventually lost the nomination to Lincoln, Seward compared himself to Moses—leading his people to the Promised Land, but forbidden to enter it himself. Seward, observes one recent Lincoln biographer, displayed "a massive savior complex."[99]

Seward overslept on the morning of February 23, when Lincoln finally arrived in Washington. He had planned to meet the president-elect at the train station at six a.m. but never made it. Seward rushed to Willard's Hotel, the busy Washington power center where Lincoln had booked a suite in the days leading up to the inauguration. To one witness who saw Seward there on the calm, cloudy morning, the New Yorker appeared "much out of breath and somewhat chagrined." It is easy to imagine the secretary of state designate, dressed in his usual rumpled black uniform, his white hair a hopeless mess, panting through the hotel lobby. To Henry Adams, son of Lincoln's minister to Britain, Seward presented "a slouching, slender figure" with a "head like a wise macaw; a beaked nose; shaggy eyebrows; unorderly hair and clothes; hoarse voice; offhand manner; free talk, and perpetual cigar."[100]

When Seward finally caught up with Lincoln, the future secretary of state "virtually kidnapped" the president-elect, dragging him from meeting to meeting throughout the capital. The two men visited President James Buchanan at the White House and attended a service at Seward's Episcopal church. (Lincoln liked to needle Seward good-naturedly about his faith. The president once told a carriage driver, "I thought you must be an Episcopalian, because you swear just like Governor Seward, who is a churchwarden.") Shortly after the president-elect's arrival, Seward hosted a small dinner for Lincoln at his home on Lafayette Square. The secretary of state's entertaining was legendary. Suppers sometimes ran to eleven courses, with endless arrays of wine and Cuban cigars—all followed by a rubber of whist under the flickering gaslights. (Seward's idol John Quincy Adams once observed that "the whole science of diplomacy consists of giving dinners.") Seward wrote home that Lincoln "is very cordial and kind toward me—simple, natural, and agreeable."[101]

Washington had changed a great deal since Lincoln's first visit in 1847. The capital now boasted formidable marble structures housing the nation's key ministries. Yet there was still a raw, incomplete quality about the place. The Mall was a mess, "a wide arc of swamp grass" dotted with pools of stagnant water and blotches of "evil-smelling mud." The whole city appeared "unhealthy, unfinished, and crude" to foreign diplomats. "To make a Washington street," observed one Englishman, "take one marble temple or public office, a dozen good houses of brick, and a dozen of wood, and fill with sheds and fields."[102]

And yet, at least some of Lincoln's young staffers saw potential in the city alongside the debris. On an unseasonably humid March day shortly after arriving in Washington, John Hay climbed to the iron-railed terrace atop the still-unfinished Capitol building and gazed out over the city. Distance, Hay observed, "lends enchantment" to the rugged American metropolis. "Seen from this point," he wrote, "the city unrolls its dusty magnificences of distance; the stupendous harmonies of its design reveal themselves in broad avenues, which converge upon the capitol as all the roads of the Roman empire converged upon that golden milestone by the Pincian gate." The city, Hay added, was "a congeries of hovels, inharmoniously sown with temples, as the Napoleonic tapestries were sown with golden bees." And yet, "something in the dust, the remoteness, the sunlight, touches them into respectability, if it does not glorify them."[103]

Three days before the inauguration, Lincoln and Seward attended a dinner at the home of Rudolf Schleiden, Bremen's minister in Washington. Schleiden was known around the capital for the quality of his wine cellar. On this night, the European diplomat served an ancient bottle—dating "but four years after the landing of the Pilgrims"—pouring it into tiny glasses. The value of the bottle "at compound interest would more than defray our national debt," one newspaper reported. Lincoln rarely imbibed. ("I am not a temperance man," he once remarked, "but I am temperate to this extent: I don't drink.") Still, the president-elect impressed his host by cracking jokes amid the gloomy circumstances. After dinner Schleiden quizzed Lincoln about diplomatic matters, presumably hoping to glean some bit of intelligence to report home. Lincoln shrewdly deflected the curious European. "I don't know anything about diplomacy," Lincoln said. "I will be very apt to make blunders."[104]

Lincoln was adept at indirection. At times he also claimed to know nothing about finance, the navy—and any number of other subjects about which he understood far more than he said.[105] Still, the president-elect complained even to friends that he wished he had spent more time "studying up" on foreign affairs. Foreign diplomats took him at his word. "Opinions about Mr. Lincoln are quite diverse—that is to say, about his character, for his mind is generally considered to be mediocre," the French minister, Henri Mercier, wrote home to his superiors in early March. "He and his wife seem like a real family of western farmers, and even in this country, where one has no right to be fastidious, their common manners and their ways expose them in unfortunate fashion to ridicule." (The feeling was not mutual; Americans were charmed by the dashing French envoy. Seward's teenage daughter Fanny breathlessly told her diary that Mercier was "tall, black-haired and quite handsome.")[106]

Even the minister from Russia—a nation that steadfastly

supported the Union during the crisis—initially had his doubts about the new American president. "Mr. Lincoln does not seem to possess the talent and energy that his party attributed to him when it named him its candidate for the presidency," the Russian envoy, Eduard de Stoeckl, reported home as the inauguration approached. "Even his supporters admit that he is a man of unimpeachable integrity but of a poor capacity." Still, when the diplomat finally met Lincoln at an early White House reception, he found the president more "pleasant and likable" than he expected. "His manners are those of a man who has spent his entire life in a small Western town," Stoeckl wrote, "but he was polite and considerate to all, and the diplomatic corps in general had nothing but praise for the reception." Power politics, however, were far more important to Russian leaders than social etiquette. The czar's house newspaper reported that his regime considered an intact United States a critical counterweight to Britain and France—a nation "necessary to the general equilibrium."[107]

The sophisticated and well-traveled Seward understood well the mechanics of the international balance of power. Still, he remained something of a wild card. Two days before the inauguration, Seward sent the president-elect a note withdrawing himself from consideration for the cabinet. Seward's motivation remains something of a mystery, but he was probably objecting to Lincoln's other choices of cabinet officers. On the cold, gray morning of Lincoln's inauguration, as the sharpshooters were taking their places on Washington rooftops (a Baltimore gang known as the Blood Tubs had been plotting to assassinate the president, according to some reports), Lincoln handed one of his secretaries a note for the New Yorker. "I can't afford to let Seward take the first trick," Lincoln explained. In his note, the president-elect appealed to both the "public interest" and his "personal feelings" in asking Seward to "countermand the withdrawal."[108]

With tensions rising across the Atlantic, Lincoln needed a competent secretary of state in place as soon as possible. On inauguration day the diplomatic corps packed into the Senate chamber in their "brilliant uniforms," Mary's cousin Elizabeth Todd Grimsley recalled. The First Lady sat in the diplomatic section with the foreign envoys. The chests full of medals and epaulette-covered shoulders offered a stark reminder that the European powers were carefully observing the new president, watching for any clues about the direction of his foreign policy. The spectators were only too aware, as Grimsley put it, of the Confederates' "strong conviction that 'King Cotton' must control the markets of the world, and thus secure foreign recognition." Southerners were counting on "that little attenuated cotton thread," in the words of one Confederate congressman, "which a child can break, but which, nevertheless can hang the world."

Lincoln must have wondered at times whether the rebels might be right about the power of the crop to sway the policies of distant empires. Mercier, for one, was not reassured by the inaugural spectacle. The "so-called simplicity" and "lack of ceremony" of the event, the French envoy reported home, was "totally out of harmony with the marble and gilt" of the unfinished Capitol building. "It's as if one wanted to inaugurate a Quaker in a basilica," he sniped. Lincoln's speech, the Frenchman added, only reinforced that impression. The new president's words lacked "that power of initiative which should characterize the hand which holds the helm in such violent circumstances." French officials were more optimistic about Seward's competence. The emperor knew the incoming secretary of state from his visit to France two years earlier and sent word through intermediaries that he remembered their *"réception tout exceptionellement amicable."*[109]

On the evening after the inauguration, Lincoln finally convinced Seward to join the cabinet after "a long and confidential talk." With his most important deputy in place, the president attempted to enjoy himself. Shortly before eleven p.m., the Lincolns entered their inaugural ball to the tune of "Hail Columbia." Mary, wearing a blue gown with a blue feather in her hair, walked in on the arm of Stephen Douglas, crossing the length of the hall and later dancing a quadrille.

The First Lady, one observer reported, would have looked at home among "the queens of the earth."

Lincoln, on the other hand, still appeared "tired and ill at ease." To Henry Adams, the president-elect presented a "long, awkward figure" with "a plain, ploughed face." Adams was struck by the "lack of apparent force" in the Illinois native. "No man living needed so much education as the new president," Adams later recalled. And yet, "all the education he could get would not be enough." John Bigelow, whom Lincoln would send to the Paris consulate later that year, agreed that the new president "was destitute of experience and withal lacks superiority of every kind except inches, though a very well disposed person and good enough president for ordinary times." Less worldly observers were more charitable. A New York clergyman "took heart" as he spotted the president's "tall form and composed face" at an early White House reception "towering above the compact crowd of foreign ministers."[110]

Office hunters seeking diplomatic posts immediately besieged the new president. Foreign-service appointments represented a key component of presidential power. They helped to inspire loyalty among allies, and amounted to one of the few levers of government that Lincoln actually controlled.[111] Still, the crush of would-be diplomats overwhelmed the president. Days after the inauguration, Lincoln complained to a newspaper editor that he felt like "a man so busy in letting rooms in one end of his house, that he can't stop to put out the fire that is burning the other." The president grumbled that he had "too many pigs for the tits." In one letter home shortly after the inauguration, Seward reported that it had become difficult to get in and out of the Executive Mansion because of all the applicants clogging the "grounds, halls, stairways, [and] closets." Lincoln joked that he was glad that God had not made him a woman, because he had always found it difficult to say no.[112]

Not all job seekers were motivated by a burning desire to serve their country. Foreign postings in the nineteenth century were often viewed as extended vacations. One Lincoln administration official recalled the time a visiting delegation had asked the president to appoint its candidate envoy to the Sandwich Islands (now Hawaii). Their man, they insisted, was "in bad health, and a residence in that balmy climate would be of great benefit to him." Lincoln understandably demurred. "Gentlemen," he told the petitioners, "I am sorry to say that there are eight other applicants for that place, and they are all sicker than your man."

The State Department maintained a tradition of assigning artists and writers to European consulates with only "light duties." The novelist Herman Melville was one of those who besieged Lincoln and Seward hoping to snag a consular post. The author of *Moby-Dick* had dispatched pleading missives to anyone he could think of asking for an assignment to Florence, Italy. On a cool, windy day in late March, Melville finally managed to slip into a White House reception and introduce himself to the president. The novelist was impressed. "There was a great crowd, & a brilliant scene," the author wrote home to his wife. "Ladies in full dress by the hundred." Melville waited in line to greet Lincoln. "Old Abe is much better looking [than] I expected & younger looking," the novelist wrote home. "He shook hands like a good fellow—working hard at it like a man sawing wood at so much per cord." The First Lady, too, was "rather good looking" and the whole scene "very fine altogether. Superb furniture—flood of light—magnificent flowers—full band of music & c." Ultimately, however, the novelist failed to win his plum.[113]

Lincoln was torn between the necessity of appointing competent diplomats, on the one hand, and the need to repay political debts, on the other. Some of the new president's closest allies were German-Americans. Seward, however, had initially indicated that no foreign-born candidate would be assigned to an American legation in Europe. The secretary of state, as Carl Schurz later explained it, feared that some of the German activists—who "had been engaged in revolutionary movements in Europe at a comparatively recent period"—might not be "favorably received" at conservative European courts. "This," Schurz added, "was of importance at a critical time when we had especial reason for conciliating the goodwill of foreign governments." The distracting diplomatic tempest filled the gossip columns of Washington newspapers. "Next to the difficulty about Fort Sumter," the *New York Herald* observed, "the question as to what is to be done with Carl Schurz seems to bother the administration more than anything else."

Indeed, the secretary of state's proposal did not sit well with Lincoln, who pressed Seward to consider key German-born allies like Schurz and Gustave Koerner for the diplomatic corps. "What about our German friends?" Lincoln asked the secretary of state in mid-March. Seward's stance, Koerner told Lincoln, was creating "the most intense sensation amongst the German Republicans all through the country." The U.S. had long appointed non-native emissaries to its diplomatic corps, Koerner argued. "Albert Gallatin—a Swiss—was our ambassador in London in former times," he reminded Lincoln, "and [Pierre] Soulé—a Frenchman—in Spain. The latter was a fool, but that was the objection to him, and not his nativity."

Lincoln ultimately overruled Seward and appointed Schurz to the Madrid post. (Koerner himself eventually took over the legation in Spain after Schurz resigned.) "By stiffening Lincoln's backbone," the scholar Michael Burlingame observes, Schurz "may have made it easier for the president to stand up to Seward" in later crises. Schurz, in any case, was thrilled. "My vanity," he later recalled, "was immensely flattered by the thought of returning to Europe clothed in all the dignity of a Minister Plenipotentiary and Envoy Extraordinary of the United States only a few years after having left my native land as a political refugee." To his wife Schurz wrote: "Next to Mexico, Spain is the most important diplomatic post—and it is mine." The whole episode was a stark reminder that international diplomacy is always a delicate undertaking in a nation of immigrants such as the United States.[114]

Mary Lincoln presented another hurdle when it came to staffing the foreign service. Her first target was Lincoln's secretary of state. "Seward in the cabinet!" she cried. "Never!" She cautioned Lincoln that Seward drew the president "around his finger as if you were a skein of thread." The First Lady derided the secretary of state as an "abolition sneak" and complained that her husband gave Seward his job only "very reluctantly." Lincoln admitted that he found it difficult to control his wife. He "constantly" worried that she would do something to "disgrace" him. Lincoln vigorously defended his secretary of state when Mary badmouthed him as an unprincipled hypocrite. "Mother, you are mistaken; your prejudices are so violent that you do not stop to reason," Lincoln protested. "Seward is an able man, and the country as well as myself can trust him."[115]

The First Lady's dislike of Seward did not stop her from shamelessly harassing him to appoint her allies to key posts. She quickly suggested that he install one of her friends as the new consul in Honolulu. On another occasion, she cornered Lincoln and insisted that he name a favorite Springfield clergyman, the Reverend Dr. James Smith, as the American consul in Dundee, Scotland. An exasperated Lincoln threw his hands in the air and demanded to know the rationale for the appointment. The preacher's résumé was certainly very thin. Even Billy Herndon, a bit of a scamp himself, later referred to Smith as "a great old rascal." Smith's son-in-law had written Lincoln in February arguing for the appointment on the grounds that the preacher "is quite advanced in life and . . . is poor in this world's goods and therefore he needs some assistance to enable him and the old lady to support themselves in Scotland." The president at first tried to steer a middle course by appointing Smith's son to the post. Still, when the younger man fell ill, the president ultimately relented under the pressure of his wife and Smith's other allies. "Send your preacher to the Cabinet Room," Lincoln told Mary. The president made his wife promise that this would be the last time she tried to box him in when it came to diplomatic appointments.[116]

Mary's influence on Lincoln's foreign policy was complex, though ultimately minimal. On the one hand, she operated as a kind of free radical—threatening to tip delicate diplomatic balances in an already unsteady capital. Mary's "natural want of tact . . . her blundering outspokenness, and impolitic disregard for diplomatic considerations," as one society reporter put it, posed a challenge for the president. She once told her old Kentucky friend Cassius Marcellus Clay, who considered himself "open enemies" with Seward, that she and the president "had no confidence whatever in Mr. Seward's friendship," and that Clay "need not fear [Seward's] influence." Lincoln, Mary told her friend, "only tolerated [Seward] for political reasons." For years after the war, Southern sympathizers taunted the First Lady (however unfairly) for her interference with diplomatic patronage. "What opulent presents were made in advance / By seekers of missions to Russia and France," jeered the Richmond *Southern Opinion.* And yet for all Mary's meddling, her influence was not entirely negative. Lincoln could sometimes be a homebody. Mary's cosmopolitan ambitions helped the president to get outside himself—a critical prerequisite for successful diplomats. "If his domestic life had been entirely happy," John Hay's uncle Milton once observed, "I dare say he would have stayed at home and not busied himself with distant concerns."[117]

Still, for Lincoln, that growth process must have been painful. Mary, in her determination to establish her husband's authority over Seward, could be maddening. "It is said you are the power behind the throne," she once told the secretary of state, according to Mary's sister, Elizabeth Todd Edwards. "I'll show you that Mr. L is president yet." She even challenged Seward on minor points of diplomatic protocol. Usually it fell to the secretary of state to host the first state dinner of an administration. In this case, however, the First Lady— who once referred to the events as "stupid state dinners"—insisted on hosting it herself.[118]

If the goal was to impress the diplomatic corps and other distinguished guests, her efforts were not entirely successful. A British journalist who attended the dinner described the First Lady as "of the middle age and height, of a plumpness degenerating to the *embonpoint* natural to her years; her features are plain, her nose and mouth of an ordinary type, and her manners and appearance homely." In any event, after Mary's guests departed for the evening, the First Lady had the $900 bill for the dinner sent over to Seward. Mary's power games were starting to irritate the secretary of state and his staff.[119]

Stress, or spring fever, or some combination of the two, seemed to afflict virtually all members of Lincoln's inner circle as April approached. As the president fell ill, Seward began to behave erratically. At one dinner party in late March, an agitated—or drunk—secretary of state threatened the representatives of England, France, and Russia, that if their ships were captured leaving Southern ports, the United States would not compensate them. The conversation had begun amiably enough, but it eventually devolved into a shouting match. Sipping whisky and puffing on a cigar, Seward gradually grew "more and more violent and noisy," the British minister reported home to his government. The American, he recalled, uttered threats that it would have been "more convenient not to have heard."[120]

God Damn Them, I'll Give Them Hell!

As March turned to April, both Lincoln and Seward had reached a breaking point. The president and his cabinet needed to make some critical decisions about how to respond to Southern intransigence—choices that, if poorly handled, risked drawing European powers into the conflict. Confederate leaders had begun to isolate the federal garrison at Fort Sumter, a brick-walled fortress just off the coast of Charleston, South Carolina. Lincoln appeared unsure about whether to send reinforcements to the troops. Confederate leaders made clear that doing so would result in war. Montgomery Blair, the postmaster general, warned Lincoln that abandoning the fort would invite recognition of the Confederacy by foreign powers. Yet Seward, trying to remain conciliatory, told Confederate representatives that he doubted Lincoln would choose to provision the garrison. Asked as April dawned whether Lincoln intended to resupply the fort, Seward told one Southern representative: "No, I think not. It is a very irksome thing to him to surrender it. His ears are open to everyone, and they fill his head with schemes for its supply. I do not think he will adopt any of them. There is no design to reinforce it."[121]

Seward was ultimately mistaken about Lincoln's resolve. To start, the president bought Blair's argument that abandoning the fort could lead to European recognition of the Confederacy. Retreating from the garrison, Lincoln later explained, "would be utterly ruinous," going far to ensure the Confederacy "recognition abroad." Abandoning the fort, he concluded, "would be our national destruction consummated." Lincoln eventually chose to send supplies (although not weapons) to the fort—a shrewd and fateful compromise that led directly to the first shots of the war and rallied the North around the president's war effort.[122]

In some ways, Seward's restraint in the face of the tremendous public pressure for action is as impressive as Lincoln's clever solution. Both men, it should be remembered, were being continually badgered by newspapers, political opponents, and their own allies, to stake out a bold position. Each day brought another wave of dire news. Critical border states like Kentucky threatened to slip out of the Union. Confederate forces continued to seize federal arsenals and garrisons, and seemed poised to attack Washington. "For god's sake do something," one correspondent urged Seward in late March. "We have been drifting too long already. I repeat for god's sake do something."[123]

Lincoln later recalled the intense pressure he felt as he tried to resolve the secession crisis. "Of all the trials I have had since I came here," he told his old friend Orville Browning later that year, "none begin to compare with those I had between the inauguration and the fall of Fort Sumpter. They were so great that could I have anticipated them, I would not have believed it possible to survive them."[124]

Shortly before the secretary of state presented Lincoln with his notorious April Fools' Day memo and "foreign war panacea," Seward complained to his wife that he too was full of "anxieties." Still, he cautioned, "they must not enter into our correspondence. Dangers and breakers are before us." Seward was right to worry. His memo to the president certainly might have been viewed as insubordination—a firing offense. Lincoln, however, chose to take the high road and retain Seward. The president "easily dismissed the incident," his secretaries later recalled.[125]

With a series of major foreign-policy decisions looming, the president needed Seward's counsel. The secretary of state was not the only observer who believed Lincoln was vacillating on international-affairs issues. "Foreign governments seem to take advantage of our difficulties; the Spanish invasion of San Domingo is an indication of what we may expect," Carl Schurz complained to the president in early April—sounding much like Seward. Schurz lamented the "dissension within and aggression from without" the Union. "It seems to me," he continued, "there is but one way out of this distressing situation. It is to make short work of the secession movement and then to make front against the world abroad." Years later, however, when Seward's April Fools' memo was revealed, Schurz marveled at the secretary of state's "incomprehensible" and "utterly delusive . . . fantastic schemes of foreign war."[126]

Spanish officials agreed that the Lincoln administration was too preoccupied to give the Caribbean much attention. Seward's bombast caused them little concern. Madrid considered Lincoln a weak president with few good options. "The Union is in agony," the Spanish minister in Washington, Gabriel García y Tassara, reported home as Lincoln prepared to take office, "and our mission is not to delay its death for a moment." Still, the conservative Spanish diplomat worried that abolitionists might seize control of Union foreign policy—and then push for reforms in Spain's Caribbean territories. Lincoln and Seward, in this scenario, were actually the moderates. Aggressively challenging the Union government risked strengthening the radicals. The American president, Tassara explained to his superiors, served as a kind of mediator between conservative constituents who valued the "old compromises" and more revolutionary figures who wanted "the complete subjugation of the South."

Tassara's analysis was not far from the mark. Expansionists had been urging Lincoln to act from the first days of the administration.

Just a month into the president's term, Washington wise men and various adventurers had begun pressing Lincoln to consider schemes to establish colonies of black Americans outside the United States— perhaps in the Caribbean or Central America. Lincoln had long been a supporter of colonization proposals, which he viewed as "a middle ground" between uncompromising abolitionists and remorseless slaveholders. Both Lincoln's idols Henry Clay and Thomas Jefferson had also supported colonization. In retrospect the schemes seem wildly impractical. Few black Americans were eager to leave the country where they had been born and raised to set out for a dangerous and untested foreign colony. Still, in the midnineteenth century, as a devastating sectional crisis threatened to tear the country apart, Lincoln honestly believed such projects had the potential to help calm domestic passions.[127]

They also presented the president with a thicket of complex foreign-policy questions. For starters, any proposals to carve colonies out of Caribbean or South American nations had the potential to alienate Latin Americans, who resented U.S. encroachment. The Lincoln administration could not afford to anger any foreign governments in the midst of a looming conflict at home. Lincoln must have recognized that many of the proposals he was asked to consider displayed a decidedly expansionist cast—a dynamic that had bothered him since his time in the House. Boosters lauded the schemes as a means of projecting American power into the Southern Hemisphere. Colonies might serve as coaling stations for the navy or footholds from which to expand export markets. In 1858, Francis P. Blair Jr. had urged colonization on Congress as a means of exploiting "the untold wealth of the intertropical region." And yet, despite the expansionist rhetoric, Lincoln was soon meeting with advocates of the ventures and assigning diplomats to look into potential locations for colonies in Guatemala and Honduras.[128]

While Lincoln was considering the colonization schemes, he also faced an urgent decision about how to handle the Southern cotton trade, which continued to fill Confederate coffers and fuel the rebellion. Lincoln was presented with two choices. In one scenario, the Federals could proclaim a blockade, enlisting their small navy to attempt to slow seaborne traffic. A second possibility consisted of closing the ports altogether. Any decision was sure to arouse the attention of European powers, which maintained a robust trade with the South. The possibility of decisive European intervention hung on Lincoln's decision.

Seward argued that the president should declare a blockade. Such a course would prove far more acceptable to Europe, the secretary of state believed, since it would only slow trade with Europe—not halt it altogether. The strategy carried risks. A blockade would offer an acknowledgment that North and South were at war—which could spur European intervention in itself. Lincoln's naval secretary, Gideon Welles, and several other members of the cabinet opposed Seward's suggestion. Yet Lincoln ultimately shared his secretary of state's view, which seemed less likely to antagonize Europe. "We could not afford," the president explained to an April 15 meeting of his cabinet, "to have two wars on our hands at once."[129]

Lincoln disingenuously pleaded ignorance when challenged by opponents of the blockade. "I don't know anything about the law of nations," Lincoln protested to one critic. "I'm a good enough lawyer in a western law court, I suppose, but we don't practice the law of nations up there, and I supposed Seward knew all about it, and I left it to him. But it's done now and can't be helped, so we must get along as well as we can."[130] Lincoln recognized the gravity of his decision, which came while Congress had not yet convened. The president was known for the lighthearted poems he sometimes composed when asked to sign autograph books. Yet on April 19, 1861, the day he announced his intention to blockade, he scribbled a single grim sentence in the book of one autograph hunter. "Whoever in later times shall see this," he wrote, "and look at the date, will readily excuse the writer for not having indulged in sentiment, or poetry."[131]

Almost immediately after Lincoln's decision to blockade, Britain proclaimed its neutrality in the conflict. "God damn them, I'll give them hell," Seward erupted. The crown's announcement did not mean London considered the Confederacy an independent nation— but Northern leaders believed it was a step in that direction. The British decision was based on a complicated calculus and carried some important advantages for the South. Neutrality, for example, would allow the Confederate government to buy weapons and borrow money from Europe. (Under international law, the proclamation meant both sides were considered "belligerents.") In reality, however, British leaders were doing their best to steer clear of the American chaos. Neutrality technically prohibited British subjects from equipping warships for use in the conflict.

Still, Seward growled "like a caged tiger" when he heard the news. Ralph Waldo Emerson once noted that the secretary of state's anger "had a curious effect on his face; his nose appeared twisted and almost corvine." But there was also a certain logic to Seward's bluster. He told his daughter that he was concerned that "Great Britain and France have lost their fear, and with it their respect for this country, in a good degree." Seward designed his threats to put the great powers back on guard. The secretary of state composed a belligerent dispatch warning London that further provocative moves could lead to conflict with the United States. American diplomats marveled at Seward's apparent impetuosity. The whole thing was "shallow madness," Henry Adams complained. Massachusetts senator Charles Sumner, who arrived in Washington while the crisis was unfolding, found "the president and every one else under the apprehension of an immediate rupture with England and France proceeding from suggestions of Mr. Seward."[132]

Lincoln wisely toned down his secretary of state's dispatch before authorizing a sanitized version. The president peppered Seward's draft with the admonition "Leave out." Lincoln challenged Seward's value judgments—replacing, for example, his secretary of state's accusation that British efforts were "wrongful" with the milder "hurtful." The president removed passages that seemed to threaten war. Seward had written that if Europe intervened in the American conflict, then "we, from that hour, shall cease to be friends and (become once more, as we have twice before been), be forced to [become] enemies of Great Britain." Lincoln softened his secretary of state's bellicose rhetoric significantly.[133]

Lincoln demonstrated that he was perfectly willing to rein in his secretary of state when necessary. And yet, as the years passed, the president eventually grew to trust Seward, delegating many quotidian duties to his chief diplomat. By the end of his first term, Lincoln signed off on some of his dispatches without even reading them. Seward's enemies thought the secretary of state had become Lincoln's "evil genius." Chicago newspaper editor Joseph Medill complained that Seward "kept a sponge saturated with chloroform to Uncle Abe's nose." The president laughed at the notion that his secretary of state was rolling him. While his critics "seemed to believe in my honesty," Lincoln observed, "they also appeared to think that when I had in me any good purpose or intention Seward contrived to suck it out of me unperceived." Actually, Lincoln cleverly managed his secretary of state.[134] "Seward," the president once remarked, "knows that I am his master!"[135]

The two men provided each other with a critical gut check and sounding board. Each acted as the other's "sober second thought."[136] Their lifelong shared approach to foreign policy kept either man from ranging too far afield.[137] Seward, like Lincoln, recognized that the patient and peaceful pursuit of commerce—not wild land grabs—would ultimately do the most to strengthen America's empire. Unnecessary foreign wars could slow the achievement of that goal.[138] By the summer of 1861, one U.S. senator observed, Seward had grown surprisingly "mild and gentle." Lincoln's secretary of state ultimately came to deeply respect his boss. "Executive skill and vigor are rare qualities," he wrote his wife. "The President is the best of us; but he needs constant and assiduous cooperation."[139]

As for the crisis that prompted Seward's "foreign war panacea"— the Spanish reoccupation of Santo Domingo—Lincoln's patient approach ultimately paid off. Shortly after the arrival of its troops, Spain

voted to annex its former colony and continued to dominate Dominican politics for many months. Yet the European nation's transatlantic
attempts to control the Caribbean eventually faltered even without
interference from the Union. Revolts broke out among those pro-
testing Spanish rule. The Dominican rebellion presented Lincoln
with a dilemma. On the one hand, if the Union openly supported the
Dominicans, it would risk aggravating tensions with Spain—an un-
needed headache. On the other hand, failing to support the protesters
against their imperial overlords would look to some like a hypocritical
abandonment of the principles elucidated in the Monroe Doctrine.

When Seward raised the conundrum with the president, Lincoln
answered by telling one of his famous stories. Once upon a time, he
began, a man in Tennessee had been consulting with his preacher.
The clergyman was not very encouraging. There were two potential
roads before his parishioner, he explained. One went "straight to hell";
the other went "right to damnation." The advice seeker, Lincoln continued, then opened his eyes wide and told the preacher that given
those options, he would blaze a third path: "I shall go through the
woods." The president compared himself to the sinner in the story.
"I am not willing," Lincoln told Seward, "to assume any new troubles
or responsibility at this time." And so, he concluded, he would "take
to the woods. We will maintain an honest and strict neutrality."[140]

It was classic Lincoln—a foreign-policy approach that the president applied with formidable patience as the disheartening first year
of the conflict ground on. For a young but growing nation, a Hamiltonian strategy in international affairs demanded tremendous forbearance on the president's part. "The virtue of patience," John Hay
later observed, was "one of the cardinal elements of his character."
Lincoln recognized that the Union would first need to survive the
rebellion, avoiding giving the European powers any pretext for intervention. Only then could the economic forces that both Lincoln and
Seward placed so much faith in propel America to world power.[141]

In the meantime, Lincoln did his best to assuage the qualms of
the diplomatic corps about the continuing chaos in the New World.

At a dinner for the foreign diplomats in June 1861, Lincoln calmly pressed the Union case with his ornately costumed audience. The White House staff tried to reinforce a sense of normalcy. Fresh-cut flowers filled vases in the Blue Room, and the elegant chandeliers were "gracefully festooned with wreaths." The dinner-table conversation occasionally grew heated. The Danish chargé d'affaires groused to Mary's cousin Elizabeth Todd Grimsley about the dangers of American sectionalism. "What is there to bind you together?" the diplomat asked. In Lincoln's own speech to the dinner guests, the president reassured them that European powers had nothing to fear from the American tumult. "Time," Lincoln declared, "would make all things right."[142]

And yet in at least one sense, neither Lincoln nor Seward left their country's future in the hands of time and fate. They feverishly worked to build a Union navy—virtually from scratch—that could successfully enforce the blockade. In the U.S. Constitution, the power to raise an army (and a navy) is vested by the Framers in Congress. Lincoln, in general, respected and valued that separation of powers. Yet in the weeks between the bombardment of Fort Sumter and the start of a special session of Congress on July 4, necessity demanded swift executive action. As the sectional crisis intensified, Lincoln issued a presidential order adding eighteen thousand men to the federal navy.

The president justified this and other early presidential directives with a vivid analogy. "Was it possible to lose the nation, and yet preserve the constitution?" he asked. "By general law life *and* limb must be protected; yet often a limb must be amputated to save a life; but a life is never wisely given to save a limb. I felt that measures, otherwise unconstitutional, might become lawful, by becoming indispensable to the preservation of the constitution, through preservation of the nation."[143]

Citing his own presidential "war power"—a concept he had invented—the president insisted that his blockade was "strictly legal." Lincoln, however, ultimately sought congressional approval for his newly minted sailors when the body finally reconvened. (The legislature rubber-stamped the measure in August.) Nevertheless, Lincoln's executive action bolstering the federal navy represents an important precedent for later presidents who have sought greater authority and maneuverability in their disputes with foreign powers.[144]

American Whigs had long obsessed over naval affairs. They viewed naval expansion as a peaceful project that would help to bolster foreign trade. Whigs had been the biggest boosters of Commodore Perry's mission to Japan in the 1850s, and their elder statesmen had been drooling for decades over the vast Asian export markets. Still, as American vessels began to swarm over the seas, they also risked clashing with the ships of the world's greatest naval power, Britain. The tensions came to a head one fateful morning in the balmy Bahama Channel, 250 miles off the coast of Cuba.[145]

CHAPTER THREE

Lincoln vs. Palmerston

T HE FEDERAL NAVY WAS THE ONLY BRANCH OF THE MILITARY THAT BROUGHT LINCOLN MUCH JOY IN THE SECOND HALF OF 1861. ONE SUNDAY AFTERNOON IN LATE JULY, THE PRESIDENT invited his old friend Orville Browning to the Executive Mansion for dinner. The two men spent several hours chatting about the progress of the war. Browning found Lincoln "very melancholy." The president acknowledged that he was depressed, but claimed there was "no special cause for it." Actually, there were plenty of good reasons for distress. A week earlier the rebel army had embarrassed Lincoln's bluecoats at Bull Run, killing more than 600, taking 1,200 prisoners, and sending the rest pouring back into Washington covered in mud, rain, and shame. Lincoln acknowledged that the whole thing looked *"damned bad."* [1]

The Union defeat at Bull Run appeared even more disturbing when viewed against the backdrop of the international stage. On the one hand, the president was eager to demonstrate to Europe that he could subdue the rebellion. All spring he had been urging his military commanders to strike. When his officers protested that the new Northern troops were still unprepared, Lincoln had responded: "You are green, it is true; but they are green, also; you are green alike." The sooner Lincoln's Federals could show their strength, the president believed, the less likely the European powers would be to throw in their lot with the Confederacy.[2]

And yet, as the disaster at Bull Run quickly made clear, that strategy had the potential to backfire. Now Lincoln's forces simply looked incompetent in European eyes. "Our prestige in Europe [is] gone," Carl Schurz wrote home to Lincoln from Spain in the wake of Bull Run. "All our efforts abroad will be of no avail if we are beaten at home." Schurz complained that the "public press all over Europe is treating us with sneering contempt or granting us the small boon of a little pitiful sympathy." The whole episode, the diplomat told Lincoln, was "bitter and humiliating in the extreme." Only military success would be capable of changing European minds. "Nowhere," Schurz concluded, "can this disgrace be washed off but on the battle-fields of America."[3]

Yet the same military strategy that Lincoln was employing to defeat the Confederacy had the potential to strain transatlantic ties. Lincoln's top general, the Mexican War hero Winfield Scott, had conceived a strategy known as the Anaconda Plan, which aimed in part to use the federal navy to strangle the Confederacy like a snake coiled around the Atlantic and Gulf coasts. Still, Scott's design also risked angering European merchants and their monarchs, who depended on cotton from the South.[4]

Now, at the White House, Browning asked Lincoln if he worried that European nations might be dragged into the war. The president admitted that he was concerned about the blockade's effect on Britain and France. If those nations chose to intervene on behalf of the Confederacy, Scott's Anaconda would be far less effective. The only thing worse than alienating the great powers would be if the small Federal navy—around forty ships at the start of the war—also failed altogether in its attempts to blockade the Southern coast. That would be like showing weakness to an already angry dog. Furthermore, the key European powers considered an ineffective "paper blockade" illegal under international law. The only solution, Lincoln had decided during one sleepless night in the wake of Bull Run, was to beef up the fleet. Browning recalled Lincoln saying that "we had better increase the navy as fast as we could and blockade such ports as our force would enable us to, and say nothing about the rest."[5]

August brought some good news from the high seas. While Lincoln's generals were still agonizing over Bull Run, the navy scored a decisive victory. Sailors patrolling the Atlantic coast off North Carolina had grown increasingly concerned about the steady flow of blockade runners launching from Hatteras Inlet. Federal commanders put together a strike force of seven ships with 141 guns to assault the Confederate stronghold. When naval officials woke Lincoln up late one night to give him the news that Hatteras had been subdued, the president was ecstatic. Wearing only a nightshirt, Lincoln wrapped one assistant secretary in a bear hug. The two men "flew around the room once or twice," recalled one witness, "and the night shirt was considerably agitated." In the wake of the naval triumph, Seward told an acquaintance that he believed the danger of European intervention was now "pretty well over."[6]

Lincoln insisted that he was ignorant about naval matters. "I know but little about ships," he told his secretary of the navy, Gideon Welles, at the beginning of the conflict. In fact, Lincoln, the former flatboat and steamboat pilot, knew plenty. In 1849 he applied for a patent for a device he had invented for lifting steamboats and other vessels over shoals. Lincoln actively pushed for innovations in the navy, signing a bill that would allow the service to develop a fleet of ironclads. That autumn a New York iron manufacturer approached Seward with a novel design. The secretary of state quickly brought it to Lincoln's attention. Some naval officers ridiculed the vessel, which resembled "a cheese box on a raft." Lincoln, however, was impressed with the design's simplicity. At one development meeting, the president hoisted a small pasteboard model of the odd-looking craft. "All I have to say," Lincoln remarked, "is what the girl said when she stuck her foot into the stocking: 'It strikes me there is something in it.' "[7]

Still, the slow job of building the navy frustrated Lincoln. In October one of the president's secretaries found him "pale and careworn, as if the perpetual wear-and-tear of the load which presses upon him were becoming too much even for his iron frame and elastic mind." As Lincoln and his team awaited completion of the ironclads, they were forced to rely on the navy's existing fleet—and its old heroes. That fall Captain Charles Wilkes, a sixty-two-year-old former Antarctic explorer, was assigned a routine mission to travel to the coast of Africa, recover the screw sloop USS *San Jacinto*, and deliver her to the Philadelphia naval yard. Wilkes was nearing the end of his career and had earned a reputation for immoderation. One naval official complained that the captain, who once burned a Fijian village to punish the theft of his crew's property, possessed "a superabundance of self-esteem and a deficiency of judgment." Naval secretary Gideon Welles agreed that the old sailor had "abilities but not good judgment in all respects," and observed that it was "pretty evident that he will be likely to cause trouble." He was, Welles added, not "as obedient as he should be."[8]

Wilkes decided to make one last stab at glory before his retirement. He disobeyed his orders, diverting the *San Jacinto* toward the Caribbean in order to hunt for Confederate blockade runners. While in port at Cienfuegos, in southern Cuba, Wilkes and his crew discovered that two Confederate envoys, James Mason and John Slidell, were scheduled to sail from Havana on November 8, heading to Europe to take up diplomatic posts in London and Paris. The Southrons made no efforts to hide their plans. Most well-informed Habañeros knew of their impending departure. Wilkes ordered his crew to position their sloop in the middle of the Bahama Channel. Then he waited for his prey.[9]

Wilkes's executive officer warned his captain that seizing the mail packet, the HMS *Trent*, might violate international law. But the aging Wilkes could not resist the opportunity. On November 8, the captain told his diary that the day was "one of the most important in my naval life." Shortly before noon, Wilkes climbed onto the deck of the *San Jacinto* and peered through a telescope. He spotted the *Trent* in the distance. Wilkes ordered his crew on deck, armed with rifles and bayonets. Then someone shouted the fateful order to fire. A cannonball soared across the bow of the British packet, dropping into the water some distance from its target. When the *Trent* continued on its course, Wilkes's men fired another shell—this one landing closer. After the British ship finally slowed to a stop, Wilkes ordered his men onto the English vessel to seize Mason and Slidell, dubbing them the "embodiment of dispatches." After a brief struggle, Wilkes's sailors hauled the Confederate diplomats back to the *San Jacinto*. The *Trent* was permitted to continue on its course— but Wilkes had his captives.[10]

And Lincoln had a mess. Northerners, at least at first, did not seem to recognize the dangers. A British journalist traveling in the United States noted the "storm of exultation sweeping over the land" when the news of the capture arrived. "The whole country now rings with applause," the *New York Times* reported. "We do not believe the American heart ever thrilled with more genuine delight. . . . As for Commodore Wilkes and his command, let the handsome thing be done. Consecrate another Fourth of July to him. Load him down with services of plate and swords of the cunningest and costliest art." Crowded theater audiences honored Wilkes with echoing ovations when he returned to shore. P. T. Barnum personally invited the captain to visit his museum. Wilkes, the *Boston Transcript* gushed, had "dealt a heavy blow" to "the very vitals of the conspiracy threatening our national existence." The U.S. Congress passed a resolution lauding the new American hero "for his brave, adroit and patriotic conduct." Americans were so eager to congratulate Wilkes that the captain's hands began to blister from too much shaking.[11]

Both Lincoln and Seward initially seemed inclined to defend Wilkes. As the early euphoria faded, however, the president and his secretary of state began to express second thoughts. "If Commodore Wilkes acted under orders," the *Richmond Inquirer* noted perceptively, "we do not see how Lincoln can possibly escape the most serious complications with the English government." Lincoln acknowledged in November that Wilkes "had no right to turn his quarter-deck into a prize court," and complained that he was losing sleep over the incident. "I fear," Lincoln told another visitor in November, "the traitors may prove to be white elephants." A State Department employee told his diary that from early on in the crisis Lincoln favored releasing the "traitors."[12]

Britons erupted when they read the initial reports of the *Trent* seizure. Londoners, reported one American in the city, were "frantic with rage, and were the country polled, I fear 999 out of 1,000 would declare for immediate war." Britain's prime minister, the irascible Lord Palmerston, called an emergency meeting of his cabinet. "I don't know whether you are going to stand this," he is said to have thundered as he threw his hat on the table, "but I'll be damned if I do!" The prime minister threatened to dispatch a fleet of gunboats to U.S. waters, and asked his war department to reconsider recent spending cuts. "Relations with Seward and Lincoln," he wrote, "are so precarious that it seems to me that it would be inadvisable to make any reduction in the amount of our military force." Palmerston demanded a halt to gunpowder and ammunition exports to the federal government, and ordered more than ten thousand redcoats to Canada. By early December, the British prime minister confidently assured his monarch that the country was well prepared for war. "Great Britain," Palmerston reported to Queen Victoria, "is in a better state than at any former time to inflict a severe blow upon, and to read a lesson to the United States which will not soon be forgotten."[13]

God Wouldn't Trust Them in the Dark

Lincoln sometimes liked to needle Britons, whom he considered stuffy and self-important. He told a favorite joke about an Englishman who hung a portrait of George Washington in his outhouse. The punch line: "There is Nothing that Will Make an Englishman Shit So quick as the Sight of Genl Washington." Another favorite knee-slapper starred an old Indian chief from the West. "He was visited by an Englishman," Lincoln explained, "who tried to impress him with the greatness of England. 'Why,' said he to the chief, 'the sun never sets on England.' 'Humph!' said the Indian. 'I suppose it's because God wouldn't trust them in the dark.' "[14]

"Nothing can be more virulent than the hatred that exists between the Americans of the United States and the English," Alexis de Tocqueville observed two decades before the Civil War. "But in spite of those hostile feelings," he noted, "the Americans derive most of their manufactured commodities from England"—a dynamic that fueled both economies. By the midnineteenth century, American interests were best served by a healthy relationship with John Bull. London held $444 million worth of American stocks and bonds, making it by far the United States' largest creditor. Lord Byron, whose poetry Lincoln admired, liked to insist that the Baring brothers and the Rothschild banking houses were "the true lords of Europe." Yet in America's case, because of the breakneck speed of economic growth, the debt figures were not particularly oppressive.[15]

Lincoln had mixed feelings about carrying debt. On the one hand, he shared the Hamiltonian view that a debt could be a "national blessing" if it helped to fund development projects and bring the country together. He had long favored a state bank in Illinois, and once jumped out a window in Springfield to avoid a vote that would put it in danger. Yet Lincoln had also experienced crushing personal obligations firsthand. As a young man, after one investment in a local dry-goods store went bad, Lincoln complained to friends about his own "national debt." On another occasion, according to a close friend, Lincoln visited a prostitute. After he "stript off and went to bed" with the young woman, the gawky Illinoisan discovered that he did not have enough cash. Lincoln dressed and called off the encounter. "I do not wish," the future president explained, "to go on credit."[16] Or so the story is told.

By the time Lincoln occupied the Executive Mansion, however, transatlantic financial and commercial ties left little room for disagreement about a wise foreign policy. A war between Britain and the

United States would likely prove disastrous to both economies. "The financial needs of the United States provided a powerful incentive for American statesmen to pursue a conciliatory foreign policy," notes the Oxford diplomatic scholar Jay Sexton. "The creditor-debtor relationship of Britain and the United States bonded the two nations together and gave them the common interest of avoiding war." Succumbing to momentary passions or old grudges would prove counterproductive.[17]

For Lincoln, the *Trent* crisis in the winter of 1861 was a high-stakes, real-world test of his lifelong belief that rational self-interest—"guided by justice"—should be the overriding principle in American foreign affairs. Lincoln believed that selfishness lay at the bottom of all human motivation. When Herndon sometimes argued that man could act disinterestedly, Lincoln ridiculed his law partner. Ultimately, the future president liked to say, "the snaky tongue of selfishness will wag out." Lincoln believed that human beings possessed little, if any, free will, and were motivated instead by what he called "the fuel of *interest.*" Freedom and progress emerged only from the clash of those interests—whether at home or among the nations of the world.[18]

What about the "better angels of our nature"—Lincoln's most often quoted phrase? Even those words, spoken in his first inaugural, were a nod to human imperfection. In an early draft of the address, which had been revised by Seward, the New Yorker had urged Lincoln to appeal to "the guardian angel of our nation." Lincoln could be an idealist, but he had little time for self-righteous crusading. The president-elect revised Seward's words, preferring a more qualified version. Lincoln believed deeply in the virtues of the American example, and he once referred to the United States as God's "almost chosen people." Yet he could never quite bring himself to slip completely into the role of national cheerleader.

Instead, Lincoln considered a kind of inexact justice the highest good. He believed that only "reason, cold, calculating, unimpassioned reason," could overcome the "basest principles of our nature." He admired British utilitarians like Jeremy Bentham and John Stuart

Mill. Careful study of the classics also shaped Lincoln's approach to foreign policy. As a young lawyer, Lincoln pored over the works of Euclid, mastering the Greek mathematician's theories of geometry by candlelight, his long legs poking out from beneath his bedcovers. Justice, Lincoln believed, was "nothing else but the best reason of wise men" applied to human affairs. For all Lincoln's genuine, almost religious faith in the power of America's republican example to reshape the world, his foreign policies also paid great heed to the Old World concept of international equilibrium. Lincoln "was always just," Herndon observed, "before he was generous."[19]

Lincoln's antagonist in the *Trent* crisis, Britain's Lord Palmerston, shared the American president's reverence for coldly rational policies that would promote the national interest. As a young man, Palmerston had been tutored by a disciple of Adam Smith, who predicted that progress would emerge from the "invisible hand" of brutal competition. As an adult, the British statesman recommended Euclid as the best training for a diplomat; the balance of power, after all, involved constant mathematical calculation and recalculation. "Nothing," Palmerston counseled, "strengthens the reasoning faculty more than geometry." Unlike Lincoln, however, the prime minister believed that a shrewd, interest-based policy was the province of well-bred, elite statesmen—not backwoods diplomats like the American president.[20]

Palmerston was not opposed to injecting morality into foreign policy—provided it served the British interest. He crusaded vigorously against the international slave trade, and assiduously cultivated ties to other constitutional governments on the Continent. Still, the prime minister was a strong believer that his nation should not "go in for chivalrous enterprises." Britain could not act as "the Quixote of the world," he insisted. Instead, self-interest should be the "shibboleth" of an English statesman's policy. Britain could "secure her own independence" from manipulating "the conflicting interests of other countries," Palmerston believed. At times, in his calls for national freedom of action, Britain's prime minister sounded like Lincoln's hero George Washington. "We have no eternal allies, and we have no perpetual enemies," Palmerston once declared. "Our interests are eternal and perpetual, and those interests it is our duty to follow."[21]

Palmerston recognized that Britain's interests lay in steering clear of the American crisis. "They who in quarrels interpose, will often get a bloody nose," he shrewdly cautioned British hawks. Yet the *Trent* affair presented the prime minister with a troubling challenge to his country's prestige. Palmerston distrusted democracies. Governments "in which the masses influence or direct the destinies of the Country," he believed, "are swayed much more by Passion than by Interest." Palmerston, too, was not always free from hot-tempered outbursts. As the American Civil War erupted, the prime minister gloated that Britain's former colonies had splintered into what he called the "Disunited States of North America." In principle, Lincoln and Palmerston were committed to reasoned, interest-based foreign policies. In practice, the *Trent* episode presented both men with the very real possibility that "emotional crisis" could sweep their nations into a devastating transatlantic war.[22]

Jupiter Anglicanus

Henry John Temple, the third Viscount Palmerston, was born in 1784, five years before the U.S. Constitution. From his first days on earth, he inhabited a world of aristocratic privilege. Even in his childhood, Palmerston found himself caught between his age's competing obsessions with order and progress. He lived through the French Revolution, and was old enough to recall a trip with his parents to revolutionary Paris in 1792. At school classmates thought Palmerston "charming," but also lacking a certain "zest." In later years students at one of the elite boarding schools he attended would concoct a song with a verse lauding "Temple's frame of iron," but as a young man Palmerston was actually somewhat sickly. Blisters pocked his pale face, and his eyes were so bad that he had trouble reading. In college at Cambridge the young man drank far less than his classmates, but he also studied little aside from geometry. Luckily, as a member of the aristocracy, he was entitled to skip exams. "Certainly philosophy was still-born in Palmerston," notes Kenneth Bourne, the best biographer of the prime minister's early years. "No one ever called him an intellectual. But he was very strong on common sense."[23]

Palmerston wangled himself a seat in the House of Commons in 1807. He still lacked a statesman's graces, stammering when he rose to speak and putting off acquaintances with his cold demeanor. The daughter of one of Palmerston's legislative colleagues found the young man "very pedantic and very pompous," adding that he "was so priggish and so sedate." His policies as a young bureaucrat during and just following the Napoleonic Wars revealed his unsentimental approach to public affairs. When popular riots erupted in London in 1815, Palmerston ordered his staff to respond to stone throwing with "a volley of small shot from a bedroom window." His invocation to "pepper the faces of the mob" raised the hackles of British liberals. Three years later, a lunatic who had cut off his own penis tried to assassinate Palmerston. The would-be killer fired a shot that tore through his target's clothes and singed his back. Palmerston simply applied ice to the burn and went back to work.[24]

The young politician quickly acquired a reputation as a ladies' man. The English press dubbed Palmerston "Lord Cupid," but his romances tended to display a quality of opportunism and rapacious conquest. At one London club, Almack's—which was so exclusive that the Duke of Wellington had once been turned away for wearing black pants instead of white—Palmerston is said to have slept with three of the seven directors of the all-female membership committee. Married women came to expect his aggressive advances. One object of Palmerston's affections recalls the future prime minister accosting her "in his impudent, brusque way, with a 'Ha, ha! I see it all—beautiful woman neglected by her husband—allow me, etc.'" The future prime minister apparently fathered more than one illegitimate child. In his diary, Palmerston used code phrases like "subscriptions & gifts" as euphemisms for child-support payments. He speckled the volumes with asterisks and phrases like "fine nights" to denote sexual conquests.[25]

In 1830, at the age of forty-six, Palmerston was named Britain's foreign minister. The viscount worked extraordinarily hard, especially for a nobleman. At first, the foreign minister felt as though he was drowning. Only when he fell ill did he take a break. "The life I lead," Palmerston told one of his diplomats in 1834, "is like that of a man who on getting out of bed every morning, should be caught up by the end of one of the arms of a windmill and whirled round and round till he was again deposited at night to rest." His goal as a government functionary, he once remarked, was to turn "night and chaos into light and order."[26]

As foreign minister, Palmerston did not easily embark on crusades. "Governments," he once said, "are not at liberty to act solely from motives of generous sympathy for the sufferings of an oppressed people." Yet he shrewdly sought to tap into Britain's liberal mood. The British foreign minister believed his nation's best interests would be served by challenging the existing order in Europe. Conservative European monarchs led by Austria's Prince Metternich had forged an alliance that aimed to suppress liberal movements on the Continent. Palmerston, as a counterweight, cast himself as a champion of constitutional government, working to cement a rapprochement between Britain, France, Spain, and Portugal. "We shall drink the cause of Liberalism all over the world," the foreign minister declared in 1830. "The reign of Metternich is over."[27]

At home, Palmerston's aggressive leadership sometimes irritated subordinates. As a boss, Palmerston could be a martinet. He scolded employees for smoking cigars at work. Poor penmanship in diplomatic dispatches drove Palmerston to distraction. "Life is not long enough to correct them," the foreign minister carped, "planting Sugar Canes would not be more labourious." The foreign minister was so annoyed with the "paleness" of the ink used by his staff in Vienna that he threatened to deny them promotions. Palmerston complained that reading another envoy's reports was "like running Penknives into one's Eyes." The foreign minister even voiced his disapproval when subordinates took off Sunday mornings to attend church. After Palmerston finally stepped down in 1834, according to tradition, his diplomats wanted to illuminate every window in the headquarters as a celebration.[28]

Queen Victoria, at least at first, was enchanted with her "tall, dark and handsome" chief diplomat. Palmerston, along with the dashing Lord Melbourne, tutored the queen in both foreign policy and chess and accompanied her on afternoon carriage rides. In one lesson Palmerston explained that the English words *aristocratic* and *democratic* both derived from the same Greek root word for "power," *kratos*. Not all members of the court approved of the queen's instructors. "She may not know their characters," griped one, "but they must know their own." In 1839, when he was fifty-five, Palmerston finally married Emily Lamb, a woman with whom he had been having an affair for thirty years. The following year the queen wed Prince Albert. Victoria and her foreign-policy tutor slowly grew apart. The queen would eventually come to refer to Palmerston as a "dreadful" old man.[29]

Palmerston could be astonishingly insubordinate. He showed up late to the queen's first state dinner and developed a lifelong habit of tardiness. He sometimes kept foreign heads of state waiting for hours. The Belgian envoy to London claimed that he had read Samuel Richardson's entire 1,500-page novel, *Clarissa*, while waiting in Palmerston's anterooms. London society had a saying to describe the lateness of the foreign minister and his wife: "The Palmerstons always miss the soup." The foreign minister was unapologetic. After showing up forty-five minutes late to a dinner at the Ottoman ambassador's home, he dismissed his host as "a greasy, stupid old Turk."[30]

Palmerston's personal amorality particularly troubled the queen and her prince consort. Once, while visiting Windsor Castle, the future prime minister burst into the bedroom of one of the queen's ladies-in-waiting, who screamed until the palace guards arrived. Albert was appalled. Palmerston, the prince told his diary, possessed a "worthless private character. How could the Queen consent to take a man as her chief adviser and confidential counselor in all matters of State, religion, society, Court, etc., he who, as her Secretary of State, and while under her roof at Windsor Castle, had committed a brutal attack upon one of her ladies? Had at night, by stealth, introduced himself into her apartment, barricaded the door, and would have consummated his fiendish scheme by violence had not the miraculous efforts of his victim and such assistance attracted by her screams, saved her."[31]

Victoria and Albert referred to Palmerston simply as the Immoral One. The British statesman's ambivalent Christianity must have irritated his devout monarch. Palmerston belonged to the official Anglican church and believed that the institution provided British society with much-needed order. Yet he attended services only irregularly. British wags joked that Palmerston treated God "as a foreign power." For political reasons the British statesman sometimes appealed to the "feelings and practices of Christian nations." But his professions of faith do not appear to have been genuine. On his deathbed, asked by a priest whether he believed in Jesus Christ, Palmerston replied laconically: "Oh, surely."[32]

Britons, however, adored their brash statesman and his muscular patriotism. In later years he acquired the sobriquet the Most English Minister. When a French official remarked, "If I were not a Frenchman, I should wish to be an Englishman," Palmerston retorted: "If I were not an Englishman, I should wish to be an Englishman." During the 1850s the viscount mastered the craft of gunboat diplomacy. He assured Britons that "the watchful eye and the strong arm" of their government would protect them anywhere in the world. "Diplomats and protocols are very good things," he remarked, "but there are no better peace-keepers than well-appointed three-deckers." A

British journalist dubbed Palmerston the "storm-compelling Jupiter Anglicanus of our Foreign Office."[33]

Palmerston did not become prime minister until 1855, when he was seventy years old. By the outbreak of the Civil War, the Most English Minister was well past his prime. Tory rival Benjamin Disraeli sniped that Palmerston "is really an imposter, utterly exhausted, and at the best only ginger-beer, and not champagne, and now an old painted pantaloon, very deaf, very blind, and with false teeth, which would fall out of his mouth when speaking, if he did not hesitate and halt so in his talk." Disraeli was right about the prime minister's failing health, but he misjudged Palmerston's resilience. France's shrewd, capable diplomat Charles Maurice de Talleyrand hit closer to the mark when he described the British prime minister as "one of the most able, if not the most able, man of business whom I have met in my career."[34]

Palmerston had no love for the United States. Memories of his tiff with Seward over the McLeod Affair in the early 1840s still rankled. Palmerston had angered Americans by dismissing the Stars and Stripes as "a piece of bunting." The prime minister had long viewed Britain's transatlantic cousin as a threat. The Manifest Destiny movement, he pointed out, was "essentially and inherently aggressive." Palmerston considered democracy a degenerate form of government. He probably would have concurred with a London *Press* editorial whose author complained that American politics combined "the morals of a horse race, the manners of a dog fight, the passions of a tap-room, and the emotions of a gambling house." Palmerston could not believe that the North would succeed in subduing the Southern rebellion. As the secession crisis worsened, the prime minister wrote to Queen Victoria lauding the "approaching and virtually accomplished dissolution in America."[35]

Britain, more than any other nation, was in a unique position to dictate terms to its quarrelsome former colonies. By the mid-1800s— dubbed "Britain's imperial century" by historians—the vast territories that Palmerston oversaw included outposts from Canada to India to Australia. After Britain defeated its chief rival, France, in the Napoleonic Wars ending in 1815, the empire's stability and dominance of Europe was stronger than it had ever been. The massive British navy, the largest in the world with its 856 ships, easily outnumbered the American force. At Queen Victoria's Renaissance-style home on the Isle of Wight, a massive fresco hung over the main staircase that depicted the god Neptune crowning the personified figure of Britannia queen of the seas. The message was clear. "At no other time in history," writes historian Niall Ferguson, "has one power so completely dominated the world's oceans as Britain did in the midnineteenth century." If Britain chose to intervene on behalf of the Confederacy, Lincoln and the Northern cause would face a new threat as perilous as anything Jefferson Davis could concoct.[36]

Still, for all the British Empire's power, Palmerston displayed a puzzling insecurity—which is partly what made him so dangerous. Britain still faced serious rivals on the Continent despite its predominance. France remained a threat, even after its defeat at Britain's hands earlier in the century. Prussia was beginning to maneuver for control of central Europe. Britain and Russia scrambled for control of Asia, a geopolitical conflict that would later come to be known as the Great Game. Finally, in North America, the prime minister was concerned that Lincoln and Seward would try to divert attention by striking at British Canada, which he believed was dangerously unprepared for an invasion. If the Confederate military proved to be "too hard a morsel for his teeth," he worried, Seward—whom Palmerston considered "a vapouring, blustering, ignorant man"—might convince Lincoln to invade their poorly defended northern neighbor. Palmerston's fears were not wholly without merit. The year before, Seward had prated that Britain's North American provinces would make "excellent states." Palmerston also feared that the war would slow shipments of cotton from the South. "We do not like slavery," he explained, "but we want cotton, and we dislike very much your Morrill tariff." (The Morrill Tariff, passed in early March 1861, raised duties significantly on European imports.)

The British prime minister, despite his advanced age, remained firmly in control of British foreign policy at the start of the Civil War. He recommended dispatching three regiments that might form the foundation of a militia to Britain's North American provinces. Such a move, Palmerston decided, would provide "a useful hint to Seward and Lincoln and their associates." Victoria agreed that it was "of great importance that we should be strong in Canada." British leaders ultimately dispatched a steamship packed with artillery to North America. As the year wore on, Palmerston argued for sending even more troops. The deployments, he suggested, were already having "a wholesome effect upon the tone and temper of Lincoln and Seward."[37]

In late May, Cassius Marcellus Clay, the president's appointee to the St. Petersburg post, stopped in London on his way to Russia and met with Palmerston at his home. The prime minister received Clay "in a very kindly spirit," the American reported home. Still, "I saw at a glance where the feeling of England was," Clay wrote in a letter to Lincoln. "They hoped for our ruin! They are jealous of our power. They care neither for the South or the North. They hate both."[38]

British opinion about the conflict was actually far more varied than Clay's analysis. Palmerston, for one, recognized that it would be folly to plunge England into America's conflict. Britain's "best and true policy," he told his foreign minister in October 1861, "seems to be to go on as we have begun, and to keep quite clear of the conflict between North and South. . . . The only thing to do seems to be to lie on our oars, and to give no pretext to the Washingtonians to quarrel with us, while on the other hand, we maintain our rights and those of our fellow countrymen." The prime minister acknowledged that there "have been cases in Europe in which allied Powers have said to fighting parties . . . 'In the Queen's name, I bid you to drop your swords.' But those cases are rare and peculiar. The love of quarreling and fighting is inherent in man, and to prevent its indulgence is to impose restraints on natural liberty."[39]

A Gross Outrage

As winter approached, however, Palmerston found it increasingly difficult to simply ignore the American conflict. "It may be," the prime minister wrote the Duke of Newcastle on November 12, "that the Washington Gov't may not wish or intend to declare war against us without adequate cause." Still, he added, "their policy is to heap indignities upon us, and they are encouraged to do so by what they imagine to be the defenseless state of our North American Provinces."[40]

The same day, the prime minister wrote the Union minister in London, Charles Francis Adams, asking for a meeting. "My Dear Sir," the prime minister began, "I would be very glad to have a few minutes conversation with you; could you without inconvenience call upon me today at any time between one and two?" Adams was surprised that Palmerston had asked to see him on such short notice. The prime minister had ignored the usual channels, including his own foreign minister. Adams showed up at Palmerston's home in London's Piccadilly district at the appointed time. He swept past a pair of flaming torches into the prime minister's darkened library, which was lit only by flickering gas lamps.[41]

Tensions between Britain and the United States had been simmering all fall. Washington and London had exchanged a series of "tart" dispatches. Lincoln and Seward worried that Britain was angling to recognize the Confederacy. Palmerston and his ministers, still spooked by Seward's belligerent spring behavior, feared the Federals wanted a foreign war. "Every report, public, official and private, that comes to us from the Northern States of America," Palmerston wrote an acquaintance in November, "tends to shew that our relations with the Washington government are on the most precarious footing and that Seward and Lincoln may at any time and on any pretence come to a rupture with us." Palmerston's foreign minister warned him a few days later that "it is the business of Seward to feed the mob with sacrifices every day, and we happen to be the most grateful food he can offer."[42]

Now, in the dark of his London library, Palmerston pressed Adams on his government's intentions. The prime minister had become particularly concerned about an American ship called the *James Adger*, which had been loitering off the coast of Britain. Palmerston feared that the *Adger* intended to seize the *Trent* and its Confederate passengers—a move that he was sure would ignite public anger in Britain. The prime minister complained, somewhat off point, that the *Adger*'s captain had been getting drunk on "some excellent brandy" during his stay in Britain. Adams later recalled that Palmerston warned of a hostile British response if the *Adger*'s captain, "after enjoying the hospitality of this country, filling his ship with coals, and with other supplies, and filling his own stomach with brandy (and here he laughed in his characteristic way)[43] should within sight of the shore commit an act which would be felt as offensive to the national flag." The prime minister stressed that seizing the *Trent* would do the Federal cause little good in Britain—and would probably inspire great "prejudice" among ordinary Englishmen. Palmerston later reported to Queen Victoria that Adams had assured him that the *Adger* "had orders not to meddle with any vessel under any foreign flag."[44]

What neither man knew was that Wilkes had already seized the *Trent* four days earlier off the Cuban coast. The news arrived in London on November 27. Karl Marx, then a journalist living in London, observed that "the electric telegraph immediately flashed" the news "to all parts of Great Britain." Rumors of war flew through the city. "Every normal Englishman," Marx reported, "went to bed with the conviction that he would go to sleep in a state of peace but wake up in a state of war." The British stock exchange plunged on war fears, becoming "a stage of stormy scenes," as Marx put it. The author of the *Communist Manifesto*, a shrewd observer of economic trends, wrote his friend Frederick Engels that he wished he had "the means to exploit the stupidity" of the stock exchange "during this fool period."[45]

Britain's most influential newspaper tried to tamp down popular passions. The London *Times* editors found it hard to believe that the Federals would intentionally provoke a conflict and counseled against responding with "an outburst of passion." Another newspaper blended swaggering nationalism with doubts about whether war would actually erupt. "We are pretty well accustomed to Yankee bluster and hot headedness," the Cardiff *Mercury* reported, "but we cannot think that they [the United States] will be so utterly blind as to provoke a collision with a power which with little difficulty could blow to the four winds their dwarf fleet and shapeless mass of incoherent squads."[46]

After ordering a review of the legal precedents, Palmerston convened a meeting of his cabinet on the afternoon of November 29. He told his foreign minister that he thought Britain should "demand from Seward and Lincoln apology and liberation of the captives." If the Americans refused, Palmerston suggested that Britain should withdraw its minister in Washington, rather than have him "remain [as] the representative of a country deliberately insulted." In the meantime, the prime minister wanted to halt all arms exports to the federal government. "We have reason to suppose that Seward and Lincoln mean a rupture with England," he told his foreign minister. Under such circumstances he considered it "folly, amounting to imbecility" to allow British weapons to reach the bluecoats. Palmerston told the queen that the cabinet believed "a gross outrage and violation of international law has been committed." He advised Victoria to "demand reparation and redress."[47]

Palmerston was convinced that Washington had planned the seizure, hoping to provoke a foreign war. The prime minister had heard rumors that the Lincoln administration had approved Wilkes's action beforehand at a White House cabinet meeting. Some Americans had initially believed the same thing; Seward's close ally Thurlow Weed wrote the secretary of state shortly after the capture of Mason and Slidell explaining that General Winfield Scott had told him in Paris that such a seizure had been discussed in Washington for weeks beforehand. "You have, I suppose, well considered [the consequences],"

Weed wrote Seward. (Scott later argued that his comments had been taken out of context.)

Palmerston was nevertheless miffed when he heard that Lincoln had dismissed the affair to a visiting Canadian official, sniffing, "Oh, that'll be got along with." The British prime minister ordered his foreign minister to draft a blunt dispatch demanding that the envoys be released within seven days of receipt of the note. The same evening he shipped the text off to Windsor Castle for the queen's approval. Palmerston believed that the British demands would come as a "Thunder Clap" to the American president.[48]

Britain's monarchs, however, were far less eager for a war. The mood at Windsor Castle was already grim. Prince Albert had been ailing for several weeks and felt "thoroughly miserable" when the dispatch arrived. The prince consort had been haunting the palace halls like a walking ghost, shivering despite the fur coat he had wrapped around his aching body. Albert felt "as if cold water were being poured down his back," Victoria worried to her diary. The prince consort "could eat no breakfast and looked very wretched." His incoming correspondence on the morning of December 1 contained nothing to lighten his mood. The prince consort complained that the Palmerston ministry's draft dispatch was "somewhat meager." Despite his illness—he could "scarcely hold his pen," Victoria reported—Albert decided to rewrite it himself.[49]

Albert softened the cabinet's language, although he still demanded a "suitable apology" from the Americans. His primary goal was to give Lincoln a way to save face. "Her majesty's government," he wrote, "bearing in mind the friendly relations which have long subsisted between Great Britain and the United States, are willing to believe that the United States naval officer who committed this aggression was not acting in compliance with any authority from his government." Or, the prince consort added, perhaps Wilkes "greatly misunderstood the instructions which he had received." Victoria and Albert then returned the text to Palmerston and his cabinet. While the British monarchs approved the text "upon the whole," they explained, they would prefer to include some "expression of hope" that Wilkes had acted alone.[50]

Palmerston, rather than picking a fight with the queen, said he thought Albert's changes "excellent." He swiftly dispatched the new text to the British minister in Washington. "What we want is a plain Yes or a plain No to our very simple demands," Palmerston's foreign minister wrote to the British envoy in Washington, "and we want that plain Yes or No within seven days of the communication of the dispatch." Over the following week the prime minister received heartening indications that American expats were urging their government to release the Confederate envoys. Still, Palmerston entertained little hope of a peaceful resolution. "The best thing," Palmerston's foreign minister mused, "would be if Seward could be turned out and a rational man put in his place." Absent such a dramatic move, the prime minister worried, "we shall not get what we ask for, without fighting for it."[51]

Not all Britons were so sanguine about the results of a prospective war. John Bright, a liberal member of Parliament who had cultivated close ties with the Lincoln White House, argued that a conflict would destroy Britain's improving relationship with its former colonies. At a speech in Rochdale on December 4, Bright lamented the British reaction to the *Trent* news—"every sword leaping from its scabbard, and every man looking about for his pistols and his blunderbusses." The statesman criticized Britons who jealously wanted to see the United States dismembered for geopolitical reasons. The American population was growing so rapidly that it would soon overtake Britain's, Bright warned. "When that time comes," he concluded, "I pray that it may not be said" that "in the darkest hour of their country's trials, England, the land of their fathers, looked on with icy coldness and saw unmoved the perils and calamities of their children."[52]

Nevertheless, two days later, on December 6, a fleet of reinforcements sailed for British Canada. Americans in London reported home to Seward that they were seeing Confederate flags unfurled throughout the city. "In the streets," wrote one correspondent, "I noticed two boys carrying miniature trays of secession flags for sale." Wagonloads of guns were spotted leaving the Tower of London. Eventually the Palmerston ministry would dispatch more than eleven thousand troops on eighteen transport ships to North America. The prime minister was satisfied with the show of force. If the Americans gave in, he told the queen, the result would be "honourable for England and humiliating for the United States." If, on the other hand, the Federals stood by Wilkes's seizure of Mason and Slidell, Britain would be well positioned to inflict a crushing blow on her former colonies.[53]

Send On Your Burial Cases

L incoln could be a melancholy man. He often expected the worst. As the autumn of 1861 unfolded, he had good reason for concern. An old Illinois acquaintance, Senator Lyman Trumbull, warned that if the Northern army did not strike decisively by winter, foreign governments would be certain to recognize the Confederacy. "Action, action, is what we want and must have," Trumbull wrote. Yet when Lincoln's army finally did move, in late October, the results were disastrous. Confederate troops crushed the Federals at Ball's Bluff, Virginia, sending the president's men retreating down a ravine toward a river at its base. Many of the Union troops simply drowned. Among the casualties: Lincoln's old Springfield friend, the English-born Edward D. Baker. Lincoln was devastated. The president sobbed when he learned of Baker's death. He walked home from the telegraph office where he got the news with his head bowed, tears streaming down his pale face. When a sentinel saluted as he passed, Lincoln just ignored him.[54]

After a brutal year, the *Trent* seizure must have initially seemed like redemption to Lincoln. The president desperately needed military victories in order to convince a skeptical Europe that the North could win the war. Furthermore, in accordance with international law, the Union blockade would be considered valid by the European powers only if it proved to be effective. Now Lincoln's growing navy was finally making him proud. The *New York Herald* reported shortly after the seizure that the president would insist on keeping the captives. Lincoln had "declared emphatically," the paper's correspondent wrote, that Mason and Slidell "should not be surrendered by this government, even if their detention should cost a war with Great Britain." The same day the president wrote to one expert on international law exultantly lauding "the capture of Mason & Slidell!" Years later Seward recalled (perhaps self-servingly) that Lincoln had "said very decidedly that he would not give [Mason and Slidell] up."[55]

Lincoln's enthusiasm did not last long. What first appeared as a rare naval victory was quickly becoming a serious crisis. After Lincoln got over his initial euphoria, he developed grave "doubts, misgivings, and regrets," reported Gideon Welles. If the *Trent* seizure inflamed British opinion, the benefits of appearing strong would be canceled out. Almost as troubling for the former prairie lawyer, British statesmen appeared to be justified in their outrage. At a cabinet meeting soon after the incident, the president worried that international law was actually on Britain's side, adding that he favored the diplomats' release. Lincoln ultimately explained that he was determined to avoid having "two wars on his hands at a time."[56]

And yet despite Lincoln's best judgment, it would be near impossible to simply set the captives free. Public opinion, Lincoln had once remarked, "is everything in this country." Now that amorphous force was running strongly in favor of keeping the Confederate envoys. The president fretted to Welles about the American public's "overwhelming" hostility toward Mason and Slidell. It would be difficult, under the circumstances, to resist their calls to harshly punish the Confederate envoys, he said. The Russian minister in Washington wrote home to his government that Lincoln wanted to release the men and issue an apology. Still, the American president desperately needed the support of his constituents if he was going to continue to maintain the war effort at home. The Russian minister complained that "demagogues" in Washington "intoxicated" by recent naval victories were urging Lincoln to hold on to the Confederate envoys.[57]

Lincoln found himself boxed in by his own subordinates. Soldiers bivouacked at Willard's Hotel, around the corner from the White House, threatened to quit the Union army if the president released Mason and Slidell. Welles wrote to Wilkes approving his actions, making the capture that much more difficult for Lincoln to disavow. The captain's conduct, Lincoln's naval secretary wrote, had the administration's "emphatic approval." State Department adviser Edward Everett, a former minister to Britain and secretary of state, began giving public speeches in support of Wilkes. "The detention," he cried, "was perfectly lawful, the capture was perfectly lawful, their confinement in Fort Warren will be perfectly lawful." A few weeks later Everett published his views of the incident in the widely read *New York Tribune*. Another State Department employee, according to a report in the *New York Times*, argued forcefully that British leaders would "not take exception to [Wilkes's] act" since international law classified both weapons and diplomatic personnel the same way— "sandwiching Mason and Slidell [together] as contraband of war."[58]

Faced with a no-win decision, Lincoln tried to punt. Such a strategy would place the ball in Palmerston's hands, and allow the American president to maintain some measure of freedom of action in the meantime. It would also give passions time to cool. While the British prime minister mulled his response, Lincoln could quietly work to prepare public opinion for the envoys' release.

The consequences of a rash decision on the president's part were too serious to ignore. Lincoln, toward the end of the war, would sometimes dream that the White House had burned down. In the winter of 1861, it was not such a fanciful prospect. All Americans who had lived through the War of 1812 could imagine the powerful British navy surging up the Potomac and laying siege to the Northern capital.[59] As the crisis reached its climax, New York mayor George Opdyke wrote Lincoln complaining about "the exposed condition of this city." He worried that "a fleet of [British] steamers might readily pass the exposed defenses of our harbor and hold this city at their mercy."[60]

Allies abroad repeatedly remonstrated with the president to release the Confederate diplomats. French author Agénor-Étienne de Gasparin implored Lincoln in a letter "to give England immediately the full satisfaction that she demands." The Frenchman acknowledged that Wilkes had a right to search the British packet, but marveled at the commander's poor judgment in seizing the diplomats. "To rouse the opinion of England and all of Europe against you! To run the risk of a new war! . . . Your wisdom will have recognized that whatever the subtleties of the law may be, it is not necessary to advance the affairs of the Richmond government. That would be suicide."[61]

Lincoln did his best to assure visiting officials that he wanted to avoid a war. In early December, the Canadian finance minister, Sir Alexander Tilloch Galt, met with the president at the White House to discuss the rising tensions between Britain and the United States. Lincoln reassured Galt that the *Trent* affair "could be arranged, and [he] intimated that no cause of quarrel would grow out of that." Galt left the White House convinced of the U.S. president's good intentions. Still, the Canadian wrote in a memo shortly after the meeting, "I cannot . . . divest my mind of the impression that the policy of the American government is so subject to popular impulses that no assurance can be, or ought to be, relied on under present circumstances. The temper of the public mind toward England is certainly of doubtful character." Galt mentioned that "the vast military preparations of the North" made him uneasy.[62]

In reality, the North had done very little to prepare for a major conflict with Britain—one more detail that has inclined some modern historians to accept Charles Sumner's contention that Lincoln was "essentially pacific" during the *Trent* crisis. When a delegation of Quakers visited the president at the White House in early December, Lincoln reiterated his desire to see the whole flap resolved peacefully.

Standing in his office in the heat emanating from his marble fire-place, the president listened as the Quakers reminded him that there were Britons like Bright who were sympathetic to the United States. Lincoln, whose "sad, yet strong countenance" had initially struck the visitors, was buoyed by the report. "These," he told the group, "are the first words of cheer and encouragement we have had from across the water."[63]

As late as a month after the *Trent* incident, Lincoln still seemed to hope that the crisis would simply go away. At a wedding on the evening of December 10, he told Orville Browning that he had heard through French officials that British experts had concluded that the seizure was legal. Lincoln predicted that there "would probably be no trouble about it." The president later suggested that if he could just meet face-to-face with the British representative in Washington, "I could show him in five minutes that I am heartily for peace." Still, at a memorial for Baker at the Capitol the following day, the president appeared wary and old. When Lincoln entered the packed Senate chamber, he looked unusually gaunt, with deep lines around his mouth. Snowflakes dotted his hair from the flurries outside. Taking his place behind the speaker's podium, John Hay observed, the president sat quietly, "leaning his shaggy leonine head upon his black-gloved hand, with more utter unconsciousness of attitude than I ever saw in a man accustomed to being stared at."[64]

Lincoln tried to put on a brave face. The *Trent* crisis did not temper the president's enthusiasm for his burgeoning navy. A week earlier, in his annual message to Congress, he had boasted that "it may almost be said a navy has been created and brought into service since our difficulties commenced." He added that "squadrons larger than ever before assembled under our flag have been put afloat and performed deeds which have increased our naval renown." The president cited a report by his secretary of the navy suggesting that the Union was prepared for battle if necessary. The federal government, Lincoln asserted, could "show the world, that while engaged in quelling disturbances at home we are able to protect ourselves from abroad."

The president, trying to calm passions, did not mention the *Trent* tension specifically in his message. "One thing is pretty certain," observed a correspondent for the *Baltimore Sun* later that month, "to wit: that the Senate is not to be consulted on the question." Lincoln's cursory remarks to Congress were one more hint of his evolving view that foreign-affairs crises often demanded executive discretion. "There is little evidence," notes one distinguished Lincoln biographer, "that the participation of Congress in this task of international adjustment would have been helpful. Heroically to take a stand, or to deliver a resounding stump speech in the form of a legislative resolution, was hardly calculated to improve the situation." Lincoln, during the *Trent* affair, confined his correspondence with Capitol Hill to "innocuous and collateral aspects" of the crisis, such as forwarding copies of the State Department's dispatches to peripheral powers like Austria and Italy.[65]

There was one particular senator, however, on whom the president relied heavily. After Seward's string of unpredictable outbursts earlier that spring, Lincoln had begun consulting regularly with Charles Sumner, the patrician chair of the Senate Committee on Foreign Relations. The pretentious senator, Lincoln once remarked, represented "my idea of a bishop." (To needle the stiff Bostonian, Lincoln sometimes asked to stand back-to-back with Sumner to compare their heights.) The Massachusetts senator, who maintained a frequent correspondence with liberal Britons like Bright and the Duchess of Argyll, was convinced that war with the Palmerston ministry would be anathema. He raised his case for conciliation with Lincoln frequently as the crisis intensified. Sumner maintained a deep suspicion of the volatile Seward. "You must watch him," the senator urged Lincoln, "and overrule him." Seward, for his part, complained that there were "too many secretaries of state in Washington."[66]

As December unfolded, the president's men filled the news vacuum with hot air. "I do not think we can be bullied into a war," Hay told readers of the *Missouri Republican* in one anonymous dispatch. "But if I understand the old gentleman who at present lives in

the Executive Mansion, there will be no sacrifice of honor or principle even to avoid a war with the swaggering bully of the United
Islands." If Britain demanded the release of Mason and Slidell, Hay
brazenly insisted, "Mr. Seward will probably reply, 'Send on your
burial cases.'"[67]

Indeed, Seward thought a new front increasingly likely as the
fall wore on. Shortly before Wilkes seized the Confederate envoys,
the secretary of state wrote home about his own "intense anxiety."
Seward worried that the pressure Southern agents were placing
on European statesmen was beginning to win sympathies. It was
"doubtful," he told his family, "whether we can escape the yet deeper
and darker abyss of foreign war. The responsibility resting upon
me is overwhelming." Like Lincoln, the *Trent* news seems to have
cheered Seward initially. According to Gideon Welles, "no man was
more elated or jubilant over the capture of the emissaries than Mr.
Seward." The secretary of state, Welles recalled, "made no attempt
to conceal his gratification."[68]

Seward's mood darkened again, however, on December 15, when
the British demands finally reached Washington. Lincoln was having tea with Orville Browning at the White House when Seward
swept in with the news. Browning reacted with indignation. "We
will fight her to the death," he vowed. But he did not really expect a
war. Lincoln, on the other hand, recognized the unpredictability of
a transatlantic game of chicken. Slidell's wife had been telling people
that Wilkes's executive officer, after boarding the *Trent*, had declared:
"Oh, John Bull would do as he had done before, he would bark, but
not bite." Lincoln was more cautious. He told a story about an aggressive bulldog he had known in Springfield. Everyone said the dog
was friendly—but was he, really? "I know the bulldog will not bite,"
Lincoln said. "You know he will not bite, but does the bulldog know
he will not bite?"[69]

Seward asked Britain's minister in Washington to withhold his
country's demands for a few days before making the official presenta-
tion. The secretary of state wanted more time to formulate a response

before the Brits turned over their seven-day hourglass. The British minister graciously obliged. Seward, meanwhile, reverted to his old blustering ways. On December 16 the secretary of state showed up loaded for bear at a dinner at the Portuguese legation. Looking "haggard and worn," with his trademark cloud of cigar smoke following him about the room, Seward boasted about the potential American reaction if Britain were to make war. "We will wrap the whole world in flames!" Seward cried. The historian George Bancroft reported that Seward "looked dirty, rusty, vulgar, and low; used such words as *hell*, and *damn*, and spoke very loud." Edward Everett, the Massachusetts statesman who had once filled the difficult job of secretary of state himself, was more forgiving of Seward's behavior that winter. The New Yorker was "really overworked," Everett told Cassius Marcellus Clay, "and every allowance must be made for him." Europe's diplomats had grown accustomed to Seward's violent outbursts. "That's all bugaboo talk," one guest at the Portuguese party had explained to a British journalist. "When Seward talks that way he means to break down. He is most dangerous and obstinate when he pretends to agree a good deal with you."[70]

Lincoln recognized that opening another front would be fatal. But first he would have to convince the public, which was still in no mood to back down. While Seward strutted about Washington's ministries, the president quietly began reaching out to friendly newspaper editors. He urged John Forney of the *Philadelphia Press* to try to counteract the popular fury. "I want you to sit down and write one of your most careful articles, preparing the American people for the release of Slidell and Mason, and for the statement that Captain Wilkes acted without the authority of his government," Lincoln told the editor. The president tried to play to the editor's vanity, adding: "I know this is much to ask of you, but it shows my confidence in you, my friend, when I tell you that I have chosen you because I can trust you, because I think you equal to the task. You will be much abused by our honest and impatient people. But when I tell you that this course is forced upon us by our peculiar position; and that the good Queen of England is moderating her own angry people, who are as bitter against us as our people are against them, I need say no more." Forney, who was a personal friend of Wilkes's, was initially full of "resentment" over the request, he later recalled. Still, "a little reflection and a fuller revelation of facts decided me," and he agreed to write the piece.[71]

Lincoln may also have enlisted his personal secretary as a propagandist. John Hay, whose anonymous newspaper reports often seemed to echo Lincoln's views, wrote that there was "little excitement and no trepidation in Washington," even after news of the British demands arrived. The capital's denizens had displayed "no serious apprehensions" about the *Trent* crisis, Hay wrote. Residents blithely strolled the shopping districts in the unseasonably warm weather, wearing their best "silk, feathers and broad cloth." Hay insisted that cool heads would prevail and war could still be avoided. A "quiet contempt" toward Britain had replaced Americans' former "intense sensitiveness," Hay observed. "Having ceased utterly to think anything of them, of course we are entirely indifferent to what they think of us." Lincoln's secretary stressed the material consequences of a pointless and destructive war.[72]

As Lincoln and Seward mulled their response to the British ultimatum, dire reports began pouring in from expats in Europe. Seward's old kingmaker, Thurlow Weed, had embarked for the Continent earlier that year to try to improve the North's image abroad. Yet now he warned that the Federals were taking a miserable beating in the French and British press. More troubling, Weed reported, Britain appeared to be preparing for a major conflict. "Everything here is upon a war footing," he wrote Seward. "Such prompt and gigantic preparations were never known." Weed advised the White House to simply release Mason and Slidell. The best policy, he insisted, would be to turn "if needs be, even the other cheek rather than smite back at present." The Confederate envoys, he insisted, "would be a million times less mischievous here than at Fort Warren." War, he warned, "unless you avert it, is inevitable."[73]

Britons were particularly hostile to Seward. The secretary of state, Weed reported, was being "infernally abused" in London drawing rooms and was "wholly misunderstood." Seward's poor reputation stemmed at least partly from an offhand comment he made to the Duke of Newcastle during his trip to England in 1859. Seward had remarked that if he should be elected president, he would go out of his way to insult Britain—or so the duke thought he had heard. Throughout the country, Weed told Seward, Britons were "ransacking" the secretary of state's collected works, looking for "every word against England." They were convinced that Seward wanted to provoke a foreign war in order to unite North and South. A number of prominent Englishmen told Weed that he should write to Lincoln demanding Seward's immediate dismissal.[74]

Meanwhile, liberal Britons like John Bright and Richard Cobden tried to influence Lincoln through other channels. Palmerston was an old antagonist of the two men. "Palmerston prime minister!" Bright had once exclaimed. "What a hoax!" Cobden referred to the prime minister as "the old dodger." Bright dubbed Palmerston "the hoary imposter." Bright and Cobden believed commercial ties bound Britain tightly to its former colonies. Palmerston, on the other hand, allowed nothing to bind him. He dismissed Bright and Cobden as unrealistic pacifists. "It would be very delightful," the prime minister wrote, "if your utopia could be realized and if the nations of the earth would think of nothing but peace and commerce and would give up fighting and quarrelling altogether. But unfortunately man is a fighting and quarrelling animal." Conflict, the prime minister insisted, was simply "human nature."[75]

Still, both Bright and Cobden also urged Washington to do its part to avoid a conflict. Cobden believed that Charles Sumner possessed "a kind of veto" on Seward's influence with the president. "At all hazards," Bright wrote Sumner, "you must not let this matter grow to a war with England, even if you are right and we are wrong." Bright urged Sumner to be "courteous and conceding to the last possible degree." He suggested that the American president might submit the affair to an international arbiter. Sumner, who met almost daily with Lincoln as the *Trent* crisis intensified, shared the letters with the president. Former president Millard Fillmore also wrote Lincoln in mid-December arguing that arbitration was the only way to avoid being "overwhelmed with the double calamities of civil and foreign war at the same time." Lincoln agreed that arbitration was the way to go. "There will be no war," the president assured Sumner, "unless England is bent upon having one."[76]

A Glutton of Gloom

With no transatlantic telegraph yet working, diplomatic dispatches took a maddening two weeks to cross the ocean by steamship. As Lincoln pondered his response to Britain's ultimatum, Palmerston waited anxiously. Finally, a dispatch arrived in London from Washington on the evening of December 16 affirming that Wilkes had acted "without instructions and even without the knowledge of the government." The news cheered some. "We shall not have war with America," said a relieved Lady Palmerston. The prime minister himself was not so sure. "As to any dispatch written by Seward before he received our demands," Palmerston told his foreign minister, "I attach very little value to it, and one cannot speculate on the nature of the answer we shall receive. We are doing all we can do on the assumption that we are to have a refusal and that is all we can be expected to do."[77]

Lincoln's diplomats, for their part, found themselves unsure about who was in charge in London. "Where is the master to direct this storm?" Charles Francis Adams asked his son as the crisis intensified. As the *Trent* affair approached its climax, the British prime minister physically broke down. Palmerston, now in his late seventies, had long walked with a stoop and could barely see. Sometimes he simply fell asleep in Parliament. For a statesman with such an outsize public image, Palmerston's deteriorating body shocked some visitors. Lord Granville thought the Most English Minister looked like "a retired old *croupier* from Baden." Now, at a moment of high tension between Britain and the federal states, an attack of gout crippled the prime minister. Rumors flew through London that Palmerston had died.

Adding to the prime minister's stress, the ailing Prince Albert finally passed away on December 14. Palmerston had often tangled with the prince consort, but Albert had earned a degree of his respect. Palmerston feared that the monarch's death at the height of an international crisis could complicate an already delicate situation. The prime minister considered it a "calamity" that was "too awful to contemplate." The entire British nation, he added, had been "plunged . . . into the deepest affliction" by the news.[78]

As Palmerston's health deteriorated, his friends began to worry. The prime minister had always led a vigorous life. In his youth Palmerston had vowed to "make exercise a religion," and preferred to work at a standing desk rather than sitting in a chair. Even in old age he "ate like a vulture." Now, however, the prime minister was "*very* far from well," Lord Clarendon reported. "He overtaxes his strength, and unless he makes some change in that respect, he cannot last long." Albert's passing had only made matters worse. "The death of the prince has affected him much," Lord Granville observed. "I never saw him so low, but there is enough to make him so, coupled with the depression always caused by the gout. Lady Palmerston appeared to me for the first time to be a little anxious about him."[79]

The rising tensions and Prince Albert's death cast a pall over London. The massive church bell at St. Paul's Cathedral filled the city with "the dull boom of its sad tones." Merchants shuttered shops, and Londoners wandered the streets wearing black under the gray winter skies. At the American legation, diplomats were instructed to write all dispatches on special black-edged paper in honor of the late prince consort. The atmosphere in London, wrote Henry Adams, the son of the American minister, would have "gorged a glutton of gloom."[80]

The American diplomats displayed little faith in their bosses in Washington. Charles Francis Adams complained that Lincoln was "unfit for his place." Seward, too, received low marks for his statesmanship. The secretary of state had once remarked that he was an enigma to himself. His actions certainly baffled his men overseas. Henry Adams acknowledged that he had no idea what the secretary of state was thinking. If he intended to provoke a war, Adams admitted, or even to "run as close as he can without touching, then I say that Mr. Seward is the greatest criminal we've had yet." The young diplomatic secretary believed Britain was wholly justified in its outrage. If the British navy had stopped an American mail packet in similar circumstances, Adams insisted, he and his countrymen would have "jumped out of our boots."[81]

The intentions of British leaders appeared equally opaque. In a letter to Frederick Engels, Karl Marx wondered what Palmerston was really thinking. "If Pam absolutely wants war," Marx wrote his friend, using the prime minister's nickname, "he can, of course, bring it about." But the German émigré did not believe Palmerston genuinely wanted one. In any case, Marx expected Lincoln to back down, removing the pretext for war. The British prime minister's real goal, Marx speculated, was to put pressure on the Americans to recognize the Declaration of Paris, a treaty guaranteeing the rights of neutrals. Neither side had an interest in a full-scale war. Still, the risk always remained that all the blustering could spin out of control. "It is, of course, possible that the Yankees will not yield," Marx told Engels, "and then Pam will be compelled to go to war by his preparations and rodomontades so far. Still, I would bet a hundred to one against it."[82]

Palmerston, still sick and in bed, believed that Lincoln and Seward were "in a Fool's Paradise about the *Trent* affair." The Federals may try to avoid a "direct refusal" of the British demands, he speculated, but he believed that Britain would ultimately be forced to fight. London's *Morning Post*, which Palmerston was said to control, wondered whether a government "elected but a few months since by the popular choice" and "depending exclusively for existence on popular support" could resist the clamor for war. "The answer to this question must, we fear, be in the negative." Palmerston's foreign minister remained more hopeful. "I still incline to think Lincoln will submit," he wrote the prime minister, "but not until the clock is 59 minutes past 11." Palmerston expected "some evasive dodge." He wondered whether Lincoln might just let the two prisoners slip across the border with Canada or Mexico.[83]

Palmerston was right in one respect. Lincoln had at first hoped to stall for time. On the afternoon of December 21, the president was visiting with Browning at the White House when the subject of the *Trent* came up again. Lincoln explained that the British minister in Washington—honoring Seward's plea for time—had still not officially presented the Palmerston ministry's demands. Still, Lincoln told Browning that "he had an inkling of what they were, and feared trouble." The president's old friend argued that it would be best to do everything possible to avoid a "rupture" with Britain, "if it could be done without humiliation and dishonor." Lincoln said that he agreed completely.

Both men believed that a neutral arbitrator might peacefully defuse the crisis. In early December the president had drafted a memo to British officials proposing arbitration and stating that "this government has intended no affront to the British flag, or to the British nation." Now, as he visited with Browning, Lincoln pulled out the document and read it to his old friend. In the dispatch, which Lincoln intended to be sent under Seward's signature, the president reiterated that Wilkes had acted "without orders from, or expectation of, the government." Although Lincoln added that he wanted to discuss several points that he considered extenuating circumstances, he did write that he would consider a British request for reparations. The text of Lincoln's document seems to have adopted some of the language of Bright and Cobden, who had been urging Sumner to lobby for such a proposal. Browning later told his diary that Lincoln's draft displayed "great force and clearness." Yet with its slippery excuses and its plea for time, the president's proposed reply would have been certain to irritate Palmerston. In the end, Lincoln thought better of sending it.[84]

Lincoln did seem to be having some success shaping public opinion at home. Someone leaked the news to the *Daily National Intelligencer* that the president was considering "a grand international . . . abitrament" in response to the British demands. The *New York Daily Tribune*, a paper with close ties to Lincoln's Republican Party, also began preparing its readers for the possibility that Mason and Slidell would be released. On December 20 the paper reported that a number of cabinet members were advocating letting the men go. Lincoln himself, the article said, anticipated "a peaceful solution." The *New York Times*, which often acted as Seward's mouthpiece, also suggested that the White House was not likely to press its case too hard.[85]

Meanwhile, Lincoln and his team scrambled to meet the British deadline. Seward assured the French minister in Washington on December 19 that "we will not have war." The rational statesmen of Britain and the United States would not fall into conflict "from mere emotion," the secretary of state maintained. Yet the delicate matter of how exactly the White House would respond to the British ultimatum remained. Even insiders like John Hay conceded that they had no idea what the president would decide. Hay observed a "bewildering flight of white envelopes" soaring "like carrier doves between the British Legation and the Department of State." The winter weather in Washington only added to the sense of gravity and impending danger. Two days before Christmas, a British journalist marveled at the "tremendous storm" that "drove over the city and shook the houses to the foundation."[86]

A Pretty Bitter Pill

As the British deadline approached, Lincoln began to doubt his own arbitration proposal. Such a scheme would simply take too long to unfold. In any case, Palmerston was not open to an equivocal response. Even Sumner, who at one time had favored arbitration, urged Lincoln to just give in. The Massachusetts senator recognized that the president was already "essentially pacific." On Christmas Eve, Sumner told the president that he favored a "complete" resolution that would avoid "mental reservations which shall hereafter be forged into thunderbolts." The *New York Tribune* reported the same day that "both civilians and military men, high in position" were urging Lincoln to release the prisoners.[87]

Lincoln called an emergency cabinet meeting for Christmas Day. On the sunny and unseasonably warm morning, the president's men assembled at the White House. Sumner read letters from Cobden and Bright, who urged the president to "make every concession that can be made" rather than risk "the breaking up of your country." Lincoln's treasury secretary worried that a war would devastate American commerce. During the four-hour meeting, a missive arrived from the French minister in Washington, who warned the men that the European powers all believed Britain was in the right. Nevertheless, to at least some members of the cabinet, the president appeared to favor holding on to the prisoners.[88]

Honest Abe may have been dissembling. Considering his recent efforts to quietly prepare the public for the release of the Confederate envoys, it seems unlikely that Lincoln had suddenly changed his mind. One scenario, historian Howard Jones suggests, is that Lincoln "wanted to go on record as standing in opposition while knowing that eventually he would have to turn them over and acknowledge a violation of international law." Another possibility is that the president, a clever manager of his headstrong cabinet, wanted to let his self-important secretary of state believe that conciliation was his own idea. Seward favored releasing the Confederate envoys outright. At the end of the meeting, Lincoln took his secretary of state aside. "Governor Seward, you will go on, of course, preparing your answer, which, as I understand, will state the reasons why they ought to be given up. Now I have a mind to try my hand at stating the reasons why they ought not to be given up. We will compare the points on each side."[89]

Lincoln knew full well that Seward would ultimately win the argument. After a Christmas dinner at the White House, the president told his old friend Orville Browning that "there would be no war with England." The following day, when the cabinet reassembled, Seward made his case. The secretary of state had "studied up all the works ever written on international law," Lincoln later recalled, "and came to cabinet meetings loaded to the muzzle with the subject." The president did not even bother to oppose him. Lincoln's secretary of state asked why the president had abandoned his own position. "I could not," Lincoln responded, "make an argument that would satisfy my own mind." The *New York Times* published an account of the "special and extraordinary session" the day after Christmas. "It is understood," the paper's Washington correspondent wrote, "that our Government is ready to disavow the act of Capt. Wilkes, and to deliver up Mason and Slidell, if that be the only means of purchasing peace with England." Still, the paper continued, "as a condition of this disavowal and restitution," Britain would be obliged to stay out of the war.[90]

Now that Lincoln had made a decision, Seward began reading in key Washington power brokers. The secretary of state hosted a dinner at his Lafayette Square home on the evening of December 27. Attendees included the British writer Anthony Trollope and Kentucky senator John Crittenden, the latter of whom showered the Sewards' carpet with tobacco spittle. Seward's daughter Fanny, who had carefully decorated the house with "Christmas greens" for the occasion, marveled at Crittenden's lack of manners. (She was also repulsed by Mrs. Crittenden, who "had trappings of gilt and velvet on her head enough to furnish a western steamboat and wore seven bracelets on her fat bare arms.") After dinner the secretary of state brought the men into his library and kicked a leg over the arm of his leather chair. He lit a cigar and read the men his dispatch, which argued that by releasing the Confederates, the federal government was simply affirming the neutral rights that America had always sought. Seward declared that Mason and Slidell would be "cheerfully liberated."[91]

As expected, the decision angered some Americans. Senator John Hale of New Hampshire complained that "surrender" would "reduce us to the position of a second-rate Power, and make us the vassal of Great Britain." Most Northerners, however, seem to have been relieved. "We believe," wrote a *New York Tribune* columnist on December 30, that "the administration is stronger with the people today than if Mason and Slidell had never been captured or their surrender had been refused." Nobody seems to have paid much attention to the fine print. If they had, they might have realized that Seward's justification was full of holes. The secretary of state had maintained that diplomats could be considered "contraband of war"—a questionable proposition at best. He also argued misleadingly that in the resolution of the affair Britian had somehow disavowed the practice of impressment, which historically had been the source of much ill will between Washington and London. Seward's response, notes one historian of the crisis, amounted to "a monument to illogic." Still, the document served its purpose. Lincoln and Seward had defused an explosive situation.[92]

Lincoln recognized that his decision had looked like weakness to some. Actually, however, it was a near-perfect illustration of the president's central foreign-policy principle. The pursuit of America's national interest, in this case, required conciliation. The United States needed British goodwill in order to survive the Civil War. Lincoln could not afford to open a second front, and any rupture of the Anglo-American relationship would make British recognition of the Confederacy that much more likely. Conveniently, the smart decision was also the just decision. Wilkes had violated international law and the world was on Britain's side. "It was a pretty bitter pill to swallow," Lincoln later recalled, "but I contented myself with believing that England's triumph in the matter would be short-lived, and that after ending our war successfully we would be so powerful that we could call her to account for all the embarrassments she had inflicted upon us."[93]

Lincoln explained his logic by telling one of his favorite stories. The president joked that he felt like "the sick man in Illinois who was told he probably hadn't many days longer to live, and he ought to make his peace with any enemies he might have." The man's greatest foe was a man named Brown, Lincoln said. "So Brown was sent for, and when he came the sick man began to say, in a voice as meek as Moses's, that he wanted to die at peace with all his fellow-creatures, and he hoped he and Brown could now shake hands and bury all their enmity." Brown, as the president told the story, eventually broke down and reconciled with the sick man. The whole thing was "a regular love-feast of forgiveness," Lincoln said. Still, as Brown was leaving the room, the sick man propped himself up on an elbow and called out after him: "But see here, Brown; if I should happen to get well, mind, that old grudge stands." Lincoln spelled out the moral of his story. "I thought," the president explained, "that if this nation should happen to get well we might want that old grudge against England to stand."[94]

For now, though, Lincoln and his secretary of state recognized that the Union was still too sick to pick a fight with Europe. Seward is generally lauded by historians for his role in peaceably resolving the *Trent* affair. The secretary of state later maintained that the crisis had been a critical moment in the war—an episode "upon which all subsequent events hinged." From the contemporary diaries of Lincoln's cabinet secretaries, it appears that at times the secretary of state was virtually the only voice in favor of unconditional release. The president, however, also urged conciliation from the beginning, and worked to prepare public opinion for the envoys' release. Lincoln's role in the episode was "of decisive importance," writes historian James Randall. The president's contribution lay "in his restraint, his avoidance of any outward expression of truculence, his early softening of the State Department's attitude toward Britain, his deference toward Seward and Sumner, his withholding of his own paper prepared for the occasion, his readiness to arbitrate, his golden silence in addressing Congress, his shrewdness in recognizing that war must be averted, and his clear perception that a point could be clinched for America's true position at the same time that full satisfaction was given to a friendly country." The president's role was "characteristic of Lincoln," Seward's son Frederick later recalled. "Presidents and kings are not apt to see flaws in their own arguments. But fortunately for the Union, it had a president at this time who combined a logical intellect with an unselfish heart."[95]

News of Lincoln's decision arrived in London by telegraph late on the afternoon of January 8, 1862. American diplomats in the city could finally exhale. For days, anxiety in the legation had been "at fever heat," one envoy recorded in his diary. The release of Mason and Slidell "lifted a load of lead from our hearts." European diplomats "sprang to their feet as if electrified" upon hearing of the decision. The following day the details were announced at London theaters between acts, "and the audiences rose like one and cheered tremendously." The telegraph beamed the bulletin from town to town as church bells pealed in celebration.[96]

Palmerston, who had been pumped full of drugs for his gout, was initially too medicated to grasp the news of Washington's capitulation. Eventually, however, he recovered enough to crow about the British victory. "The peaceful settlement of the difference with the Federal Government," he wrote Queen Victoria, "is indeed a happy event." While a war with the Federal government would have been "most successful," he told the queen, it also would have come at a heavy cost. Any conflict, even a victorious one, would have involved "much embarrassment to commerce" and "painful sacrifices of the lives and blood of brave men." The *Morning Post*, Palmerston's mouthpiece, lauded "the mingled firmness and courtesy" of British policy.[97]

Still, the whole episode irritated the British prime minister. Palmerston was still "wary of the Yankees," even after Mason and Slidell had been handed over. He wrote one of his most scathing assessments of the American Civil War less than two weeks after the release of the Confederate envoys. If the United States were dismembered and Mexico became a monarchy, Palmerston argued, "I do not know any arrangement that would be more advantageous for us." John Bright believed Palmerston was simply blustering to maintain public support. The prime minister's reputation, he wrote to Lincoln's man in Paris, John Bigelow, depended on the public belief that "he is plucky and instant in the defense of English honour." Conflict, Bright insisted, would help keep Palmerston in power. "If foreign affairs are tranquil," the British liberal wrote, the prime minister's government would fall.[98]

The Bottom Is Out of the Tub

Lincoln, meanwhile, worried that his own government was teetering. At a New Year's reception at the Executive Mansion, the president presented a genial face, joking and shaking hands. Still, Lincoln appeared "perceptibly older" than he had when he took office, one journalist observed. Ten days later the president complained to General Montgomery Meigs about the flood of new crises pouring into his office. Americans were growing "impatient" with the war's progress, he explained. His top general had typhoid. "The bottom is out of the tub," Lincoln wrote. "What shall I do?"[99]

Union finances were one major cause for concern. All fall Lincoln's treasury secretary, Salmon P. Chase, had been trying to secure loans from European financiers to bolster the war effort. Chase had not been having much luck, even before the *Trent* crisis. Yet after the capture of the mail packet, that prospect vanished completely. "Not a dozen battles lost could have damaged our good cause as much as the ill-judged, and overzealous act of Capt. Wilkes," August Belmont, the American agent of the European Rothschild banking family, complained to Chase. To make matters worse, the uncertainty spawned by the crisis caused Americans to hoard gold and silver. The U.S. treasury, which paid its debts in specie, went virtually broke.[100]

One dramatic solution propounded by Lincoln and his allies in Congress was to issue a national paper currency. Aside from precious metals, the country's primary form of money until now had been notes issued by some 1,600 state banks. Chase had originally been concerned that a measure to print federal greenbacks would be unconstitutional. Lincoln had his own anxieties about such a revolutionary step. The president, however, convinced Chase that the exigencies of the war justified the move, according to one recollection. Congress ultimately passed the Legal Tender Act—a law that eventually pumped more than $450 million in federal greenbacks into the economy during the war—in late February 1862. As the new paper money began rolling off the presses, Lincoln's bodyguard observed, the president was "in high spirits" and "seemed to feel happier than I had seen him for a long time."[101]

The greenbacks were not enough to reverse the Union's financial fortunes on their own. Yet the measure went a long way toward building a more powerful and centralized American state. The Legal Tender Act, notes one modern historian, amounted to a "major innovation increasing the economic influence of the national government—linking Americans with ever stronger economic sinews." The creation of the first national income tax also made it easier for the central government to tap the resources of the wider country. Finally, Lincoln pushed hard to establish a national bank, which Congress finally created in 1863. These sweeping modernizations of the nation's financial system were critical prerequisites to America's rise to world power.[102]

Foreign affairs and global finance, Lincoln had learned over the course of his first year in office, were a serious and complex business. European chancelleries were no place for dilettantes or slouches. Still, it was always difficult for Lincoln to resist the pleas of his friends. In January, Billy Herndon traveled from Springfield to Washington to see his old law partner. According to Springfield tradition, Herndon had made the trip to ask the president to appoint him to a diplomatic post in London or Rome. Considering the gravity of the international crisis, Lincoln could not in good conscience have obliged his volatile partner. Whether the rumors about Herndon's intentions are true or not, the younger man ultimately left Washington without a foreign posting from the tense and "considerably careworn" president. (Herndon did, however, ask the president if he could borrow $25.)

In later years Lincoln liked to tell the story of an office seeker who at first demanded a diplomatic post—and then, when the request was denied, asked for a series of lesser jobs. Eventually, the office seeker said he'd settle for a pair of old trousers. It is not hard to imagine Billy Herndon playing the role of diplomatic supplicant in the joke. According to one newspaper report, Herndon returned to Springfield "very sour on Lincoln." If Herndon wanted an English or Italian vacation, he would have to make the trip on his own.[103]

In the wake of the *Trent* affair, Lincoln and his team did their best to project the insouciance of would-be victors. One State Department assistant observed the "confidence in the certainty of triumph" that was "growing and deepening" in Washington. "The only fear now," he continued, "is of foreign interference. If that can be warded off it is felt all is safe." On January 28 the aide attended a reception at the Executive Mansion—"the largest and most brilliant of the season," as the *Baltimore Sun* described it. In the Blue Room the president and First Lady greeted French, Prussian, and Swedish diplomats (along with "one notable looking personage," observed the *Washington Evening Star*, who was dressed in a "peculiar uniform, which consisted of purple tights and jacket, with a dragoon sword, wearing a cock's feather in his left breast"). The State Department functionary reported that Lincoln appeared "care worn but in good spirits. Indeed, such are the prevailing feelings."[104]

As winter faded, the navy once again buoyed the president's spirits. On January 30, the first ironclad finally launched. The news panicked Britons. The London *Times* worried that the innovation had made Britain's fleet of 149 "first-class warships" obsolete. Only its two experimental ironclads would now be of any use in a war with the United States. "There is," the *Times* reported, "not now a ship in the English navy apart from these two that it would not be madness to trust to an engagement with that little *Monitor*."

The *Monitor*, Henry Adams observed from London, "has been the main talk of the town ever since the news came, in Parliament, in the clubs, in the city, among the military and naval people. The impression is that it dates the commencement of a new era in warfare, and that Great Britain must consent to begin over again." News of the ironclad's launch spread rapidly through a reception hosted by Lady Palmerston. Henry's father spotted the prime minister at the event, and noted in his diary that Palmerston, whose arm was still in a sling from his gout, "certainly looks badly." The American minister marveled at the "revolution in opinion concerning the formidable character of the United States." Still, he added, the "feeling of jealousy" was "all pervading here, and scarcely covered with a decent veil."[105]

Cassius Marcellus Clay, who had met with Palmerston in London the year before, told Seward that he still "very much fear[ed] England's interference," even after the resolution of the *Trent* affair. "My first impressions in Europe are not changed nor weakened, but rather strengthened," Lincoln's man in St. Petersburg confided. "Nothing but quick and effective success will save us from foreign enemies." Clay, ever the firebrand, suggested that the Lincoln administration "fortify our coast lines everywhere. We ought to commence at once a war navy of iron vessels, on the seas and the lakes—first capable of protecting the seaport towns, and next taking the ocean against all enemies."[106]

With transatlantic tensions building once again, the Lincoln administration did its best to smooth ruffled feathers. A month after releasing Mason and Slidell, Seward wrote to Queen Victoria under the president's signature offering his condolences on Prince Albert's death. "The People of the United States are kindred of the People of Great Britain," Seward wrote. "With all our distinct national interests, objects, and aspirations, we are conscious that our moral strength is largely derived from that relationship, and we think we do not deceive ourselves when we suppose that, by constantly cherishing cordial friendship and sympathy with the other branches of the family to which we belong, we impart to them not less strength than we derive from the same connection. Accidents, however, incidental to all States, and passions, common to all nations, often tend to disturb the harmony so necessary and so proper between the two countries, and to convert them into enemies."[107]

Four days later, Mary Lincoln threw a huge party at the White House. All the diplomats were there, chests dripping with colorful decorations. The First Lady had hired the renowned (and expensive) Maillard's to cater the affair. The assembled diplomats could not have missed the tributes to America's burgeoning navy. Mary's centerpieces included a model of the steamship *Union* made out of confectionary sugar, as well as a large Japanese punch bowl that Commodore Perry had brought back as a souvenir from the East. As the diplomats mingled under the elegant gaslight chandeliers, the Marine Band played the "Marseillaise," the French revolutionary anthem. To show her sympathy for Queen Victoria, Mary's white silk gown included dozens of black flowers in remembrance of Prince Albert.[108]

Even as the Lincolns paid tribute to the British monarch's grief, they were about to sink into a family horror of their own. While the diplomats mingled in the East Room, the Lincolns' eleven-year-old son, Willie, was lying sick with a fever in his bedroom upstairs. Both the president and First Lady frequently left the party to check on Willie. Mary's seamstress, Elizabeth Keckley, spotted the president upstairs in Willie's room with his back to the fireplace, hands locked behind him, staring solemnly at the carpet.

Willie died on February 20. Both Lincolns were disconsolate. "Well, Nicolay," the president told his secretary, his voice cracking, "my boy is gone—he is actually gone!" As Keckley was dressing Willie's dead body, Lincoln walked in to take a last look at his child. He lifted the sheet, uncovering the boy's face—and then broke down. "It is hard, hard to have him die!" the president cried, burying his face in his hands. "His grief unnerved him," Keckley recalled, "and made him a weak, passive child. I did not dream that his rugged nature could be so moved." For months afterward, Mary, too, would burst into tears whenever someone mentioned Willie's name. She could not get out of bed for weeks.

Still, the First Lady took some comfort in the elaborate rituals of Victorian mourning. Mary had carefully studied the etiquette of the British royal family. One of her favorite books was Agnes Strickland's multivolume *Lives of the Queens of England*. Now Mary deliberately imitated the example of Queen Victoria's sorrow over Albert. Among other mourning clothes, Mary sent away to New York for a black bonnet of "the *finest, jet black* English crape," specifying that it must be "exceedingly plain and genteel." She also began holding séances in an effort to contact Willie through spiritualist mediums—a practice that Victoria had reportedly also tried in an effort to commune with the late prince consort.[109]

With their son's death, both Lincoln and his wife grew increasingly superstitious. At night, the president told friends he sometimes dreamed of "a sweet communion" with "my lost boy Willie." The First Lady, for her part, chose absurdly disreputable mediums for her séances. She invited Charles J. Colchester, who went by the sobriquet Lord Colchester and claimed to be an English peer, to the Executive Mansion in an effort to contact Willie. White House aides soon lost their patience. The journalist Noah Brooks recalled attending one such session, in which he eventually rose from his seat and "grasping in the direction of the drumbeat, grabbed not a disembodied spirit, but rather the very solid and fleshy hand of the Lord Colchester himself who was beating a drum in the darkened Red Room." The president, after learning of the meetings, eventually put a stop to the charade.[110]

Mary's reverence for all things European often displayed a pathetic insecurity. And yet for the president, there were plenty of good reasons to carefully study trends on the Continent. American statesmen had long prided themselves on their independence from European affairs. Time and experience, however, had undermined that treasured principle. It was impossible, Lincoln's diplomats were discovering, to withdraw from the world. Throughout the spring, Cassius Marcellus Clay continued to urge the Lincoln administration to bolster its defenses. "Since steam can throw, in twelve days or less, the entire navies of Europe upon our country," he argued, "it is useless to deceive ourselves with the idea that we can isolate ourselves from European interventions. We become, in spite of ourselves—the Monroe Doctrine—Washington's farewell—and all that—a part of the 'balance of power'. . . . We must then strengthen ourselves like other nations."[111]

At the same time, however, Lincoln and Seward began to look for new ways to bolster the "cordial friendship and sympathy" between the Union and the European powers. One source of persistent tension remained America's lackluster enforcement of its bans against the international slave trade. Radical Republicans had long advocated using the power of the federal government to stanch the continuing flow of slaves from West Africa. Earlier that year Lincoln had refused to commute the sentence of Nathaniel Gordon, an American who had been condemned to death for engaging in the trade. "It had to be done," the president later recalled, adding that he sought to make "an example" of Gordon. "Any man," Lincoln remarked as the Civil War unfolded, "who, for paltry gain and stimulated only by avarice, can rob Africa of her children to sell into interminable bondage, I will never pardon, and he may stay and rot in jail before he will ever get relief from me."[112]

Palmerston, too, vigorously opposed the slave trade. Now British leaders proposed crafting a treaty that would create a joint U.S.–British force to stop and search U.S. vessels off the coast of Africa—a sensitive subject, considering the history of Anglo-American animosity over impressment. The Lincoln administration acquiesced, as long as the idea could be made to appear to have originated in

Washington. Britain's minister in the capital, Lord Lyons, observed an eagerness at the White House "to rally the anti-slavery feeling in England to the northern cause." Lincoln and the vast majority of his cabinet were "warmly in favor" of the measure, which the White House submitted to Congress in April. Seward was reclining on his couch in his office at the State Department when Charles Sumner arrived to tell him that the Senate had unanimously ratified the treaty. "Good god!" the secretary of state cried as he jumped off the sofa. "This is the greatest act of the administration."[113]

Lincoln continued to look for additional ways to sway European public opinion. The leaders of Britain and France were generally hardheaded realists and would act primarily in what they perceived as their own selfish interests. And yet they were also human, susceptible to the same passions and romantic feelings as the rest of us. Furthermore, ordinary Britons and Frenchmen might have some power to sway their aristocratic statesmen if Lincoln could somehow appeal directly to the masses. In a game of brinksmanship in which European recognition of the Confederacy could mean the difference between the life and death of the Union, Lincoln would need to seek foreign goodwill wherever he could find it.

The president may have seen a dispatch published February 1, 1862, in the *New York Tribune* titled "English Public Opinion." The article, by the paper's special correspondent in London, argued that the English war furor had been misleading. The exultant reaction of ordinary Britons to the release of Mason and Slidell proved "the unpopularity of the apprehended war." The "venal and reckless" British press may have tried to gin up a conflict, the correspondent wrote. Still, it "ought never to be forgotten in the United States that at least the *working classes* of England, from the commencement to the termination of the difficulty, have never forsaken them." The *Tribune*'s editors published the dispatch without a byline, but it was written by one of the paper's most provocative and controversial contributors. The author, Karl Marx, was about to urge Lincoln to make his boldest foreign-policy stroke yet.[114]

CHAPTER FOUR

Lincoln vs. Marx

ON THE SUNNY, COOL MORNING OF JANUARY 1, 1863, A LINE OF FOREIGN DIPLOMATS PARADED INTO THE WHITE HOUSE "ARRAYED IN GOLD LACE, FEATHERS, AND OTHER TRAPPINGS." The envoys, one journalist remarked, presented "a truly gorgeous appearance." Seward's daughter Fanny marveled at the diplomats' "full court dress." The whole reception, she told her diary, was "very brilliant." After the foreign representatives had entered, sentries opened the gates to the general public. A chaotic mob pushed its way through the north portico. Inside, Mary Lincoln hovered in a black velvet dress with lozenge trimming. The president stood in the corner of the Blue Room, stiffly shaking each hand as the receiving line passed.[1]

The president was exhausted. He had not slept at all the night before. Over the past several weeks, Lincoln had sunk into a deep depression. "His hair is grizzled," reported one journalist who met Lincoln that winter, "his gait more stooping, his countenance sallow, and there is a sunken, deathly look about the large, cavernous eyes."

The Union's continuing military setbacks weighed heavily on the commander in chief. In mid-December the Army of the Potomac had launched an ill-advised assault on a dug-in Confederate position near Fredericksburg, Virginia. Southern forces, occupying the high ground and bristling with more than three hundred pieces of artillery, drove back repeated Union charges. During two days of battle, the Confederate defenders killed or wounded 12,653 Union men. (The Southern forces lost less than half the Federal tally.) The rest of the Northern troops fell into a panicked retreat under a driving rain. Lincoln was disconsolate. "We are now on the brink of destruction," the president told an old friend after the battle. "It appears to me the Almighty is against us, and I can hardly see a ray of hope."[2]

There was, however, one bright spot on this New Year's afternoon. After Lincoln retired to the White House residence, Seward arrived with a copy of the Emancipation Proclamation for Lincoln's signature, unrolling the document onto a table. Lincoln dipped a pen in ink—but then he hesitated. He had been greeting guests and shaking hands since early that morning. Now the president found that his arm was numb. The signature, he worried, would be carefully scrutinized. "If they find my hand trembled," he said, "they will say 'he had some compunctions.'" Lincoln waited for a moment for the shaking to subside. Then he swept the pen firmly across the paper. "That will do," he said with a smile.[3]

The president had long opposed slavery, which he considered "founded on both injustice and bad policy." As the Civil War unfolded, he also began to view antislavery as a tool of foreign relations. The Emancipation Proclamation, Lincoln believed, "would help us in Europe, and convince them that we are incited by something more than ambition." It was aimed particularly at England's textile workers, who were the most likely to be affected by the cotton shortages produced by the war—and also the most likely to respond to a moral appeal. The popular energy produced by the proclamation, he believed, could help to apply pressure on Britain's aristocratic ruling class, many of whom supported the Confederacy. After Lincoln signed the proclamation, Seward's State Department quickly printed copies and shipped them abroad to the diplomatic corps.[4]

Presidents before Lincoln had long been reluctant to use the office as a platform to influence public opinion. They considered it undignified to engage in the rough-and-tumble of democratic politics once in high office. But the telegraph and other innovations in communication had changed the world dramatically in the first half of the nineteenth century. "Our government," Lincoln told a Chicago banquet in 1856, "rests in public opinion. Whoever can change public opinion, can change the government." Two years later the future president was even more emphatic. "In this age, and this country, public sentiment is every thing," he wrote. "*With* it, nothing can fail; *against* it, nothing can succeed." Billy Herndon later recalled that his law partner "made efforts at all times to modify and change public opinion." As a new force in foreign affairs, "soft power" had arrived.[5]

And yet, soft power was a volatile thing. In the globalizing world it was a weapon that could be wielded by skillful individuals and like-minded groups—not just heads of state. Karl Marx, a bohemian German philosopher living in exile in London, was one of those feverishly dabbling in the nineteenth century's new mass media. Marx spent much of his time in the decade before the Civil War squirreled away in the British Museum reading room working on his economic treatises. Yet philosophy alone left the agitator unsatisfied. "The philosophers of the past," Marx once wrote, "merely interpreted the world in various ways. The point, however, is to change it." Marx thought writing for the world's quickly proliferating newspapers could help effect political change. The world's most powerful statesmen, Marx insisted, would only respond to what he called "pressure from without." Starting in the early 1850s, Marx took a job writing regular dispatches for the *New York Tribune*—the world's largest newspaper.[6]

Over the course of the decade, Marx grew to become one of the paper's most respected correspondents. Marx and the *Tribune* shared elements of a common vision. The newspaper's nickname was the Great Moral Organ, and its editors pushed an ambitious slate of reformist policies. Lincoln had carefully pored over the *Tribune* for years. The president considered its editor, Horace Greeley, so important that he kept a special mail slot in his desk to hold correspondence with the mercurial newspaperman. With more than two hundred thousand readers, the *Tribune*'s role in "the particular drama which ended with the Emancipation Proclamation" was "as great as any statesman's save Lincoln," notes Allan Nevins, the distinguished scholar of the Civil War. Lincoln appreciated the influence of Greeley and his newspaper. "In print," the president once remarked, "every one of his words seems to weigh about a ton."[7]

Marx sometimes complained that his bosses on the foreign desk of the *Tribune* were "impudent" and complained that they represented "the industrial bourgeoisie of America." Yet he ultimately bragged to friends about writing for "the foremost English-language American newspaper." Both the paper and its special correspondent in London aggressively lobbied to end slavery in America. When the artist Francis Carpenter painted his famous scene of Lincoln and his cabinet issuing the Emancipation Proclamation, Carpenter considered the role of the *Tribune* so important that he included an issue of the newspaper in the portrait. Marx declared that the Civil War was the first stage in a worldwide working-class revolution. "As the American War of Independence initiated a new era of ascendancy for the middle class," he predicted, "so the American anti-slavery war will do for the working-classes."[8]

Diplomacy and Imagination

Karl Marx was certainly not a player in the diplomacy of the Civil War in the same sense that men like Seward and Palmerston were. Lincoln had never met Marx, and they corresponded only indirectly. And yet, observing the two men side by side does reveal something important about the international arena in the midnineteenth century. In the years immediately following the 1815 Congress of Vienna, which ended the Napoleonic Wars, a tight-knit fraternity of highly conventional elites had come to dominate European statecraft. Stability in the international arena meant adhering to a common set of moral principles that would prevent any one nation from upsetting the balance of power. Foreign envoys refined an elaborate system of etiquette. Revolutionary change was frowned upon. Diplomacy had become a game for the orthodox.

By the Civil War, however, that system had broken down. After the outbreak of the Crimean War in the mid 1850s, nations began to act increasingly as free radicals—common moral principles be damned. Scientific progress and new theories of evolution seemed to justify a brutal competition for power and resources. And yet morality had not really disappeared from the international arena. It had simply fractured, diffused, and changed shape. Operating in such a global context required leaders who could make sense of the world for their followers, who could pick up the pieces and craft new narratives that would provide purpose and meaning. Survival, above all, demanded imagination.[9]

Lincoln and Marx were both creative geniuses who understood better than most that the old rules of foreign affairs were changing. (The word *genius* has a proactive, slightly spiritual connotation. The Latin root word, *gignere*, means "to beget"; the French version, *génie*, evokes its own type of otherworldly presence.) Marx, of course, is known for his materialistic conception of history. Lincoln, too, was a careful student of the concrete elements of power. Yet neither man could ultimately afford to ignore the less tangible elements in foreign affairs. Both enlisted the media of their times to help strengthen the resolve of their acolytes. Each ultimately managed to create a measure of order from the chaos of a changing world.[10]

Lincoln and Marx, in some ways, were temperamentally similar. Both could be fun-loving and warm; both sometimes sunk into bouts of gloom and pique. Focused on the activity between their ears, both sometimes neglected outside appearances. The prairie lawyer stored important documents in his stovepipe hat; the bohemian intellectual occupied an office covered with dust and tobacco ash. Above all, both men were revolutionaries who believed in the power of money and markets to reshape the world.

Lincoln, however, saw bourgeois life as a guarantor of social mobility; Marx viewed it as a prison. For the U.S. president, a Northern victory in the Civil War would redeem the American promise. The country's free-labor system, Lincoln believed, was partly what differentiated the United States from the Old World. For Marx, on the other hand, the Union's success represented the first step toward the revolution's final stage: proletarian revolt. In the newly interconnected world, the American Civil War had the potential to rally European workers. The sooner middle-class America triumphed over the country's Southern aristocrats, Marx believed, the sooner the world's workers could triumph over both. "Labor in white skin," Marx explained, "cannot emancipate itself where it is branded in black skin."[11]

In the near term, however, the aims of Lincoln and Marx were the same. Both sought the defeat of the Confederate States of America, even if the two men disagreed strongly over philosophy and strategy. Marx believed that the North held a key (and underutilized) advantage that had nothing to do with its material resources: the moral high ground. He recommended that Lincoln should use every means at his disposal—including the abolition of slavery—to win global sympathies. Only "the *revolutionary* waging of war," Marx believed, would give the Union war effort the ideological consistency it needed to carry the day.

That, of course, was easy for Marx to say from his journalistic perch safely across the Atlantic. Lincoln was the one with the near-impossible task of actually managing the revolution. In the war's first days, the Union's enemies seemed dangerously close to home. Secessionists in northern Virginia appeared poised to strike Washington. For all Lincoln knew, Kentuckians might be next. If the president wanted to placate border-state slaveholders, he would need a strategy that was far more subtle and pragmatic than Marx's prescription. Lincoln decided to save the moralizing for a later date. "The President *wanted* God on his side," observed one contemporary, "but he *must* have Kentucky." To accomplish that aim, Lincoln originally maintained that the North was fighting to preserve the Union—not to eradicate slavery.[12]

Lincoln's early strategy had not impressed the German dissident. The American president was "a man without intellectual brilliance," Marx lamented—one of the New World's "mediocrities of merely local influence." His cautious war making angered the philosopher. Marx complained that the president was always "hesitant, resistant, unwilling." Lincoln lacked originality, the journalist believed. Only a public outcry was likely to shift his stance. "Lincoln," Marx observed as the debate over slavery intensified, "yields only hesitantly and cautiously to this pressure from without."[13]

Actually, Lincoln and Marx were headed in the same direction. They were just taking different paths. Lincoln believed that it would have been counterproductive to issue a proclamation freeing the slaves if ordinary Americans were not yet "educated up to it," as he put it. By early 1862, however, he had come to recognize that the Northern effort needed a morale boost. Although the Union armies had won some major victories—the Battle of Shiloh, in April, was one example—the death tolls on both sides were growing to horrifying proportions. Northern and Southern forces had each lost more than 10,000 men at Shiloh—almost seven times the casualties at Bull Run. Shiloh, notes one historian, was the battlefield on which Americans' "Romanticism expired." The Union war effort desperately needed a leader to make sense out of the carnage.[14]

In the international arena, too, the human suffering was becoming unbearable. Although Southern threats about the power of King Cotton had been overstated, by the middle of 1862, Europeans were beginning to feel the pinch. Factory owners slashed working hours dramatically, throwing tens of thousands of Britons and Frenchmen out of a job. The economic turmoil threatened to turn European workers—many of whom otherwise loathed slavery—against the Union effort. Lincoln feared that the workers might put pressure on decision makers in London to stop the fighting. The president came to believe that a dramatic gesture that revised the war's aims to include the abolition of slavery might reassure suffering European workers—and buy the North the time to finish the war.

With the Emancipation Proclamation, the strategies of Lincoln and Marx finally began to converge. Each man recognized that only a bold moral appeal would infuse the Union effort with purpose and meaning—both at home and abroad. "National power," the diplomatic scholar Thomas A. Bailey points out, "is moral as well as physical." Yet in the tumultuous Victorian era—in which leaders increasingly found themselves amid a wasteland of ideological debris—marshaling the moral elements of power demanded audacious acts of reinvention. Throughout the conflict, both men struggled to manage and manipulate public opinion—a new and unpredictable force in the global arena. Amid the maelstrom of the Civil War, Lincoln and Marx rose to the challenge of their age.[15]

The Wild Boar

Karl Marx had been trying to reinvent himself—and the rest of the world, for that matter—for almost his entire adult life. He was born in the Prussian Rhineland city of Trier, a picturesque spot filled with vineyards situated along the banks of the Mosel River. He later studied law and philosophy at a series of German universities. The brilliant young scholar was captivated by the philosophy of G. W. F. Hegel, and in particular his concept of historical dialectic. But much of his time was devoted to drinking and carousing. Classmates elected Marx co-president of the Trier Tavern Club, and university police once arrested him for disturbing the peace during a drunken spree. The rowdy student took to carrying a gun, and was wounded above the eye in a saber duel. Marx's father complained about his son's "musty brooding under a gloomy oil-lamp" and "unsociable withdrawal with neglect of all decorum."[16]

In between drinking, fighting, and reading, Marx managed to find time to court Jenny von Westphalen, the daughter of a Prussian baron. With her green eyes and auburn hair, Jenny was far out of Marx's league. Her aristocratic family descended from the Earls of Argyll. Marx descended from a line of rabbis (although his father had converted to the state religion of Protestantism). Still, the passionate philosopher captivated the beautiful and well-bred young woman. The two became secretly engaged in 1836. Marx later boasted that he had snagged "the most beautiful girl in Trier." Jenny affectionately referred to her short, hairy husband as her "little wild boar."[17]

Marx earned his doctorate in 1841. Yet the young philosopher was never satisfied with pure theory. The day was approaching, he insisted, when philosophy must come into contact with "the real world." Marx turned to journalism. In the early nineteenth century, the profession remained a dumping ground for "the disreputable, the meretricious, the unstable." Still, Marx saw potential. He moved to the German city of Cologne, where he joined the staff of a newly formed newspaper, the *Rheinische Zeitung*, which was financed by the city's rising business class. One of the paper's founders recalls the young Marx as "a powerful man of twenty-four whose thick black hair sprung from his cheeks, arms, nose and ears. He was domineering, impetuous, passionate, full of boundless self-confidence."[18]

Marx quickly went to work eviscerating both the Prussian aristocracy and his colleagues in the opposition. For a young journalist whose professed goal was to change the world, Marx could be surprisingly detached. After rising to the editorship of the *Rheinische Zeitung*, Marx warned his writers that he considered it "unsuitable, indeed immoral, to smuggle communist and socialist doctrines into casual theatre reviews." Still, the young editor relentlessly advocated the liberalization of Prussian society. Eventually, the Prussian authorities began censoring Marx's subversive newspaper. Soon they shut it down altogether.[19]

Marx fled to Paris, then a hotbed of European revolutionaries. It was there that he got to know Frederick Engels, the son of a German industrialist whose parents owned a cotton mill in Britain. In August 1844, Marx and Engels met at a Paris café, then spent ten days drinking red wine and comparing notes at Marx's apartment. Engels was soon contributing articles to Marx's publications, and he wrote some early rough drafts of the *Manifesto of the Communist Party.* Marx was eventually ordered to leave Paris by the French authorities. Jenny quickly sold the furniture, and the family set off for Belgium in the frigid winter weather. Finally ensconced in his new home in Brussels, Marx chain-smoked cigars as he completely rewrote Engels's draft of the *Communist Manifesto.*[20]

The document was a political call to action, but it was also a profound portrait of the globalizing world. Marx and Engels observed that with the rise of the industrial classes, the constant quest for new markets meant that capitalism was destined to spread across the entire planet. The bourgeoisie, Marx and Engels insisted, "must nestle everywhere, settle everywhere, establish connections everywhere." New technologies like the steamship and the telegraph had the power to transform public opinion, spawning "a world literature." As a result of the "immensely facilitated means of communication," they continued, national differences were disappearing by the day. Ultimately, Marx and Engels concluded, "national one-sidedness and narrow-mindedness become more and more impossible." With the publication of the manifesto in 1848, the German exile and his partner had established themselves firmly as the leaders of a new global movement.[21]

Only a month after Marx completed the *Communist Manifesto,* revolution erupted in Paris. Soon the entire continent was aflame. Liberal protests attempted to topple autocratic regimes throughout Europe. For decades, conservative European statesmen had maintained a surprisingly sturdy peace on the Continent in the wake of the Napoleonic Wars. Now, however, Europeans from Switzerland to Sicily were beginning to demand press freedoms and voting rights. The changes were partly fueled by the tremendous advances in communication spawned by the steam press and the telegraph that Marx had described in the *Communist Manifesto.* In a single month in Paris, 171 separate newspapers began publishing. Marx, however, was not taking any chances. He sent revolutionaries in Prussia cash to pay for daggers and revolvers. On their own, Marx wrote in the years before the uprisings, "ideas can accomplish absolutely nothing. To become real, ideas require men who apply practical force."[22]

Marx moved back to Cologne to help lead the effort in Prussia. He borrowed money to restart his newspaper; this time he named it the *Neue Rheinische Zeitung*. His employees stocked the offices with rifles and bayonets. Marx resumed his practice of carrying a pistol. Engels recalled that Marx ran the newspaper as "a simple dictator-ship," and wondered whether his abrasive partner was really tem-peramentally suited to the profession. "He is no journalist and will never become one," Engels complained. "He pores for a whole day over a leading article that would take someone else a couple of hours as though it concerned the handling of a deep philosophical problem. He changes and polishes and changes the change and owing to his unremitting thoroughness can never be ready on time."[23]

As the European revolutions intensified, the *New York Tribune*, which sympathized with the insurgents, dispatched one of its young writers, Charles A. Dana, to cover the protests. Dana wandered around Paris gathering string and dodging batteries of artillery in the streets, fearing visits from the secret police. The young *Tribune* reporter was particularly taken aback by the reactionary crackdowns in Germany and Austria. With the spread of press freedoms and uni-versal education, Dana did not see how the old regimes could sur-vive. "It is vain for barbarism and tyranny to attempt to regain the conquests of liberty," he wrote home. "They may seem to triumph for a while, but they are destroyed by their triumph." Dana was eager to see the revolutions succeed. The goal of the protests, he under-stood, was "not simply to change the form of government, but to change the form of society." The *Tribune* reporter, a fluent German speaker, eventually left Paris for Berlin. Later, in Cologne, Dana met Marx through a mutual friend.[24]

Prussian authorities finally crushed the liberal revolt. Marx and his family fled to London amid the counterrevolution. At one point,

Marx had actually considered moving to the United States—to newly annexed Texas—but he discovered it was "hellishly expensive" and dropped the idea. Work as a radical communist, he was learning, did not pay the bills. "It is a pity," Marx's mother once remarked, "that Karl doesn't make some capital instead of just writing about it." The family eventually moved into a dingy, two-bedroom apartment on London's Dean Street.

Marx and his group in London, biographer David McLellan notes, displayed a ferocious zeal, behaving "like the early Christians awaiting the Second Coming." A Prussian spy who infiltrated one of the meetings found Marx's home full of broken furniture and covered in a thick layer of dust and tobacco ash. "If you sit down," the spook reported, "you risk a pair of trousers." According to the agent, Marx led "the existence of a real bohemian intellectual. Washing, grooming and changing his linen are things he does rarely, and he likes to get drunk." The whole place reeked so badly of cigar and coal smoke that the Prussian spy found his eyes watering.[25]

One of the group's first tasks, the revolutionaries decided, would be to form a newspaper as part of their "secret propaganda society." Yet Marx's heart was not really in it. Both Marx and Engels were chastened by the failure of Europe's liberal moment. "From now on," Engels wrote Marx in 1851, "we are answerable for ourselves alone." Marx, who had taken to wearing a fashionable scarf and a monocle in one eye, spent time teaching fellow German refugees political economy. Still, the philosopher could not stay away from the newspaper business for long. He remained convinced that the reactionary crackdown could not survive the swift pace of technological change. "King Steam," a friend recalled Marx saying, "was being superseded by a still greater revolutionary—the electric spark."

In 1851, a letter arrived from Charles Dana offering Marx a job writing for the *Tribune*. The paper wanted two articles each week, and would pay five dollars per piece. Marx immediately agreed to join the paper's staff.[26] The *Tribune* offer could not have come at a better time. Marx's home life was on the verge of falling apart.

Money was so tight that Jenny sold their beds to pay the bills. Meanwhile, Marx had impregnated the family's nanny, who had been a childhood friend of Jenny's back in Prussia. The tension had become unbearable in the tiny Dean Street apartment. Nothing could soothe the pain of Marx's betrayal, but at least the newspaper job allowed Marx to support his family. Jenny Marx later recalled that the family paid off old debts with the new income and managed to live a somewhat "less anxious life" free of their old "nagging daily worries."[27]

Marx complained about the job, but he was increasingly fascinated by North America. His philosophic forebear, Hegel, considered America "the land of the future." Soon, Hegel wrote, "the center of world-historical importance will be revealed there." After gold was discovered in the American West in 1848, Marx identified the United States as the new "fulcrum of world commerce." He complained about "the moneybag republicans of North America," but he also marveled at the accelerating wave of technological innovation emerging from the United States. At one industrial exhibition, Marx wrote Engels in 1851, the Americans displayed new weapons, reapers, and sewing machines—alongside "a colossal lump of California gold ore." The natural resources of North America were spawning a brisk trade across the Pacific, the economist observed. The New World was filling the role that Italy had played in the Middle Ages and England had taken on in recent years. America was still something of a backwater when it came to the issue of human bondage. Other countries in Europe and Latin America had emancipated their slaves years before. Still, there was no denying the increasing material strength of Britain's former colonies. Marx considered America the rising "center of gravity of world trade."[28]

Grinding Bones and Making Soup

Marx recognized that his dispatches for the *Tribune* had the power to influence two hundred thousand Americans each week. Still, he had to hold his nose to work for a newspaper that he considered the house organ of the American bourgeoisie. "It's truly nauseating," Marx wrote, "that one should be condemned to count it a blessing when taken aboard by a blotting-paper vendor such as this. To crush up bones, grind them and make them into soup like paupers in the workhouse—that is what the political work to which one is condemned in such large measure in a concern like this boils down to." Marx had no respect for Horace Greeley, despite the editor's crusading editorial policies. He considered Greeley a second-rate thinker. Still, it was hard to beat the reach of the *Tribune*. Readers particularly looked to the paper for its international coverage, provided by a network of eighteen foreign correspondents.[29]

From his perch in London, Marx covered the entire world. He wrote about British trade with China. He analyzed the Greek insurrection against Ottoman rule. He composed dispatches on revolutions in Spain and revolts in India. Lincoln, as a lawyer in Springfield during the 1850s, carefully pored over the *Tribune*, noting that it was "extensively read in Illinois." He sometimes wrote Greeley to complain about individual stories with which he disagreed. We have no record of whether Lincoln actually read Marx's dispatches. But they would have been difficult to miss. Marx contributed more than 350 articles to the newspaper over the course of the decade. Many were printed on the front page under his own byline. It is certainly easy to imagine Lincoln stretching out on his couch in the offices of Lincoln & Herndon, reading Marx aloud, to the annoyance of his partner. Herndon often noted the power of the *Tribune* in letters to associates, referring to Marx's employer as a "great paper" with a "wide-spread and almost universal circulation."[30]

Despite the high profile, Marx complained that the "newspaper muck" irritated him. He often wrote through the night, then napped on his sofa once the sun rose. When he was done, Marx's wife would copy the philosopher's illegible scrawl into a readable format. Marx referred to the reports as his "letters." The *Tribune* sometimes felt the need to apologize for its controversial contributor. The editors

cautioned readers that they did not always agree with their opin-
ionated London correspondent. And yet, Marx's bosses continued,
"those who do not read his letters neglect one of the most instructive
sources of information on the great questions of current European
politics." Marx, for his part, complained that the *Tribune* editors
ruthlessly chopped up his material. In later years, they often printed
his contributions as unsigned editorials. The *Tribune*, Marx wrote
Engels in 1854, "has again appropriated all my articles as leaders and
published only trash under *my* name." In many cases the frustrated
Marx simply farmed out the work to Engels, who was working at his
father's textile mill in Manchester.[31]

The urban underclass of Manchester would one day play its own
highly unlikely role in the international affairs of the Civil War.
Diplomacy, in many ways, was still the province of kings and their
representatives. Yet over the course of the nineteenth century, common people outside the world's chancelleries were becoming increasingly capable of exerting pressure on high officials. The burgeoning
culture of political activism in Britain, coupled with the boom in
newspaper publishing, meant that organized groups of workers could
manage to have some voice—however soft—in global politics.

Lincoln may have ultimately given this group too much credit for
its ability to sway the sympathies of cold-eyed British statesmen. Still,
as the Civil War intensified, the American president would eventually find himself appealing directly to British laborers, convinced that
any bonds of affinity would help the Union's cause. Textile workers
in cities like Manchester would bear the most painful burdens of any
potential cotton shortage. If they grew desperate enough, British officials might feel pressure to intervene to stop the war. Furthermore,
Lincoln believed (correctly, this time) that a moral appeal could ener-
gize this constituency. Many of the same workers, after all, had mo-
bilized to help abolish West Indian slavery earlier in the nineteenth
century.[32]

As for Engels, working at his father's mill provided an opportunity to stay in close contact with labor leaders and observe the

deprivations of English workers firsthand. The city, Engels observed, consisted of "a planless, knotted chaos of houses" situated along "a narrow, coal-black, foul-smelling stream, full of debris and refuse." The creek ultimately emptied into "the most disgusting blackish-green slime pools." Pigs rolled in the slop, and the stench of the local tanneries was oppressive. The disgusting conditions did not keep Marx from coming to visit regularly throughout the 1850s. Manchester, he found, was a convenient location to hide out from his creditors. Marx's wife, Jenny, teased Engels that he had become "a great cotton lord." Actually, Engels stole hundreds of dollars from his father's company to send back to his collaborator in London. Marx was elated when he heard the postman knock. "There's Frederick!" the philosopher would cry. "Two pounds extra! Saved!"[33]

Marx had withdrawn from politics during much of the 1850s. He maintained some contacts with the Chartists, a movement of British workers that sought voting rights and labor reforms. But he was frustrated by the failure of the working class to rise up. Instead he focused primarily on journalism and his longer economic treatises. Marx devoured European newspapers as research for his *Tribune* articles. He was ever on the lookout for signs of impending revolution. The outbreak of the Crimean War in 1853 offered one potential spark. The whole situation was "bubbling and boiling," he wrote. A foreign crisis, Marx understood, could induce Manchester's workers to take to the streets and demand change. "The times," he wrote optimistically in 1856, "seem to me to be hotting up."[34]

Marx's financial situation improved slightly as the decade progressed. When two of Jenny's aristocratic relatives died, the family inherited a couple of hundred pounds. They moved to more spacious accommodations near London's Hampstead Heath. The new place, with its view of St. Paul's Cathedral, "is truly a prince dwelling compared with the holes we used to live in," as Jenny put it. Marx, whom his children called Moor because of his dark complexion, found time to relax a little, carrying the tots around on his back like a horse. But money ultimately remained tight. Marx felt that he deserved a higher salary from the *Tribune.* "With three pounds per article," he wrote Engels, "I could at last get out of the muck." At first his bosses in New York agreed to raise his rate. But in 1857 they cut his weekly contributions from two articles to one—defeating the purpose of a raise. Marx, writing in his unique mishmash of German and English, complained to Engels that he was "from all sides *gebothert.*" He groused about the "lousy Yankees." Marx's wife was forced to cart their remaining linen and furniture to the local pawnshop.[35]

Marx, despite his poverty, never pulled his punches as a journalist. He reserved some of his most vehement criticism for Britain's Lord Palmerston. The German radical considered the Most English Minister the tool of Britain's bourgeoisie. Palmerston was a great phony, Marx believed. If he was too weak to confront a "strong enemy," he predicted, Palmerston would find a straw man to knock down instead. In Palmerston's vision, Marx wrote, "the movement of history is nothing but a pastime, expressly invented for the private satisfaction of the noble Viscount Palmerston of Palmerston." Still, Marx observed, the aging statesman had become a hero to the middle class. His chief supporters consisted of Britain's lords of industry, whom Marx derided as "vampyres, fattening on the life-blood of the young working generation." The irresponsible Palmerston and the "industrial slaveholders" who supported him, Marx complained, sought foreign wars to distract from troubles at home.[36]

Marx, despite his uncompromising rhetoric, was actually willing to support middle-class revolutions if he thought they would lead to an uprising of the working class. The growing tension in North America on the slavery question enthralled him. By the winter of 1860, Marx considered the rising conflict over slavery one of "the biggest things now happening in the world." He recognized that a Civil War across the Atlantic could have profound consequences in Europe. English textile mills like the one Engels helped operate depended on a steady supply of raw cotton from the slaveholding states in America. A shortage could lead to massive unemployment, perhaps even revolution. "If things gradually get serious," Marx wrote Engels in January 1860, "what will become of Manchester?"[37]

Marx was a careful student of the material elements of national power. The more he analyzed the state of play, the more a Northern victory appeared inevitable. In a letter to Engels in July 1861, Marx cited census figures to make the case that the burgeoning population of the American Northwest (including the modern-day Midwest) alone now far exceeded the total population of the seceding states. Northwesterners, Marx insisted, would not simply hand over the Mississippi Delta to a foreign power. Still, the war would be no easy victory. Marx believed that the South—teeming with angry, poor "adventurers"—would win some early battles. In the long run, however, the North was sure to prevail—not least, Marx observed, because it could always "play the last card, that of a slave uprising."[38]

A Snake in the Bed

M arx considered the antislavery agitation in America part of a worldwide trend toward abolition. He saw parallels in Russian czar Alexander II's emancipation of the serfs in 1861. Antislavery had in fact been sweeping the globe for decades prior to the American Civil War. In 1814 Mexico had abolished slavery, and a decade later Central America did the same. Britain banned the slave trade in 1807, and prohibited slavery altogether in 1833. In the 1850s, Colombia, Argentina, Venezuela, and Peru all joined the movement. The United States was well behind the times.[39]

Lincoln, of course, loathed slavery. For years he had been speaking out eloquently against the institution. Yet he also believed that the Constitution protected the property rights of slaveholders. As the secession crisis deepened, therefore, he made his goal the preservation of the Union—not abolition, which he initially believed would be both illegal and counterproductive. Furthermore, racism remained prevalent, even in the North. Lincoln recognized that he needed to take those views into account. "A universal feeling," he once remarked, "whether well or ill founded, cannot be safely disregarded." Freeing slaves might alienate otherwise loyal plantation owners in border states like Kentucky. With territory slipping out of the Union by the day, the president could not afford to forfeit any supporters. "I think to lose Kentucky," he wrote Orville Browning, "is nearly the same as to lose the whole game. Kentucky gone, we can not hold Missouri, nor, as I think, Maryland. These all against us, and the job on our hands is too large for us. We would as well consent to separation at once, including the surrender of this capitol."[40]

Lincoln further clarified his position by reciting a parable. If "out in the street, or in the field, or on the prairie I find a rattlesnake," he began, "I take a stake and kill him. Everybody would applaud the act and say I did right. But suppose the snake was in a bed where children were sleeping. Would I do right to strike him there? I might hurt the children; or I might not kill, but only arouse and exasperate the snake, and he might bite the children." On another occasion, Lincoln compared the country to a sick man with a tumor on his neck. Remove the tumor, he warned, and the patient might die in the process.[41]

In Lincoln's first inaugural, the new president went out of his way to reassure slaveholders in the border states. He had no intention, he explained, "directly or indirectly, to interfere with the institution of slavery where it exists." Seward relayed the message to his diplomats in the field: Slavery was not to be mentioned at all as a rationale for the war. (A frequently overlooked line in the secretary of state's April Fools' memo urges the president to "change the question before the public from one upon slavery" to "a question upon Union or disunion." Lincoln agreed with this part of Seward's counsel— at least at first.) Europe's ruling classes took Lincoln and Seward at their word—not least because it was convenient for them. Europeans disliked slavery, but they also depended upon cotton from the Confederate states. If the war transformed into an antislavery crusade, it would complicate matters immensely. Marx, in his *Tribune* dispatches, tried to expose the hypocrisy in the attitudes of European aristocrats. He argued persuasively that slavery actually lay at the foundation of the conflict.[42]

Marx, in some ways, operated like a modern blogger. He did little original reporting. Instead, he pored over the proliferating English newspapers and magazines—and then critiqued them. Marx once revealingly complained that he could not do his job because he did not have enough money to buy newspapers. When he did have the money, there was never a lack of material. The number of American newspapers alone had more than doubled in the three decades before the Civil War.[43]

Lincoln, too, was a shrewd observer—and manipulator—of the media. Even before he became president, he worked carefully to control his own image.[44] He spent a great deal of time in newspaper offices. He often lurked in composing rooms, watching as his speeches were set in type to make sure no mistakes crept in. Once, back in Illinois, he bought a printing press in an attempt to woo German voters. Sometimes he tried to bribe newspaper publishers. As president, Lincoln quizzed visiting correspondents for intelligence from the battlefield.

The flood of newspaper commentary sometimes overwhelmed Lincoln. He complained that he lost sleep over hostile editorials. At the White House on one occasion, an acquaintance observed that newspapers were not always "reliable." Lincoln shot back that he agreed. "That is to say," the president added, that "they '*lie*,' and then they '*re-lie*'!" As the war unfolded, Lincoln soured particularly on the editor in chief of the *Tribune*. "Greeley is so rotten," the president told his cabinet on one occasion, "that nothing can be done with him."[45]

And yet the power of Greeley's newspaper was impossible to ignore. Lincoln believed that emancipation would help the United States in Europe, but he could not shift America's war aims without risking a backlash at home. The pressure from the *Tribune* and other newspapers—however aggravating—could help change American minds. Still, Lincoln recognized that public opinion moved glacially. Any move toward emancipation, the president later explained, would have to wait for the "great revolution in public sentiment" that was "slowly but *surely* progressing." Lincoln compared his approach to watching a pear ripen on a tree. Pick it too soon and the fruit is spoiled. Wait patiently, on the other hand, and the pear would fall on its own.[46]

By the fall of 1861, Lincoln was coming under increasing pressure to pluck the pear. In August, General John C. Frémont, the president's commander in Missouri, issued a proclamation to free slaves in the territory he controlled. There was a certain logic to letting military commanders do the emancipating in a local, piecemeal fashion. It would dodge the border-state pitfalls, allow the president to stay above the fray, and avoid publicly shifting the war aims to an antislavery crusade. Yet the order deeply troubled the ever-cautious Lincoln. For one, such a gradual approach would be far less likely than a bold proclamation to make an impact on European powers. Lincoln let his dissatisfaction be known, and Frémont's wife, Jessie—daughter of the renowned Missouri senator Thomas Hart Benton—eventually traveled to Washington to defend her husband. When she arrived in the capital, she sent the president a note asking when would be a good time to call. "Now, at once," Lincoln wrote back.

In the White House, Frémont's wife later recalled, the president did not even offer her a chair. She protested that Lincoln did not understand European opinion and complained that "we were on the eve of England, France and Spain recognizing the South." The European powers, she added, "were anxious for a pretext to do so; England on account of her cotton interests, and France because the emperor dislikes us." The president brusquely dismissed the pleas. "You are quite a female politician," Lincoln said. The encounter, the president later explained to John Hay, "taxed me so violently with many things that I had to exercise all the awkward tact I have to avoid quarreling with her." Lincoln ultimately countermanded Frémont's order.[47]

Many abolitionists, however, agreed with Frémont and his wife.

"No wonder Europe looks on the struggle with indifference," one Delaware resident wrote to Lincoln. Billy Herndon once again questioned his law partner's judgment. "What is Lincoln doing?" Herndon wrote to an Illinois acquaintance in the wake of the Frémont countermand. "Does he suppose he can crush—squelch out this huge rebellion by pop guns filled with rose water?" Lincoln tried to assure his former partner that he favored ultimate emancipation—if public opinion would help him get there. "I am moving slowly outward," Lincoln explained, "as if pressing iron rings [were] riveted on me." And yet, even after Lincoln's assassination, Herndon was still insisting that Lincoln "never ran in advance of his age."[48]

The president felt the timing was still not right. "We didn't go into the war to put down slavery, but to put the flag back," Lincoln told one acquaintance shortly after his Frémont decision. "This thunderbolt will keep." Lincoln insisted that it was better to follow public opinion, rather than leading it. Radicals complained that Lincoln was squandering an opportunity. Charles Sumner grumbled that it was "vain to have the power of a god" and "not to use it godlike." Lincoln simply counseled patience. "Wait," he told Sumner. "Time is essential."[49]

In London, Karl Marx was mystified by Lincoln's "fainthearted" decision to revoke Frémont's proclamation. Still, he considered such caution in character for the American president. "Lincoln," Marx complained, "in accord with his lawyer's tradition, has an aversion for all originality, clings anxiously to the letters of the Constitution, and fights shy of anything that could mislead the 'loyal' slaveholders of the border states." The German radical also blamed Seward. Marx thought that the secretary of state wanted to eliminate Frémont as a political rival. Seward, Marx insisted, "has provided fresh proof that virtuosos of the tongue are dangerously insufficient statesmen. Read his state dispatches! What a revolting mixture of greatness of phrase and pettiness of mind, of postures of strength and acts of weakness!"[50]

Seward's counsel, however, was not the only foreign-affairs advice that Lincoln was listening to in the early months of the war. Other members of Lincoln's inner circle argued that the impact abroad of a proclamation would outweigh the domestic risks. Carl Schurz frequently dropped by the White House in the early days of Lincoln's presidency, before he left for his post in Madrid. The two men would spend long evenings talking in the library. Schurz plinked at the piano keys as the sun slowly dropped below the horizon. On one occasion, Schurz suggested that a proclamation of emancipation would be the most effective weapon to prevent foreign intervention. Lincoln sat in silence for a moment, and then replied: "You may be right. Probably you are. I have been thinking so myself. I cannot imagine that any European power would dare to recognize and aid the Southern Confederacy if it becomes clear that the Confederacy stands for slavery and the Union for freedom."[51]

Schurz had once met Marx when the latter was still a young revolutionary back in Cologne. Lincoln's man in Spain considered Marx "intolerable." His brusque demeanor irritated Schurz. "Everyone who contradicted him," Schurz later recalled, "he treated with abject contempt; every argument that he did not like he answered either with biting scorn at the unfathomable ignorance that had prompted it, or with opprobrious aspersions upon the motives of him who had advanced it." Schurz recalled the "cutting disdain" with which Marx pronounced the word "bourgeois." The future communist railed wildly against his enemies. Schurz thought Marx probably alienated many potential acolytes.[52]

By early 1861, Marx was also beginning to repel his bosses at the *Tribune.* They had already significantly scaled back his contributions when the war erupted. Jenny Marx recalled that "Old Europe with its petty, old-fashioned pigmy struggles ceased to interest America." The salary cut was particularly painful for the Marxes because their daughters had entered their teenage years, and were more conscious than before of the deprivation. "For me personally," Marx wrote his uncle, "the American events are, of course, rather harmful, as for the time being the transatlantic readers have eyes and ears only for their own story." The qualms of the *Tribune* editors, however, went beyond simply self-absorption. Greeley thought Marx had wandered far off the reservation. He tried to have the philosopher fired. Dana agreed that Marx's dispatches sometimes displayed "too German a tone." Yet he refused to let him go. Finally, however, Dana relented—before being forced out himself by Greeley. Engels later referred to Greeley in letters to his partner as an "old jackass."[53]

Marx was devastated by his dismissal from the *Tribune*. His family was already impoverished, even when he had a job. "I'm now stone-broke," he had complained to Engels as the Civil War loomed. "As you see," he wrote Engels, "I am as tormented as Job, though not as god-fearing." His health was also failing. Marx signed some letters "Your Hemorrhoidarius," and adhered to a diet of lemonade and castor oil. Jenny was stricken with a bout of smallpox that left her face covered in ugly purple scars. As the family's fortunes worsened, she told her husband that she wished she were dead. "I really cannot blame her," Marx told Engels, "for the humiliations, torments and alarums that one has to go through in such a situation are indeed indescribable."

Marx desperately tried to raise cash. He reported that his wife had to drag "everything that was not actually nailed down" to the pawnbroker's. To Engels, he lamented his increasingly dire straits. "If only I knew how to start some sort of business!" the scourge of the bourgeoisie wrote in the summer of 1862. "All theory, dear friend, is gray, and only business green. Unfortunately, I have come to realize this too late."[54]

Marx, meanwhile, remained obsessed with the Civil War. He continued to sift through newspapers at an American coffeehouse in London. The conflict was such a part of his daily life that his children began to share his enthusiasm. Marx's daughter Eleanor, whom he called Tussy, quizzed her father about news of the battles and diplomatic reports. "At that time," she later recalled, "I had the unshakeable conviction that Abraham Lincoln could not succeed without my advice." The six-year-old wrote the American president long letters, which Marx promised to take to the post office. Marx, however, longed to once again write his own "letters" with advice for the American president. For all his gripes, the communist had come to appreciate the powerful megaphone of Greeley's paper. "I painfully miss contributing to the *Tribune*," he wrote Engels in the spring of 1862. Marx eventually took a job writing for a conservative Austrian newspaper called *Die Presse*. At least, Marx insisted, it was one way to continue to spread "correct views" about the American conflict in Europe.[55]

A Thunderbolt in a Clear Sky

Lincoln, too, began looking for new ways to influence the European public. For months his diplomats had been urging the administration to expand the scope of the war. Lincoln's man in Belgium wrote Seward shortly after the fall of Fort Sumter demanding that the White House begin "an antislavery crusade" that would appeal to British workers. "You must bear in mind," he added, "that any popular sympathy we have now here or in England is solely on the ground that the war we are entered upon is supposed to be for the *extinction of slavery*." From Spain, Schurz complained that even journalists "who in their papers work for us to the best of their ability" were "secretly troubled with serious scruples" about the limited Union war aims. He argued that Washington's foreign policy should establish "a stronger foothold in the popular heart." Schurz urged the Lincoln administration to put the war "upon a higher moral basis and thereby give us the control of public opinion in Europe. . . . Every step done by the government toward the abolition of slavery is, as to our standing in Europe, equal to a victory in the field."

Charles Sumner, the chair of the Senate committee on foreign relations, relentlessly hectored the president on the slavery issue. From the first days of the war, Sumner urged Lincoln to use his war powers to abolish slavery. The senator's entreaties tried Lincoln's formidable patience. "Mr. Sumner, I will not issue a proclamation freeing the slaves now," the exasperated president finally declared. Sumner stormed out of the room, slamming the door as he left.[56]

Now Lincoln was beginning to see the wisdom of a more radical approach. As the blockade raised transatlantic tensions, the president assured Sumner that they were not so far apart after all. "Well, Mr. Sumner," Lincoln told him in November 1861, "the only difference between you and me on this subject is a difference of a month or six weeks in time." In the wake of the *Trent* affair, the president redoubled his efforts to win hearts and minds in Europe. In January, Sumner brought a delegation to visit Lincoln, some of whom urged the president to begin a program of compensated emancipation. Lincoln said he thought the idea had merit. Still, he felt that any such measure remained premature. "Perhaps we may be better able to do something in that direction after a while than we are now," the president told his visitors.[57]

Lincoln's men were offering him conflicting advice. The potential effects of a proclamation of emancipation remained uncertain— even in Europe. On the one hand, such a move could help win the sympathies of workers in France and Britain. Yet it could also spook the Continent's aristocratic decision makers, who feared the disorder of a slave revolt. Britons warily recalled the Indian Mutiny of 1857 and 1858, when sepoys working for the British East India Company had rebelled, assassinating imperial officers and sometimes murdering their families. Some of Lincoln's aides insisted that a conservative approach would actually most impress the European powers. Lincoln was sensitive to the qualms of the conservatives, even if he ultimately rejected their advice. While Lincoln reassured radicals like Sumner that he shared their goals, he also insisted that he did not want the war to "degenerate into a violent and remorseless revolutionary struggle."[58]

The middle-of-the-road policy of compensated emancipation offered one potential solution. Early on the morning of March 6, 1862, Lincoln sent his secretaries to fetch Sumner and ask him to come to the White House. The senator dressed hurriedly and made his way to the Executive Mansion. The president showed Sumner the draft of a proposal that would compensate border states if they used the funds to help plantation owners free their slaves. "I want you to read my message," Lincoln said. "I want to know how you like it." Lincoln read Sumner the document and then handed it over to the senator. Sumner later complained about Lincoln's "aboriginal, autochthonous" language. He disliked Lincoln's use of the word "abolishment," for example. Still, Sumner was heartened by the message. Lincoln eventually took back his draft. "There, now," he told Sumner, "you've read it enough, run away. I must send it in today." Notably, Lincoln apparently did not consult his own secretary of state on the plan.[59]

Newspapers across the country lauded Lincoln's message as a blow to the North's enemies in Europe. The *New York Tribune* cheered the scheme, calling it "perhaps the most important document ever addressed to Congress." The president wrote to Horace Greeley in March thanking him for his support. Lincoln was eager to see his program passed, he told the editor, "but you have advocated it from the first, so that I need say little to you on the subject." Abolitionists were elated. The radical Wendell Phillips praised Lincoln's decision as "a thunderbolt in a clear sky."[60]

Yet even as Lincoln moved steadily toward emancipation, he continued to rein in rogue subordinates. In early May, General David Hunter followed Frémont's lead and freed the slaves in the Department of the South. Treasury secretary Chase, a strong advocate of the piecemeal approach, argued that the order would help change minds overseas. Carl Schurz also supported Hunter. Lincoln, however, again countermanded the order. If abolition became a "necessity indispensable to the maintenance of the government," the president insisted, it was a policy that "I reserve to myself, and which I can not feel justified in leaving to the decision of commanders in the field." Lincoln took the opportunity to once again push for compensated emancipation. "You can not if you would, be blind to the signs of the times," the president argued. "The change it contemplates would come gently as the dews of heaven, not rending or wrecking anything. Will you not embrace it?"[61]

Despite the flap with Hunter, reactions to Lincoln's proposal generally encouraged the president's team. John Hay was relieved that Americans were finally beginning to consider slavery a question "to be discussed and settled coolly"—not a hobbyhorse "to ride into place and power upon." An issue that was once the province of "passion and prejudice" had matured into "a thing to be discussed and decided in the light of reason and common sense," Hay observed. On the Hill, Charles Sumner reassured radicals that the president was sincerely committed to promulgating "the principles of the Declaration of Independence." Still, Lincoln could not seem to get much traction on his initiative from legislators. In June the president sent his compensated emancipation proposal to Congress. The body adjourned without taking it up.[62]

The president made one final effort to woo border-state representatives. On July 12 he invited them to the White House. Lincoln insisted that the war would have virtually ended if they had voted for his proposal. "How much better for you, as seller, and the nation as buyer, to sell out, and buy out, that without which the war could never have been, than to sink both the thing to be sold, and the price of it, in cutting one another's throats," the president said. Lincoln, noting Hunter's recent proclamation, argued that public agitation for abolition was actually intensifying. "The pressure, in this direction, is still upon me, and is increasing," he said. Ultimately, however, the border-state representatives concluded that Lincoln's plan would be too expensive. Nothing came of the president's proposal.[63]

Finally, on July 13, Lincoln resolved to take even more drastic measures. In a carriage on the way to the funeral of the son of Secretary of War Edwin Stanton, the president told Seward and Naval Secretary Gideon Welles that he was considering issuing a more ambitious proclamation. Lincoln said it was the first time he had mentioned the matter to anyone. As the carriage rolled through the streets of Georgetown, the president explained that he considered it a "military necessity" that "we must free the slaves or be ourselves subdued." Seward said he needed more time to mull over the "vast and momentous" proposal. But Lincoln kept returning to the issue. Before the men parted ways, Lincoln told Seward and Welles to give the matter "special and deliberate attention."[64]

The dramatic new policy proposal had important implications for foreign affairs. "By framing a proclamation rather than allowing events to take their course, [Lincoln] could appeal specifically to the antislavery feeling of foreign nations," notes the scholar Hans Trefousse. Still, European opinion remained immensely diverse; courting it was maddeningly complex. If the timing was wrong, the strategy had the potential to backfire spectacularly, stoking British fears of disorder and ultimately damaging the Union cause.[65]

News of Lincoln's change of heart seems to have slowly filtered through the White House. On July 20, John Hay wrote to a friend insisting that Lincoln would not preserve the peculiar institution for long. For a year, Hay wrote, the president had acted as "the bulwark of the institution he abhors." Next time Lincoln mentions the subject, the president's secretary predicted, "it will be with no uncertain sound." Two days later, Lincoln alerted the full cabinet to his decision. The president gathered his inner circle in the oval-shaped library of the White House residence. Lincoln read the men his proclamation, which he had copied out onto two oversize sheets of paper.[66]

When the president had finished, Seward complained that the order might have the opposite of its intended effect in Europe. The move, he cautioned, could well prompt the powers to intervene. Emancipation would "break up our relations with foreign nations . . . for sixty years," Seward insisted. At the least, the secretary of state argued, Europeans would see the move as a sign of weakness. The North's military efforts had been stalled for weeks. General George B. McClellan, Lincoln's commander of the Army of the Potomac, had conceived a plan to march his troops—more than a hundred thousand—up the Virginia Peninsula, hoping to capture Richmond. Yet by midsummer his forces had bogged down near the outskirts of the city. During the Seven Days' Campaign in late June and early July, troops commanded by Confederate general Robert E. Lee audaciously attacked McClellan's forces, charging across the Chickahominy River. Although the Union army ultimately stopped the Confederate assault, McClellan was forced to withdraw his forces. Lee and his men had dramatically shifted the war's momentum.

A proclamation freeing the slaves now, Seward argued, "may be viewed as the last measure of an exhausted government, a cry for help." The secretary of state feared that Europeans would consider the measure the North's "last *shriek*, on the retreat." The New Yorker advised Lincoln to hold off until the army scored more decisive victories on the battlefield. Seward's arguments, the president later recalled, "struck me with very great force."[67]

The secretary of state did not seem sanguine about the proclamation, no matter when it would be issued. "Proclamations are *paper* without the support of armies," Seward complained to his wife a week after the cabinet meeting. "It is mournful to see that a great nation shrinks from a war it has accepted, and insists on adopting proclamations, when it is asked for force. The Chinese do it without success."[68]

Lincoln felt that his Federals had already demonstrated their prowess on the battlefield and was nonplussed by the lack of faith in Europe. In late July the Frenchman Agénor-Étienne de Gasparin wrote to Lincoln from Europe uging the president to avoid "revolutionary measures" like "precipitate emancipation." The administration should remain neither "indifferent to abolition" nor "carried away by the extreme abolitionists," he said. Either position might

inspire European powers to meddle in the war. Gasparin asserted
instead that clear battlefield victories would be the key to avoiding intervention. "You are quite right," Lincoln shot back, "as to
the importance to us, for its bearing upon Europe, that we should
achieve military successes. . . . Yet it seems unreasonable that a series of successes, extending through half-a-year, and clearing more
than a hundred thousand square miles of country, should help us so
little, while a single half-defeat should hurt us so much. But let us be
patient."[69]

Still, there was truth in Gasparin's missive. Henry P. Tappan,
the president of the University of Michigan, had been traveling
through France in the summer of 1862. "To the minds of Frenchmen," Tappan wrote Lincoln, "our government has shown only
weakness and irresolution. To them, we have exhibited no military ability. They regard our conduct of the war as a grand failure."
The situation was much the same in Britain. "It is too late now to
change these sentiments by diplomacy," the educator told Lincoln.
"We can reestablish ourselves abroad only by manful and successful doing at home. . . . The thunder of victorious cannon on the
Potomac is the only diplomatic agency that can prevail on the Seine
and the Thames." Another American, William T. Dahlgren, wrote
to Lincoln from London that summer emphasizing that the U.S.
"must sooner or later establish their status by force of arms. It is
all very well talking—or rather dreaming—of 'fraternity' etc., but
might more than ever rules the day, and the sooner we make ourselves understood, the better."[70]

At home, public opinion was approaching a tipping point. The rising swell of abolitionist sentiment emboldened Horace Greeley. "Do
you remember that old theological book containing this: 'Chapter
One: Hell; Chapter Two: Hell Continued'?" Greeley asked Charles
Sumner in early August. "That gives a hint of the way Old Abe *ought
to be* talked to in this crisis." The abolitionist Wendell Phillips, like
Marx, lamented that the president "is not fighting vigorously and
heartily enough." If the government were only true to its ideals, he

argued, the Northern states alone might form "the strongest nation on the face of the globe." In Lincoln, however, the Union was led by "a first-rate *second-rate* man." The only way to get movement from the president, Phillips complained, was by applying intense pressure. "We have constantly to be pushing him from behind," he said. The abolitionist later quipped that if Lincoln grew in office, it was only "because we have watered him."[71]

Marx believed the conflict had reached a critical moment. Until now, Lincoln's regard for the border states had "blunted the Civil War's points of principle," Marx wrote in August, and "deprived it of its soul." Slavery, he argued, had been "transformed from the Achilles' heel of the South into its invulnerable horny hide." Observing the North's faltering military efforts, Marx took the opposite lesson from Seward. "The long and the short of the story seems to me to be that a war of this kind must be conducted in a revolutionary way," he wrote Engels in August, "whereas the Yankees have been trying so far to conduct it constitutionally." Engels went even further, arguing that the South had virtually won the war. Marx disagreed, but he took his collaborator's criticisms in stride. "In regard to the North's conduct of the war," he wrote Engels, "nothing else could be expected from a *bourgeois* republic, where swindle has been enthroned for such a long time."

Still, Marx viewed public opinion as a potential savior of the North. The president could be bullied into adopting what Marx called "the great radical remedy." The war was about to take "a revolutionary turn," Marx predicted. He noted the public pressure from abolitionists like Wendell Phillips that was building in the American press. The Northwest and New England would push Lincoln to abandon his "diplomatic methods of waging war," Marx wrote Engels. The philosopher predicted that there would be a new American revolution if Lincoln did not cave in to the abolitionists. "Up to now we have witnessed only the first act of the Civil War—the *constitutional* waging of war," he wrote. "The second act, the *revolutionary* waging of war, is at hand."[72]

A Masterpiece of Art

Marx rightly perceived the shift in American public opinion. Yet he underestimated Lincoln's media savvy. Marx had always considered the American president something of a backwoods dunce, thrust into power by the vagaries of demographics and buffeted by the unpredictable winds of democratic politics. Lincoln himself sometimes felt as if he had lost control. Once, when the president was asked to describe his policy, Lincoln replied, "I have none. I pass my life in preventing the storm from blowing down the tent, and I drive in the pegs as fast as they are pulled up." In the case of abolition, however, Lincoln was actually shrewdly and quietly preparing the public for a major transformation of the war aims.[73]

On August 20, Greeley published an editorial in the *Tribune* titled "The Prayer of Twenty Millions." The newspaper editor complained that Lincoln was acting too slowly on the slavery issue. Greeley griped that the president was "unduly influenced" by "certain fossil politicians hailing from the border slave states." The men, the editor insisted, were providing Lincoln with only "timid counsels." The North's preservation of slavery was causing its war efforts to founder. "On the face of this wide earth, Mr. President, there is not one disinterested, determined, intelligent champion of the Union cause who does not feel that all attempts to put down the rebellion and at the same time uphold its inciting cause are preposterous and futile," Greeley wrote.

Lincoln responded two days later, writing a letter to Greeley—and then leaking it to a rival newspaper. The president began magnanimously. If Greeley's letter displayed "an impatient and dictatorial tone," Lincoln wrote, he would ignore it "in deference to an old friend, whose heart I have always supposed to be right." Then the president offered a defense of his cautious position on slavery. "My paramount object in this struggle *is* to save the Union, and is *not* either to save or to destroy slavery," Lincoln wrote. "If I could save the Union without freeing *any* slave I would do it, and if I could save it by freeing *all* the slaves I would do it; and if I could save it by freeing some and leaving others alone I would also do that. What I do about slavery, and the colored race, I do because I believe it helps to save the Union; and what I forbear, I forbear because I do *not* believe it would help to save the Union. I shall do less whenever I shall believe what I am doing hurts the cause, and I shall do *more* whenever I shall believe doing more will help the cause."[74]

On the surface, Lincoln's response to Greeley appears to be a defense of the president's original, limited war aims. Actually, as Lincoln's conversations with his cabinet earlier that summer reveal, the president had already determined on a policy of emancipation more than a month before Greeley's "Prayer." Why, then, would the president seem to resist the editor's plea? First, despite Lincoln's assurances, he must have been miffed by Greeley's impetuosity. That the president printed his response in a rival newspaper offers one clue to his true feelings. Second, Lincoln wanted to prepare border-state holdouts for the inevitability of emancipation. By defining abolition as a tool of national salvation, he tried to address their fears that the shift would degenerate into a slave revolt. Finally, Lincoln still needed to temporize. The president may have convinced himself of the necessity of emancipation, but he saw the logic in Seward's pleas to await military success.[75]

Yet the victories remained elusive. In late August, with a small force of only thirty-two thousand men, Union general John Pope attacked a unit of Stonewall Jackson's rebel troops dug in around Manassas, Virginia. Reinforcements eventually arrived, but by the time the battles were finished, the Federals had taken more than sixteen thousand casualties. Rain poured down on Lincoln's defeated troops as they streamed back toward Washington. The battle, later known as Second Bull Run, was one more blow to Lincoln's plans. When one radical Republican complained to the president on August 31 about the slow pace of the emancipation effort, Lincoln shot back: "You would not have it done now, would you? Must we not wait for something like a victory?"[76]

The battle disheartened Lincoln and his men. "You could scarcely find a gloomier city than Washington is today," John Hay wrote on August 31. The whole capital was depressed and despondent. Even the sky was gray. The summer rain soaked clothes and dampened moods. Lincoln brooded around the Executive Mansion. "Well, John," he told Hay, "we are whipped again, I am afraid." The president, according to one of his cabinet secretaries, "seemed wrung by the bitterest anguish." Lincoln complained that he felt like hanging himself.[77]

The president had good reason for concern. In Europe the cotton shortages produced by the blockade were finally beginning to take their toll on workers. The livelihoods of more than two hundred thousand Frenchmen and a million Britons were tied up with the industry. In the early months of the war, British and French textile manufacturers had been able to draw on existing cotton surpluses and additional supplies from countries like India. Yet by September cotton stocks had plunged to crisis levels. Roughly three quarters of British textile workers were unemployed or underemployed. The *New York Times* reported that English laborers were pawning their clothes and blankets to survive. In London, Charles Francis Adams tried to remain sanguine. He was "inclined to believe," he wrote home to the State Department, "that we are at the crisis of the difficulty, and from this time things will rather mend than grow worse." Just days later, however, Adams was forced to revise his estimate, sheepishly informing Washington that "the distress in the manufacturing districts is rather on the increase."[78]

As the crisis deepened, Britain's Lord Palmerston began to question the wisdom of nonintervention. The prime minister had long been reluctant to get involved. Yet momentum in the conflict seemed to be shifting. The Federal troops "got a very complete smashing" at Manassas, Palmerston wrote to his foreign minister in September. The British prime minister thought a mediation proposal that would settle the conflict by separating the combatants might finally be a good idea. France would go along if Britain took the lead, Palmerston predicted. If the North lost one more battle, the prime minister wrote, "the iron should be struck while it is hot." If the Federal troops managed to eke out some more victories, on the other hand, the prime minister was willing to take a wait-and-see approach.[79]

Lincoln's men seem to have at least dimly perceived the impending peril. John Hay boasted that, despite the Confederate troops on Washington's doorstep, the capital remained safe. Hay attributed the city's lack of alarm to the "truculent-looking" fleet of Northern gunboats protecting the Potomac. Still, Hay recognized that if Confederate forces did manage to capture Washington, European intervention was sure to follow. "We would find the whole world about our ears," Hay wrote. Such a turn of events, Hay believed, would amount to a death blow for the nation.[80]

On September 13 a delegation representing "Chicago Christians of All Denominations" visited Lincoln at the White House. The men presented the president with a petition favoring emancipation that had resulted from a meeting of Chicago abolitionists a week earlier. The clergymen argued that a proclamation abolishing slavery "would secure the sympathy of Europe and the whole civilized world. . . . No other step would be so potent to prevent foreign intervention." Lincoln conceded the point. Still, he wanted to make sure that any such proclamation was taken seriously. "I do not," the president protested, "want to issue a document that the whole world will see must necessarily be inoperative, like the Pope's bull against the comet!"[81]

And yet only four days later, Lincoln changed his mind. Near Sharpsburg, Maryland, on September 17, Union and Confederate armies clashed in an epic fourteen-hour battle that produced more than twenty thousand casualties. Lincoln recognized that a Union victory was critical. If the Federals had been driven back, the president later recalled, Lincoln would have found himself "in a bad row of stumps." Northern generals spun the battle as a triumph for their cause. McClellan believed that he had produced "a masterpiece of art." Seward dashed off a letter to Charles Francis Adams in London lauding the "renewed and reinvigorated forces of the Union." The battle at Antietam Creek was indeed a Union victory. Yet McClellan's men ultimately allowed the Confederate troops to escape rather than pursuing them and inflicting a crushing blow. The outcome, however, was good enough for Lincoln. He believed he had finally found an excuse to issue his proclamation.[82]

Lincoln misjudged European reactions to Antietam. The president believed that the battle would weaken the interventionist camp across the Atlantic. In fact, as the diplomatic scholar Howard Jones has convincingly shown, in the short term it did nothing of the kind. European statesmen were indeed carefully awaiting the battle's results, but they were less impressed by the outcome than Lincoln. When Palmerston got the news, he dashed off a letter to his foreign minister. The prime minister considered the battle "just the case for the stepping in of friends. One thing must be admitted and that is that both sides have fought like bulldogs." Still, just days later, Palmerston reverted to his prior vacillation. "The whole matter is full of difficulty," he wrote his foreign minister. An armistice now, Palmerston argued, "would only be like the breathing time allowed to boxers between the rounds of a fight, to enable them to get fresh wind." More decisive battles would be needed to change his mind.[83]

Karl Marx, on the other hand, shared Lincoln's view that Antietam represented a "decisive" moment in the conflict. "The brief campaign in Maryland," Marx told the readers of *Die Presse*, "has decided the fate of the American Civil War." The German émigré had no love for McClellan, whom he derided as a "military incompetent." Yet Marx remained unshaken by the setbacks of 1862. No single commander could ruin the Northern war effort. The Federals still possessed far greater resources than the Confederacy. Marx repeatedly assured Engels that the North would prevail. The philosopher would "wager my head" on the prospect, he wrote to his collaborator. "In world history," Marx insisted, "reason does conquer."[84]

The Last, Best Hope of Earth

Five days after Antietam, on September 22, Lincoln sent his cabinet an urgent message instructing them to report to the Executive Mansion. The men were given only a few hours' notice. When they arrived, Lincoln began by reading a comedic sketch by one of his favorite writers, Artemus Ward. Then he got down to business. The president told the men that he was ready to issue a preliminary proclamation announcing that slaves in the Confederacy would be freed within a matter of months. "I think the time has come now," Lincoln said. "I wish it were a better time. I wish that we were in a better condition." He acknowledged that the result of Antietam was not "quite what I should have best liked." Still, Lincoln felt that he had to do something. The president appeared a little superstitious to some members of his cabinet. "I made the promise to myself," Lincoln told the men—and then, after hesitating a little, he added, "and . . . to my Maker."[85]

Lincoln's cabinet was giddy after the meeting broke up. The men joked around, calling one another abolitionists. John Hay noted in his diary that the cabinet officers "seemed to enjoy the novel sensation of appropriating that horrible name." Seward, falling in line behind his boss, quickly sent copies of the preliminary proclamation to his diplomats in the field. "The interests of humanity have now become identified with the cause of our country," he told his minister in London. Yet the secretary of state was still not completely convinced of the wisdom of emancipation. He wrote to his daughter wondering whether the proclamation might be premature. Seward lamented the "confused" state of American foreign relations. Even Lincoln later conceded that he had serious doubts about the timing.[86]

Abolitionists responded with an outpouring of emotion. "It is the beginning of the end of the rebellion; the beginning of the new life of the nation," Greeley exulted in the *Tribune*. "God bless Abraham Lincoln." The following day the newspaperman wrote that the proclamation took a nation "sunk in the semi-barbarism of a medieval age to the light and civilization of the Nineteenth Christian Century." On the night of September 24, a huge crowd arrived at the White House and spilled onto the front lawn. John Hay looked on as revelers hurdled the iron gates and "filled every nook and corner of the ground entrance as quietly and instantly as molten metal fills a mold." To Hay, the mass of elated merrymakers appeared "lucid and diaphanous in the clear obscure like the architecture of a dream." When Lincoln appeared at the window over the north portico, he appeared unusually dignified, Hay reported. The president obliged the crowd with a few brief remarks. "It is now for the country and the world to pass judgment" on the proclamation, Lincoln told the demonstrators, "and, may be, take action upon it."[87] The president would not sign the final version of the document until New Year's Day, 1863—a hundred-day interval that was intended partly to give Confederate states the opportunity to return to the Union fold before the proclamation was final.

Lincoln, meanwhile, was making other plans to try to simultaneously sway public opinion in Europe. In late September he repeatedly summoned Edward Everett, the cosmopolitan former secretary of state and minister to Britain, to the Executive Mansion. The president's allies had been urging him to send Everett to Europe as an unofficial envoy "to exercise a salutary influence to discourage hostile intervention." The former diplomat was not a big advocate of Lincoln's emancipation proposal. "The matter," Everett wrote Charles Francis Adams in London, "stood better without any proclamation. . . . It raises many troublesome theoretical questions and augments the difficulties under which Union men already labor in the Border States." Nevertheless, Everett was a strong supporter of the president and the Union war effort. At the White House, the former secretary of state found Lincoln still grumbling about Antietam. The president acknowledged the campaign was well fought, but complained that "he did not know why McClellan did not follow up his advantage," as Everett later described the meeting in his diary.

Lincoln told the former secretary of state that he was doing his best to maintain a "good temper" nonetheless.

The president explained to Everett that he wanted to send him to Europe—but the appointment would be tricky. If Lincoln named the distinguished former diplomat to an official post as special envoy, the president's regular men in the field might balk. On the other hand, if he gave Everett an unofficial role, Seward—who was already complaining about the freelancing of Sumner and others—might feel slighted. Lincoln tried to walk a thin line, ultimately drafting an "excessively non-committal and curiously characteristic" letter of introduction, and making an effort to keep Seward in the loop. Everett, however, ultimately declined the appointment, arguing that he was not the right man for the job.[88]

Lincoln badly needed help explaining his policy to Europeans. The continent's ruling classes reacted warily to the preliminary proclamation. Palmerston complained that the document was a piece of "trash." The London *Times* wrote that Lincoln was acting like some sort of "moral American pope." The president, the paper proclaimed, was like "a Chinaman beating his two swords together to frighten his enemy." The British newspaper published increasingly lurid and provocative editorials suggesting that Lincoln sought to unleash a slave revolt. "He will appeal to the black blood of the African," the paper warned, "he will whisper of the pleasures of spoil and of the gratification of yet fiercer instincts; and when blood begins to flow and shrieks come piercing through the darkness, Mr. Lincoln will wait till the rising flames tell that all is consummated, and then he will rub his hands and think that revenge is sweet." *Blackwood's* magazine sniped that the document was "monstrous, reckless, devilish."[89]

Lincoln was infuriated by European reactions to his proposal. The president's son Robert later recalled that "what chiefly astonished and grieved" Lincoln during the war was that "the organs of English opinion which had censured Americans for slavery, turned round and condemned them when actual steps were taken for putting it down." The hypocrisy of it all, Robert added, seriously undermined American respect for the island nation.[90]

Still, the president listened when allies urged him to tweak his draft to make it more palatable to Europeans. The language of Lincoln's preliminary proclamation worried Marx's old editor at the *Tribune*, Charles A. Dana. Dana told Seward that the document could be read as if it encouraged slave revolts. The phrasing, he wrote the secretary of state, "*jars* on me like a *wrong tone in music*. . . . This is the only 'bad egg' I see in 'that pudding'—and I fear may go far to make it less palatable than it deserves to be." In the final draft, the president ultimately altered the text to address the qualms of Dana and others.[91]

If Marx had similar concerns, they have not been recorded. He wrote to Engels that October lauding the "world transforming" turn of events across the Atlantic. There was "nothing more disgusting," he told Engels, than the outcry among British elites over the preliminary proclamation. If anything, Marx thought the American president seemed too timid. "All Lincoln's acts," he insisted, "seem like the mean, pettifogging conditions that one lawyer puts to his opponent." Still, Marx added, "this does not change their historic content."[92]

The proclamation prompted the president to intensify his efforts to establish overseas colonies of American blacks. If slaves were going to be freed, Lincoln believed, they needed somewhere to go. The president had told a delegation of black activists earlier that year that he considered it "selfish" of them to remain in the United States after emancipation. Separation and colonization, he explained, would be "better for us both." Shortly after taking office, Lincoln had dispatched his brother-in-law, Ninian W. Edwards, to investigate one potential site in what is now Colombia. Edwards, in his report to the president, stressed the economic and geopolitical advantages of the site. It offered a strategically located lagoon that might "save whole squadrons" of American ships in need of refuge. Edwards also lauded the "inexhaustible" coal supply and "vast saving" that the venture might bring the U.S. government. Yet after some members of Lincoln's cabinet—including his naval secretary, Gideon Welles—had objected to the plans, Lincoln had temporarily set the project aside.[93]

Now, two days after issuing the preliminary proclamation, Lincoln called another meeting of the cabinet to discuss colonization once again. Welles still opposed such a move, as did Seward. "I am always," the secretary of state explained, "for bringing men and states *into* this Union, never for taking any *out*." Seward's longtime secretary, George Baker, later explained that colonization was the only substantive issue on which Lincoln and Seward strongly disagreed. Still, at Lincoln's request, the secretary of state canvassed diplomats in France, Britain, and the Netherlands to determine whether the European powers might possess suitable territories in the Caribbean for colonies of free blacks. Lincoln, meanwhile, asked Congress to pass a constitutional amendment that would fund potential colonies. "I cannot make it better known than it already is," Lincoln said, "that I strongly favor colonization."[94]

Even as Lincoln tried to refine such ambitious projects, nettlesome smaller diplomatic flaps distracted him. In October, Charles Sumner wrote Lincoln urging him to fire his envoys in the Sandwich Islands. The local government had been complaining about the "intemperate habits" and inability to focus of David L. Gregg—an old friend of Lincoln's who was now advising King Kamehameha IV. Close trade ties with the Sandwich Islands were particularly important to the northeastern merchants that Sumner represented. Union leaders also worried that Confederate agents might use the islands to outfit privateers. To make matters worse, French forces were rumored to be working to enhance their clout on the archipelago. "Our influence in the Sandwich Islands," Sumner told Lincoln, "is seriously impaired by the character of our representatives there. . . . For the sake of our good name and of our just influence there, and especially of those commercial interests in which Massachusetts has so large a share, I trust that the present commissioner will be recalled."

Lincoln's old friend Gregg tried to shift the blame onto Thomas J. Dryer, the American commissioner on the islands. "He is rude, rough and repulsive to genteel society," Gregg complained to Lincoln. Dryer's "backwoods style" might be "appreciated at County Court gatherings, where whiskey more than reason is the convincing argument," Gregg said. But Dryer's behavior the last time he was invited to the palace was so disruptive that he would not be invited again. "I do not deem it necessary to mention particulars," Gregg told the president. "They are almost too bad to mention. . . . Pray send us a gentleman who will not disgrace his character or give countenance to the idea that we are inferior . . . to the rest of the world in our diplomacy." Lincoln ultimately replaced Dryer in January, admonishing Seward to appoint "a tip-top man there next time."[95]

As Lincoln sought to reform the diplomatic corps abroad, he also pushed for a more aggressive strategy on the battlefield at home. The president finally tired of McClellan's cautious war making. For a year and a half, Lincoln had patiently tolerated the general's inaction. He barely protested when McClellan—who privately referred to his commander in chief as "the original gorilla"—insulted him. Lincoln complained that McClellan had the "slows." But the president had always indulged the pompous officer. McClellan, a Democrat who opposed abolition, had complained to his wife that he would not fight for a slave revolt. He had been warning Lincoln that abolition would alienate European decision makers. Now Lincoln decided that he had heard enough from his insubordinate general. The day after the 1862 election, Lincoln dismissed McClellan. To Marx, who was convinced of the cautious general's "mediocrity," the decision amounted to another promising step toward "the *revolutionary* waging of war."[96]

That is precisely what worried Europeans. On October 7, the British Liberal William Gladstone gave a speech to a raucous mass meeting in England in which he seemed to recognize the legitimacy of Confederate independence. "We may have our own opinions about slavery," Gladstone declared, "we may be for or against the South;

Lincoln believed that defining America's place in the world was at the core of the Union's mission. The "central idea" of the Northern effort, he explained, was to prove "that popular government is not an absurdity."

Left: As an ambitious young politician in Springfield, Lincoln cultivated the support of the powerful Edwards family, which held weekly salons where guests were greeted in French. *Right:* Mary Todd Lincoln had grown up in a Kentucky house adorned with French mahogany furniture and Belgian rugs. She attended a boarding school run by Parisian aristocrats who had fled the country in the aftermath of the French Revolution.

Lincoln's impetuous law partner Billy Herndon complained that his friend was harming himself politically by his opposition to the Mexican War. "I will stake my life," Lincoln responded, "that if you had been in my place, you would have voted just as I did."

Lincoln was almost certainly in the audience in Lexington, Kentucky, in November 1847, as an elderly Henry Clay delivered a moving speech opposing the Mexican War.

Left: Lincoln initially worried that he was unprepared to manage foreign affairs. "I don't know anything about diplomacy," he told one European envoy. "I will be very apt to make blunders." *Right:* Secretary of State William Henry Seward proved to be a capable statesman—yet he also possessed an outsize ego and a sometimes volatile temperament. "When he was loaded," recalled the son of one of Lincoln's diplomats, "his tongue wagged."

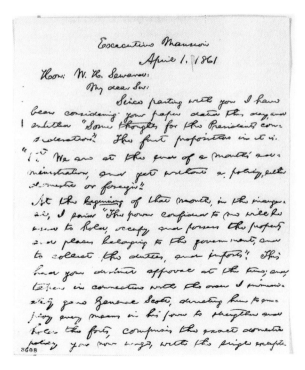

Holograph of Lincoln's response to Seward's "foreign war panacea."

As First Lady, Mary Lincoln meddled in diplomatic appointments. She urged Seward to name her personal choice to a post in the Sandwich Islands and demanded that Lincoln appoint one of her favorite clergymen to a consulship in Scotland.

Left: Lincoln's minister to Russia, Cassius Marcellus Clay, was an old friend of the First Lady's. The president came to believe that Clay possessed "a great deal of conceit and very little sense." *Right:* Charles Sumner, the powerful Massachusetts senator who chaired the foreign-relations committee, often tangled with Seward, who complained that there were "too many secretaries of state in Washington."

Britain's Lord Palmerston generally opposed intervening in the Civil War. Britain's "best and true policy," he wrote his foreign minister in 1861, would be "to keep quite clear of the conflict."

As a journalist in London, Karl Marx steadfastly supported the Union. The sooner bourgeois America defeated the slaveholding aristocracy, Marx believed, the sooner the proletariat could triumph over both.

Foreign observers were baffled by the inscrutable French emperor Napoleon III. One Lincoln aide dubbed him the Sphinx of the Tuileries. Otto von Bismarck described the French monarch as "a great unfathomed capacity."

The influential French empress Eugénie was troubled by the rise of the United States. "Sooner or later," she said, "we shall have to declare war on America."

Left: Tall, blue-eyed General Joseph Hooker—nicknamed Handsome Captain by local women during the Mexican War—longed to invade Mexico again. The general, recalled one contemporary, was "very eager to raise an army on the Pacific coast for a fight with a foreign nation." *Right:* Radical Republicans such as Maryland congressman Henry Winter Davis urged Lincoln to take a harder line over the French occupation of Mexico. Davis used the issue—unsuccessfully—to try to unseat the president during the 1864 campaign.

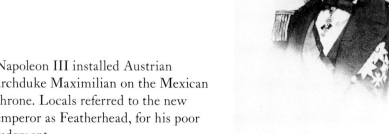

Napoleon III installed Austrian archduke Maximilian on the Mexican throne. Locals referred to the new emperor as Featherhead, for his poor judgment.

Left: Lincoln's glib young personal secretary John Hay thought the president's foreign envoys were "generally men of ability," but also "not always of that particular style of education which fits men for diplomacy." *Right:* More than thirty years after Lincoln's assassination, Hay was appointed secretary of state—a position he held under presidents William McKinley and Theodore Roosevelt. Hay once gave Roosevelt a ring with a lock of Lincoln's hair encased in it.

As the war drew to a close, Lincoln's demeanor alternated between relief and melancholy. "There has been war enough," the president told a reporter who wondered whether the Union and Confederacy would now unite to invade Mexico.

but there is no doubt that Jefferson Davis and other leaders of the South have made an army; they are making, it appears, a navy; and they have made what is more than either—they have made a nation." Throughout the fall, British interventionists appeared to be making headway in convincing Palmerston to take action. A few days after the chancellor of the exchequer's speech, Palmerston remarked that Gladstone was "not far wrong in pronouncing by anticipation the National Independence of the South." Only days later, however, the prime minister backtracked once again. By October 22, Palmerston wrote that he had "very much come back to our original view of the matter." British statesmen, he concluded, "must continue merely to be lookers-on till the war shall have taken a more decided turn." By November, the likelihood of European intervention had lessened considerably.[97]

As the New Year approached, however, the pressure on Lincoln only increased. The defeat at Fredericksburg in mid-December shattered Northern morale. Radicals, emboldened by Lincoln's decision to issue the proclamation, made a determined effort to oust the cautious Seward. The president found himself besieged by Congress, his own cabinet, and the press. "If there is a worse place than hell," Lincoln complained, "I am in it."[98]

Greeley's minions, meanwhile, worked feverishly to gin up support for emancipation. In early December, Sumner wrote Greeley's deputy in New York urging abolitionists to help strengthen public opinion "by argument, persuasion, appeal[s] of all kinds." Two days later, in a *Tribune* editorial, Greeley downplayed the notion that emancipation could induce a European intervention. With tensions rising in Italy, Austria, and Poland, the Continental powers had too much on their plates already. "The greater the danger of collision among themselves," Greeley wrote, "the less European governments will feel an inclination to meddle in transatlantic strife." The *Tribune* editor's analysis, for once, was dead-on.[99]

For all the winter tensions, by December, Lincoln and Seward actually had reason for optimism when it came to international relations. "A year ago," Seward wrote to Lincoln's emissary in Paris, "it seemed that any foreign nation might assail and destroy us at a blow. I am sure that no one foreign nation would now conceive such an attempt, while combination of several powers for that purpose is impossible." According to Seward, the president was the most content with foreign affairs that he had ever seen him. The secretary of state reported that the continued "warnings of danger" from U.S. diplomats in the field embarrassed Lincoln, who was otherwise "disposed to take a more cheering view of our foreign relations, at this time, than he has allowed himself to indulge at any previous period since the Civil War commenced."[100]

Part of the reason for Lincoln's optimism may have been that the president finally had an opportunity to reconcile his realism with his idealism. Even as Lincoln pursued America's national interest, he also appealed to what Thomas Jefferson had dubbed "a decent respect to the opinions of mankind." With the burgeoning mass media shrinking the world, such considerations were more important than ever. At the suggestion of his treasury secretary, Lincoln added a line to the Emancipation Proclamation invoking "the considerate judgment of mankind, and the gracious favor of Almighty God." (Charles Sumner wrote one correspondent shortly after the New Year arguing that while the "last sentence was actually framed by Chase . . . I believe I first suggested it to him and to the President. I urged that he should close with 'something about *justice* and *God*.'")[101]

In his annual message to Congress, Lincoln acknowledged that American foreign relations remained tenuous but claimed they were not as bad as might be expected considering how "unhappily distracted" the country appeared to Europeans. In any case, Lincoln believed that he was about to unleash a potent new weapon. With the looming Emancipation Proclamation, the president would attempt to bridge the Atlantic and speak directly to British workers. If Americans could only finish the job at home, Lincoln told Congress, the result would resonate across the globe.

"Fellow-citizens," the president declared, "*we* cannot escape history. We of this Congress and this administration, will be remembered in spite of ourselves. No personal significance, or insignificance, can spare one or another of us. The fiery trial through which we pass, will light us down, in honor or dishonor, to the latest generation. We *say* we are for the Union. The world will not forget that we say this. We know how to save the Union. The world knows we do know how to save it. We—even *we here*—hold the power, and bear the responsibility. In *giving* freedom to the *slave*, we *assure* freedom to the *free*—honorable alike in what we give, and what we preserve. We shall nobly save, or meanly lose, the last best, hope of earth. Other means may succeed; this could not fail. The way is plain, peaceful, generous, just—a way which, if followed, the world will forever applaud, and God must forever bless."[102]

The Labor Kings of London

The American press, led by the *New York Tribune*, had helped set the stage for emancipation. Newspapers printed editorials lauding abolition. Fiery orators like Wendell Phillips riled up huge crowds. The whole dynamic fed on itself. The papers reported on the speeches, the public debated the editorials—and soon the entire country had become a massive echo chamber. Lincoln raised his own megaphone at key moments, writing public letters and corresponding with influential editors. Yet in the new art of public relations, the old laws of power did not neatly apply.[103]

Marx had long recognized that power politics had taken on new rules. The novel technologies of the telegraph and the steam press had helped fuel the European revolutions a decade earlier. One of Marx's earliest editorials as a young journalist had been an analysis of press freedoms in Prussia. Yet despite the proliferation of new media, he remained frustrated by the failure of Britain's working classes to revolt. Part of the problem, he was convinced, was that the nation's newspapers remained in the hands of venal tycoons. Marx considered the London *Times*—dubbed the Thunderer by Britons—the worst offender. He derided the paper's editors as "public opinion-mongers" and their reports as "paid sophistry."[104]

Marx found it difficult to control even smaller newspapers that catered to Britain's working classes. One of them, the *Bee-Hive*, persistently abused Lincoln and the Union in the early years of the Civil War. The American president, the newspaper's editors insisted, was a "mindless man." His cabinet consisted of "atrocious jobbers, who live better by hostilities than they ever do in peace." Even in the wake of the preliminary Emancipation Proclamation—which was intended, after all, partly to shift the opinions of British workers— the *Bee-Hive* remained antagonistic. How could Marx successfully spread "correct views" in America and on the Continent, he must have wondered, if he could not even shape public opinion in his own backyard?[105]

Frustrated by the hard line of the labor movement's house organs, labor leaders in Britain's industrial districts began looking for other methods of expressing their support for the Union. One solution was to organize "monster meetings" of workers. Prominent speakers would laud the Northern cause, and the raucous audiences could then vote on resolutions of support. Newspapers—even hostile ones—would be forced to cover the meetings. The organization of mass gatherings, therefore, offered one novel means of co-opting Britain's conservative media. Marx, for one, appreciated the new tool. Monster meetings, he wrote to Engels the day after Lincoln issued the Emancipation Proclamation, "cost nothing" but "bring in a great deal 'internationally.'"[106]

Starting in November 1862, a cascade of popular demonstrations rolled across Britain. Over the following two years, British workers held more than a hundred such gatherings. The Emancipation Proclamation, Charles Francis Adams observed, had "rallied the sympathies of the working classes." The London *Times* sniped that the crowds consisted of "nobodies." But Lincoln's diplomats reported home that the meetings were actually organized by a combination of religious dissenters and middle-class agitators. In London, huge halls were packed to capacity. Swarms of demonstrators spilled out into the streets. Inside, the mere mention of Lincoln's name inspired euphoric whelps. "I think in every town in the Kingdom," John Bright wrote to Sumner in January, "a public meeting would go by an overwhelming majority in favor of President Lincoln and of the North."[107]

Marx wrote newspaper dispatches about the meetings, helping to bolster the impression that popular enthusiasm was building. He believed that such demonstrations were the key to wresting concessions from Britain's ruling class. "No important innovation," he wrote, "no decisive measure, has ever been carried out in this country without pressure from without." The new burst of working-class energy was a positive omen. Marx saw the meetings as "a splendid new proof of the indestructible soundness of the English popular masses." Still, if the workers wanted change, he insisted, they would have to remain visible on the national stage.[108]

Lincoln, too, did his best to encourage the demonstrators. Any sympathy he might win from ordinary Britons and Frenchmen, he believed, could help to exert pressure on European decision makers to support the North—or at least stay out of the war. The resolutions passed in at least some of the gatherings had actually been carefully crafted by Lincoln and his team. The messages contained a decidedly moral appeal. In one example, Lincoln's men offered a resolution declaring that no slaveholding nation should be recognized by "the family of Christian and civilized nations." Sumner shipped the text across the Atlantic to Bright. In some cases, the Lincoln government actually sent secret payments to help fund the meetings, which the president believed could help convince British statesmen that intervention would be an unpopular policy.

Lincoln, meanwhile, wrote public letters appealing to the sympathies of workers. "I have understood well," he told laborers in Manchester, "that the duty of self-preservation rests solely with the American people. But I have at the same time been aware that favor or disfavor of foreign nations might have a material influence in enlarging and prolonging the struggle with disloyal men in which the country is engaged. A fair examination of history has seemed to authorize a belief that the past action and influences of the United States were generally regarded as having been beneficent toward mankind. I have therefore reckoned upon the forbearance of nations. Circumstances . . . induced me especially to expect that if justice and good faith should be practiced by the United States, they would encounter no hostile influence on the part of Great Britain." Lincoln told the demonstrators that his hopes now appeared to be well placed, and thanked the workers for their "sublime Christian heroism." The meetings, he declared, provided "an energetic and reinspiring assurance of the inherent power of truth and of the ultimate and universal triumph of justice, humanity, and freedom."[109]

Seward continued to privately resent the proclamation. At an intimate dinner with the president's old friend Orville Browning in late January, the secretary of state complained (as Browning later told his diary) that he "regretted the policy of the administration—thought the proclamations were unfortunate, and that we would have been nearer the end of the war and the end of slavery both without them." Still, Seward sighed that the decision was "now past, and we must look to the future." At least relations with the European powers seemed to be improving. The secretary of state recalled that "it was not alone the abolition clamor at home that induced the president to issue [the Emancipation Proclamation], but that he was farther influenced by the wishes of foreign nations who could not be made to understand our condition." Seward acknowledged that "there was no prospect of foreign interference now—that France and England were jealous of each other and neither had any intention of interfering with us."[110]

On March 26, 1863, British workers organized their most ambitious meeting yet, at St. James's Hall in London. Marx was among the spectators in the throbbing, cheering crowd. Some historians have speculated that the communist actually helped to put together the event. Henry Adams, who also attended and sent a report home to Washington about the meeting, later recalled that he had assumed Marx had taken the lead. Modern scholars are less certain about what role—if any—Marx played in organizing the gathering. We do know, however, that the emotional demonstration impressed the ornery philosopher. "The workers," Marx reported to Engels two weeks later, "spoke *excellently*." The following year Marx lauded the St. James's Hall demonstrators as the "labor kings of London." The meeting, Marx maintained to a friend, "prevented Palmerston from declaring war upon the United States."[111]

Marx's analysis was far too simplistic. Palmerston could be combative and at times seemed to favor the dissolution of the United States, yet the British prime minister actually acted as a realistic check on more interventionist members of his cabinet. At first, the news of the Emancipation Proclamation seemed to push Palmerston closer to the interventionist position. Eventually, however, worries about proliferating crises closer to home kept him from reaching out. The popular enthusiasm unleashed by the Emancipation Proclamation further cemented the British prime minister's resolve to refrain from intervention.[112] Lincoln's men in London gleefully took note of the shift in opinions. "The Emancipation Proclamation," Henry Adams wrote home to his brother, "has done more for us here than all our former victories and all our diplomacy. It is creating an almost convulsive reaction in our favor."[113]

Marx discovered that the War Between the States had dramatically reinvigorated European workers—a goal that he had been trying to accomplish for two decades. "It would, indeed, be difficult to over-estimate the importance of the Civil War for the subsequent history of the British Labour movement," writes Royden Harrison, a leading scholar of socialism. "Even more than the Polish and Italian national movements, the Civil War helped to widen the horizons of the British workers, and prepared their leaders for participation in [international organizations of workingmen]."[114]

In Britain's industrial districts, laborers were becoming politically active out of necessity. When newspapers were delivered, workers would read the dispatches out loud, attracting a crowd. City employees posted the latest issues on the walls of railroad stations and public buildings. Almost every edition contained details of the American conflict. With mills shuttered, out-of-work laborers attended special schools and learned to read. The rise in literacy helped to fuel political awareness and demands for change. Still, political leaders found the new readers of Britain's textile districts difficult to propagandize. Nineteenth-century newspapers, modern scholars emphasize, mirrored public attitudes as much as they guided them.[115]

In the case of the *Bee-Hive*, public attitudes seem to have actually played a role in ousting the paper's pro-Confederate editor. In January, as the public pressure was intensifying, the *Bee-Hive*'s editorial board fired its chief. The paper quickly swung its support behind Lincoln and the North. It attacked Britain's ruling class, which it derided as "a few effete aristocrats who love their moneybags more than their fellow men." The paper reserved an entire page for the massive meeting in St. James's Hall. Lincoln was portrayed as a hero to the workers, many of whom considered themselves "wage slaves." Marx worked feverishly to gain control of the paper for his increasingly active international organization of workers. "It is impossible," he later wrote Engels, "to have a movement here without a press organ."[116]

Marx and the political program he supported were gaining ground. He had always insisted that it was imperative that the working classes "master themselves the mysteries of international politics" if they were to succeed. Now Marx began to put his theories into action. Marshaling the workers was exhausting. The philosopher spent days at mass meetings, late nights at committee meetings, and hours signing new membership cards in London pubs. Marx told Engels that he was overwhelmed. His organizing work "haunts me like a nightmare," he complained. His health continued to fail. Uncomfortable boils spread across his body, as they did almost every winter. Marx complained to Engels that he had grown a "second Frankenstein on my back." Marx sometimes took "medicines," including opium, arsenic, and Spanish fly in an attempt to cure the sores.[117]

Marx, meanwhile, was beginning to gain a greater respect for Lincoln. But his support had never been a sentimental thing. The philosopher's careful analysis of economic and demographic trends told him that the Federal government was sure to overwhelm the Confederacy eventually. Although Marx supported the "bourgeois republic" in the short run, he believed a Union victory would ultimately bring about the system's demise. "Most observers who spoke of the promise of America," notes the scholar Laurence Moore, "found that promise in America's difference from Europe. Marx and Engels turned this vision on its head. America could become a promised land to the extent that it became just like Europe—and multiplied its vices." Marx's old boss Horace Greeley had once complained about "the unprincipled egotism that is the soul of European diplomacy." Marx, on the other hand, believed that America—like all capitalist countries—was also drowning in "the icy water of egotistical calculation."[118]

Lincoln believed strongly that human beings, whether American or European, tend to act in their own self-interest. Yet that worldview—and, in fact, his entire approach to foreign affairs—took on dramatic new dimensions with his decision to issue the Emancipation Proclamation. Until now, Lincoln had maintained that "reason, cold, calculating, unimpassioned reason" should be the principle that guides policy, including global affairs. During the Mexican War, he had coolly worked to avoid upsetting the sectional balance. In the first days of the current conflict, Lincoln had calmly reined in his hot-tempered secretary of state. After the seizure of the *Trent*, the president had tamped down passions and ultimately made a deeply unsatisfying—but also eminently reasonable—decision to release the captives.[119]

Yet with the Emancipation Proclamation, Lincoln reimagined his core principle—an innovation that the new world of the mid-nineteenth century demanded. The decree still represented a calculation of national interest. Lincoln hoped that freeing slaves in the Confederate states would both preserve the Union at home and win sympathies abroad. The decision, he later explained, was "not a question of sentiment or taste, but one of physical force which may be measured and estimated as horse-power and Steam-power are measured and estimated." Lincoln, to be sure, had long opposed slavery. Yet he had also believed that the Constitution protected the institution. Now, however, the president merged his old attempt to preserve the Union with the new tool of the Emancipation Proclamation. The synthesis, he argued, would help to defeat the Confederacy while fundamentally improving the Union in the process.[120]

Crafting—and ultimately selling—that policy required a creative genius who could marshal all the tools of his age to convince his countrymen of its merits. The proclamation's efficacy as an instrument of foreign relations is still contested by historians. There is, however, no debating that the measure marked a major step forward in the evolution of presidential power. "The effectiveness of the President's personal propaganda warfare could not be measured," writes historian David Donald, "for it was not so much public statements or popular rallies as the internal dynamics of British and French politics, plus fears of ultimate American reprisal, that determined a course of neutrality for the two major European powers. But for Lincoln the opportunity to use the White House as a pulpit, to speak out over the dissonant voices of foreign leaders to the common people, daringly broadened the powers of the Presidency."[121]

Yet even as Lincoln expanded executive influence, the office was taking its toll on the man. In February 1863, as the monster meetings in Britain intensified, a White House staff member found Lincoln looking "worn and haggard." The president's hands trembled as he attempted to write a letter. Lincoln, the staffer observed, was "growing feeble." The president would need his strength in the months to come. The Emancipation Proclamation may have ended the threat of British intervention. But it did not end Lincoln's foreign-affairs troubles. The proclamation may have actually emboldened France's emperor, Napoleon III, to challenge Lincoln's government for control of North America.[122]

Marx considered the French emperor "clumsily cunning, knavishly naïve, doltishly sublime, a calculated superstition, a pathetic burlesque, a cleverly stupid anachronism, a world-historic piece of buffoonery and an undecipherable hieroglyphic." In the realm of foreign affairs, however, Napoleon III could also be a dangerous man. The French emperor, Marx told readers of the *New York Tribune*, was "a reckless gambler, a desperate adventurer, who would as soon dice with royal bones as any other if the game promised to leave him a winner." As the war ground on, France's gambling emperor prepared to bet against Abraham Lincoln.[123]

Lincoln vs. Napoleon

A S THE CIVIL WAR ENTERED ITS FINAL DAYS, MARY LINCOLN WORRIED THAT HER HUSBAND WAS BEGINNING TO LOOK "SO BROKEN-HEARTED, SO COMPLETELY WORN OUT." IT WAS A judgment that many visitors shared during those last months of the president's life. When the abolitionist preacher Henry Ward Beecher dropped in on Lincoln at the Executive Mansion in late winter 1865, he found the exhausted president alone in his receiving room. Lincoln's hair was shooting up "every way for Sunday," the minister recalled. "It looked as though it was an abandoned stubble field." The president wore a pair of slippers, and his suit vest flapped free. Lincoln welcomed the minister, and then sank into his chair. The president, Beecher later recalled, "looked as though every limb wanted to drop off his body."[1]

In one sense, Lincoln had little reason to be weary. For a year and a half now, his armies had been relentlessly on the offensive. The early days of tentative war making were long past. The president had replaced hesitating figures like George B. McClellan with effective new generals like Ulysses S. Grant and William T. Sherman. Within one week in July 1863, Union forces had bested their Southern foes at both Gettysburg and Vicksburg, decisively shifting the war's momentum. Fierce fighting continued for more than a year in the wastes of northern Virginia. Yet by the last months of the war, Union success appeared all but inevitable. Lincoln's army, led by the irascible Sherman, finally captured both Atlanta and Savannah in late 1864. As the New Year dawned, Sherman's troops were still on the move, cutting a devastating path through the American South.

By the start of 1865, the president had also subdued the most dangerous of his personal critics. Throughout the previous year, Lincoln's antagonists—including members of his own party and cabinet—had been angling to defeat him in his bid for reelection. Even some of Lincoln's diplomats in Europe threatened to come home and campaign against him. Buoyed by the success of his armies in the weeks leading up to the election, however, Lincoln had ultimately won a second term by a huge margin. Grant forwarded a message of congratulations to the victorious candidate saying that in Europe, Lincoln's reelection would be "worth more to the country than a battle won." The "importance of this event, in its influence upon the reputation of the nation," agreed Charles Francis Adams in London, "would be difficult to overestimate."[2]

Meanwhile, a series of crises on the Continent unrelated to the Civil War were preoccupying the great powers. In early 1863, Polish rebels had revolted against Russian domination of their country, begging in vain for British and French assistance. The following year, Prussian and Austrian armies had invaded the Danish-controlled duchies of Schleswig and Holstein—a move that shocked European liberals and threatened to upset the region's fragile balance of power. Palmerston had once vowed to defend the territories against aggressors. Yet in the final calculus, he determined that it would be wiser to stand aside. The whole drama undermined the Anglo-French relationship and exposed the surprising weakness of the world's most powerful nation. By the early months of 1865, the threat of British intervention in the American Civil War had vanished.[3]

And yet, the French emperor, Napoleon III, remained one lingering cause for anxiety. The Confederacy, he warned Lincoln's representative in Paris, would be too "difficult to subdue." The emperor believed that North and South "would never come together again." Napoleon had been working steadily, almost since the start of the American conflict, to extend French influence into North America. As the Union and Confederate armies began to clash, he convinced British and Spanish policy makers to join a three-way intervention in Mexico, advertised as a mission to recover unpaid debts. Actually, Napoleon's scheme was an ambitious project to restore France's imperial prestige, improve its economy, and bolster its geopolitical position.

Within months Britain and Spain cooled on the adventure and withdrew their forces. Napoleon, on the other hand, decided to double down on Mexico. Even as the Polish and Danish crises simmered, he continued to send troops across the Atlantic. Ultimately the emperor installed his puppet, the Austrian archduke Maximilian, on the Mexican throne. "No more sinister project, in terms of American interest, American influence, and American ideas," writes historian Dexter Perkins, "has ever been conceived in the history of the Monroe Doctrine."[4]

Lincoln recognized that Napoleon's troops just south of the border (and the emperor's desire to mediate an end to the war raging north of it) represented serious foreign-policy problems. Still, as Lincoln's army—and his power—grew, the president's options for confronting Napoleon also increased dramatically. Lincoln saw that the tumult on the Continent severely limited the European powers' freedom of maneuver in the New World. The president told one visitor in a moment of frustration that he would "be d[amne]d if he wouldn't get 1,000,000 men if France dares to interfere."[5]

As the Union victories mounted, support for a dash south of the border built. In Congress, hawks like Henry Winter Davis urged Lincoln to challenge the French. The Northeastern penny press egged on the radicals. The *New York Herald*, a forceful advocate of a Mexican expedition, suggested "forming together a grand army to drive the invaders into the Gulf." By early 1865, Russia's minister in Washington reported home that "a sure source" told him that

Lincoln's men were urging an invasion. Some Northerners viewed a joint expedition as a means of welcoming Confederate soldiers back into the Federal fold. France's chargé d'affaires in the capital wrote his superiors that a war with French troops in Mexico could serve as a "pivot of reconciliation" between North and South.[6]

The Progress of Our Arms

N ow, in early 1865, Lincoln finally had to make a decision. Francis P. Blair Sr., the distinguished former Democrat and the father of Lincoln's postmaster general, had arranged a summit with Confederate representatives at Hampton Roads, Virginia, in part to consider the prospect of a joint invasion. The president boarded a train south to attend the conference with just one aide and a small bag. Seward had already gone ahead, carrying with him two bottles of champagne and three more of whisky to help lubricate the negotiations. On February 3—just over two months before his assassination—Lincoln and his secretary of state met the Confederate commissioners in the saloon aboard the *River Queen*, a steamboat that had been draped in red-white-and-blue bunting for the occasion.[7]

The Confederate delegation included Vice President Alexander Stephens, who had served with Lincoln in the House of Representatives. Back then, like Lincoln, Stephens had given a passionate speech in the House chamber challenging Polk's conduct of the Mexican War. At the time, Lincoln had written to Herndon lauding Stephens's remarks as "the very best speech, of an hour's length, I ever heard. My old, withered, dry eyes, are full of tears yet." Now, however, seventeen years later, the circumstances in Mexico had changed dramatically. Stephens prepared to urge his old legislative ally to send his armies into Mexico to oust the French forces.[8]

Stephens—whom Lincoln had once described as "a little slim, pale-faced, consumptive man"—argued that a joint invasion could help bring the warring factions together. It was important, the

Confederate vice president suggested, to find some issue that would "divert the public mind" from the conflict, in which both sides shared "a common feeling and interest." Stephens held forth for some time about "the so-called Monroe Doctrine," as one witness put it. The tiny man who had once eloquently opposed an American invasion of Mexico now proposed taking "the whole of the North American continent by the states of the two confederacies." Such a move, Stephens argued, could engender "fraternal feelings" while at the same time keeping foreign powers from establishing a foothold in the New World.[9]

Both Lincoln and Seward acknowledged that they were concerned about the French emperor's invasion. Seward seemed particularly sympathetic to Stephens's plan. The proposal was not so different, after all, from the secretary of state's own "foreign war panacea." Yet Lincoln, despite his earlier outburst about raising a million-man army, remained wary. The president pointed out that Congress would need to authorize any new conflict. And the Union could not afford to undermine its own war effort at home. Even if North and South could settle their domestic differences, Lincoln added, he feared the two sides might turn against each other again during any potential Mexican operation. The whole scheme, Lincoln finally concluded, simply "could not be entertained."[10]

After four hours, the meeting broke up. Stephens asked Lincoln one more time to reconsider his Mexico proposal. "Well, Stephens," Lincoln replied, "I will reconsider it; but I do not think my mind will change." The president said that he had already "maturely considered" the scheme and had decided that it was unworkable. The conference at an end, the Confederate commissioners then boarded a small boat and headed back to their own craft. As the Southerners drifted away, Seward decided to send them one of the leftover bottles of champagne as a goodwill gesture. The secretary of state dispatched a black aide in a small rowboat after the Confederates to deliver the gift. When it arrived, the commissioners thanked Seward by flourishing their handkerchiefs. Lincoln's secretary of state lifted a boatswain's trumpet and bellowed good-naturedly across the water, "Keep the champagne, but return the negro!"[11]

Lincoln, in one sense, got lucky with the outcome of the Mexican crisis. He benefitted, at least in part, from fortunate circumstances. The European ferment over Poland and Schleswig-Holstein, combined with Napoleon's own hubris, certainly made the episode more manageable for the president. Lincoln, a lifelong fatalist, often felt as though he were being buffeted by powerful winds that he could not fully control. "I claim not to have controlled events," he once explained, "but confess plainly that events have controlled me." Sometimes that worldview inspired hopelessness and melancholy. Yet in other cases, like the French thrust into Mexico, it engendered patience and long-term thinking. In international affairs, where major shifts in the power grid are often the product of vast, impersonal forces, a little healthy fatalism is not always such a bad thing.[12]

And yet the Mexican crisis also demanded a series of determined acts of will from the president. Lincoln understood that the Union military effort at home had a profound impact on his diplomacy abroad. Nothing would unnerve Napoleon as effectively as the massive Northern army surging south through the hills of Georgia. As the Civil War progressed, the president delved deeply into military affairs, studying thick tomes on the subject that he had borrowed from the Library of Congress. John Hay recalled hearing Lincoln's creaking footsteps pacing in the White House late at night as the president examined the latest volume. As the fighting intensified, Lincoln began to devise strategy himself. He relentlessly questioned his generals and demanded that Union tactics remain consistent with his overriding political goals—including keeping foreign powers like France out of the war. The stakes, he realized, were enormous. Upon "the progress of our arms," Lincoln declared, "all else chiefly depends."[13]

Lincoln's approach to military strategy was subtle, original—and ruthlessly effective. The president, especially after the Army of the Potomac's maddeningly slow start, was eager for decisive engagements. Still, while impetuous generals like Joseph Hooker longed to seize the great prizes—Richmond, for example, and later Mexican territory—the president took a more measured approach. Lincoln's careful study of both war and economics had led him to believe that occupying territory was far less important than depleting the material resources of his foes. As the conflict intensified, the president peppered his generals with notes insisting that they focus on destroying enemy armies, not necessarily capturing cities. This strategy, argues historian Gabor Boritt, was "the most original and probably most significant of Lincoln's military contributions."[14]

A wild lunge into Mexico, he had come to realize, would do nothing to empower America in the long run. Lincoln ultimately chose to keep his massive army north of the Rio Grande in the face of powerful headwinds from the penny press, important military officers, and some members of Congress, who at times were all urging an invasion. The Mexican episode is a critical illustration of Lincoln's ability to use the powers of his office to direct foreign policy in a crisis. In 1864, as Napoleon was redoubling his efforts to secure Mexico, the U.S. House of Representatives passed a resolution condemning the venture. Yet Lincoln's State Department, eager to avoid unnecessary trouble while the war was ongoing, privately assured the French through diplomatic channels that the clamor on Capitol Hill was simply noise.

Legislators objected to being sidelined. They passed another measure maintaining that "Congress has a constitutional right to an authoritative voice in declaring and prescribing the foreign policy of the United States." Yet Lincoln and Seward's insistence that the protests were not binding is the legacy that has endured. The outcome, notes Arthur Schlesinger Jr., author of *The Imperial Presidency*, "helped confirm the practice of regarding such [congressional] resolutions . . . as purely advisory." Lincoln and Seward had once again helped to shape an executive office that was better suited to the country's role as an emerging world power.

Ultimately the whole episode also served to refine and crystalize one of the key tenets of American foreign policy. For propriety's sake, both Lincoln and Seward shied away from using the term "Monroe Doctrine" during the Mexican crisis. Still, while prior to the Civil War the Doctrine "had not yet attained the importance of a truly national principle," in the words of one historian, by the end of the Mexican drama "it emerged . . . immensely strengthened, and firmly anchored in the thought of the American people and in the policy of their government." And yet, a clean break from the fallen Old World—as the authors of the Monroe Doctrine had hoped for— remained elusive. Independence, after all, is sometimes just another word for power.[15]

Monsieur Oui-Oui

Napoleon III was deeply troubled by the American debate over whether to invade Mexico. His protégé Maximilian wrote Napoleon shortly before the conference at Hampton Roads lamenting that the French troop levels in the country were "barely sufficient" to maintain his hold on the place. Napoleon was a risk taker, but he was also pathologically insecure. As a young man, the pale, stocky future emperor would lurch awake in the middle of the night convinced that burglars had broken into his home. Once he was enthroned in the Tuileries Palace, Napoleon's crown never rested comfortably on his head. He fretted that European monarchs did not take him seriously as a peer. The French leader's outsider status, noted one Austrian diplomat, was "the worm that eats at the heart of Emperor Napoleon." Now, despite Lincoln's forbearance, Napoleon had one more cause for self-doubt. The French emperor's most ambitious foreign-policy scheme was crumbling about his ears.[16]

The emperor's insecurities seem to have begun in his youth. Louis Napoleon, the future Napoleon III, was a nephew of Napoleon Bonaparte. His father was Bonaparte's brother, and his mother, Hortense de Beauharnais, was a daughter of Napoleon's first wife,

Josephine, from her previous marriage. Some of Louis's earliest memories consisted of outings with his celebrated uncle. The Gallic conqueror did his best to toughen up his young nephew. At family gatherings, Bonaparte would clamp one hand on each of the boy's ears and lift him up onto the table by his head—as Louis's mother watched in horror.[17]

Louis was a quiet and introverted boy. His family called the child "Monsieur Oui-Oui," mocking the toddler's pronunciation of his own name. Louis was only seven in June 1815, when the Duke of Wellington and his armies crushed his uncle's forces at Waterloo. Fearing that her children were in danger, Hortense sent Louis and his brother to hide out in a small Paris apartment belonging to her dressmaker. In the tumult following the Napoleonic Wars, the family fled to Switzerland, where they settled in a château surrounded by pine trees and vineyards along the shores of Lake Constance.[18]

Louis found Swiss provincial life dull. During lessons with his tutor, he would sometimes imagine that he was a bird and could soar out through the window to freedom. He amused himself by flirting with the local girls around Lake Constance, serenading the young women and reading to them from pulp romance novels. His youthful flirtations may have been one more balm for his insecurities. If so, his mother did nothing to bolster his self-esteem. She admitted that her child was "not attractive enough to make the women run after him."[19]

The exiled prince occasionally escaped the sleepy Swiss village for excursions to Italy with his family. On his way home from one journey, Louis stopped at the Rubicon River and filled a bottle with water as a keepsake. Eventually the young man's Italian adventures got him into trouble. As a twenty-two-year-old, Louis traveled to Italy with his family and established contacts with Italian nationalists who were conspiring against the pope. Roman authorities finally confronted the young man and expelled him from the city. Louis's mother eventually had to travel across northern Italy to rescue her son.[20]

By the time he reached his late twenties, the future emperor was plotting more ambitious schemes. In the summer of 1835, he joined a group of collaborators and began planning a coup that he hoped would oust King Louis Philippe in France. One morning in late October of the following year, Louis told his mother that he was going to visit a cousin. Actually, the young man slipped into the French city of Strasbourg, in the country's northeast corner. After a sleepless night, he dressed in epaulettes and a cocked hat and crept out into the city in the early morning hours. Over a thin blanket of snow, Louis and his co-conspirators fanned out toward key power centers like the army barracks and telegraph office. At first the plot seemed to come off well. Louis led a column of soldiers through the town, past crowds cheering, "Vive l'Empereur! Vive Napoléon!" Yet the coup unraveled quickly. After a loyalist army officer shouted that Louis was an imposter, the king's men swiftly rounded up the conspirators.[21]

Louis was exiled to America. He spent two and a half months in the United States soaking up the culture. The future French emperor ensconced himself in the Washington Hotel in New York and mingled with the city's social elite. Gotham in the 1830s was a small metropolis of three hundred thousand—"only a child," Louis wrote home to a friend. Still, he took note of the young country's "immense material forces." The nation was clearly in the throes of a revolutionary transformation. "Every day," he wrote, "the transition continues: the caterpillar is shedding its cocoon and taking wing." And yet he believed American expansion could not avoid some growing pains. By the time he arrived, a financial panic was gripping the city. "I do not think," he wrote, "the transition will be completed without crises and convulsions."[22]

After learning that his mother was ill, Louis left America and made his way back to Switzerland. French authorities continued to harass him, however, and after her death he ultimately left for Britain. The future French emperor was captivated by the changes wrought by the industrial and market revolutions. He toured Britain's industrial heartland, taking notes as he wandered through the impoverished region. With his Savile Row suits and giant ruby thunderbolt

pendant, he would not have blended in. He was probably more comfortable in London, socializing with dignitaries like Charles Dickens
and future British prime minister Benjamin Disraeli. Once, when he
was out rowing on the Thames with the Disraelis, his boat got stuck
on an embankment. "You should not undertake things which you
cannot accomplish," Disraeli's wife, Mary Anne, chided Louis. "You
are always, sir, too adventurous."[23]

The future emperor embarked on his next adventure in the
summer of 1840, when he once again attempted to seize the French
throne. Louis chartered a steamship, piled it high with guns and
ammunition, and attempted a landing in Boulogne, on France's
northern coast, accompanied by "a motley throng" of a few dozen
"malcontents and adventurers." At one point a crew member bought
a vulture that looked like an eagle. Louis's enemies later claimed that
the would-be emperor placed a piece of bacon under his hat, hoping
to keep the bird circling around his head like a portent. Ultimately,
Louis's second coup attempt proved as disastrous as his first. After
landing in France, the conspirators once again met resistance from
skeptical loyalists. Louis's gun accidentally discharged, wounding a
soldier and further raising tensions. Finally the plotters were chased
back to the seashore. Louis's escape boat capsized, and the emperor-
to-be had to be fished out of the water.[24]

French authorities locked up the hapless plotter in the dank,
fifteenth-century Château de Ham, which had once held Joan of
Arc. Louis spent the next five and a half years in captivity. He complained to a friend that prison was like "a death in life." Actually, it
was not all that bad. Louis had abundant time to study and write,
and his guards allowed him occasional horseback rides. He even
took a mistress—the prison's twenty-two-year-old chambermaid,
whom he eventually impregnated (twice).[25] As the years passed,
however, he began to plot once again. He memorized the prison
floor plan. Then he smuggled in a workman's clothing and shaved
off his trademark moustache. He donned a wig and threw a wooden

plank over his shoulder. Finally he slipped past the prison guards— eventually escaping to London.[26]

Louis did not return to France until 1848, when the liberal revolutions erupted across the continent. Even after King Louis Philippe fled in February, French internecine politics remained ruthless. Socialists bickered with more conservative factions for control of the government. Louis's supporters concocted a pithy campaign slogan ("HIM!") and plastered the country with posters. Still, French authorities continued to dangle the threat of arrest. Not until autumn did the French exile run for—and win—an empty seat in the National Assembly. When Louis's English landlord went to check on his tenant in the wake of the victory, he discovered that the future emperor had already set out for France—absentmindedly leaving his marble bathtub full of water in his haste.[27]

The former exile immediately captured the attention of Parisians. Charles A. Dana, Marx's editor at the *Tribune*, covered Napoleon's first appearance in the Assembly. Dressed all in black, Bonaparte's nephew looked surprisingly small and weak, Dana reported, and the ladies in the gallery sniped that he wore "a bad-looking moustache." And yet the former exile became "instantly the sole object of attention of every person in the House." Only three months later, Frenchmen elected Louis Napoleon president of the republic. There was no doubt in Dana's mind that "he would much rather be emperor than president."[28]

Dana was right. Louis assiduously courted key players in French society as he worked toward his goal. He plied military officers with champagne and cigars. He hired organ grinders to sing Bonapartist songs. Marx, frustrated by Napoleon's outmaneuvering of the socialists, complained that the president was "an adventurer blown in from abroad, elevated on the shield by a drunken soldiery, which he has bought with liquor and sausages, and which he must continually ply with sausage anew." Victor Hugo derided the president as "Napoleon the Little."

Still, ordinary Frenchmen embraced their renowned conqueror's nephew. On December 2, 1851, the anniversary of his uncle's coronation, Louis Napoleon led one final coup attempt. He gave the operation the codename Rubicon and ordered mass arrests of his political enemies. This time the power grab was successful. Louis proclaimed himself Emperor Napoleon III. Americans marveled at the news. Mary's old friend Cassius Marcellus Clay had once considered the hapless plotter a joke. "Who," Clay wrote to one acquaintance, "thought that Louis Napoleon at one time would ever have been the emperor of the grand nation!"[29]

Napoleon III's reign, in some sense, heralded the birth of modern France. He came to power just as the industrial and market revolutions were beginning to transform societies throughout the world. The new emperor supported the establishment of large banking houses, which in turn funneled capital into French businesses. As the country's wealth grew, the emperor enlisted his aide Baron Haussmann in a series of plans to make over Paris. Napoleon and his adviser reshaped the Parisian landscape, carving wide boulevards out of the city's tangle of alleyways. The innovations were designed partly to make the streets harder to barricade. They ended up giving Paris the unique character we know today.[30]

By the time Napoleon seized the French throne, he had earned a well-deserved reputation as a womanizer. In London he had taken up with an English actress and courtesan with whom he fathered two illegitimate children. When he returned to Paris in 1848, he brought his mistress with him, moving her into a house near the Elysée Palace. Still, such arrangements did not prevent the emperor from making awkward advances at whomever struck his fancy. "Each new woman is brought to the Tuileries in a cab," reported one Parisian diarist, "undressed in an ante-room, and taken naked into the room where the Emperor, likewise naked, is waiting for her." Then a chamberlain would announce: "You may kiss His Majesty anywhere except on the face." European statesman quickly homed in on the emperor's fondness for the flesh. Count Camillo Cavour, the Piedmontese prime minister, once dispatched his voluptuous eighteen-year-old cousin, Virginia di Castiglione, to the Tuileries with the instructions "to flirt with and if necessary seduce the Emperor." The teenage bombshell did manage to seduce him, although historians doubt whether the affair influenced his Italian policy. "If we did for ourselves what we do for our country," Cavour remarked as a postscript, "what rascals we should be."[31]

Louis Napoleon spent the first forty-five years of his life as a bachelor. In January 1853, however, Napoleon finally married Eugenia de Montijo—the Spanish beauty who would become the influential Empress Eugénie. The wedding, at the Cathedral of Notre Dame, was lit by fifteen thousand candles. Eugénie, with her penetrating blue eyes, elegantly braided red hair, and perfect figure, had enchanted the emperor. European statesmen, however, immediately panned the match. Disraeli mocked the empress's "Chinese eyes" and "perpetual smile or simper which I detest." Britain's Lord John Russell—Palmerston's future foreign minister—dubbed her an "*intrigante.*" Even the French stock exchange plunged. On one visit to Paris, the Austrian archduke Maximilian described the emperor's bride as "essentially lacking in the august quality of an empress." The whole imperial scene, Maximilian wrote home, left the impression of "a make-believe court, the various offices of which are occupied by amateurs who are not very sure of their parts." The emperor himself—with "his shuffling gait, his ugly hands, the sly inquiring glance of his lusterless eyes"—disgusted Maximilian, at least at first. The Austrian archduke noted that Napoleon often cast "reproving glances" at his free-spirited wife.[32]

Eugénie is often portrayed as a femme fatale, a powerful behind-the-scenes power broker who managed to roll her weak and distracted husband. That picture is exaggerated, although the French empress was both influential and strong-willed. As a girl, Eugénie was so talkative that she found it difficult to remain silent at the dinner table with adults. If she drew disdainful glances, she would sometimes banish herself to a corner of the room and continue the conversation alone. As she grew into womanhood, an acquaintance described the future empress as "short-tempered and bossy." She once plunged a dagger into her arm to prove her toughness—or so the story is told. As an adult, she scandalized polite society with her affection for bullfights. The empress—an essentially conservative aristocrat raised in a Roman Catholic country—had no love for the increasingly powerful United States. "Sooner or later," she told European diplomats, "we shall have to declare war on America."[33]

An Impassable Barrier

Both Napoleon and Eugénie had long dreamed of reviving France's role in the New World. The future emperor had begun imagining such a scheme while still imprisoned in the Château de Ham. As the Civil War loomed, Napoleon was also looking for excuses to strengthen France's relationship with Austria, which had been strained by Napoleon's past support for Italian nationalists. Installing a Hapsburg monarch on the Mexican throne was one potential way to tighten those ties. Eugénie maintained her own relationships with prominent Mexican diplomats. One childhood acquaintance, Don José Manuel Hidalgo, had grown up to become one of the most forceful advocates of European intervention in Mexico. As the sectional crisis in North America intensified, the suave, handsome Mexican pressed his case once again with the French imperial couple.[34]

Mexico had been mired in political and economic chaos for decades. Local factions were battling for control of the country. Yet by the 1850s, Mexico was not much of a prize. The nation had fallen deep into debt. Meanwhile, American filibusters had been slipping across the border, establishing a foothold south of the Rio Grande. During one meeting at the imperial palace in Compiègne in 1858, as Napoleon sipped a glass of wine, Hidalgo warned the emperor that the Americans were already plundering Mexican silver mines. The emperor insisted that he would like to get involved, but added that he could not take any action on American questions without England's blessing. "I wish I could," he told the Mexican diplomat on another occasion, "but how?"

Then, in the summer of 1861, Mexico suspended payments on its debts to the European powers. Hidalgo thought he saw his opportunity to reengage the imperial couple. When the Mexican diplomat got the news, he was visiting Napoleon and Eugénie at their villa on the beach in Biarritz—a pleasant spot with a trail leading down to a cluster of bungalows by the water. After dinner, Hidalgo approached the empress. "Your Majesty," he said quietly, sitting down on a stool next to her, "I have just received some very interesting letters; events are moving in our direction, and I believe that the idea of intervention and of an empire may be realized." Eugénie agreed and brought the Mexican diplomat into Napoleon's study. "Tell the Emperor what you just told me," she said. Napoleon lit a cigarette as Hidalgo related the latest developments. The Mexican suggested that the time was finally ripe for French intervention. The United States, caught up in its own war, would find it impossible to challenge the move—particularly if France could enlist Britain and Spain to go along with the plan.[35]

Napoleon, who had been considering such a scheme on his own, was intrigued. With Hidalgo, the imperial couple brainstormed a list of European princes whom they might be able to install on the Mexican throne. At first, all three agreed that Austria's Maximilian—the archduke who had earlier found Napoleon's court so distasteful—would probably refuse. Then, however, the empress suddenly tapped herself on her chest with her fan. Eugénie could be superstitious. Like many of her nineteenth-century contemporaries, she believed in palm readers and psychics, and would listen intently to the prophesies of gypsy fortune-tellers. Now, in her seaside villa with the emperor and Hildago, Eugénie explained that she had a "presentiment" that the Austrian archduke would accept an offer.[36]

Napoleon began lobbying European heads of state to support a

Mexican venture. In October he wrote a family friend asking him to make the case to Palmerston. Europeans had a "common interest" in seeing Mexico stabilized, the emperor insisted. Mexican guerrillas had been raiding British and French convoys in the country, making off with millions of dollars' worth of European silver. An invasion could help secure key trade routes. Napoleon also offered a geopolitical rationale for his scheme. A joint invasion would establish "an impassable barrier" to American southward expansion, Napoleon argued. "The American war," the emperor concluded, "has made it impossible for the United States to interfere in the matter, and, what is more, the outrages committed by the Mexican Government have provided England, Spain and France with a legitimate motive for interference in Mexico." The emperor made sure to send a copy of the letter to Maximilian in Austria.[37]

Maximilian saw the Mexican venture as a personal opportunity. At the start of the Civil War, the Austrian archduke was "29 and jobless," as one account puts it. His prospects were not promising. The young man was "extravagant and ever in debt"—hardly the ideal savior for insolvent Mexico. Maximilian also suffered from a number of illnesses, many of them probably psychosomatic. When he finally arrived in Mexico, locals gave the slender, bearded European the nickname Featherhead, for his poor judgment. Maximilian had married Princess Charlotte, the pretty daughter of Belgium's King Leopold. Both young Europeans quickly began to see themselves as the leaders of a divine mission. As European troops set out for Mexico, Charlotte wrote to Eugénie lauding the operation as a "holy one." The French empress, Charlotte continued, had been "marked out by Providence" to revive Catholicism in North America.[38]

Spanish troops began arriving in Mexico in early December 1861, followed by French and British reinforcements in January. The joint operation was a critical step forward in Franco-British relations. Despite a rapprochement between Palmerston and Napoleon III in the 1850s, mistrust still lingered from the era of the Napoleonic Wars. Even after Waterloo, France remained "a considerable power" in

Europe for decades, the historian Paul Kennedy has noted. Innocuous celebratory gunfire in British port towns could still spark a panic that the French armies were about to invade. The French, too, remained wary of disrupting the continental balance of power.[39]

Napoleon sought to constrain the growth of the United States—but that is not the same as wanting the Union dismembered. America's rising influence provided Napoleon with a critical counterweight to Britain's naval predominance. It was all a delicate balancing act. "We are interested in seeing the United States powerful and prosperous," the emperor told one of his generals in mid-1862, "but we have no interest in seeing that republic acquire the whole of the Gulf of Mexico, dominate from this vantage-point the Antilles and South America, and become the sole dispenser of the products of the New World." Still, the safest thing for Napoleon would be to first win British support for any potential foreign-policy schemes.[40]

Marx observed that the French emperor preferred to carry out "his overseas adventures under English aegis." Napoleon himself used a homey metaphor to describe the relationship. "I regard England as my wife," the emperor remarked, "and the others as mistresses." Palmerston was wary. "Our good friend and ally in Paris may mean well and keep quiet," he had written one correspondent as the Civil War loomed, "but there is an awkward leer in his eye which forbids overconfidence and his ears are a little laid back as if to forewarn a kick or a bite."[41]

As news of the scheme filtered through London society, Marx told readers of the *New York Tribune* that he considered the operation "one of the most monstrous enterprises ever chronicled in the annals of international history." The philosopher blamed Palmerston for the expedition. Still, Marx added that the plan's "insanity of purpose" and "imbecility of . . . means" seemed out of character for "the old schemer." Marx considered the Most English Minister basically competent, even if he was also venal. Napoleon, on the other hand, was simply a political charlatan, lashing out in an effort to keep his public amused.[42]

Lincoln was understandably troubled when reports of the French-led operation in Mexico reached the White House. The whole matter, Seward wrote the American minister in Paris, had "awakened some anxiety on his part." Since the first days of his administration, Lincoln had been struggling to manage the delicate relationships with other European powers like Spain and Britain. First he had been confronted with the Spanish reoccupation of Santo Domingo. Then he had been faced with Britain's declaration of neutrality and the tensions that his blockade had spawned. Now the French emperor, too, seemed to be threatening to overthrow the balance of power in the New World.

Union loyalists feared that the operation might be a prelude to full-scale foreign intervention in the Civil War. A Parisian newspaper report, picked up and reprinted in the *New York Times*, warned that the French maneuvering was only "a pretext for getting into the American waters a large force, ready to act in liberating cotton when the time comes." Lincoln administration officials did their best to prevent that outcome. They "spoke the language of the Monroe Doctrine," as one historian puts it—without ever using the loaded phrase itself. "In the president's opinion," Seward wrote his envoy in Paris in March, "the emancipation of this continent from European control has been the principal feature of its history during the last century."[43]

Matías Romero, the charming and well-connected young emissary who represented Mexico's government in Washington, cleverly reinforced Lincoln's views on hemispheric independence. The Mexican diplomat declared that the principles of the Monroe Doctrine "seem to be written for the present occasion." Early in Lincoln's term Romero had visited the new president at the Executive Mansion to give the Illinoisan a primer on Mexican affairs. The Mexican diplomat explained that there were two main factions in his country—a "liberal" party that aimed "to imitate the United States," as Romero put it; and a "reactionary" wing "composed of the clergy, the demoralized part of the old army, some moneychangers, and a few other illusionaries and fanatics who collectively are in an evident minority." Napoleon, Romero told Lincoln, would seek to ally himself with the latter faction; the United States, he argued, should work closely with the former.

The American president listened quietly with "marked attention," Romero told his superiors, and assured the Mexican that he considered the country a priority. Yet he offered no practical proposal for keeping France out of Mexico. Lincoln, Romero noted, seemed to "lack confidence" that he could do much of anything abroad with a war already raging at home. Privately, Lincoln and Seward were even more nonplussed by the Mexican turmoil than they let on. "The actual condition of affairs in Mexico," Seward had written to Thomas Corwin, the Union minister to the country, "is so imperfectly understood here that the President finds it very difficult to give you particular and practical directions for the regulation of your conduct during your mission."[44]

An American invasion of Mexico was out of the question, particularly at such an early stage in the war. The president's forces had demonstrated at Bull Run, Ball's Bluff, and other early skirmishes that they could not defeat a band of Confederate rebels, much less the military of one of the world's great powers. "Since the United States, for the present, must allow no foreign complication to interfere with their war for the Union," wrote Marx, "all they can do is to *protest*." Any serious response to the French-led operation would have to wait until Lincoln's armies had made more headway against their domestic foes. "Upon the settlement of this family quarrel," the *New York Times* promised, "the case of Mexico will be attended to."[45]

In the meantime, the White House lodged a perfunctory complaint with the Tuileries. "We cannot look with indifference," Seward wrote to the U.S. minister in Paris, "upon an armed European intervention for political ends in a country situated so near and connected with us so closely as Mexico." Lincoln sent Congress a proposal to float a loan to the Mexican government so the country could continue to make payments on its debt. British policymakers, for their part, were cool to the idea. "A mortgage of Mexico to the United States," Palmerston believed, "would certainly lead to foreclosing."

Lincoln's diplomats countered that Palmerston had it the wrong way around. Corwin argued that if the American aid package was rejected, England would then "own" the country, directing Mexican affairs "as fully as she does the policy of India or Canada." In that event, Corwin told another correspondent, "England and France will absorb Mexico, and we shall have less to do with it than we have with the African Kingdom of Dahomey." Lincoln, however, seemed lukewarm about the whole enterprise, and sent word that he "could suggest no plan by which aid could be given to Mexico." The reluctant U.S. Senate eventually tabled the measure and the loan proposals ultimately went nowhere.[46]

As the spring unfolded, the news improved for the Lincoln administration. In April, Britain and Spain decided to withdraw their troops from Mexico, leaving Napoleon on his own. Foreign-affairs crises closer to home demanded the attention of the European powers. Meanwhile, yellow fever stalked the French troops who remained behind in Mexico. Napoleon's army was badly weakened by May 5, when it marched on the Mexican town of Puebla. Though the French soldiers were far better armed, Mexican guerrillas hiding in the town's baroque churches rained bullets on the invaders. The Mexicans ultimately drove the French forces out of town. (The Mexican holiday Cinco de Mayo celebrates the victory at Puebla.) The French army survived to fight another day. Yet the expedition was off to an unimpressive start.[47]

Nevertheless, Napoleon's army of thirty-five thousand continued its steady march toward Mexico City. Lincoln's inner circle grew increasingly alarmed. In July, John Hay published an anonymous article in the *Missouri Republican* arguing that if the United States did not shore up its relationships with Mexican republicans, great powers like France would step into the void. A "grasping European dynasty" on America's southern border would gravely threaten U.S.

security, Hay insisted. It was "almost impossible," he wrote, "to over-estimate the importance" of keeping the "continent free from the footsteps of European absolutism." As the New Year approached, with French forces slowly cementing their hold on the country, that prospect looked increasingly unlikely. Meanwhile, Napoleon III was about to present Lincoln with his boldest challenge yet.[48]

The Sphinx of the Tuileries

P russia's iron chancellor, Otto von Bismarck—a future antago-nist of Napoleon's—once described the French emperor as "a great unfathomed capacity." The French statesman's contemporaries found it notoriously difficult to make sense of his whims. Even those closest to him found him hard to read. "Had I married him," recalled one youthful flame, his cousin Mathilde, "I think that I might have broken his head open just to see what was in it." To Europe's statesmen, increasingly steeped in the logic of Realpolitik, the French emperor's romantic scheming seemed baffling. "Ideas proliferated in his head like rabbits in a hutch," Palmerston com-plained. Americans, separated by a vast ocean, were even more per-plexed by the inscrutable Frenchman. John Hay wrote of the "plots and schemes that lurk in the tortuous brain of the impassive and silent emperor of the French." Hay called Napoleon the Sphinx of the Tuileries.[49]

Lincoln had once defended the French emperor against his radical foes—at least rhetorically. In 1858 a band of conspirators led by Ital-ian nationalist Felice Orsini had attempted to assassinate Napoleon III, throwing bombs at the emperor's coach. Lincoln, in his memo-rable speech at New York's Cooper Union in 1860, had compared the attackers to zealous abolitionists like John Brown, who had repeat-edly attacked American slaveholders. "Orsini's attempt on Louis Na-poleon," the Illinoisan told the crowd, "and John Brown's attempt at Harper's Ferry were, in their philosophy, precisely the same." Both crimes, Lincoln explained, had been committed by "an enthusiast" who "imagines himself commissioned by Heaven."[50]

By the summer of 1862, however, Napoleon's meddling in the Americas had begun to grate on Lincoln and his deputies. John Bigelow, the president's consul in Paris, complained that Napoleon had "lost pretty much all of the little faith he had in our ability to reduce the South to obedience." The emperor, Bigelow continued, was "hovering over us, like the carrion crow over the body of the sinking traveler, waiting till we are too weak to resist his predatory instincts." His unpredictability was unsettling. With Europe wracked by its own crises, most of the Continent's power brokers found it difficult to justify far-flung adventures. Yet just as the other European powers were pulling back their commitments in the New World, Napoleon redoubled his efforts to meddle in the Western Hemisphere. In early January 1863, the French emperor floated an offer to mediate between North and South. To Lincoln, the proposal represented one of the most dangerous moments in the war.[51]

Part of the problem was that many of Lincoln's own erstwhile supporters embraced the French offer. The president had always viewed the volubility of his own constituents as one of his weaknesses. Lincoln's bodyguard once compared the president's situation to that of the great French statesman Cardinal Richelieu. Lincoln did not see the similarities. Richelieu, the president pointed out, "had a united constituency; I never have had." Lincoln assumed that any French effort to mediate would end with the division of the United States. As French troops closed in on Mexico City, that prospect seemed particularly troubling.

Still, with Federal armies bogged down in the winter of 1863, many Americans just wanted to stop the bleeding. Horace Greeley argued in the *New York Tribune* that Napoleon III was now "more popular with his people than any other European monarch." In the past, Greeley had been convinced that the autocratic Napoleon could never be a fair judge of events in republican America. Yet by late January, after intense lobbying efforts from an American businessman,

Greeley suddenly shifted his stance. The emperor, Greeley was now convinced, "is inspired by the most friendly feelings to the Federal Government and the loyal states." The mercurial editor advocated taking the French emperor up on his offer.[52]

The French mediation proposal also coincided with a revival in the popularity of peace Democrats, known as Copperheads. (The activists, who got the name from sniping Republicans, cut the figures of Liberty from copper pennies and proudly wore them in their lapels.) The group eagerly sought to end the war, even if it meant the preservation of slavery. The Copperheads' most charismatic spokesman was Clement Vallandigham, a tall, slender Ohioan with dark hair and skin that accentuated his "light flashing eyes." In speeches throughout the country, Vallandigham derided the president as a tyrant, railing against "King Lincoln."[53]

On January 14, 1863, Vallandigham rose in the House of Representatives and urged the warring parties to accept the French offer. The Copperhead congressman insisted that he was not defeatist. America's emergence as a world power, he believed, was simply contingent on stopping the war. "Union," he told the chamber, "is empire." In some ways, Vallandigham's underlying rationale was not so different from Seward's own conciliatory position during the secession winter. Yet the Ohioan's means were vastly different. Vallandigham implored his colleagues to consider Napoleon III's proposal. "It would be churlish to refuse," he declared. "As proposed by the Emperor of France, I would accept it at once. Now is the auspicious moment. It is the speediest, easiest, most graceful mode of suspending hostilities."[54]

Lincoln, already worn down by the winter's battlefield defeats, was shaken by Napoleon's mediation proposal. When he got the news, recalled one newspaper correspondent, the president appeared "so careworn and dejected." The dispatches coming in from Lincoln's diplomats in the field did nothing to improve his mood. Henry Sanford reported that talk of a rivalry between the "Latin race" and American republicans was being repeated "*ad nauseam* in Parisian salons." State Department adviser Edward Everett warned that he had heard murmurs that France was attempting to wrest control of "a larger Texas" for an imperial possession. Lincoln's minister in Paris complained that Americans were beginning to "distrust" the emperor. His countrymen, he protested, "do not like to see His Majesty's hand always in this business." Alexander Hamilton's son James wrote Lincoln urging him "to throw a large force without delay into Texas" in order to "admonish the emperor" over "his magnificent designs" on the continent. Such a move, Hamilton argued, "would perhaps shake his throne." Yet with increasingly desperate battles raging with Southern forces at home, there was little else Lincoln and his diplomats could do.[55]

Lincoln, meanwhile, once again intensified his efforts to establish overseas colonies of American blacks. After failing to arouse much interest among the European powers for colonization, the president turned instead to Bernard Kock, an American businessman who wanted to establish a colony on the Île à Vache, a small island off the coast of Haiti. Kock told the president that the island was "beautiful, healthy, and fertile" (adding that it was "known to be free from reptiles"). The president was intrigued. Seward suggested delaying the venture in the wake of the Emancipation Proclamation, but Lincoln ultimately overruled him. Kock, flush with promises of U.S. government funds, set sail in April from Virginia with a band of 453 colonists.

Historians have often viewed Lincoln's colonization proposals as something of a public-relations ploy. His support for overseas settlements, the thinking goes, was largely an effort to conciliate Northern racists who were angry about emancipation. More recently, however, scholars have questioned this "lullaby thesis." Evidence suggests that Lincoln continued to pursue colonization long after the Emancipation Proclamation. "Lincoln," historians Phillip Magness and Sebastian Page observe, "likely saw colonization as one of many avenues to approach an anguishing difficulty that had no simple resolution." Embarking on a "second wave" of such schemes in 1863, the president met repeatedly over the course of the year with British officials whom he believed might be convinced to help facilitate new colonies in Central America.[56]

At home, Lincoln's men did their best to put a positive spin on the continuing fighting. Seward audaciously compared America's burgeoning forces to those of Julius Caesar or Napoleon Bonaparte. "Our armies," the secretary of state declared on the second anniversary of Fort Sumter, "are moving on with a firmer step than those of the Roman Empire or the French Republic ever maintained." In reality, the situation remained perilous throughout the spring. In May, Confederate forces led by General Robert E. Lee defeated Lincoln's army at Chancellorsville, Virginia. The news devastated the president. "Clasping his hands behind his back," recalled one witness, "he walked up and down the room, saying, 'My God! my God! What will the country say! What will the country say!'" In the process, however, Confederate general Thomas (Stonewall) Jackson had been fatally wounded. Lincoln's diplomats clung to any sliver of positive news from the battlefield. "The truth is," Henry Adams wrote from the legation in London, "all depends on the progress of our armies." Lincoln acknowledged as much to Mexico's man in Washington, Matías Romero. The Mexican recalled Lincoln once telling him that he "had always believed . . . that the settlement of Mexico's present difficulties depended upon the course events would take here [at home]."[57]

In Mexico, meanwhile, Napoleon's forces were finally making their own progress. On June 7, 1863, French troops broke through the remaining Mexican defenses and poured into Mexico City. The scene was somewhat reminiscent of the American conquest less than two decades earlier. Officers jumped off their horses near the cathedral and listened to a performance of the Te Deum, the ancient Christian hymn of praise. Supporters threw flowers and affixed posters of the emperor and empress to every wall in the city. Back in Europe, the emperor of the French wept with joy upon hearing news of the conquest.[58]

For Lincoln, the French occupation of Mexico City could not

have come at a worse time. Lee's Confederate forces were inching closer to the Federal capital. Lincoln was growing despondent. A former State Department employee who spotted the president walking the streets of the capital in June 1863 reported that he looked "exhausted, care-worn, spiritless, extinct." A visitor to the White House around the same time described Lincoln's "drooping eyelids, looking almost swollen; the dark bags beneath the eyes; the deep marks about the large and expressive mouth; the flaccid muscles of the jaws." In the depths of that summer, Mary Lincoln's seamstress recalled the president walking with a "slow and heavy" step into the First Lady's dressing room, collapsing onto the sofa, and then covering his eyes with his hands—"a complete picture of dejection." He consoled himself by reading the Book of Job. Even Mary began to worry about her husband. "What do you think of Mr. Lincoln?" she asked her half sister as the year wore on. "Do you think he is well?"[59]

Mary, for her part, did not do much to ease the president's anxieties. Even as Lincoln fretted over Napoleon's troops in Mexico, the First Lady was busy taking French lessons and mimicking the empress's fashions—a particularly expensive taste. Eugénie's innovation had been to increase the size of the steel hoops supporting her skirts—which also doubled the amount of fabric necessary to make them. Mary was not entirely successful in her attempts to imitate Eugénie. A relative of Napoleon III's who visited Washington toward the beginning of the war told his diary that Mary had received him "dressed in the French style without any taste." Nor was Lincoln thrilled with the fashions. Aside from the expense, the dresses could be scandalously low cut. One U.S. senator complained that the First Lady "had her bosom on exhibition" at one reception. She seemed determined, he added, "to exhibit her milking apparatus to public gaze." The president sometimes told Mary that he wished she would show a little more restraint. "Whew," Lincoln said on one occasion, "our cat has a long tail tonight. Mother, it is my opinion, if some of that tail was nearer the head, it would be in better style."[60]

Abraham Rex

As 1863 unfolded, Lincoln finally began to get comfortable in his role as commander in chief of the military. "Some well-meaning newspapers advise the president to keep his fingers out of the military pie," John Hay wrote to a colleague as the Union war effort gathered momentum. "The truth is, if he did, the pie would be a sorry mess." Lincoln understood that the war effort at home and the work of his diplomats abroad were intricately linked. European statesmen were closely watching results of key battles as they debated whether to intervene and stop the fighting. Only a steady string of victories would ultimately deter the cold-eyed great powers.[61]

The president, from the first days of the war, had begun cramming on military affairs. "He gave himself, night and day, to the study of the military situation," Hay recalled. "He read a large number of strategical works. He pored over the reports from the various departments and districts of the field of war. He held long conferences with eminent generals and admirals, and astonished them by the extent of his special knowledge and the keen intelligence of his questions."[62]

Back in January, after enduring a string of lackadaisical commanders, Lincoln had decided to elevate the energetic and dynamic General Joe Hooker to command of the Army of the Potomac. With his rust-colored hair, rosy cheeks, and blue eyes, the tall and lean Hooker cut a striking figure. (During his service in the Mexican War, local women referred to Hooker as Handsome Captain.) Lincoln liked Hooker, but he was also wary of the zealous officer. One of the president's acquaintances recalled that Lincoln loved Hooker "as a father might regard a son who was lame." The president told his secretary of the navy that he thought "as much as you or any other man of Hooker, but I fear he gets excited." Lincoln was not afraid to level with the hot-blooded officer, who once declared that he thought the Federal government needed a dictator. "Beware of rashness," the president wrote Hooker upon his appointment.

"Beware of rashness, but with energy, and sleepless vigilance, go forward, and give us victories."[63]

The president frequently cabled Hooker and other officers, laying out his vision for a successful Union war effort. In one exchange, in early June, Hooker telegraphed Lincoln, reporting that he saw an opportunity to march on Richmond "at once," hammering the Confederate capital with a "mortal blow." Lincoln swiftly responded by reminding Hooker that such a maneuver would not be consistent with the Union strategy: "I think *Lee's* Army, and not *Richmond*, is your true objective point." The implication was that territorial gain was far less important than depleting the enemy's human and material resources. Furthermore, the president understood, "[i]f our army can not fall upon the enemy and hurt him where he is, it is plain to me it can gain nothing by attempting to follow him over a succession of intrenched lines into a fortified city."[64]

The same point applied to the standoff with Napoleon. Lincoln believed that a determined show of force in Texas might serve as a warning to the French emperor. Yet while Hooker and many of Lincoln's other generals itched to surge into Mexican territory, the president persisted in wearing down his enemies north of the Rio Grande. The French emperor was far more likely to be deterred by a Union defeat of the Confederacy. A Mexican adventure would divert resources from the main event and offer too many opportunities for something to go wrong. Furthermore, if the United States invaded Mexico, the French public—which had long been skeptical of the emperor's North American scheme—might decide to rally around its monarch.

In the first days of July, Lincoln's commanders at long last turned the tide of the war—bolstering Northern diplomatic efforts. After a brutal, three-day battle, Federal forces halted the rebel army at Gettysburg, Pennsylvania. The following day, the Union armies finally took the Mississippi city of Vicksburg as well. The victories deflated the Copperheads, who had been so forcefully pushing the French intervention scheme. They also immediately buoyed

Lincoln's diplomats in the field. "I wanted to hug the army of the Potomac," recalled Henry Adams in London. "I wanted to get the whole of the army of Vicksburg drunk at my own expense. I wanted to fight some small man and lick him."[65]

Lincoln recognized that the successes had reinforced his diplomacy at a key moment. Yet the president and his cabinet remained anxious about the French maneuvering in Mexico. "The Mexican Republic has been extinguished," naval secretary Gideon Welles told his diary in late July, "and an empire has risen on its ruins." The supercilious Welles believed that Mexico was "[t]orn by factions, down-trodden by a scheming and designing priesthood, ignorant and vicious," and "incapable of good government." He added, however, that "I don't expect an improvement of their condition under the sway of a ruler imposed upon them by Louis Napoleon." British aristocrats, too, remained full of "malignant and disgraceful hatred of our government and people," in Welles's view. "Palmerston and Louis Napoleon," he sneered, "are as much our enemies as Jeff Davis."[66]

Lincoln shared Welles's concerns about France, but he believed that war with Britain was actually now unlikely. The victories at home had also encouraged the president. Washington that summer was dull, Hay reported—"dismal as a defaced tombstone." And yet, Hay told one correspondent, the president was in "fine whack. I have rarely seen him more serene and busy. He is managing this war, the draft, foreign relations, and planning a reconstruction of the Union, all at once. I never knew with what tyrannous authority he rules the Cabinet, till now. The most important things he decides and there is no cavil. I am growing more and more firmly convinced that the good of the country absolutely demands that he should be kept where he is till this thing is over. There is no man in the country so wise, so gentle and so firm. I believe the hand of God placed him where he is."

Hay credited Lincoln's proactive management of the war for the summer's successes on the battlefield. "The old man," Hay wrote to Lincoln's other secretary, John G. Nicolay, in early September, "sits here and wields like a backwoods Jupiter the bolts of war and the machinery of government with a hand equally steady and equally firm." Hay began referring to the president in his letters as "Abraham Rex."[67]

The reinvigorated American president unsettled the chronically insecure French emperor. Maximilian wrote to Napoleon in early August worrying that the revival of Northern fortunes presented a "most serious difficulty" for the French effort. The North, Maximilian believed, was both "bent upon expansion" and "hostile to the monarchical principle." The archduke argued that only more French troops in Mexico would prevent an American thrust southward. The United States, Maximilian predicted, "will doubtless be unable to await its own internal stabilization before proceeding to the overthrow of the throne erected at its gates."[68]

By midsummer Lincoln was pushing hard to challenge Napoleon—even if he was not willing to send American troops all the way into Mexico. Lincoln's allies were alarmed by rumors of French designs on Texas. Considering the "movements of France in Mexico," Francis P. Blair Sr. implored Lincoln, it was "of vast importance" to get an army down to Texas as soon as possible. Lincoln had already begun quietly advocating the same course. "Can we not renew the effort to organize a force to go to Western Texas?" the president asked his secretary of war on July 29. "Please think of it. I believe no local object is now more desirable." Two days later, Lincoln called a meeting of his inner circle to discuss the matter further. The president ultimately ordered one of his favorite officers, General Nathaniel Banks, to begin the planning. "Recent events in Mexico, I think, render early action in Texas more important than ever," Lincoln wrote the general. The president made the same point to whomever he could get to listen that August. "I am greatly impressed," Lincoln wrote to Grant on Aug. 9, "with the importance of re-establishing the national authority in Western Texas as soon as possible."[69]

For the first time in months, Lincoln seemed to be cheering up. Mary and the kids had fled the hot, dry Washington summer, leaving Lincoln alone with his staff at the White House. Lincoln's family—particularly Mary—sometimes drove the president to distraction. Still, he missed them when they were away. Even as Lincoln was mulling a show of force along the Mexican border, he found the time to write Mary an affectionate letter with news of their son Tad's pet goat, Nanny. The boy was known for terrorizing the White House staff with the animal, disrupting state dinners and parading her through the grounds. Now, Lincoln reported, the goat had gone missing. "This," the president wrote Mary, "is the last we know of poor 'Nanny.' "[70]

"With Mary out of town," Doris Kearns Goodwin writes, "Lincoln found John Hay a ready companion." Hay was almost like an adopted child—"far more intimately connected to the president than his own eldest son." Both John Hay and John Nicolay would go on to work in the foreign service in overseas postings in the years following the Civil War. Hay, in particular, distinguished himself as a diplomat, serving as ambassador to Britain and secretary of state under presidents William McKinley and Theodore Roosevelt. As a foreign-policy education, it was hard to beat the crucible of the American Civil War. From Seward, Hay learned about the hard realities of international politics at the elbow of one of America's greatest diplomats. From Lincoln, the president's young secretary learned something more subtle but just as critical—how to wield great power with grace.[71]

That was certainly easier when things were going well. By late summer, Hay told his diary, Lincoln was "in very good spirits. He thinks the rebel power is at last beginning to disintegrate—that they will break to pieces if we only stand firm now." One Sunday afternoon in August, the president took Hay to Alexander Gardner's photo studio to have their picture taken together. Even on Sabbath outings, the president remained obsessed with the French emperor's plotting. Hay reported that Lincoln was "very anxious that Texas should be occupied and firmly held in view of French possibilities." The president, his secretary recorded, believed that mission even more important than efforts to subdue Mobile, Alabama—a move that some of Lincoln's generals were advocating instead. Any attack on Mobile would have to wait until "the Texas matter is safe," Lincoln believed.[72]

The president, however, remained opposed to a full invasion of Mexico. "I'm not exactly 'skeered,'" one of Lincoln's military commanders later recalled the president saying about the French intervention, "but [I] don't like the looks of the thing. . . . My policy is, attend to only one trouble at a time. If we get well out of our present difficulties and restore the Union, I propose to notify Louis Napoleon that it is about time to take his army out of Mexico. When that army is gone, the Mexicans will take care of Maximilian." Lincoln repeated his favorite old story about the man on his deathbed who was feuding with a friend. Since he was already ill, he agreed to reconcile. But, went the punch line, "I want it distinctly understood that if I get well the old grudge stands."[73]

At least some of Lincoln's commanders proposed more radical remedies. Hooker, for one, was eager to take the war south of the Rio Grande. In Washington on September 9, Hooker dined with Hay and other Lincoln administration officials. The general, Lincoln's secretary told his diary, "was in a fine flow" during the meal. Hooker bragged about the quickly growing Federal army. It was, the general insisted, "the finest on the planet," Hay recalled. "He would like to see it fighting with foreigners." The general quizzed Hay "very anxiously about our relations with France. He seems very eager to raise an army on the Pacific coast for a fight with a foreign nation. His eye brightened as he talked of it." Lincoln's secretary noted that although Hooker did not drink much at the dinner, "what little he drank made his cheek hot and red and his eye brighter."[74]

The following night, Hooker seemed even more determined to pick a fight with a foreign power. The general dined again with Hay and naval official Gustavus Fox, this time at Wormley's, a Washington watering hole on I Street that would become renowned during the Gilded Age for its wine cellar. Whatever the men were drinking sparked a raucous conversation about foreign affairs. Fox stated that

Britain would have to atone for all the "insults and wrongs" she had committed during the war—"of ports closed to us and opened to the enemy—of flags dipped to them and insultingly immovable to us—of courtesies ostentatiously shown them and brutally denied us—that will make the blood of every American boil in his brain-pan. We shall have men enough when this thing is over."[75]

Hooker agreed. "We will be the greatest military power on earth," the general told the table, "greatest in numbers, in capability, in dash, in spirit, in intelligence of the soldiery. These fine fellows who have gotten a taste of campaigning in the last three years will not go back to plowing, and spinning and trading, and hewing wood and drawing water. They are spoiled for that and shaped for better work." Hooker said that if there were no domestic war, the men would look abroad for their next conflict. Before the dinner broke up, the men reminisced a little, sharing stories about their Mexican War adventures. The young Hay was clearly caught up in the romance. As Hooker was preparing to return to the field from Washington later that month, Hay scrawled in his diary, "I wish to God I was able to go with him."[76]

Cooler heads in the Lincoln administration counseled a less belligerent approach to Mexico. While Hooker was crowing about raising an army of invasion, Seward wrote to his consul in Paris, John Bigelow, admitting that Napoleon's troops were not really such a threat. The secretary of state told Bigelow that the Federal government was too busy trying to put down the rebels to pick a fight with France. Seward suggested that he thought Napoleon probably also had his hands full trying to subdue Mexico. In the meantime, the emperor would be unable to cause much trouble for the Union. "I may be wrong in the latter view," the secretary of state told Bigelow. "But, if I am, there is likely to be time enough for us to change our course after discovering the error."

Seward was so eager to reassure French policy makers that he hinted to French minister Henri Mercier that the United States might be willing to distance itself from Mexican republicans. In mid-September, the secretary of state dragged the French minister to the White House for an audience with Lincoln, during which the president "reiterated very cordially the assurance of his government's neutrality." The president, Hay and Lincoln's other personal secretary, John G. Nicolay, later recalled in their joint biography, "if he erred at all," was determined "to err on the side of strict neutrality."[77]

Washington was full of rumors that France sought to seize parts of Texas and the Mississippi River. In the event of a "rupture with France," argued Frank Blair, the son of Francis P. Blair Sr. and the brother of Lincoln's postmaster general, "it may be necessary to march into Mexico and relieve that country." Blair asked his brother to lobby Lincoln to send him to Texas and place fifty regiments under his command. (Lincoln declined.) Some diplomats whispered that Maximilian's representatives were plotting with Confederate agents. Lincoln tried to turn a deaf ear to the gossip. "He does not allow himself to be disturbed by suspicions so unjust to France and so unreasonable in themselves," Seward explained to one correspondent, "but he knows, also, that such suspicions will be entertained more or less extensively by this country, and magnified in other countries equally unfriendly to France and to America; and he knows also that it is out of such suspicions that the fatal web of national animosity is most frequently woven."[78]

Secretly, however, some Americans with ties to the State Department were quietly working outside standard channels to aid the Mexican liberals. At the request of Mexican minister Matías Romero, American Mexico expert Edward Lee Plumb reached out that autumn to what he later described to Romero as "various gentlemen of great wealth and of very high position . . . gentlemen whose names I am not at liberty to mention in this letter, but who are known to you by reputation." Plumb urged the men, "whose capital would enable them to act swiftly and secretly," to sponsor between 25,000 and 50,000 mercenaries that could be slipped into Mexico to assist the liberals. The businessmen, however, thought the operation would be too expensive, and "the final decision was unfavorable," Plumb explained. Still, the episode reveals the lengths to which opponents of Lincoln's conciliatory foreign policy were willing to go.[79]

Napoleon, meanwhile, was concerned that anarchy in Mexico was already threatening his North American project. He urged Maximilian not to worry so much about an American invasion. Lincoln and Seward fully understood that France was backing the venture, the emperor reminded him. The United States could not send its armies south into Mexico "without at once making an enemy of us." In the meantime, Napoleon urged Maximilian to begin thinking about how he might bring greater order to chaotic Mexico. He said the project would require a firm hand. "A state which is sunk in anarchy is not to be regenerated by parliamentary liberty," Napoleon wrote. "What is wanted in Mexico is a *liberal* dictatorship."[80]

Meanwhile, Lincoln's efforts to make a show of force near the Mexican border ran into trouble. In early September, a flotilla of four Federal gunboats attempted a landing near Sabine Pass, on the Texas-Louisiana line. The Confederate post, manned by only about fifty troops with six light guns, was highly vulnerable. Yet the invasion immediately foundered. Southern gunners quickly shot out the boiler in one of the Union vessels. A second gunboat washed up in shallow water—making an easy target for the Confederate guns. By the time Lincoln anxiously wrote to Banks late that month expressing his "strong hope that you have the old flag flying in Texas by this time," the invading force had long since retreated. It was not until November that Banks's seven thousand troopers finally took Brownsville, Texas, and established a foothold just north of the Mexican boundary. "The importance of Texas," Banks later wrote to Lincoln, "will be felt if we imagine it to be in possession of the French." In that event, Banks argued, the territory might become "a nucleus for all the enemies of the country."[81]

Lincoln needed—and got—a break that autumn, when a group of six Russian warships showed up off the Atlantic coast. The ships' arrival looked to the world like a show of solidarity with the Union cause—and a not-so-veiled threat to the French, their old antagonists in the Crimean War. Actually, Russian commanders had ordered the fleet into open waters for its own protection. If rising tensions in eastern Europe should erupt into all-out hostilities, the ships would be safely out of the line of fire. Yet the Russian strategy was poorly understood at the time. French officials had long been wary of any potential U.S.-Russian alliance. Decades before the Civil War, Alexis de Tocqueville had warned that the United States and Russia seemed "to be marked out by the will of heaven to sway the destinies of half the globe." Napoleon III shared that view, rightly believing that the two countries would rise to dominate the world stage by the twentieth century.[82]

Lincoln and Seward did their best to spin the arrival of the Russian fleet to their advantage. Northerners welcomed the Russian sailors with huge rallies and elegant balls. In New York, the seamen paraded down Broadway as cheering spectators thronged the surrounding streets and rooftops. "The moving pageant," the *Times* reported, "rolled in a glittering stream down the broad thoroughfare between banks of upturned human faces, the trappings of the equipages, the gold and silver epaulets of the Muscovite guests and the sabers, helmets, and bayonets of the escort reflecting back in unnumbered dazzling lines the glory of the evening sun." Mary Lincoln, who was visiting New York that fall, climbed aboard a Russian frigate to welcome the visitors. Surrounded on the quarterdeck by a crowd of sailors braced by Turkish cigarettes and Italian wines, she offered a toast to Czar Alexander II.

At a ball in honor of the officers at the New York Academy of Music, champagne corks popped as women dressed in velvet and crinoline spun the diminutive Russian sailors around a hall decked out in Russian and American flags. The whole place was flickering with diamonds. The night's caterer, Delmonico's, had constructed portraits of Lincoln and Alexander out of confectionary sugar. It was almost possible to forget that a devastating war was still raging in the American heartland. "The good feeling of the people of Russia,"

Cassius Marcellus Clay reported home from St. Petersburg, had been "greatly heightened by the cordial reception given by our country-men to the Russian officers."[83]

For a time, the whole Northeast was "seized with a Russian mania," the *New York Herald* reported. The sailors eventually made their way south to Washington, where Lincoln's cabinet officers made sure to flaunt them as conspicuously as possible. The secretary of the navy, Gideon Welles, threw an event for the Russians in early December. John Hay noted that the sailors "have vast absorbent powers and are fiendishly ugly." The following night, Hay spotted the Russians at the theater. The men, he told his diary, "were disgustingly tight and demonstrative."

Members of Lincoln's inner circle were initially unsure about what impression the visit would make on French statesmen. Welles told his diary that there was "something significant" in the maneuver, but added that its "effect on France and the French policy we shall learn in due time. It may moderate; it may exasperate." Still, he exulted: "God bless the Russians." The sailors' presence, along with the North's continuing good fortunes on the battlefield, eventually seemed to work a kind of magic on foreign diplomats in Washington. The French minister, Henri Mercier, appeared to be gaining a grudging respect for Seward. *"Il est très sage,"* Mercier was heard saying of Seward—"He is very clever." Hay noted that by mid-December the diplomats had "stopped blackguarding and abusing" the secretary of state. Even those who still did not like Seward, Hay noted, had been "forced to respect."[84]

Napoleon, too, was beginning to respect the burgeoning power of the North. "I realize that I have got myself into a tight place," he admitted as winter approached. He complained, according to one visitor, about the "great mistakes" that had been made in the North American project. The French emperor acknowledged privately that he could no longer maintain control of Mexico. "The affair," he insisted, "has got to be liquidated." The emperor hoped to withdraw most French troops, while at the same time training Mexicans to fill the foreigners' role. Napoleon's "Mexicanization" plan, one historian has noted, bears eerie similarities to Vietnamization plans of the 1970s—and, it should be said, modern American efforts to train the Iraqi and Afghan militaries.[85]

With Banks's troops camped out along the Mexican border, the risk of miscalculation on both sides posed a serious threat. "If raids were to take place on Mexico from Texas," Napoleon worried to Maximilian, "I might suddenly find myself at war with the Americans—a war which would spell disaster to the interests of France and would have no possible object."

Lincoln and Seward shared the French emperor's fears. In late November, the American consul in Matamoros—the Mexican town just across the border from Banks's men in Brownsville—asked the American commander for protection. Banks trained his guns on the Mexican castle just opposite his encampment. An exasperated Seward later briefed the president on the incident. "Firing on the town," the secretary of state complained to Lincoln, "would involve us in a war with the Lord knows who."

"Or rather," the president shot back, "the Lord knows who not."[86]

The Imperial Cat's Paw

On December 3, 1863, horses attached to ropes and pulleys hoisted Thomas Crawford's bronze statue *Freedom* to the top of the just-completed Capitol dome in Washington. Cannon from all the Union forts surrounding the city rumbled in tribute. As a symbolic gesture of the Federal government's rising strength, the ceremony was hard to top. The president, meanwhile, was finally beginning to win the respect he sought from foreign powers. New Jersey politician James Scovel wrote Lincoln from London reporting that British liberal Richard Cobden had been speaking "most warmly in praise of you," lauding the American president's "coolness and forecast at the time of the *Trent* affair. He highly approves of your policy of 'one war at a time.' " Scovel, who had traveled Britain that autumn speaking at mass meetings, told the president that his audiences "always applauded at the mention of Abraham Lincoln's name."[87]

On December 8, five days after the Capitol dome was completed, Lincoln sent his annual message to Congress. The section on foreign affairs made note of the North's improving fortunes. The Union alone now possessed more "armored vessels" than "any other power," according to the message. American iron and timber supplies were also "superior to any other nation." As recently as the last session of Congress, Europeans had looked upon the war-torn United States with "pity." Now, however, the "tone of public sentiment" abroad was "much improved." Naval secretary Gideon Welles observed in his diary that autumn that the American ironclads and "heavy ordnance" were having "a tranquilizing effect" on the "tone and temper" of British and French statesmen.[88]

And yet the French presence in Mexico continued to trouble the president and his inner circle. Even Sumner, who went out of his way to placate the French emperor, found himself tangling with Napoleon's representative in Washington. When Mercier argued to the Massachusetts senator around Christmastime that "a division of the Union is inevitable," Sumner "snapped his fingers at" Mercier and "told him he knew not our case," Welles wrote in his diary. "Palmerston and Louis Napoleon," the naval secretary scribbled, "are the two bad men in this matter. The latter is quite belligerent in his feelings, but fears to be insolent towards us unless England is also engaged."[89]

Lincoln, too, remained preoccupied with Mexico. On New Year's Day 1864, the president held his annual reception at the White House. A former State Department employee recorded in his diary that Lincoln quietly quizzed the Mexican minister about his country's affairs as the receiving line wound its way through the ground floor. The entire exchange was accomplished "stealthily and *sotto voce*," the diarist observed, "in a manner as if Lincoln was afraid of the other diplomats." The Mexican, who supported the republican forces that were fighting to oust the French, explained to the president that the rebels were making good progress. "Oh, I am very glad," Lincoln replied, somewhat undiplomatically. "I wish you may have the best of the invaders."[90]

Some hawks in Congress, however, were determined to launch an invasion of their own. In January 1864, they renewed their efforts to pass a resolution calling for Napoleon's expulsion from Mexico. James A. McDougall, a California senator and old acquaintance of Lincoln's from his days as a lawyer on the Illinois circuit, authored a motion condemning the Mexican venture. The French emperor, McDougall insisted, should be immediately ordered to withdraw his forces. If he refused, "on or before the 15th day of March next it will become the duty of the Congress of the United States of America to declare war against the Government of France."[91]

McDougall was not one of the Senate's shining lights. Lincoln's friend Orville Browning once recalled watching the California Democrat stumble "quite drunk" onto the chamber floor. A correspondent for the *Sacramento Daily Union* reported that McDougall "has only been in the Senate a few times this winter, then drunk, booted like a dragoon and spurred like a Spanish *vaquero*. He falls drunk from his horse on Pennsylvania Avenue. In a word, he is the first drunkard in Washington." A dedicated expansionist, for months McDougall had been challenging Lincoln to take on Napoleon in Mexico. He warned that French forces could easily establish a foothold on the Colorado River and then swiftly conquer San Diego. "We have nothing of value to lose by a French war," McDougall declared in a speech on the Senate floor. "We have everything to gain, and for one I am unwilling to avoid it."[92]

Even if McDougall was only "little more than a drunken clown," as one historian puts it, his blustering unnerved French diplomats. Seward was forced to dispatch a stream of letters to the American representatives in Paris emphasizing that Lincoln did not share Congress's belligerent stance. The congressional resolutions, the secretary of state told his minister in France, were "not in harmony with the policy of neutrality, forbearance, and conciliation which the president has so faithfully pursued." A few weeks later, he again warned his men in the field that there would be a "legislative demonstration" against the French project in Mexico. Seward insisted that only "executive moderation" was managing to restrain the popular animosity toward Napoleon.[93]

In some cases, however, even members of Lincoln's own diplomatic corps had been urging Congress to take a harder line. The previous autumn James Shepherd Pike, Lincoln's envoy to the Netherlands, had written home to a Maine senator complaining about the submissive tone "which seems to be taken in the United States over the suppression of Mexican independence and the erection of an empire upon its ruins." In late January, Edward Lee Plumb, the businessman who sometimes worked as a State Department translator, urged Charles Sumner to "let it be known to the world that the people of the United States have not abandoned the Monroe Doctrine, that they do not and cannot look with favor or indifference on the attempt of a European power to overthrow republican institutions and introduce a European form of government into their neighborhood and sister republic."[94]

Lincoln and Seward did their best to hold a firm line against the hawks in Congress, the State Department, and elsewhere. Sumner backed them up. "Sir," Sumner complained to one hard-liner, "have we not war enough already on our hands, without needlessly and wantonly provoking another?" He managed to kill McDougall's resolution, complaining that there was "madness in the proposition" of taking on Napoleon while still fighting a war at home. Mexican envoy Matías Romero, meanwhile, was growing increasingly impatient with the Lincoln administration's refusal to take on Napoleon. He groused to his superiors that Sumner's "fear of France makes him as condescending with that nation as Seward."[95]

The tug-of-war over Mexico wore Lincoln down. To one journalist, Noah Brooks, the president complained that the senators trying to gin up a war with France sapped his strength. Lincoln imagined himself as the target of a pack of hungry predators. The president told Brooks that he dreaded the encounters, in which pushy senators "darted at me with thumb and finger, picked out their especial piece of my vitality, and carried it off."[96]

Lincoln's scheme for colonization off the coast of Haiti gave Congress more ammunition to attack the president. Lincoln had authorized U.S. funds for Kock's adventure on the Île à Vache but had not paid much attention to the details of the contract. As it turned out, conditions on the island were miserable. Colonists, attacked by disease-carrying bugs, begged to come home; many of them died on the island. The rest forced Kock to flee. Lincoln eventually had to order a Union ship to the Caribbean to clean up the bungled operation. Congress, already on Lincoln's case over Mexico, pounced. The body eventually launched an investigation and froze further funds for colonization amid a frenzied round of bureaucratic politics.[97]

Still, newspaper correspondents in the capital marveled at the way Lincoln personally seemed to escape from the most strident criticisms. More often, Seward found himself taking the blame for the administration. While Lincoln and Seward crafted their foreign policies together, a writer for the *Philadelphia Sunday Dispatch* observed, "President Lincoln is not held responsible" when plans unfolded badly. Part of the reason, the reporter speculated, was Lincoln's clever style of meeting individually with Seward or other cabinet ministers, rather than in large councils: "This way of doing business is not relished by the old fogies; but it relieves the administration, and, consequently, the president. It was not Lincoln's administration, but Seward, who let the French set aside the Monroe Doctrine in Mexico"—or so the thinking went, which probably suited the president just fine.[98]

Across the Atlantic, meanwhile, the French emperor was preparing to begin the next stage of his Mexican operation. Maximilian and Charlotte had remained in Europe—at their castle in Miramar, along the Adriatic coast of present-day Italy—while French forces worked to pacify Mexico. Now, just as Napoleon was losing interest in the project, they finally prepared to depart and claim their thrones in the New World. Maximilian's father-in-law, King Leopold of Belgium, warned the Austrian archduke that the mission was looking increasingly perilous. Napoleon, Leopold cautioned, was "bent upon withdrawing his troops from Mexico, for if things go badly, then he is exonerated." Leopold urged his son-in-law to get a promise "officially and in writing" from the emperor confirming French support for the venture. Otherwise, Leopold warned, Maximilian would simply be acting as the imperial "cat's-paw."[99]

Maximilian, perhaps convinced by his father-in-law's warning, began to get cold feet. Napoleon no longer seemed committed to maintaining the French military presence. The Austrian government, meanwhile, was also growing wary of the project. Maximilian's family told the archduke that if he proceeded to Mexico, he would have to renounce his place in line for the Austrian throne. Wags on both sides of the Atlantic began referring to Maximilian as the Archdupe.

Maximilian wrote to Napoleon and tried to back out. The French emperor, however, viewed the Austrian archduke as his best hope for sloughing off the project. Napoleon scolded Maximilian that it was now "impossible" for him to give up on the mission. "Your Imperial Highness," the emperor wrote to Maximilian in March, "has entered into engagements which you are no longer free to break. What would you really think of me, if, when Your Imperial Highness had already reached Mexico, I were suddenly to say that I can no longer fulfill the conditions to which I have set my signature!"

Finally, in mid-April, Maximilian agreed to renounce the Austrian throne and depart for Mexico. On April 14, 1864, he prepared to board the Austrian vessel *Novara* and sail for the New World. Crowds thronged the streets in Miramar, and a hundred porters carted the imperial baggage onto the ship. Women threw flowers and a band played the Mexican imperial anthem as Maximilian and Charlotte strode under an elegant red-and-gold sunshade and onto the *Novara*. For the imperial couple, it was an emotional parting. As their boat slipped away from the shore, past a flotilla of tiny fishing boats, Charlotte cried out, "Look at poor Max! How he is weeping!"[100]

As Maximilian and Charlotte were preparing to depart Miramar, the Union armies suffered a series of troubling setbacks. General Banks, after finally establishing a foothold near the Mexican border, launched an ill-advised campaign along Louisiana's Red River (named for the color of its muddy water). Union commanders wanted to send Banks up the river to Shreveport, in the state's northwest corner, a maneuver designed at least partly to place the French emperor on guard. From there, Banks and his men could join a Union attack on strategically critical Mobile, Alabama.

Banks's men, however, never reached their destination. As the spring rain poured down on the Union troopers, they sank up to their ankles in red slime. On April 8, Confederate defenders launched a counterattack near Mansfield, Louisiana. The Federals, one witness recalled, degenerated into "a disorganized mob of screaming, sobbing, hysterical, pale, terror-stricken men." Banks found himself desperately waving his sword in the air, trying unsuccessfully to convince his men to hold fast. The officer's troops ultimately mocked their commander as "Napoleon P. Banks."[101]

The Red River debacle frustrated Lincoln. After the president got the news of the campaign's failure, he read aloud from "The Fire-Worshippers," a section of Thomas Moore's romantic epic, *Lalla Rookh*, including the lines "Oh! ever thus, from childhood's hour, / I've seen my fondest hopes decay. . . ."[102] In Congress, Henry Winter Davis, chair of the House Committee on Foreign Affairs, had already been scolding Lincoln for his hapless Mexican policy. The congressman convinced the House of Representatives to pass a measure denouncing "the deplorable events now transpiring in the Republic of Mexico"—a provocative gesture that Lincoln and Seward would have preferred to have avoided. The secretary of state grumbled that "party politicians think that the Mexican question affords them a fulcrum, and they seem willing to work their lever reckless of dangers to the country." Some members of the national media also chimed in. The *New York Herald* complained of "the namby-pamby, wishy-washy foreign policy of the administration."[103]

Seward continued to assure his diplomats in Paris that the White House did not share the aggressive posture of Congress and the penny press, although the secretary of state acknowledged that the French occupation remained "a source of continued irritation." Legislators, he wrote, were only reflecting widespread popular pressure to confront the French armies. Seward predicted that—as in the case of the *Trent* affair—the executive would ultimately be able to steer the ship of state safely through the crisis. In any case, he added, if the most determined expansionists would just display a little patience, they would ultimately get their way. "Five years, ten years, twenty years hence," Seward wrote in a confidential dispatch to his consul in Paris, "Mexico will be opening herself as cheerfully to American immigration as Montana and Idaho are now. What European power can then maintain an army in Mexico capable of resisting material and moral influences of emigration?"[104]

In the spring of 1864, however, it sometimes seemed as if the war would never end. Grant plunged his army south through Virginia, but the campaign was slow going. Northern and Southern troops battled fearsomely in the Wilderness—a bleak stretch of land near the Rapidan River consisting of little more than scrub trees and tangled vines. As Grant's forces bogged down in their drive south toward Petersburg, casualties mounted dramatically. By June more than sixty-five thousand Union troops had been killed, wounded, or had simply vanished—more than half as many as had been lost in the preceding three years.[105]

Lincoln took the setbacks hard. He found it difficult to get any sleep during the Wilderness campaign. One visitor to the White House that May, the artist Francis Carpenter, found Lincoln in the residence dressed only in a "long morning wrapper," pacing in front of a window, "his hands behind him, great black rings under his eyes, his head bent forward upon his breast—altogether such a picture of the effects of sorrow, care, and anxiety as would have melted the hearts of the worst of his adversaries." During those tense days, Carpenter noted, the president would usually take his dinner upstairs, alone. "I *must* have some relief from this terrible anxiety," Lincoln complained, "or it will kill me." Lincoln observed that no matter how much rest he got, it "seemed never to reach the *tired* spot."[106]

The president had neither the energy nor the will to confront Napoleon over Mexico now. Seward, too, found it baffling that some people still wanted to divert troops needed to defeat the Confederate rebellion. The secretary of state, Gideon Welles reported in late May, "is becoming very anxious in view of our relations with France." Seward continued to resist taking a harder line. "I think," the secretary of state protested in late May to Bigelow in Paris, "with our land and naval forces in Louisiana retreating before the rebels instead of marching towards Mexico, this is not the most suitable time we could choose for offering idle menaces to the Emperor of France. . . . Why should we gasconade about Mexico when we are in a struggle for our own life?" Seward insisted that the American people would never forgive the administration if the country slipped into a new war over "a contingent and merely speculative issue like that of the future of Mexico."[107]

Lincoln and Seward could never completely drown out the calls for the French emperor's head, but they did try to placate Napoleon in small ways. In May Lincoln relaxed the blockade somewhat, permitting the export of the type of horses "as have been bought for the personal use of the Emperor of the French." Napoleon—whose squat legs and awkward gait made him prefer making his public appearances on horseback—undoubtedly appreciated the gesture.[108]

Yet even as Lincoln was making efforts to normalize trade ties with Napoleon, activists were pressing the First Lady to boycott French goods. Washington was full of Continental fashions that spring. The wives of diplomats and legislators happily strolled Pennsylvania Avenue "in full Parisian attire," one newspaper reported. As the season unfolded, a representative from a group calling itself the Ladies' National Covenant approached Mary and urged her to avoid buying European "web-velvets and plushes, satins, white and black thread laces, foreign embroideries, foreign artificial flowers and feathers, ermine, camel's hair shawls, French hats, bonnets, caps, and head-dresses." The women even tried to ban champagne from Washington parties. At first Mary was receptive. She "impulsively" agreed to sign the pledge, one activist later recalled. Lincoln, however, was outraged at the First Lady's freelancing on critical trade issues. "You have no idea what a hornets' nest you are stirring up," he told his wife. Considering the delicate "state of our foreign relations," the president explained, signing the boycott "will never do."[109]

The Day of Reckoning

On May 28, 1864, the *Novara*, carrying Maximilian and Charlotte, finally made landfall in Veracruz, Mexico, after the six-week transatlantic journey. At least at first, the European monarchs were discouraged by what they found. As they climbed ashore, Maximilian and Charlotte had to pass the carcass of a wrecked French ship and a cemetery full of French yellow-fever victims. Vultures picked at garbage alongside the dilapidated ruins of the customs houses. Someone had erected a few arches made of flowers by way of welcome. But on their first night in the country, a furious windstorm blew the arches down.[110]

The trip to Mexico City was no more encouraging. The views were breathtaking; they drove past acres of mango, banana, and coconut groves. Yet the road was pocked with pits and rocks and the rainy weather was depressing. Few locals turned out along the route to welcome their new head of state. "Everything in this country calls for reconstruction," Charlotte wrote to Eugénie after finally arriving in the capital two weeks later. "Nothing is to be found, either physical or moral, but what nature provides." The whole venture, she told the French empress, "remains a gigantic experiment, for one has to struggle against the desert, the distance, the roads, and the most utter chaos."[111]

Once in Mexico City, however, Maximilian and Charlotte warmed to their surroundings. As they entered the capital, residents peppered the imperial couple with flowers from the balconies, waved sombreros, and shot off firecrackers. To Charlotte, the capital actually seemed vaguely cosmopolitan. "In Mexico City," she told Eugénie, "it is very much as in Europe." Maximilian bragged to his brother about the beauty of Mexican women. The couple particularly enjoyed the palace at Chapultepec—the magnificent castle perched atop a basalt cliff just west of Mexico City. From the top, the views stretched out toward huge volcanoes and snowcapped peaks. Hummingbirds and butterflies fluttered between giant, thousand-year-old cypress trees. Elaborate gardens filled the air with the scent of rose blossoms and oranges.[112]

In Washington, meanwhile, Lincoln was beginning to pick up the scent of a second term in office. "No man knows what *that gnawing* is till he has had it," the president admitted of his rising desire. On June 7–8, Lincoln supporters gathered in Baltimore to re-nominate the president. The delegates took the opportunity to launch one more rhetorical volley at Napoleon. They passed a resolution declaring that the party would "view with extreme jealousy, as menacing to the peace and independence of their own country, the efforts of any such power to obtain new footholds for monarchical governments, sustained by foreign military force, in near proximity to the United States." The statement, Hay and Nicolay later recalled, "was a wider and more energetic extension of the Monroe Doctrine than had ever before been put forward in so authoritative a form by any body representing the majority of the people of the United States."[113]

Lincoln found himself pushing back against his own party to avoid antagonizing the French emperor. The president "heartily approved" the resolutions passed by the convention but went to great lengths to assure the convention committee that he would stand by his cautious approach to the occupation. "While the resolution in regard to the supplanting of republican government upon the Western continent is fully concurred in," he wrote the delegates, "there might be misunderstanding were I not to say that the position of the government, in relation to the action of France in Mexico, as assumed through the State Department, and approved and indorsed by the convention, among the measures and acts of the Executive, will be faithfully maintained, so long as the state of facts shall leave that position pertinent and applicable."[114]

The convention also dumped Lincoln's vice president, Hannibal Hamlin, and replaced him with Tennessee's military governor, Andrew Johnson. Some observers believed that Lincoln had favored Johnson because he thought a Southerner on the ticket would bolster support for the Union overseas. (Lincoln's secretaries denied that he had in any way influenced the choice.) In any case, Johnson almost immediately gave Lincoln heartburn when it came to Mexican diplomacy. Shortly after learning of his nomination, Johnson appeared at a huge rally in Nashville. "The day of reckoning is approaching," the vice-presidential nominee told the cheering crowd. "The time is not far distant when the rebellion will be put down, and then we will attend to this Mexican affair and say to Louis Napoleon, 'You can get up no monarchy on this continent.'" The crowd broke into wild applause. Johnson sneered that an American invasion of Mexico would be "a sort of recreation" for the battle-hardened troops. "The French concern," Johnson declared, "would quickly be wiped out."[115]

By the middle of 1864, Lincoln was increasingly buoyed by the Union military. "The national resources are not at all exhausted," the president told one crowd in Philadelphia. "This war has taken three years. . . . We are going through on this line if it takes three years more." The audience whooped in delight. Having riled up the throng, the president then asked if he could count on them if he needed even more recruits for Grant's armies. "Will you give them to me?" he asked. The crowd roared back: "Yes!"[116]

Throughout the summer, however, Congress continued to press

Lincoln on Mexico. The attacks gradually grew more serious. Organized Radical Republicans—not just individual agitators—began using Lincoln's foreign policy as an election-year cudgel. In late June the Senate sent the president a resolution demanding information about potential arms shipments to Mexican republicans. John Hay asked Seward what to do about the request. The secretary of state was miffed. "Our friends are very anxious to get into a war with France, using this Mexican business for that purpose," Seward told Hay. "They don't consider that England and France would surely be together in that event. France has the whip hand of England completely." The Union was fortunate that England had abandoned its part in the Mexican project, the secretary of state told Hay. Since then, the European powers had been kept apart through "good management" on behalf of Northern diplomats. Why reunite England and France now? "Worse than that," Seward added, "instead of doing something effective, if we must fight, they are for making mouths and shaking fists at France—warning and threatening and inducing her to prepare for our attack when it comes."[117]

There was little chance that any attack would come before the November elections, which were quickly approaching. By the late summer of 1864, Lincoln's prospects for reelection seemed dim. If things did not improve on the battlefield, Napoleon and Mexico would be someone else's problem in a matter of months. The president, noted one visitor to the White House in July, "shows marks of mental overwork." Lincoln felt that his administration had "no friends" in Washington. On August 23, he gathered his cabinet in the Executive Mansion. The president passed around a folded sheet of paper, and, without revealing the contents, asked each cabinet officer to sign the back. "This morning," Lincoln had written inside, "as for some days past, it seems exceedingly probable that this Administration will not be re-elected. Then it will be my duty to so cooperate with the President elect, as to save the Union between the election and the inauguration; as he will have secured his election on such ground that he cannot possibly save it afterwards." The president did not reveal the contents until weeks later, when the campaign was finally over.[118]

Even some of Lincoln's erstwhile admirers in the diplomatic corps had begun to turn against him. Matías Romero, the increasingly frustrated Washington-based representative of the anti-Maximilian Mexican liberals, met over the summer with James McDougall, the drunken California senator who had been aggressively advocating a harder line on Mexico. McDougall complained to Romero that the president's reelection would be a "calamity" for Mexico. The senator grumbled about his one-time acquaintance Lincoln's "very objectionable conduct of United States foreign affairs, most especially his policy in regard to Mexico." Romero, who was eager for a new American administration that might challenge Maximilian's regime more forcefully, agreed to help McDougall compile opposition research—a dossier that would help Mexico hawks "vigorously to attack the government on the subject."[119]

Lincoln's reelection prospects improved instantaneously, however, with the arrival of a telegram from General William Tecumseh Sherman on September 3. "Atlanta is ours, and fairly won," the dispatch read. Lincoln's armies finally dominated the heart of the Southern Confederacy. From the Hague, the U.S. minister to the Netherlands reported that the news had effected "a marked change in the public sentiment of Europe in regard to our affairs." The capture of Atlanta "suddenly destroyed the illusion" that the major Confederate cities were invulnerable. As a result, the diplomat observed, "the public judgment on the whole subject fell to pieces."[120]

Seward was in the library of his home in Auburn, New York, when he got the news. Euphoric revelers poured into the park across from his house, as cannon thundered and church bells tolled in celebration. The secretary of state gave an hour-long speech lauding the victory. In a reference that Napoleon III would not have missed, Seward compared Lincoln's secretary of war to the military mastermind of the French Revolution. American newspapers began comparing Sherman to the French emperor's conquering uncle.[121]

Actually, imperial adventures remained the last thing that Lincoln and Seward wanted in the autumn of 1864. With the final defeat of the Confederacy in reach, only some unpredictable event like an unwanted war with France had the potential to scuttle the Union victory. In late September, Seward wrote to a Union military commander in New Orleans, reiterating that he should avoid provoking a conflict with France at all cost. "On no account," Seward wrote, "and in no way, must the neutrality of the United States in the war between France and Mexico be compromised by our military forces." The president sent a good-natured letter to Napoleon congratulating him on the birth of a second son to his cousin Prince Napoleon Joseph Bonaparte and Marie Clotilde of Savoie. Lincoln wrote that he hoped God would protect the royal family, warmly signing the missive, "Your Good Friend." Mention of the Monroe Doctrine was nowhere to be found.[122]

Gratuitous threats were unnecessary. The events of the fall spoke for themselves. Lincoln's reelection on November 8 could not help but impress the European powers. Around seven p.m. on a drizzly election night, the president and a small band of supporters left the White House and walked over to the War Department to get the returns. Lincoln, despite the wet weather, was in a good mood. In the warmth of the war office, the president joked around and served fried oysters to his guests. The news was all good. Telegram after telegram arrived announcing wide margins for Lincoln. The party did not break up until well after midnight, when Lincoln's reelection appeared sure. The president ended up winning by more than four hundred thousand ballots and nearly two hundred electoral votes.[123]

Two nights later, a euphoric crowd arrived at the White House after dark, pushing up to the front gates and then spilling onto the front lawn. The revelers dangled lanterns and hoisted banners, while a band played military marches. The concussion from a pounding cannon shivered the windows of the Executive Mansion, delighting eleven-year-old Tad. The boy flew from window to window taking in the scene.

Lincoln dreaded serenades. "I never know what to say on these occasions," he once remarked. Nevertheless, he scratched down several dozen lines of a short speech in his clear, looping hand. Then he walked to a window above the north portico, gazing out at the dim shape of the crowd shifting in the dark below. When the revelers spotted the president's tall, gaunt figure, they erupted in "the maddest cheers"—a "deafening racket" that lasted for several minutes.[124]

As he began to speak, Lincoln reminded his audience of the Civil War's global significance. The progress of the war shows "how *sound*, and how *strong* we still are," the president cried, in his shrill, piercing voice with a hint of a Kentucky drawl. The Union victories were not just a message to the Confederacy, Lincoln insisted, but a demonstration to the world. "We have more men now, than we had when the war began. Gold is good in its place; but living, brave, patriotic men, are better than gold." The London *Times* considered Lincoln's brief remarks "one of the best speeches he has ever made." Lincoln's secretaries, too, thought the serenade response "one of the weightiest and wisest of all his discourses." It contained, Hay and Nicolay later held, "the inmost philosophy of republican governments."[125]

Meanwhile, congratulations flooded in from supporters at home and abroad. From London, Karl Marx wrote on behalf of the International Working Men's Association to congratulate Lincoln on "the triumphant war cry of your reelection." In a private letter to a relative a few weeks after the election, Marx marveled at the "gigantic transformation" in American politics. The results, Marx declared, would "have a beneficent effect on the whole world." John Lothrop Motley, Lincoln's minister in Vienna, saw Lincoln's reelection as a victory for the New World at the expense of Old Europe. Motley told the president that it had been naïve of Union diplomats at the start of the war to think they could change the minds of "the privileged classes of Europe." Public opinion in elite quarters remained "depraved," Motley wrote Lincoln. And yet, the diplomat added, the Union effort had managed to secure "the sympathy of the uncounted millions of mankind throughout the civilized world, who would be left without a hope if the great transatlantic commonwealth should go down in this struggle."[126]

In Atlanta, meanwhile, Sherman prepared to jump off on his commanding March to the Sea. The disheveled, chain-smoking former banker had recognized the international implications of the war early on. Shortly before Lincoln's reelection, Sherman telegraphed Grant, suggesting that if they could manage to march an army straight through Confederate territory, it would provide "a demonstration to the world, foreign and domestic, that we have a power which Davis cannot resist." Lincoln, however, was not initially so sanguine. He later admitted to being *"anxious,* if not fearful" as Sherman's army of sixty thousand departed Atlanta on November 15 for the Georgia coast.[127]

Indeed, as Sherman's forces plunged on to Savannah, stomping through the red-clay roads with bands blaring "John Brown's Body," Europeans seemed puzzled by the maneuver. "Military history," the London *Times* observed, "has recorded no stranger marvel than the mysterious expedition of General Sherman, on an unknown route against an undiscoverable enemy." Henry Adams reported from London that Britons remained skeptical. Still, he added, the "interest felt in his march is enormous." If Sherman were to succeed, Adams wrote, "you may rely upon it that the moral effect of his demonstration on Europe will be greater than that of any other event of the war. It will finish the rebs on this side."[128]

The tens of thousands of battle-hardened Federal troops hurtling southward must have unnerved Napoleon. The Mexican adventure had long since lost its charm for the French emperor. He insisted that Maximilian should abandon any illusions of liberal reforms and first try to get a grip on his country. "I consider," the French emperor wrote to Maximilian in November, "that Your Majesty is bound to keep the absolute power in your hands for a long time." From Chapultepec, Maximilian and Charlotte begged the emperor to avoid further drawdowns of French troops. Charlotte complained to Eugénie that their efforts to control the country were "much hampered" by the shrinking French forces. As the New Year dawned, Charlotte reported that the Mexican monarchy was passing through "a grave crisis." Only "big battalions," she insisted, would save Napoleon's project.[129]

There Has Been War Enough

As Northern armies laid siege to the last bastions of Confederate power, Lincoln began to feel his oats. With Grant's army stalled near Petersburg, Virginia, a delegation visited the White House, complaining about the Union army's progress. Lincoln walked over to a map and explained to the visitors how close Grant actually was to victory. The president then broke into one of his ribald stories— this one about "a wicked and lascivious sinner" in Indiana who had asked to be baptized. The preacher took the man to the local river and dunked him in. When the sinner came up for air, "gasping and rubbing his face," he immediately asked to be dunked again. The preacher was puzzled but ultimately obliged. When the man emerged the second time, he exclaimed, "Now I've been baptized twice, and the Devil can kiss my ass." Lincoln jabbed a finger at a place on the map, and insisted that when his army arrived at that spot, the Union would finally be victorious. "And then," Lincoln told his visitors, "the Southern Confederacy can kiss my ass."[130]

The same went for Napoleon III. Fortunately, by early 1865, French public opinion had also turned violently against the adventure in Mexico. Auguste Laugel, a French correspondent for *The Nation* magazine, wrote about the changing national mood in his country—and urged U.S. policymakers to avoid sending the military south of the Rio Grande.

Charles Sumner brought Laugel to the White House to see Lincoln in January. The Frenchman found Lincoln in his second-floor office, running one of his huge hands through his coarse, disheveled hair. Through two large windows Laugel could make out "the white streak of the Potomac, the Virginia heights, the unfinished Washington obelisk." Lincoln displayed an "almost paternal gentleness," Laugel told his diary. The Americans did not seem inclined to challenge the French emperor. At a dinner at Seward's the following night, the secretary of state sounded even more sympathetic. "It is not my judgment that the emperor is hostile to us," Seward said. "It seems to me that I could bring him over."[131]

Still, ordinary Americans did not appear so magnanimous. In late January the French journalist visited the Federal armies in the field. There he found "great irritation against England" in the ranks. "Sir," one young soldier from Vermont told Laugel, "if war were declared against England, were it ten years hence, or twenty, I would not wait a day to enter a regiment, as a private if need be." Laugel suspected that the troops harbored as great an anger against France—but concealed it "out of politeness." With each day that passed during his travels, Laugel became more convinced that France should be courting America rather than provoking it. "America has felt her strength," he later wrote, "and will want to make use of it like a bird who feels its wings." France, he insisted, should be positioning itself to "profit by this new force"—not antagonize it.[132]

Back in France, Napoleon seemed to be slowly getting the message. "What I really want," the emperor told Bigelow in February, "is to get out of Mexico altogether." The French emperor alleged that his efforts had done some good in Mexico. Maximilian's regime, Napoleon said in a speech from the throne in February, was "establishing itself, the country is becoming peaceful, its immense resources are being developed; a happy effect of the bravery of our soldiers, the good sense of the Mexican population, and the intelligence and energy of the sovereign." And yet later in the same speech, Napoleon announced a dramatic reduction in French troop levels around the world. "Thus," the emperor continued, "all our overseas expeditions are reaching an end." The French army in Mexico, Napoleon said, "is already returning to France."[133] In the meantime, the French emperor did his best to reassure his protégés in Mexico. "We have been rather uneasy at the news from America," Napoleon wrote. "However, it looks as if the war will still last a long time, and when peace comes, the United States will think twice before declaring war on France and England."[134]

High above Mexico City, in their palace at Chapultepec, Maximilian and Charlotte tried to whistle past the graveyard. With his empire crumbling around him, Maximilian did his best to distract the diplomatic corps in the city. Each Monday Charlotte would throw a ball and invite the "boring" local diplomats. The former Belgian princess would fill the events with "a bevy of the loveliest women," Maximilian told his brother. Guests at the balls could often hear the rumbling cannon from battles with guerrillas in the distance over the music. The former Austrian archduke resorted to stuffing the foreign envoys with rich cuisine and wines from the imperial cellars. "The diplomatists gorge and swill to such an extent," Maximilian told his brother, "that as a rule after dinner they can only mumble inarticulate sounds."[135]

Lincoln, too, could barely speak as the war entered its final days. Shortly before the second inaugural, the president's old friend Joshua Speed visited the White House and found Lincoln "worn down in health and spirits." Lincoln complained that he felt ill. "I am very unwell," he told Speed. "My feet and hands are always cold. I suppose I ought to be in bed." The poet Walt Whitman spotted the president at the White House the following week. Lincoln, he reported, appeared "very much worn and tired; the lines indeed of vast responsibilities, intricate questions, the demands of life and death cut deeper than ever upon his dark brown face; yet all the old goodness, tenderness, sadness, and canny shrewdness [remained] underneath the furrows."[136]

Lincoln's tragic sensibility seemed to pervade even his public pronouncements. On the cool, cloudy morning of March 4, Lincoln delivered his second inaugural in the shadow of the newly completed Capitol dome. The president, appearing "gaunt" and "skeleton-like" to one observer, perched his steel-rim glasses on his nose and gathered together the oversize sheets of foolscap on which he had written the 703 words of the speech. Lincoln's audience included Washington's diplomatic corps—one of whom, a journalist reported, "was so stiff with gold lace" that he could barely sit down. (In his own address, before Lincoln's, a drunken Vice President Andrew Johnson had insulted the gathered diplomats, mocking the "fine feathers and gewgaws" of their ornate uniforms.) Now, as Lincoln began his own address, a ray of sun emerged from the clouds.[137]

Lincoln's second inaugural should be considered one of America's seminal foreign-policy documents. The only explicit reference to global affairs comes in the last line, with its appeal for a just and lasting peace "with all nations." Yet the president's words can be read as a profound meditation on America's place in the world. Both North and South, Lincoln told the crowd, "read the same Bible, and pray to the same God; and each invokes his aid against the other. It may seem strange that any men should dare to ask a just God's assistance in wringing their bread from the sweat of other men's faces; but let us judge not that we be not judged. The prayers of both could not be answered; that of neither has been answered fully. The Almighty has His own purposes."[138]

France, England, Spain, Mexico, and Russia, of course, also read the same Bible and prayed to the same god. Understood one way, then, the address trenchantly sets forth a worldview in which Lincoln's Union is portrayed as one nation among others—not as God's chosen people on earth. If morality were to be found in international relations, it would emerge from a just balance of competing national interests—not romantic crusades. The theologian Reinhold Niebuhr, a shrewd thinker about the place of love and justice in global affairs, later observed that Lincoln's second inaugural proclaimed the "partiality of all historic commitments." The president's address, Niebuhr concluded, "put the enemy into the same category of ambiguity as the nation to which his life was committed."[139]

Europeans appreciated the appeal to international justice. From tense Paris, the *Chicago Tribune* correspondent reported that

Lincoln's speech "has been received here with unmitigated satisfaction." Frenchmen praised the address for "its moderation of tone, its wise reticence with respect to the war, the absence of all boasting either as regards the glorious past or the hopeful future." Bigelow wrote home from the French capital to say that the address "has enjoyed a rare distinction for an American state paper of being correctly translated and almost universally copied here. This, I think, is less due to its brevity than to its almost inspired simplicity and Christian dignity."[140]

America's penny press, on the other hand, did not universally laud the oration. The *New York Herald* scolded Lincoln for saying nothing about the French presence in Mexico. Lincoln later dismissed the gripes. "Men are not flattered," the president explained, "by being shown that there has been a difference of purpose between the Almighty and them."[141]

And yet even as Lincoln proclaimed his government's humility, the president celebrated the occasion in high style. One fashion magazine reported on the "august assemblage" of "foreign ministers with their wives" that paraded through the inaugural ball. Mary wore a white satin dress with a matching lace flounce. Heavy silk cords and tassels swung from the garment, and white-and-purple flowers adorned her hair. The scene, the correspondent continued, "impressed us as being fully equal to the . . . pageants of the Old World." As March progressed, even the president began to loosen up a little, occasionally taking Mary out to the opera. "Mr L.," the First Lady told a friend, "when he throws off his heavy manner, as he often does, can make himself very, very agreeable."[142]

Not all Europeans were comfortable with the rejoicing across the Atlantic. The American president now commanded the world's largest army and a navy shimmering with ironclads. Any cold analysis of the new balance of power could not fail to take note of the colossus of North America. From Mexico, Charlotte wrote to Eugénie pleading that Napoleon's regime not be "too optimistic" about their prospects in Mexico. Maximilian's government was like "ivy,"

Charlotte told the empress—"we shall grow into a tree, but for the moment we still need a trunk to cling to." Austria's minister in Washington, Baron Wydenbruck, also cautioned against taking American power lightly. "It is certain that the inexhaustible resources at the disposal of the American people have developed in an eminent degree its sense of its own power and of the part reserved for it in the events of the world," he warned. "The naval powers of Europe will in future have to reckon more and more with this proud and sensitive people."[143]

As the spring unfolded, the news only improved for Lincoln. In the first days of April, Grant's Army of the Potomac finally penetrated the Confederate defenses around Richmond. Lincoln had traveled from Washington to the front lines with his son Tad to witness the fall of the Confederate capital. From City Point, Virginia, the president watched as Grant's men made their final assault on a rainy, moonless night. Lincoln could hear the pounding of the cannon and see their flickering light reflected against the clouds. On the warm, sunny Sunday morning of April 3, Grant's men finally broke the Confederate lines and barreled into Richmond. "Thank God that I have lived to see this," Lincoln exulted. "It seems to me that I have been dreaming a horrid dream for four years, and now the nightmare is gone. I want to see Richmond." The president and his son walked the shattered streets of the Confederate capital, surrounded by cheering crowds.[144]

On April 6, Mary Lincoln joined her husband at City Point. She was accompanied by the Marquis de Chambrun—a young grandson of Lafayette's who was visiting the United States. Mary, long a Francophile,[145] had renewed her French studies once again in the last days of the war. She peppered Chambrun with flowers and invitations. Now Mary and the Marquis joined Lincoln in the saloon of the *River Queen*—the same space in which Stephens had pressed his case for an invasion of Mexico earlier that year. Lincoln showed Chambrun around the room, pointing out where each of the delegates to the conference had sat.

Chambrun thought the sunburned Lincoln's eyes looked sunken and full of "deep sadness." He marveled at the way Lincoln would shift, in the course of a single evening, from mirth to melancholy— one moment regaling his company with jokes, and the next clos- ing his eyes to "retire within himself." One night the Frenchman counted more than twenty "of these alternations and contrasts." The president's demeanor left Chambrun with an odd, slightly unsettling feeling. "Every time I have endeavored to describe this impression," he later recalled, "words, nay, the very ideas, have failed me."

The Frenchman quizzed the president about his intentions with regard to Mexico. Would he invade? "There has been war enough," Lincoln replied. "I know what the American people want, but, thank God, I count for something, and during my second term there will be no more fighting." Still, the president could not resist a subtle jab at his imperial antagonist in the Tuileries. With Chambrun looking on, Lincoln told the band to strike up the "Marseillaise"—the French revolutionary standard that Napoleon III had prohibited. When the band had finished, Lincoln told them to play it again.[146]

With Richmond finally secure, relief broke over Washington. Seward, for once, was pleased with the outlook for American foreign relations. On the sunny afternoon of April 5, he closed up shop at the State Department and went for his usual afternoon carriage ride, tak- ing along his son Frederick, his daughter Fanny, and one of Fanny's friends. But as their carriage rattled up Vermont Avenue, the door kept flapping open, and the driver suddenly lost control of his horses. The secretary of state lurched for the reins—but then caught a heel and tumbled into the street.

The fall knocked Seward unconscious, dislocating his shoulder and breaking his jaw on both sides. Blood poured from his nose as he lay in the street with his heavy overcoat thrown over his head. Frederick, along with a clutch of bystanders, carried the secretary of state's limp body up the stairs to his bed. Fanny sat by her father's side as he muttered incoherently in his sleep. When he woke up, the secretary of state was in excruciating pain. Seward's wife, when she arrived at his bedside, found his face "so marred and swollen and discolored that one can hardly persuade themselves of his identity; his voice so changed; utterance almost entirely prevented by the broken jaw and the swollen tongue. It makes my heart ache to look at him." The secretary of state remained incapacitated for days.[147]

After Lincoln heard the news, he returned to Washington. Inside the secretary of state's Lafayette Square home, the president found the gaslights turned down to a dim flame. The house was filled with whispers. As Lincoln entered Seward's sickroom, he found his secretary of state completely wrapped in bandages. He sat down on the edge of Seward's bed. The New Yorker could hardly speak. "You are back from Richmond?" Seward whispered to the president. "Yes," Lincoln said, "and I think we are near the end, at last." The president then told stories from the front until Seward drifted off to sleep.[148]

Lincoln, despite his early tension with Seward, had grown fond of his secretary of state. He had come to rely on the New Yorker's foreign-affairs counsel.[149] Fortunately, the threat of a foreign war now seemed distant. Euphoric Washingtonians paraded through the streets waving flags and exploding fireworks over Lafayette Square. Lincoln even allowed himself to daydream about traveling abroad. He fantasized about taking his family on a vacation to Europe. The president, who came into office with virtually no experience with the world outside America's borders, explained that he had a strong desire to spend time "moving and traveling." He also wanted to visit the Middle East. Mary later recalled her husband telling her that "there was no city on earth he so much desired to see as Jerusalem."[150]

In the meantime, Lincoln satisfied his escapism by going to the theater.[151] The president was particularly captivated by the tales of jealousy, murder, and guilt in Shakespeare's histories and tragedies. Lincoln was attending the theater so often in the spring of 1865 that aides worried he would make an easy target for an assassin. His security was so light, one friend lamented, that "any able-bodied woman in this city" would be able to make an attempt. An Iowan had once written to Lincoln's personal secretary offering to construct a special shirt made of gold-plated chain mail to protect the president. "I am told that Napoleon III is constantly protected in this way," he explained, "and that his life was thus saved from small pieces of the Orsini shells, which killed his horses and several persons. I shall be very happy to get this done for Mr. Lincoln if he will accept of it." Lincoln declined the eccentric offer.[152]

On the night of April 14—Good Friday—the president attended the performance of *Our American Cousin* at Ford's Theatre with Mary, along with a young Army major and his fiancée. It was a comedy, and loud and frequent peals of laughter filled the theater. Few patrons paid much attention to the twenty-six-year-old actor who crept upstairs toward the president's box. As the audience tittered and guffawed, the young man peered at the president through a small peephole that had been cut into the door of the box.[153] Then he pushed through the entrance and lifted his snub-nosed pistol.[154]

John Hay was in his bedroom in the residence of the Executive Mansion that evening, when an anxious, hurried crowd came pouring through the compound's east gate. Lincoln's twenty-six-year-old secretary, the White House doorkeeper later recalled, was "a handsome young man with a bloom on his cheeks just like that of a beautiful young lady." When the doorkeeper told him that Lincoln had been shot, Hay "turned deathly pale, the color entirely leaving his cheeks." Now the stricken young man hurried down the White House stairs alongside the president's son Robert, with whom he had been studying Spanish earlier that night. They hustled into a carriage and sped off toward the boardinghouse across from Ford's Theatre where Lincoln was being treated for his gunshot wound.[155]

Hay had once dismissed the threat of Lincoln's assassination. It would be impossible to prevent, the young man told his diary, and so was not worth worrying about. Now, however, the nightmare scenario was unfolding before his eyes. When Lincoln's secretary arrived at the boardinghouse, he found his mentor lying diagonally on the bed, his hair caked with blood. Robert wept uncontrollably. Mary, also wailing, was finally taken from the crowded room. As the sun rose, Lincoln's breathing grew shallower. Hay was at Lincoln's bedside when the doctor pronounced the president dead at 7:22 a.m. "Now he belongs to the ages," said the secretary of war, Edwin Stanton.[156]

The assassination, as it turned out, was part of a coordinated plot to strike at key figures in the Lincoln administration. Late on the same evening that the president had gone to Ford's Theatre a tall, dapper figure showed up at the front door of Seward's home on Lafayette Square, claiming that he brought a message from the secretary of state's doctor. Despite the late hour, the man was brought upstairs through the dim, gas-lit corridors. Most of the family had already gone to bed. Seward's son Frederick explained that his father was off limits for the night. At first the messenger seemed ready to depart. "Very well, sir, I will go," he muttered, and turned back toward the stairs.

Then, in a flash, the man pulled out a revolver and lunged toward Seward's son. A gunshot cracked in the quiet house—but the assailant had missed his mark. Now the intruder brought the pistol crashing down onto Frederick's head, shattering his skull and fracturing the gun itself. In another instant he dashed into Seward's room, where the bandaged secretary of state was still recovering from his carriage accident. The would-be assassin drew a bowie knife and slashed at Seward's face and neck. A pool of blood spread across the bed. After the commotion drew the screams of the secretary of state's family, the attacker fled down the stairs, flailing wildly at anyone who tried to stop his escape. He jumped on a horse and galloped off, leaving Seward for dead.[157]

The assailant had cut Seward's throat on both sides. "His right cheek," the secretary of state's wife later recalled, was "nearly severed from his face." In the commotion, the bandaged and bleeding

Seward had tumbled from his bed. Yet the metal frame that had been immobilizing his head after the carriage accident had protected him somewhat, parrying at least some of the knife blows.

In the days that followed, Seward's family propped their recovering patriarch on pillows in his darkened room so he could look out the window at Lafayette Square. They were careful, at first, not to tell him about the president's assassination. But then Seward spotted a lowered flag fluttering in tribute outside his window. "The president is dead," he told his nurse. "If he had been alive, he would have been the first to call on me. But he has not been here, nor has he sent to know how I am; and there is the flag at half-mast."[158]

Evil Days

With Lincoln dead and Seward slowly recovering, the White House team did its best to maintain a steady keel on Mexican policy. Shortly before the assassination, Lincoln and Seward had appointed John Hay as the secretary of legation in Paris. With Napoleon's troops lingering in Mexico, it was more important than ever that the president and secretary of state have men they could trust in France. Hay was more than willing to make the trip. He was "thoroughly sick of certain aspects of life" in Washington, he had told his brother in March. Lincoln's young secretary considered the move "a pleasant and honorable way of leaving my present post which I should have left in any event very soon."[159]

After the assassination, Washington became intolerable for Hay. He found the "shadow of recent experiences resting on everything," he wrote to Robert Lincoln in the months after the president's death. Hay seemed vaguely disgusted that life could go on after the tragic events of the spring. When he visited Andrew Johnson's White House shortly before leaving for Paris, Hay found the Executive Mansion "full of new faces." The specter of the "evil days" of Lincoln's assassination, Hay told Lincoln's son, still haunted his former home. Returning to the Executive Mansion was "worse than a nightmare," Hay wrote. "I got away as soon as I could from the place."[160]

By July, Hay was in Paris. The American legation—with its imperial intrigue and high-stakes diplomatic drama—was a good place to try to forget the "evil days" surrounding Lincoln's death. With the enormous material strength of the Federal armies on full display, U.S. diplomats were exultant in the summer of 1865. At a Fourth of July party in the French capital, diplomats danced by the light of flaming candelabras as red-white-and-blue fireworks burst overhead. Ecstatic American expats hurrahed and raised their hats as a band blared "Yankee Doodle" and "Hail, Columbia."[161]

Hay, who possessed a melancholy streak similar to Lincoln's, could not quite bring himself to enjoy the celebrations. Even in Paris, images of Lincoln were everywhere. Shops sold badly drawn portraits of the American president; Hay complained that they were "mere caricatures" of the man he had known. "When I see anything that you would like in Paris," Hay wrote to Robert Lincoln in August, "for a moment I wish you were here, and then I think how the light and the noise and the gaiety of this town would jar more heavily on your spirit than it does on mine, and I envy you that you are at home."[162]

With tensions rising over Mexico, Franco-American relations were "not in a state to talk about," Hay wrote home to his brother. On the one hand, the massive Federal army had largely demobilized over the summer. And yet Johnson's military still possessed eight times as many men as France had under arms in Mexico. Some former American soldiers had already begun slipping across the border on their own, joining Mexican republicans. Meanwhile, Grant ordered Sheridan to the Rio Grande with fifty thousand troops to make a show of force along the Mexican boundary. Sheridan began smuggling tens of thousands of muskets across the border to Maximilian's enemies.

Senior generals, including Grant, Sherman, and Sheridan, all seemed eager to invade. Grant considered Napoleon's actions in Mexico "a direct act of war against the United States." Sheridan warned in August that it was "no use to beat around the bush in this Mexican matter; we should give a permanent government to that republic. Our work in crushing the rebellion will not be done until this takes place. . . . Most of the Mexican soldiers of Maximilian's army would throw down their arms the moment we crossed the Rio Grande."

Seward, who had by now largely recovered from the assassination attempt, pushed back against the hawkish generals. At a cabinet meeting attended by Grant in June, the secretary of state "was emphatic in opposition" to the military proposals, Gideon Welles recorded in his diary. The French-sponsored monarchy "was rapidly perishing," Seward maintained. American interference would only "prolong [Maximilian's] stay and the Empire also," he said. The secretary of state, Hay and Nicolay later recalled, "carried on with the same unswerving skill, dignity, and forbearance the policy inaugurated in the lifetime of Mr. Lincoln." Still, the army was now wildly popular in the wake of the Union victory. The belligerence of its senior officers posed serious new risks to what had been the Lincoln administration's conciliatory strategy.[163]

By the fall of 1865, Napoleon and Eugénie were feeling heavy pressure to end the Mexican adventure. "I hope that America will not trouble the new empire," Napoleon wrote to Maximilian in August. The emperor advised his protégé to "cause us no embarrassment, since France is making such sacrifices for your support." Eugénie complained that American diplomats were starting to get "discourteous" in their demands to end the Mexican venture. "It is very necessary," Eugénie wrote to Charlotte in late September, "not to give rise to any complications in that quarter."[164]

From London, Lord Palmerston tried to reassure Maximilian. Despite the bellicose American rhetoric, Palmerston wrote, Johnson's men would "have enough to do reorganizing their immense territories and repairing the calamities following the disastrous war" that they would probably "refrain from disturbing your majesty."

But then in October, the legendary British statesman died. It was "strange," wrote Queen Victoria, "to think of that strong, determined man, with so much worldly ambition—gone!" British liberals were less forgiving. "I wish," wrote John Bright, whose portrait Lincoln had kept in his anterooms, that "there were more to be said in his praise." Modern historians use Palmerston's death to mark the beginning of the British empire's relative economic decline.[165]

By the holiday season, the French imperial couple were doing everything they could to try to charm the Americans in Paris. At a dinner party on Christmas Eve, the emperor confided to Bigelow that he was eager to withdraw his troops from Mexico. It was "too expensive," Napoleon said with a smile, to keep French soldiers there indefinitely. Bigelow assured the emperor that the Johnson administration would do "nothing to embarrass him." Both Napoleon and Eugénie were all sweetness and light with the American. The empress told Bigelow that she was eager to travel to the United States now that the war was over. (Her doctor had recommended a trip across the Atlantic to treat a persistent cough.) Recounting the evening in a confidential letter to Seward, Bigelow wrote that he "derived the impression from these conversations that the Emperor had made up his mind to seize the first available opportunity to close his accounts with Mexico and Maximilian, and was anxious that we should do nothing to render his task more difficult."[166]

As the New Year dawned, even the relatively junior Hay found himself showered with invitations to the Tuileries. On the morning of January 1, Hay was presented at the imperial court for the first time. His uniform, he wrote home to his mother, included "more gold than broadcloth. I was as gorgeous as a drum-major." Hay and the other diplomats lined the walls of the emperor's throne room, which was filled with imperial officials dressed in "shining raiment." Napoleon slowly worked the room, speaking a few words to each guest. "He is a short, stubby looking man," Hay told his mother, "not nearly so tall as I." (Hay was five foot two.) The emperor "wore a rotten threadbare uniform with tarnished epaulettes." Napoleon's face, Hay wrote, "is just as you see it in the pictures, only older and more lifeless. I never saw so dead a looking eye." When the emperor arrived at the American delegation, he quizzed Hay about life in Washington. "Were you present," Napoleon quietly asked Hay, "at the death of President Lincoln?"[167]

In the summer of 1866, the Empress Charlotte made a surprise trip to Paris to press her case one last time with the imperial couple. Eugénie complained to a friend that the visit was "like a bolt out of the blue." Charlotte, too, was taken slightly aback when Eugénie arrived at her suite at the Grand Hôtel. "The Empress," Charlotte wrote home to Maximilian, "has lost much of her youth and strength since I last saw her." Charlotte was put off by the ignorance of French officials about conditions in Mexico. "What struck me," she told Maximilian, "was that I know more about China than these people here know about Mexico, where they have ventured upon one of the greatest enterprises in which the French flag has ever been involved."[168]

As Charlotte pressed her case, Hay scrambled to gather what intelligence he could. Lincoln's former secretary met with the French foreign minister and quizzed him about the visit. The official assured Hay that despite Charlotte's visit, there would be no change in the French government's promise to withdraw its troops. The French foreign minister, Hay explained, "was so emphatic in his assertion of the continued intention of the Emperor's Government to adhere to the arrangement already announced and so careful to say nothing of the objects for which the princess [Charlotte] is in Paris, that I did not deem it prudent to insist upon an answer on that point." Still, Hay reported that he was hearing in "informed circles" that Charlotte was complaining that without "timely assistance" from France, the Mexican venture would be "at an end." Other confidants of the emperor assured Hay that Napoleon had no intention of changing his plans as a result of Charlotte's pleas.[169]

With Charlotte's mission at an end, Napoleon finally decided to level with Maximilian. "We had the great pleasure," the emperor wrote on August 29, "in receiving the Empress Charlotte, and yet it was very painful to me to be unable to accede to the requests which she addressed to me." The Mexican venture was approaching "a decisive moment," Napoleon admitted. "It is henceforward *impossible* for me to give Mexico another *écu* or another man. . . . Can you maintain yourself by your own strength? Or will you be forced to abdicate?" Rising tensions on the Continent were taking all the French emperor's energies. "We can no longer lull ourselves with illusions," he told Maximilian, "and it is necessary that the Mexican question, in so far as it concerns France, should be settled once for all."[170]

Napoleon's decision to abandon Mexico marked a significant, if posthumous, vindication of Lincoln and Seward's foreign policy. Both the American president and his secretary of state saw that the shifting geopolitical landscape in Europe, combined with the Union's ruthlessly efficient war effort at home, would make any French venture in Mexico a nearly hopeless endeavor. The best policy would be, as Lincoln once put it, simply to "take to the woods." A strategy of delay would give the president the time to consolidate his strength north of the Rio Grande. At the same time, the powerful, impersonal forces that were combining to scuttle the French emperor's plans would be left alone to work themselves out.

And yet successfully maintaining that policy of restraint actually demanded determined leadership. Lincoln and Seward—confronted with hawks in Congress, the military, the press, and representatives of the Confederate States—firmly resisted calls for an invasion to oust the French-supported regime. An invasion, at the least, would have risked drawing Napoleon's forces into the American conflict. Lincoln and Seward's conciliatory policy gave Napoleon enough political cover to pull out on his own. The whole episode left a lasting imprint on the American diplomatic tradition. Lincoln and his team had proven that the American chief executive and his State Department could shrewdly manage a dangerous foreign-policy crisis, even in the face of stiff opposition from his own countrymen.

The emperor Maximilian was less successful at beating back his domestic foes. The former Austrian archduke decided to remain in Mexico for the denouement of his short-lived empire. As republican forces closed in on the capital in the early months of 1867, Maximilian fled the city with 1,500 men and a few pieces of artillery. He made a last stand at Queretaro, one of the final bastions of imperial support. Guerrillas ultimately surrounded the village, intimidating the inhabitants by sending dead bodies floating into town on the currents of the local river. Finally they captured the emperor, locking him in a makeshift prison cell in a convent with little more than a crucifix and a couple of candlesticks. On the morning of June 19, Maximilian's captors marched him to a hill along the outskirts of Queretaro. "I forgive everybody," the Mexican monarch cried as he faced his firing squad. "Long live Mexico, long live independence!" Then, under a clear blue sky, a team of riflemen fired six bullets into his body.[171]

CHAPTER SIX

Lincoln vs. Lincoln

JOHN HAY WAS IN VIENNA ON THE DAY OF MAXIMILIAN'S FU-
NERAL, IN JANUARY 1868. THE FORMER HAPSBURG PRINCE HAD
BEEN VIRTUALLY DISOWNED BY AUSTRIA'S ROYAL FAMILY AFTER
he accepted the throne of Mexico. Now, however, ordinary Austrians
respectfully welcomed home his lifeless body, lining the route as the
solemn cortege carrying the former archduke's corpse wound its way
to its crypt. "All the streets and adjoining squares were filled with a
vast crowd of citizens and strangers," Hay wrote home to Seward.
Lincoln's former secretary was struck by the "genuine and touching"
sympathy for Maximilian that spilled into the streets. Still, despite
the nationwide mourning, Hay told Seward that he considered the
whole affair a vindication of republican principles—"a sensible blow
at the prestige of kings."[1]

In the years following the Civil War, Hay was uniquely positioned to observe the conflict's international fallout. After his stint
in Paris, the young Illinoisan took diplomatic posts in both Madrid
and Vienna. Along the way, he stopped in London to watch the
wrangling in the British Parliament over the Reform Bill of 1867—a
measure that would ultimately double the number of Britons eligible
to vote. Hay sat spellbound in the gallery as legendary figures like
William Gladstone and Benjamin Disraeli debated the legislation.

The bill had been inspired by far more than just the Civil War. Still, the redemption of the world's most prominent democracy had indeed chastened many English aristocrats and softened their resistance to reforms. "It is probably no exaggeration," notes the scholar James McPherson, "to say that if the North had lost the war, thereby confirming Tory opinions of democracy and confounding the liberals, the Reform Bill would have been delayed for years."[2]

Lincoln had believed strongly in the power of America's example. In the years following the American Revolution, the president's idol George Washington had once warned his countrymen that "the eyes of the whole world" were "turned upon them." The nation's first president believed that the republican experiment in North America was being carefully observed by both autocrats and liberals across the globe. "With our fate," Washington had declared in 1783, "will the destiny of unborn millions be involved." Lincoln took that message to heart. The outcome of the Civil War, he told Congress in his first address to the body in July 1861, "embraces more than the fate of these United States. It presents to the whole family of man, the question, whether . . . a government of the people, by the same people—can, or cannot, maintain its territorial integrity, against its own domestic foes."[3]

During the Civil War, embracing that faith in democratic government had required the suspension of disbelief. In the midnineteenth century, reasoned observation alone did not necessarily suggest that democracy was on the march. Lincoln, as the crisis deepened, had found himself making an almost mystical appeal to his countrymen. Hay, for one, found himself eagerly worshipping at the side of the new high priest of freedom. "I consider Lincoln Republicanism incarnate, with all its faults and all its virtues," he wrote in a letter to Billy Herndon shortly after Lincoln's assassination. "As, in spite of some evidences, Republicanism is the sole hope of a sick world, so Lincoln, with all his foibles, is the greatest character since Christ."[4]

Lincoln's presidency and the outcome of the Civil War had resoundingly affirmed American ideals. They also positioned the

nation for a dramatic leap onto the world stage. The country's astonishing expansion in the postwar years—helped along, at least in part,
by economic policies crafted by Lincoln, Seward, and their allies—
soon placed the United States amid the ranks of the world's largest
and wealthiest countries. In the years between 1860 and 1900, the
U.S. population doubled. By 1874 the nation began to export more
than it imported—a dynamic that lasted for almost the next century.
Annual crude oil production ballooned from 3 million barrels in 1865
to over 55 million barrels in 1898, and the country saw a more than
fivefold increase in the production of steel rails. "The figures," President William McKinley declared in 1901, "are almost appalling."

As the economy surged, Hay began to advocate a greater world
role for the United States. More than thirty years after the end of
the Civil War, he would help to preside over the birth of American
imperialism. In late 1898, in the wake of the Spanish-American War,
McKinley chose Hay to be his secretary of state. By then, the United
States had become an unquestioned economic and political colossus.
Power and prosperity sometimes seemed to turn American idealism
on its head. Hay, in one letter to Theodore Roosevelt, described the
conflict with Spain as "a splendid little war." Lincoln's former secretary had traveled a long way from the "terrible war" that his boss had
once lamented.[5]

There is, then, a natural tension embedded in a Lincolnian foreign policy.[6] On the one hand, Lincoln's moral vision represented American idealism at its best. The Railsplitter, who had never
been overseas, understood better than most of his countrymen how
slavery undermined the nation's prestige in the international arena. "I
hate [slavery]," Lincoln told one Springfield audience long before he
became president, "because it deprives our republican example of its
just influence in the world—enables the enemies of free institutions,
with plausibility, to taunt us as hypocrites—causes the real friends
of freedom to doubt our sincerity." Lincoln's later justification of the
war in his Gettysburg Address rings with reformist overtones. Only

through a cleansing "new birth of freedom," he declared, would the United States take its rightful place on the world stage.[7]

Yet the Union victory also left a more disconcerting imprint on American foreign policy. In the decades that followed, blind faith in American ideals would sometimes come to inspire intolerance and dogmatism. In his 1962 classic, *Patriotic Gore*, the iconoclast Edmund Wilson acidly derides the "insufferable moral attitudes" spawned by the War Between the States. The outcome of the conflict, notes one modern diplomatic scholar, "purged some old myths only to fuse nationalism even more inextricably with a cult of material progress disguised as a holy calling. That coalescence of Union and creed, power and faith, rendered Americans ever since uniquely immune to cynicism and uniquely prone to sanctimony."[8]

The American foreign-policy tradition is riven by this identity crisis. The mercurial nature of the U.S. approach to diplomacy, former senator William Fulbright has observed, "is not an accident but an expression of two distinct sides of the American character. Both are characterized by a kind of moralism, but one is the morality of decent instincts tempered by the knowledge of human imperfection and the other is the morality of absolute self-assurance fired by the crusading spirit."[9]

Lincoln, on his best days and at his most mature, was the personification of the former type. He infused his moralism with a highly disciplined sense of justice. He was not constitutionally prone to emotional crusades. While his countrymen crowed about regenerating the world, from Mexico to Hungary, Lincoln took a more reasoned, pragmatic approach. "Did Mr. Lincoln rule himself by the *head* or heart?" Billy Herndon once asked rhetorically. "He was great in the *head* and ruled and lived there." Lincoln's patience and sense of human frailty usually prevented his democratic sympathies from sounding sententious.[10]

Lincoln's foreign-affairs legacy is marked by one other "peculiar paradox," as the scholar David Donald has labeled it. Lincoln and Seward were both shapers and products of the Whig ethos, which historically had defined itself in opposition to presidential excess. And yet amid the national emergency of the Civil War, Lincoln and his secretary of state firmly—if temporarily—enlarged the powers of the executive to direct global affairs. The president swiftly proclaimed a blockade and expanded the navy by executive order. After his ships clashed with Britain's on the high seas, he confined Congress's role in the *Trent* affair to private consultations with key members. As the conflict intensified, Lincoln used his bully pulpit to speak directly to the British and French publics. In the war's final days, he resolutely defied hawks in Congress who were eager to invade Mexico. Yet at the same time, the president steadfastly supported congressional measures like the Legal Tender Act, the Homestead Act, and the Pacific Railroad Act, which worked to strengthen the bonds that united the state. Those legislative reforms, combined with Lincoln's executive innovations, ultimately helped to boost the country to greater global prominence.[11]

Hay found himself caught between the competing traditions that Lincoln's presidency had helped to inspire. On the one hand, Lincoln's former secretary had once proclaimed himself "a republican until I die," strongly dedicated to a belief in popular government. And yet he also plunged into the heady expansionist currents of the late nineteenth century, marrying the daughter of a business tycoon and lusting after what he once called "the pole-star of humanity, $!" As secretary of state, he was a firm advocate of executive power, tangling repeatedly with Congress over foreign policy. Hay's life was defined by the tension between the individual conscience that Lincoln had helped to shape and the rise to global power that the president had helped to touch off. In the life of his secretary, Lincoln did battle with himself.[12]

After his diplomatic travels in the wake of the Civil War, Hay returned to the United States in 1870. He eventually settled in a massive, brick-and-mahogany mansion on Lafayette Square, just

across from the White House. Hay's new home soon became a gathering place for the city's power brokers. (His dining room was larger
than the one at the White House.) He filled his oak-paneled library
with souvenirs from his days as Lincoln's secretary. Hay particularly
liked to show off two different bronze life masks of Lincoln's face
that he kept in the library—one made in 1860 and the other in 1865.
Lincoln's former secretary pointed out to visitors how much his boss
had aged during his time in office.[13]

From the windows of his home, Hay could see both his old bedroom at the White House and Seward's former place on Lafayette
Square. Henry Adams later recalled an aging and wistful Hay gazing
out his windows at the Civil War–era officers walking in the park.
Lincoln's former secretary "would break off suddenly the thread of
his talk," Adams recalled, "as he looked out of the window on Lafayette Square, to notice an old corps commander or admiral of the
Civil War, tottering along to the club for his cards or his cocktail:
'There is old Dash who broke the rebel lines at Blankburg! Think of
his having been a thunderbolt of war!'" For his children, Hay would
turn old Civil War songs into lullabies, sending them off to bed amid
the strains of Federal battle hymns.[14]

Hay eventually made a name for himself as a writer, first for the
New York Tribune—the same "Great Moral Organ" that had employed Karl Marx—and later as a poet, novelist, and historian. His
most ambitious literary undertaking was the ten-volume biography
of Lincoln that Hay produced with the former president's other secretary, John G. Nicolay. The serialized version began to appear in
Century magazine in 1886. The whole venture gave Hay the opportunity to reexamine and reevaluate the key episodes in Lincoln's foreign
policy—sometimes in light of surprising new documents unearthed
in the president's private papers.[15]

Writing at the height of the Gilded Age, Hay and Nicolay were
not reflexively opposed to American expansion. In their section covering the annexation of Texas, Lincoln's former secretaries suggested

that the absorption of the territory was probably inevitable. "Here was a great empire offering itself to us," they wrote. "It may be doubted whether there is a government on the face of the earth, which, under similar circumstances, would not have yielded to the same temptation."

Yet at the same time, Hay and his coauthor lauded Lincoln's Mexican War stance for its prudence. In the process, Lincoln's former secretaries kneecapped Billy Herndon, who happened to be at work on his own Lincoln biography. Hay and his coauthor criticized the president's former law partner for his overemotional defense of the war. Herndon was "young, bright, and enthusiastic," Hay wrote, but in his letters to Lincoln during the Mexican War, he had also displayed "more heart than learning, more feeling for the flag than for international justice." Lincoln had repeatedly tried to convince Herndon of "the difference between approving the war and voting supplies to the soldiers," they wrote. Yet Lincoln's law partner had remained "obstinately obtuse."[16]

Perhaps the book's most important contribution to understanding the foreign policy of the Civil War was its section on Seward's "foreign-war panacea."[17] Nicolay and Hay had discovered Seward's April 1, 1861, memo, "Some Thoughts for the President's Consideration," buried in the cache of papers provided by Robert Lincoln. Seward's influence on Hay was arguably as important as Lincoln's, and Lincoln's former secretary owed much of his diplomatic career to the New Yorker. Yet Seward's April Fool's power play clearly startled Hay. Lincoln's former secretaries described Seward's memo as an "extraordinary state paper," and suggested that the secretary of state intended to "heal a provincial quarrel in the zeal and fervor of a continental crusade." Still, they added, Seward quickly understood "how serious a fault he had committed." In any event, the president magnanimously let the episode pass.[18]

Hay and Nicolay also wove a slightly subtler foreign-policy message through their book. Lincoln and Hay were both reformers, convinced that democracy was on the march throughout the world. Yet they both also balked when reform appeared too self-righteous. Lincoln had given Hay a signed copy of his second inaugural—that mystical appeal for justice. Now Hay included in his history another document that he had discovered among Lincoln's papers after his assassination. "In the present civil war," Lincoln had written in a memo to himself in 1862, "it is quite possible that God's purpose is something different from the purpose of either party—and yet the human instrumentalities, working just as they do, are of the best adaptation to effect His purpose." Hay gave the fragment the title: "Meditation on the Divine Will." Applied to the international arena, the document's message could be understood as an indictment of sanctimonious crusades. There was a difference between, on the one hand, embracing progress and setting an example for "the eyes of the whole world," as Washington put it, and on the other hand, trying to reshape the globe in one's image at the point of a gun.[19]

Billy Herndon, for his part, derided Hay's Lincoln biography as "unimportant trash." Herndon's own *Life of Lincoln*, released in 1889, carried a slightly different foreign-policy message. After Lincoln's death, Herndon had adopted an increasingly liberal worldview—and one often at odds with Lincoln's Whig reticence. Whereas Lincoln had favored a tariff, Herndon described himself as "a radical free trade man." Herndon's global vision was full of millennial overtones. Republicanism, Lincoln's former law partner told his readers, was "destined to overshadow and remodel every government upon the earth. The glorious brightness of that upper world, as it welcomed [Lincoln's] faint and bleeding spirit, broke through upon the earth at his exit—it was the dawn of a day growing brighter as the grand army of freedom follows in the march of time."[20]

Herndon died in 1891, "poor as Job's turkey," as he once put it. Hay, on the other hand, continued to thrive professionally. Flush with funds from book royalties and investments, he donated large sums of money to Republican political candidates as the nineteenth century came to a close. In 1897, President William McKinley, one of the key beneficiaries of Hay's largesse, sent Lincoln's former secretary into the diplomatic swirl once again. McKinley named Hay ambassador to the Court of St. James in London—an increasingly critical post as the United States began to supplant Britain as the world's preeminent power.[21]

Back in December 1861, at the height of the *Trent* affair, Hay had complained that "the arrogance of England must be distinctly met and tamed, and I think Providence has specially detailed the United States for that particular duty." Yet by the last decades of the nineteenth century, Hay had come to love and respect Britain. He had traveled to the island nation frequently throughout the 1880s and once even thought of buying a country house there. As he aged, Hay— who had once proclaimed himself full of "democratic bigotry"— now increasingly began to appreciate British elitism. Compared to the wild tumult of American political life, Hay found the stability in Britain comforting. He believed strongly that the world's shifting power relationships also demanded closer ties with London. American jingoes did not always see things the same way. Theodore Roosevelt complained the year before Hay left for London that Lincoln's former secretary had become "more English than the English."[22]

Hay recognized that as British power was waning, the United States would need to fill the vacuum. Though Hay had long been somewhat cautious about territorial expansion, he understood that America's new role would mean extending U.S. influence in ways that would help maintain the worldwide balance of power. By the 1890s, Hay favored annexing the Hawaiian Islands—a position he had opposed earlier in his career. Hay had come to admire Britain's management of its empire, studying the mechanics of the "Pax Britannica" in places like India and Egypt. The transition to American preeminence, Hay believed, would require a "partnership in beneficence" between Britain and the United States. In one speech at a banquet in London, Hay remarked that there was "a sanction like that of religion" that bound the two nations. "We are joint ministers," he told his audience, "of the same sacred mission of liberty and progress." Queen Victoria praised Hay as "the most interesting of all the ambassadors I have known."[23]

Hay was on vacation in Cairo in February 1898 when news arrived that the USS *Maine* had exploded in Havana Harbor, killing more than 250 American servicemen. American hawks immediately raised a war whoop. Theodore Roosevelt, then an assistant secretary of the navy in the McKinley administration, complained about the president's slow pace of retaliation. McKinley had "no more backbone than a chocolate éclair," Roosevelt sniped. When war finally erupted in April, the assistant secretary of the navy joined a regiment of American troops and shipped off for Cuba. Hay mocked Roosevelt for enlisting in "a cowboy regiment," and initially appeared far less eager for a war. Still, Hay wrote home to McKinley, informing him that British opinion was overwhelmingly supportive of a conflict. "The commonest phrase," Hay reported, "is 'We wish you would take Cuba and finish up the work.' " The American ambassador recognized that a conflict might well draw Britain and the United States even closer together.[24]

Hay's detractors have used his description of the Spanish-American conflict as "a splendid little war" to paint him as a rabid imperialist. Actually, the phrase was in part a plea for moderation. The war, Hay added in the same missive, "is now to be concluded, I hope, with that fine good nature, which is, after all, the distinguishing trait of the American character." Still, by the end of the conflict, Hay had turned into an energetic cheerleader for the American effort. When the war eventually expanded to Southeast Asia, Hay ultimately supported the annexation of the Philippines. Lincoln's former secretary was primarily attracted by the commercial and strategic advantages of possessing the islands. Yet as he attempted to justify the expansionist policies, he could sometimes be as vigorous a crusader as Herndon. "I cannot for the life of me," he told one correspondent, "see any contradiction between desiring liberty and peace here and desiring to establish them in the Philippines."[25]

Historians have long found it difficult to neatly categorize Hay's foreign-policy views. On the one hand, Lincoln's former secretary could proclaim himself a die-hard republican; on the other, he could laud British elitism. On some days he might plead for international justice; on others he might herald American power. Hay himself recognized that his views were not always coherent. "I do what seems possible every day," he once wrote Henry Adams, "not caring a hoot for consistency and the Absolute." At his worst, Hay could appear an unprincipled hypocrite. And yet on his best days, he displayed some of the magic of his one-time mentor—skillfully pursuing American interests while simultaneously appealing to the "considerate judgment of mankind."[26]

In late 1898, McKinley appointed Hay secretary of state, bringing him home to Washington. From the windows of Hay's large, bright office, he could gaze out onto the Ellipse and the Washington Monument. He had come a long way from the uncertain hours of the Civil War. Now the Union was not only safe—it was in a position to challenge the greatest powers in the world. Still, Hay could not entirely bring himself to breathe easily. Lincoln had once remarked that when he had finally fulfilled his deepest ambitions, he had discovered that power consisted of only "ashes and blood." Now Hay acknowledged the same. "Like many another better man before me," he wrote one correspondent, "I find power and place when it comes late in life, not much more than dust and ashes."[27]

As secretary of state, Hay moved quickly to shore up U.S. commercial interests. Hay's foreign-policy mentors had long coveted Asian export markets. Seward had once dreamed of a commercial empire extending "beyond the Pacific Ocean." Lincoln, too, had strongly supported naval expansion. Now, with the acquisition of the Philippines, the East seemed more accessible than ever. Hay believed China held "the key to world politics for the next five centuries."

And yet even as the United States was beginning to make its presence felt in Asia, Hay found that the European powers were also scrambling to carve out "spheres of influence" on the continent. In response, Hay issued his Open Door notes in 1899, condemning the heavy-handed behavior of the powers. The new statement of policy maintained that all countries must have equal access to Chinese markets. Historians debate the ultimate effectiveness of the notes. Yet they did provide a vivid illustration that the Hamiltonian foreign policy of Lincoln and Seward was alive and well in Hay. It is possible to draw a straight line from the commercial reciprocity policies favored by Lincoln's idol Henry Clay and other Whigs to the Open Door notes of the McKinley era.[28]

Despite the paroxysm of violence unleashed by the Spanish-American War, the devout McKinley actually preferred to advance American interests by peaceful expansion. "There is nothing in this world," the president declared in 1901, "that so much promotes the universal brotherhood of man as commerce." (McKinley knew the horrors of battle firsthand. As a young Union soldier during the Civil War, he had driven a sandwich cart on the battlefield at Antietam.) Hay recognized that support for America's burgeoning industry also demanded "a stabilization of the existing political order," in the words of one historian. As secretary of state, he worked carefully to bring the great powers into what Henry Adams later described as "a combine of intelligent equilibrium."[29]

To many, such a scheme—starting with closer U.S. ties to Britain—seemed suspiciously like an acceptance of the balance-of-power system of alliances and treaties that so many past American diplomats had rebelled against. America had become a great power on a vast wave of economic growth—but had the old republican values that Lincoln had nurtured in Hay vanished in the process? Before 1899, Hay's biographer Tyler Dennett notes, "the United States had been less interested in the *status quo* of European Powers than in the spread of republican principles." The same, of course, had once been true of Hay. Now, as McKinley's secretary of state, Hay seemed to be inverting his old republican faith. "In 'McKinleyism,' " writes Dennett, "there was no place for crusading." America's new world role startled even those closest to Hay. "History," wrote Henry Adams, "broke in halves."[30]

On September 6, 1901, an assassin shot President McKinley at the Pan-American Exposition in Buffalo. A little more than a week later, the president died, propelling Vice President Theodore Roosevelt to the nation's highest office. Roosevelt retained Hay as secretary of state, and on the surface at least, they seemed to get along well. In the wake of the Spanish-American War, Hay had written to Roosevelt admitting that the Rough Rider had been right after all about Cuba. Hay, who was old enough to be Roosevelt's father, would regale the new president with stories of Lincoln reading Shakespeare to him as he drifted off to sleep. Roosevelt once described the charming Hay as "the most delightful man to talk to I ever met." After Roosevelt was elected president in 1904, Hay gave the president a ring with a lock of Lincoln's hair encased inside. Roosevelt wore it proudly at his inauguration.[31]

Hay deferred to Roosevelt when necessary and helped the president to gain control over the modern-day Panama Canal Zone. Yet Hay actually preferred McKinley's careful diplomacy to the belligerent style of the new president. Roosevelt made little effort to help Hay push commercial reciprocity treaties through the intransigent Senate. The new president also encouraged Hay to take a harder line with Britain in a dispute over the Canadian boundary, and he ultimately sent troops to Alaska to drive home his message. Hay complained privately that there was "no comfort" in trying to reason with Roosevelt face-to-face. "When McKinley sent for me," he told his wife, "he gave me all his time till we got through; but I always find T.R. engaged with a dozen other people, and it is an hour's wait and a minute's talk—and a certainty that there was no necessity of my coming at all." Roosevelt later complained that Hay was not "a strong or brave man."[32]

Hay simply had a different conception of strength. Like his

mentors Lincoln and Seward, Hay believed the roots of American power lay in a healthy economy and a brisk trade. The proliferating new media also had the ability to shape the environment in which statesmen maneuvered. Toward the end of his life, Hay gave a speech in St. Louis to a group of journalists called "The Press and Modern Progress." Every day, Hay told his audience, he did business with the most influential men in the world. And yet all of them recognized that "behind the rulers we represent, there stands the vast, irresistible power of public opinion." No single human—or even a political party—could resist the impersonal elements that defined an age. Hay referred to such forces as the "cosmic tendency."[33]

And yet as a survivor of the Civil War, Hay also understood that cosmic tendencies could be maddeningly hard to read. He knew well, from his careful study of the classics, that empires rise and fall, glories fade and vanish. These were lessons he had learned not from visions of the future, but from echoes of the past. "Men make their own history," Karl Marx had once written in an essay about Napoleon III, "but they do not make it just as they please; they do not make it under circumstances chosen by themselves, but under circumstances directly found, given, and transmitted from the past. The tradition of all the dead generations weighs like a nightmare on the brain of the living. And just when they seem engaged in revolutionizing themselves and things, in creating something entirely new . . . they anxiously conjure up the spirits of the past."[34]

Hay knew that every decision he made as secretary of state was circumscribed by the past—by economic influences he could not fully control, by a public with myths and minds of its own. Luckily for Lincoln's former secretary, the spirits of the past also included some benevolent souls. By the summer of 1905, Hay had become chronically ill. He was sixty-six, and with each day he appeared a little thinner and grayer. His doctors recommended that he take a leave of absence from the State Department and travel to Europe to restore his health. He took their advice, returning to the United States by steamship in early June. In his cabin aboard the RMS *Baltic*, Hay slipped in and out of consciousness. One evening he had a dream that he had been called to the White House by the president. The commander in chief in his dream was "kind and considerate, and sympathetic about my illness," the secretary of state told his diary. The president gently assigned Hay a bit of menial work, perhaps to make him feel important. The whole episode left Hay haunted by a feeling of "overpowering melancholy." He had dreamed that the president was Abraham Lincoln again.[35]

ACKNOWLEDGMENTS

I owe a special debt to the distinguished scholars of the Civil War and American foreign policy who read early versions of this manuscript (some of them twice) or offered guidance and encouragement, especially Michael Burlingame, James Cornelius, Norman Ferris, Amanda Foreman, George Herring, Howard Jones, James McPherson, and Frank Williams.

I am also deeply fortunate to have been able to work closely with some of the country's finest biographers and foreign-policy thinkers during my time at *Newsweek*. Jon Meacham, the magazine's top editor during several of my years there, has been a longtime booster of my work. I am grateful for his suggestions and encouragement on this project. I am indebted also to Jon's predecessor as editor, Mark Whitaker, and Mark's then-deputies Mark Miller and Marcus Mabry, for agreeing to send a green twenty-six-year-old off to cover the world. Evan Thomas, perhaps the single best writer I know, has been reading and critiquing my work for years and has been a steady source of sage counsel. I have learned an enormous amount about telling true stories from Evan's advice and example.

My thinking about U.S. foreign policy was shaped by years of working with dozens of accomplished current and former editors and foreign correspondents at *Newsweek*, including Jeffrey Bartholet, Joanna Chen, Babak Dehghanpisheh, Deidre Depke, Christopher Dickey, Tony Emerson, Dan Ephron, Alexis Gelber, Arlene Getz, Nisid Hajari, Joshua Hammer, Michael Hastings, Michael Hirsh, Scott Johnson, Larry Kaplow, Daniel Klaidman, Adam Kushner, Melinda Liu, Nuha Musleh, Andrew Nagorski, Rod Nordland, Debra Rosenberg, Steven Strasser, Jonathan Tepperman, Tom Watson, Lally Weymouth, and Fareed Zakaria.

I began this project while working as a foreign correspondent posted in Jerusalem. Hebrew University of Jerusalem on Mount Scopus, where I did some early research, holds a formidable collection of books in English on U.S. and European history. I am grateful to the staff of the interlibrary loan office there, especially Jenny Chahanovski and Gila Emanuel, who cheerfully assisted me in borrowing a number of books from the University of Haifa and Tel Aviv University. While posted overseas I also benefited greatly from Internet Archive (archive.org), an invaluable resource that provides user-friendly access to an enormous selection of nineteenth-century memoirs, diaries, and reminiscences.

Once back in Washington, D.C., where my family and I moved in early 2012, my home base became Gelman Library at George Washington University. I am grateful to the good people of the Foggy Bottom Association, particularly Asher Corson and John Woodward, for facilitating my membership in their neighborhood organization, which made my research at GW possible. Thanks also to Joey Fones at Gelman for helping to arrange admission during my period of transition to the U.S. from abroad.

At the Library of Congress, the wonderful Michelle Krowl offered a number of useful suggestions and helped me to navigate the Lincoln Papers. During research trips to Springfield, Illinois, I enjoyed getting to know the superb staff at the Abraham Lincoln Presidential Library and Museum, including James Cornelius, Debbie Hamm, Eileen Mackevich, Mary Michals, Jan Perone, Patrick Russell, Cheryl Schnirring, and Glenna Schroeder-Lein. Lori Birrell at the University of Rochester, Anna Cook at the Massachusetts Historical Society, B. J. Gooch at Transylvania University, and Holly Snyder at Brown University skillfully helped me with their respective collections. I am particularly grateful to Desiree Butterfield-Nagy at the University of Maine, Orono; Juanita Walker at Prairie View A&M University; and Michelle Ganz at Lincoln Memorial University—who went out of their way to send me copies of materials when I could not visit their libraries myself.

My family and friends have been reliable sources of inspiration, reassurance—and occasionally research. My brother Jim, a graduate student in architecture, took time from his busy schedule to plunge deep into the stacks of Harvard's Widener Library to look for a decaying pamphlet on free trade written by William Herndon. My brother-in-law Tony Ninan let me stay at his apartment during early trips to the Library of Congress. My brother-in-law Joe Musumeci somehow found time to read and critique my manuscript despite the pleasant distraction of twin baby girls at home. (Joe saved me from an alarming tendency to overuse semicolons; although in my defense, Lincoln once remarked, "I have a great respect for the semi-colon; it's a very useful little chap.") Thanks also to Joanna Musumeci, Mathew and Molly Ninan, Seena Ninan, Sean Cassels, Jeremy Saks, Mike and Laura Faga, Jonathan Carpenter and Caroline Nolan, Kevin and Nassrin Flower, and David and Jori Meyer, who, each in their own way, have been sources of support and inspiration over the years. Finally, I am lucky to have a large extended family that has provided willing readers since I was a boy.

Chad Frazier, a talented doctoral student in the Georgetown University history department, assisted me in running down sources and checking citations. Chad's thoughtful suggestions, scrupulousness, and attention to detail made this a far better book. My thanks also to Karen Needles, director of the Lincoln Archives Digital Project, who read an early draft of the manuscript. Aviel Roshwald at Georgetown and Tyler Anbinder at GW also each provided useful recommendations as I prepared to begin the fact-checking process.

My original editor, Sean Desmond, is one of the stars of the book-publishing world. His sharp eye and creative mind significantly improved this book, and he made the whole process a pleasure. When Sean took another job in early 2013, Vanessa Mobley stepped in. Smart, funny, and a tireless advocate, Vanessa is every author's dream. Thanks also to Sarah Breivogel, Danielle Crabtree, Stephanie Knapp, Maya Mavjee, Claire Potter, Annsley Rosner, Jay Sones, Molly Stern, and the rest of the team at Crown.

My agent, Amanda Urban, is a font of wise counsel and encouragement. I feel truly lucky for the opportunity to work with Binky, who offered her unerringly shrewd guidance and warm fellowship throughout this project. I am grateful also to the staff of ICM Partners, including Liz Farrell and Colin Graham, for their assistance.

My parents, Sam and Donna Peraino, have nurtured my desire to write since about the first grade. They have patiently tolerated my interest in foreign affairs, even when it meant reporting from dangerous places—a form of devotion that I am only beginning to appreciate now that I am a father myself. I am endlessly grateful to them.

My most important debt is to my wife, Reena. Researching a book is a time-consuming process, and the work has sometimes taken me away to dusty archives when I would have preferred to be at home. Reena's patience and encouragement have been the bedrock upon which this book was built. I love her more than I can say.

Both my children, Jack and Kate, were born during the research and writing of this book. It is almost impossible to believe that Jack is now old enough to recognize photos of Lincoln (whom he cheekily refers to as "Old Babe"). Kate, I fear, is not far behind. My interest in foreign affairs, at its most basic, is driven by the hope of a better world in their lifetimes.

Source Notes

Abbreviations

AKM . . . . Archiv Kaiser Maximilians von Mexiko, Haus-, Hof- und Staatsarchiv (Vienna, Austria). The Library of Congress holds selected photostatic copies from this archive.

ALP . . . . Abraham Lincoln Papers, Library of Congress, Washington, D.C.

ALPLM . . . . . . Abraham Lincoln Presidential Library and Museum, Springfield, Illinois.

BNA . . . . British National Archives, Kew, England.

CG . . . . *Congressional Globe.* The Library of Congress provides online access to the volumes at http://memory.loc.gov/ammem/amlaw/lwcg.html.

CWL . . . . Basler, Roy P., ed. *The Collected Works of Abraham Lincoln*, 8 vols. (New Brunswick, N.J., 1973).

FRUS . . . . *Foreign Relations of the United States.* The series is listed in the bibliography under its nineteenth-century title, *Papers Relating to Foreign Affairs.*

Hay, *Diary* . . . . Burlingame, Michael, and John R. Turner Ettlinger eds. *Inside Lincoln's White House: The Complete Civil War Diary of John Hay* (Carbondale: Southern Illinois University Press).

HI . . . . Wilson, Douglas L., and Rodney O. Davis, eds. *Herndon's Informants* (Urbana and Chicago, 1998).

HL . . . . Wilson, Douglas L., and Rodney O. Davis, eds. *Herndon's Lincoln* (Urbana and Chicago, 2006).

HW . . . . Herndon-Weik Collection, Library of Congress, Washington, D.C.

KMIR . . . . McLellan, David, ed. *Karl Marx: Interviews and Recollections* (Totowa, N.J., 1981).

ALAL . . . . Burlingame, Michael. *Abraham Lincoln: A Life.* 2 vols. (Baltimore, 2008). For the "director's cut" of Burlingame's work, available on the website of the Lincoln Studies Center at Knox College (www.knox.edu/lincolnstudies.xml), I have used the abbreviation *ALAL-DC.*

LOC . . . . Library of Congress, Washington, D.C.

MECW . . . . *Karl Marx, Frederick Engels: Collected Works* (New York, 1975).

NARA . . . . National Archives and Records Administration, College Park, Md.

MAC . . . . Padover, Saul K., ed. *Karl Marx on America and the Civil War* (New York, 1972).

RW. . . . . Fehrenbacher, Don E., and Virginia Fehrenbacher. *Recollected Words of Abraham Lincoln* (Stanford, Calif., 1996).

Welles, *Diary* . . Beale, Howard K., ed. *Diary of Gideon Welles.* 3 vols. (New York, 1960).

I have also identified the following sources in the notes by the author's last name only: **BAKER**, Jean, *Mary Todd Lincoln* (New York, 1987); **BANCROFT**, Frederic, *The Life of William H. Seward*, 2 vols. (New York, 1900); **BAUER**, Karl Jack, *The Mexican War* (New York, 1974); **BELL**, Herbert, *Lord Palmerston* (London, 1966); **BEVERIDGE**, Albert J., *Abraham Lincoln, 1809–1858*, 4 vols. (Boston, 1928); **CORTI**, Count Egon Caesar, *Maximilian and Charlotte of Mexico* (Archon Books, 1999); **GABRIEL**, Mary, *Love and Capital* (New York, 2011); **GOODWIN**, Doris Kearns, *Team of Rivals* (New York, 2005); **HANNA AND HANNA**, *Napoleon III and Mexico* (Chapel Hill, 1971); **HERRING**, George C., *From Colony to Superpower* (New York, 2008); **JENKINS**, Brian, *Britain and the War for the Union* (Montreal, 1974); **JERROLD**, Blanchard, *Life of Napoleon III* (London, 1874); **MAHIN**, Dean, *One War at a Time* (Washington, 1999); **MERRY**, Robert W., *A Country of Vast Designs* (New York, 2009); **MONAGHAN**, Jay, *A Diplomat in Carpet Slippers* (Lincoln, 1997); **PALUDAN**, Phillip Shaw, *The Presidency of Abraham Lincoln* (Lawrence, 1994); **VAN DEUSEN**, Glyndon, *William Henry Seward* (New York, 1967); **WARREN**, Gordon H., *Fountain of Discontent* (Boston, 1981); and **WHEEN**, Frances, *Karl Marx* (New York, 1999).

PROLOGUE

1. For Mary Lincoln's temper see, for example, Jesse Weik interview with Margaret Ryan, Oct. 27, 1886, Weik Papers, box 2, memo book 1, ALPLM. The most complete collection of Mary Lincoln's outbursts is in Burlingame, "The Lincolns' Marriage," *Inner World*, p. 277. For Mary's desire to visit Europe, see Mary Lincoln to Emilie Todd Helm, Sept. 20, [1857,] in Turner and Turner, *Mary Todd Lincoln*, pp. 49–50.

2. Lincoln's promises to take his wife abroad are in Noyes W. Miner, "Personal Reminiscences of Abraham Lincoln," p. 54, Miner Papers, ALPLM; and William Henry Herndon interview with Mary Todd Lincoln, [Sept. 1866,] in *HI*, p. 359. See also Bradford, "The Wife of Abraham Lincoln," *Harper's*, pp. 496–97; Bryan, *Great American Myth*, p. 177; Goodwin, p. 733; White, *A. Lincoln*, p. 673; Donald, *Lincoln*, p. 570.

3. Mary Lincoln interview with Herndon, [Sept. 1866,] *HI*, p. 357; Heidler and Heidler, *Henry Clay*, p. xx; French, *Witness to the Young Republic*, p. 497 ("airs of an empress"); John Lothrop Motley to his wife, June 20, 1861, in Curtis, ed., *The Correspondence of John Lothrop Motley*, p. 387 ("sir"); John Bigelow Diary, v. 35, entry for July 9, 1861, John Bigelow Papers, New York Public Library ("Tres poo"). See also Burlingame, "The Lincolns' Marriage," p. 270; Baker, pp. 41–42; *ALAL*, v. 2, p. 259.

4. Herndon to Jesse Weik, Jan. 12, 1886, HW, LOC ("toothache"). For Lincoln's desire to travel abroad, see Weik Papers, box 2, memo book 2, ALPLM; Wilson, "Recollections of Lincoln," *Putnam's Magazine*, v. 5, no. 5, Feb. 1909, p. 517; Reminiscences of George Hartley, *Chicago Daily News*, Jan. 28, 1909, cited in *ALAL-DC*, ch. 1, pp. 2–3. The quote about "a great empire" is in Lincoln's "Speech at Kalamazoo, Michigan," Aug. 27, 1856, *CWL*, v. 2, p. 364. On the conflict's global importance see Thomas, *Abraham Lincoln*, p. 268; and Hay, *Diary*, p. 20, entry for May 7, 1861.

5. Kennedy, *Rise and Fall of the Great Powers*, pp. 179–181; McPherson, *Battle Cry*, p. 816; Jones, *Blue and Gray Diplomacy*, p. 1; *Chicago Tribune*, Apr. 12, 1865, in White, *Lincoln's Greatest Speech*, p. 196; Van Deusen, p. 360; Adams, *Great Britain and the American Civil War*, v. 2, p. 239n1 ("despotic ferocity").

6. For eyewitness accounts of the assassination, see "Major Rathbone's Affidavit," in J. E. Buckingham Sr., *Reminiscences and Souvenirs of the Assassination of Abraham Lincoln*, p. 73; Taft, "Abraham Lincoln's Last Hours," *Century*, p. 634; Charles A. Leale to Benjamin Butler, July 20, 1867, in Good, ed., *We Saw Lincoln Shot*, p. 60; Horatio Nelson Taft Diary, entry for Apr. 30, 1865, LOC. See also Brooks, " 'The Deep Damnation of His Taking-Off,' " in Burlingame, ed., *Lincoln Observed*, p. 190; Helm, *Mary, Wife of Lincoln*, pp. 257–58; Randall, *Mary Lincoln*, p. 382; Goodwin, p. 738; Donald, *Lincoln*, p. 595–96; *ALAL*, v. 2, p. 809–810,

816–819; White, *A. Lincoln*, pp. 673–74; Baker, p. 248; Oates, *With Malice Toward None*, locs. 8490–8502.

7. Notable exceptions include the work of Jay Monaghan, whose 1945 classic, *A Diplomat in Carpet Slippers*, emphasizes Lincoln's command of foreign policy. Though Monaghan's account exaggerates Lincoln's role, it is still the best jumping-off point for examining Lincoln's involvement in Civil War diplomacy. After decades of revisionism de-emphasizing Lincoln's role as a diplomat, more recent studies by Howard Jones and Dean Mahin treat Lincoln as a diplomat by nature. Mahin's study finds that "Lincoln set the major foreign policy goals of the Union government, determined U.S. responses to a series of diplomatic developments and crises, and made a number of other presidential decisions designed to reduce the chance of war with England or France." And yet, as Jones notes, Lincoln the human being tends to get lost in Mahin's comprehensive survey of Civil War diplomacy. Jones's own excellent studies argue that Lincoln "personified a diplomat, as shown in his appointments, his realization that international (and domestic) law became flexible in wartime, and his ability to make meaningful public pronouncements." Jones's work, however, is not intended to be a holistic portrait of Lincoln. See Mahin, p. 3 and passim; Jones, "Forgotten 'Near War': Lincoln's Civil War Diplomacy," *American Diplomacy*, v. 6, no. 1, 2001; and Jones, *Blue and Gray Diplomacy*, p. 322. For more on Lincoln's diplomatic role, see Jones, *Abraham Lincoln and a New Birth of Freedom*, and

Jones's introduction to the 1997 Bison Books edition of *A Diplomat in Carpet Slippers*. George Herring, in his magisterial history of American foreign policy, *From Colony to Superpower*, also admires Lincoln's "uniquely American brand of practical idealism." See Herring, pp. 5, 228, and 963.

8. Lincoln visited Canada on a trip to Niagara Falls. See Mary Lincoln to Emilie Todd Helm, Sept. 20, [1857,] in Turner and Turner, *Mary Todd Lincoln*, pp. 49–50. See also *Lincoln Lore*, No. 319, May 20, 1935 (copy in Ruth Painter Randall Papers, LOC); Herring, p. 228; Monaghan, p. 13. On Lincoln's lack of European friends, see Lincoln to Forney, July 28, 1864, in *CWL*, v. 7, p. 468. See also Lincoln to Jesse W. Fell, Dec. 20, 1859, *CWL*, v. 3, p. 511 ("wizzard"); Barlow A. Ulrich to William Henry Herndon, Sept. 21, 1866, in *HI*, p. 352 (immigrant voters); *ALAL*, v. 1, p. 584 ("Beans"). For the Colombian diplomatic post see Bullard, "When John F. Stuart Sought to Send Lincoln to South America," p. 21. See also Ninian W. Edwards interview with William Henry Herndon, Sept. 22, 1865, in *HI*, p. 133 ("crazy").

9. Russell, *My Diary North and South*, p. 36, entry for Mar. 27, 1861 ("effect of a smack"); Hay, *Diary*, p. 14, entry for Apr. 30, 1861 ("When go back Iowa?"); Nordholt, "The Civil War Letters of the Dutch Ambassador," p. 361 ("laughs uproariously"); Bayne, *Tad Lincoln's Father*, pp. 168–69 ("glittered grand"); Lutz, "Rudolph Schleiden and the Visit to Richmond, April 25, 1861," p. 210 ("apt to make blunders").

10. On the character of Lincoln's diplomatic corps, see Jones, *Blue and Gray Diplomacy*, p. 29; *ALAL*, v. 2, pp. 93–95; Monaghan, p. 68. Both Monaghan and Jones point out that there was also a logic in appointing abolitionists to foreign posts: it sent a message to European countries that the U.S shared their antislavery sympathies. See also Foner, *Fiery Trial*, p. 193. The "sot/rake/swindler" quote is from the *New York World*, Mar. 12, 1861. See also Adams Jr., *Autobiography*, p. 62 ("wagged"). Adams adds, however, that despite Seward's loose lips, he never saw the New Yorker "approaching drunkenness."

11. Hay, *Missouri Republican*, Nov. 17, 1861, in Burlingame, ed., *Lincoln's Journalist*, p. 140 ("Hottentot" etc.); Perkins, *History of the Monroe Doctrine*, pp. 125–26 ("public business"); Sandburg, *Abraham Lincoln*, p. 637 ("not his wife"); Bigelow, *Retrospections*, v. 2, pp. 234–35; Hay, *Diary*, p. 8, entry for Apr. 22, 1861, and p. 116, entry for Nov. 22, 1863 ("wonderful ass"); Pease and Randall, eds., *Diary of Orville Hickman Browning*, v. 1, p. 595, entry for Dec. 12, 1862 ("little sense").

12. For a nuanced, if slightly dated, treatment of European attitudes toward the war, see Nevins, *The War for the Union*, v. 2, pp. 242–74. Nevins notes that "the danger of Anglo-French involvement did not arise from Machiavellianism in high places. It arose, fundamentally, from the fact that when the supposedly short war of 1861 was converted into the patently long war of 1862, without any grand moral purpose to justify it, without any prospect that either side could rationally impose its will on the other, and with steadily increasing hardship to other lands,

impatience inevitably seized foreign peoples and leaders." Nevins, *The War for the Union*, v. 2, p. 272. See also Lord Palmerston to Lord John Russell, Jan. 19, 1862, Russell Papers, BNA. The London *Times*, Norman Ferris suggests, offered "echoes of English aristocratic thought" in its editorials, arguing, "Instead of a great, united, irresistible nation, they [the North and South] will be two jealous States watching each other." (London *Times*, Sept. 18 and 19, 1861, quoted in Ferris, *Desperate Diplomacy*, p. 132.) Still, there's a subtle nuance between simple Schadenfreude and actively working toward the dismemberment of the republic. As D. P. Crook and others have noted, it is a "cliché" and speculative to conclude that Britain in general (and even Palmerston, at other times) necessarily wanted "a breakup of the Union for realpolitik reasons, to destroy a rival in the hemisphere" (Crook, *The North, the South, and the Powers*, p. 374). Howard Jones points out that Palmerston "could not see how England could derive the same commercial profits from a divided North and South as from a unified nation" (Jones, *Union in Peril*, p. 85). On Bagehot see *Economist*, Mar. 2, 1861, quoted in Crook, *Diplomacy During the American Civil War*, p. 32 (expected North to win); *Economist*, Jan. 19, 1861, quoted in Jones, *Blue and Gray Diplomacy*, p. 32 ("less irritable"). The final quote is from LaFeber, *The American Age*, p. 150 ("a single . . . mistake").

13. Mencken, H. L. *Prejudices: Third Series*, pp. 172–73; Brooks, Noah, "The Final Estimate of Lincoln," in *New York Times*, Feb. 12, 1898, quoted in

Peterson, *Lincoln in American Memory*, p. 97. See also Peterson, p. 196.

14. Hughes is quoted in Peterson, p. 197. On the "great age of European realpolitik," see Herring, p. 229. "Aristocratic, antirevolutionary, and self-interested, whether economic or imperial, these two powerful European figures [Napoleon III and Palmerston] sought to restore the halcyon days when iron rule assured international order," notes Howard Jones (Jones, *Abraham Lincoln*, pp. 2–3). "While not yet the age in Europe of blood and iron," D.P. Crook writes, "it was an age of muscular patriotism" (Crook, *The North, the South, and the Powers*, p. 73). See also Bell, v. 1, p. 97; Ridley, *Palmerston*, p. 334; Kissinger, *Diplomacy*, pp. 96, 129 (Bismarck); Ridley, *Napoleon III*, p. 309.

15. William Henry Herndon to Jesse Weik, Nov. 17, 1885, HW, LOC (chess); Lincoln, "Address Before the Young Men's Lyceum of Springfield, Illinois," Jan. 27, 1838, *CWL*, v. 1, p. 115 ("reason"); *HL*, p. 264 ("realist") and pp. 352–53 ("precise shape"). For a fascinating discussion of Lincoln's "depressive realism," see Shenk, *Lincoln's Melancholy*, pp. 133–35, 171. The final quote is from Swett to William Henry Herndon, Jan. 17, 1866, in *HI*, p. 162.

16. Kennedy, *Rise and Fall of the Great Powers*, pp. xxi, 73, 197; Kissinger, *Diplomacy*, p. 803. Fareed Zakaria's 2008 *The Post-American World* is an analysis of the modern multipolar international arena. The quote is from Kissinger, *Diplomacy*, p. 810.

17. Herring, pp. 225 and 920. Herring, citing Norman E. Saul, *Distant*

Friends, p. 329, notes the juxtaposition of nineteenth-century nationalism and globalization: "The steamship, telegraph, and trade brought nations closer at the same time nationalism was highlighting differences and provoking conflict. . . . Americans were more aware of events elsewhere because of increased immigration, faster and cheaper communication, growing literacy, and mass-circulation newspapers." For the nexus of liberalism, nationalism, and journalism, see also McDougall, *Throes of Democracy*, pp. 398–99; and Carwardine and Sexton, eds., *Global Lincoln*, p. 6. The literature on the nineteenth-century information age and transportation revolution is voluminous. See Blackett, *Divided Hearts*, pp. 142–43; Carwardine, *Lincoln*, p. ix–x; Carwardine, "Lincoln and the Fourth Estate," p. 2; Crook, *Diplomacy During the American Civil War*, p. 69; Guelzo, *Abraham Lincoln: Redeemer President*, pp. 22–24; Holzer, *Lincoln President-Elect*, pp. 3, 7, 33–4; Howe, *What Hath God Wrought*, passim; Jones, *Blue and Gray Diplomacy*, p. 220; Kissinger, *Diplomacy*, p. 160; McDougall, *Throes of Democracy*, pp. 154–55, 357; McPherson, *Battle Cry of Freedom*, pp. 12–13; Monaghan, p. 47; Mott, *American Journalism*, p. 216; Peterson, *Lincoln in American Memory*, p. 386; Thomas, *Abraham Lincoln*, p. 164; Vidal, "Vidal's Lincoln: An Exchange," p. 34; White, *Lincoln's Greatest Speech*, p. 186. Richard Carwardine adds a fascinating twist to this story, noting that "the dissemination of Lincoln's story at times tells us as much about networks of communication, transnational movements, and geopolitics as it does about the man himself." Carwardine, "Lincoln's Horizons," in *The Global Lincoln*, p. 21; see also pp. 16–17. Despite the revolutionary developments, some scholars also highlight the relatively slow speed and unreliability of nineteenth-century communications. See Jones, *Blue and Gray Diplomacy*, pp. 110, 303; Jones, *Union in Peril*, p. 83; Mahin, pp. 25–6 and 115.

18. Harold Holzer has noted that the "scrutiny" Lincoln faced during the secession winter "was no less intense during this age of politically motivated broadsheet newspapers than it is in today's world of all-day broadcast news and Internet blogs." On the telegraph, Holzer recommends Tom Wheeler's *Mr. Lincoln's T-Mails: The Untold Story of How Abraham Lincoln Used the Telegraph to Win the Civil War* (New York, 2006). See Holzer, *Lincoln President-Elect*, pp. 3, 501. See also LaFeber, *The American Age*, pp. 136–37 (Japan); McDougall, *Throes of Democracy*, p. 154 (periodical stats); Hay, *Missouri Republican*, Oct. 19, 1861, in Burlingame, ed., *Lincoln's Journalist*, p. 108 ("enthralled by newspapers"); Carwardine, "Abraham Lincoln and the Fourth Estate," pp. 1–2; Marx, "The Eighteenth Brumaire of Louis Bonaparte," in *The Marx-Engels Reader*, p. 599 ("sheet lightning"); Marx, "Manifesto of the Communist Party," in ibid., p. 477 ("immensely facilitated"); ibid., p. 488 ("vanishing"); Empress Eugénie to the Empress Charlotte, undated, 1864, in Corti, v. 2, p. 834 ("no secrets"); Howe, *What Hath God Wrought*, p. 2.

19. Harold Holzer argues that "Lincoln was the first campaigner and President to be aware of the potential

of mass communications" (Holzer, "If I Had Another Face, Do You Think I'd Wear This One?" p. 57). David Herbert Donald notes that "[t]he effectiveness of the President's personal propaganda warfare could not be measured, for it was not so much public statements or popular rallies as the internal dynamics of British and French politics, plus fears of ultimate American reprisal, that determined a course of neutrality for the two major European powers. But for Lincoln the opportunity to use the White House as a pulpit, to speak out over the dissonant voices of foreign leaders to the common people, daringly broadened the powers of the Presidency." See Donald, *Lincoln*, p. 416. Michael Burlingame writes that Lincoln also likely used his personal secretaries as propagandists (Burlingame, "Lincoln Spins the Press," p. 65). See also Jones, *Blue and Gray Diplomacy*, p. 322; Monaghan, pp. 274–94.

20. John Bigelow to Hippolyte Taine, Oct. 19, 1864, in Bigelow, *Retrospections*, v. 2, pp. 222–23. See also Crook, *The North, the South, and the Powers*, pp. 29–30; Crook, *Diplomacy During the American Civil War*, p. 18 (PR value).

21. William H. Herndon to [?], Nov. 24, 1882, printed in the *Washington Post*, Feb. 4, 1883 (copy in the Barbee Papers, Georgetown University); Harper, *Lincoln and the Press*, p. 97 ("escape of gas"); Nye, *Soft Power*, p. 30 ("less coercive"); Paludan, p. xvi ("everything in this country").

22. For an insightful and thorough comprehensive history of Union and Confederate foreign relations, see Jones, *Blue and Gray Diplomacy*

(Chapel Hill, 2010). For a panoramic and vivid recent account of the British role in the war, see Foreman, *A World on Fire* (New York, 2011).

23. Randall, *Lincoln the President*, v. 2, p. 29, quoted in Current, "Comment," p. 47.

24. McKee, *Story* (New York, 1997), p. 101.

25. Kennedy, *Rise and Fall of the Great Powers*, p. 17. Kennedy adds that "[i]ndividuals still counted" as late as the twentieth century, "but they counted in power politics only because they were able to control and reorganize the productive forces of a great state." See p. 197. On America's rising economic strength in the Civil War era see also pp. 149 and 179.

26. LaFeber, *The New Empire*, pp. 1, 60; and Sexton, *Debtor Diplomacy*, p. 3; Davis and Wilson, eds., *The Lincoln-Douglas Debates*, p. 47 ("not generally opposed"). Gabor Boritt argues that this statement is "meaningless," because there was no more territory that could be honestly had. See Boritt, *Lincoln and the Economics of the American Dream*, p. 140. See also McDougall, *Promised Land, Crusader State*, p. 97 (expansionist measures); Foner, *Free Soil, Free Labor, Free Men*, pp. 27, 312, 316. Mark Neely Jr. writes that Lincoln "did not share . . . the Whig party's concerns about expansion" and "did not oppose expansion properly achieved" (Neely, "Lincoln and the Mexican War," pp. 13–15). Boritt, on the other hand, contends that Lincoln's economic outlook "sharply clashed with expansionism" but then adds, "Perhaps he was not as much against territorial expansion *per se*, as he was in favor

of concentrating the people's energies *within the country*, to make *it* flower, to build *it* up." See Boritt, *Lincoln and the Economics of the American Dream*, pp. 138–39. See also Herring, p. 238; *CWL, Supplement 1832–1865*, p. 45; Foner, *Fiery Trial*, p. 117 ("go to escape"); Lincoln, "Speech in the U.S. House of Representatives on Internal Improvements," June 20, 1848, *CWL*, v. 1, p. 483 ("nothing else").

27. Hay to John G. Nicolay, Sept. 11, 1863, in Burlingame, ed., *At Lincoln's Side*, p. 54 ("backwoods Jupiter"); Donald, *Lincoln*, p. 310; and Donald, *"We Are Lincoln Men,"* p. 187 (shoguns); Hay, "Life in the White House in the Time of Lincoln," in Burlingame, ed., *At Lincoln's Side*, pp. 139–40 ("great rapidity").

28. On Lincoln's guilt see, for example, the analysis of Richard Hofstadter in *The American Political Tradition*, pp. 171–73, and cf. Burlingame, *Inner World*, pp. 254–55; Hay, *Diary*, pp. 75–76, entry for Aug. 23, 1863 (drifted off to sleep); Lincoln to James H. Hackett, Aug. 17, 1863, in *CWL*, v. 6, p. 392; Hay, "Life in the White House," in *At Lincoln's Side*, p. 137 ("death of kings"); Chambrun, "Personal Recollections," *Scribner's*, p. 35 ("envy the sleep"). See also Donald, *Lincoln*, p. 569; Guelzo, *Abraham Lincoln: Redeemer President*, pp. 317–18, 329; and Carwardine and Sexton, eds., *Global Lincoln*, pp. 35–36.

29. On the Romantic era, see Winger, *Lincoln, Religion, and Romantic Cultural Politics*, passim; Donald, *Lincoln's Herndon*, p. 185; and McDougall, *Throes of Democracy*, pp. 167–71. Robert W. Johannsen deftly analyzes the Mexican War in the context of the

Romantic era; see Johannsen, *To the Halls of the Montezumas*, passim, but esp. pp. 31, 57–78, 108–11. On Lincoln and Byron, see William Henry Herndon interview with Joshua F. Speed, *HI*, p. 30; Joshua F. Speed to William Henry Herndon, Jan. 12, 1866, in ibid., p. 156; Henry C. Whitney to William Henry Herndon, Nov. 20, 1866, in ibid., pp. 403–4; Henry C. Whitney to William Henry Herndon, Aug. 27, 1887, in ibid., p. 632; Wilson, *Honor's Voice*, pp. 190–97; Shenk, *Lincoln's Melancholy*, pp. 27–31; *ALAL*, v. 1, p. 353 (kick feet up); Byron, "Childe Harold's Pilgrimage," in McGann, *Lord Byron*, pp. 10, 21, 40, 47. Doris Kearns Goodwin, noting Lincoln's affection for Byron and other writers, observes that "[i]t was through literature that he was able to transcend his surroundings. . . . Lincoln, this acolyte of pure reason and remorseless logic, was also a romantic" (Goodwin, pp. 51–53).

30. Jon Meacham writes particularly skillfully about the intersection of the "personal" and the "political." See, for example, Meacham, *American Lion*, p. xvii, and passim. Allen Guelzo, citing an observation by Mark Neely Jr., observes that Lincoln biographies tend to "travel either the road of personality-history (as blazed by William Henry Herndon) in which Lincoln's achievements are explained in terms of temperament or genealogy; or else the road of public-history (the model for this being the ten-volume biography by Lincoln's White House secretaries, John G. Nicolay and John Hay) in which Lincoln is lauded mostly for his public management skills as a president, a politician, or a commander-in-chief." Guelzo offers

his brilliant "intellectual biography" of Lincoln as a "model" for other writers who aim to integrate "the old political Lincoln with the revived subjective Lincoln." See Guelzo, *Abraham Lincoln: Redeemer President*, pp. 19 and 472.

31. Adams, *The Education of Henry Adams*, pp. 147 ("victim's sympathies"), 418 ("Power is poison" and "society at large"), 421 ("struggle . . . of forces"); Adams, *Mont-Saint-Michel and Chartres*, p. 276 ("door of escape"). See also Niebuhr, *Moral Man and Immoral Society*, p. 6.

32. Tocqueville quoted in Schlesinger, *Imperial Presidency*, pp. 125–26. George Herring, noting the "distinctive cast" of foreign policy in a democratic system that divides power between the executive and legislative branches, quotes another passage from Tocqueville arguing that democracies "obey the impulse of passion rather than the suggestions of prudence" and "abandon a mature design for the gratification of a momentary caprice" (Herring, pp. 7–8).

33. Russell, *My Diary North and South*, p. 43, entry for Mar. 28, 1861; Carpenter, *Inner Life*, p. 150.

34. For a trenchant analysis of Lincoln's innovations in executive power, see Schlesinger, *Imperial Presidency*, pp. 58–69. Schlesinger draws in part on the work of historians Edward Corwin and Quincy Wright. See, for example, Corwin, *The President*, pp. 263–69; and Wright, *Control of American Foreign Relations*, pp. 33 and 280. The Lincoln quote is in Oates, "Abraham Lincoln: *Republican* in the White House," p. 99. For a study of Union and Confederate state building during the Civil War, see Bensel, *Yankee Leviathan* (Cambridge, 1990), ch. 3.

35. Howard Jones sees Lincoln as "a born diplomat" with "a calm and patient demeanor, a trusting yet careful and genteel temperament, unquestioned integrity, an interest in listening to advice and learning from those who disagreed with him, and a willingness to compromise on issues requiring no sacrifice of principles." (Jones, *Blue and Gray Diplomacy*, p. 21.) Dean Mahin finds that Lincoln's "experience as a lawyer, politician, legislator, and debater had honed his skills in communication, negotiation, and compromise" (Mahin, p. 9).

36. Palmerston quoted in Bourne, *Palmerston: The Early Years*, p. 308 ("occult science"). On Washington's farewell, evidence suggests that Lincoln likely read more than one biography of Washington that included the full text of the document. See Bray, "What Abraham Lincoln Read," for a careful analysis of Lincoln's reading habits. Bray considers Washington's farewell to be "of obvious importance in the formation of Lincoln's mature thought." See also Lincoln, "Proclamation for Celebration of Washington's Birthday," Feb. 19, 1862, *CWL*, v. 5, p. 136; and Edward Haight to Lincoln, Feb. 17, 1862, ALP, LOC. Walter Lippmann, in his 1943 classic, *U.S. Foreign Policy: Shield of the Republic*, makes much of Washington's advice, and takes the famous phrase about "our interest guided by justice" as his epigraph. (Lippmann, *U.S. Foreign Policy*, epigraph and p. 177.)

37. Lincoln to George Robertson, Aug, 15, 1855, *CWL*, v. 2, p. 318.

38. Allen Guelzo, himself a top-notch Lincoln scholar, sees the past 15 years as the "golden age of Lincoln studies." For a more thorough discussion of the methods used by Burlingame and other modern Lincoln biographers, see Guelzo, "The Bicentennial Lincolns," *Claremont Review of Books*, v. 10, no. 1 (winter 2009–2010), pp. 45–46.

39. Frederic S. Cozzens to Manton Marble, Oct. 12, 1867, Manton Marble Papers, LOC. A transcript of this letter is in the Ruth Randall Papers, LOC. Cozzens recalls in this letter that the Polish Count Adam Gurowski, who worked as a translator at the State Department for nearly two years, used to refer to Mary as "that 'Sprinkfieldt B—ch,' " imitating the count's accent. Since this is a recollection of a spoken phrase, I have regularized the spelling in the text. In 1862 Gurowski published a candid diary that was critical of many administration figures (including the president, who he wrote possessed a "rather slow intellect"). He was eventually fired from the State Department—which may account for some of his animosity toward Mary Lincoln. President Lincoln himself worried to his bodyguard that Gurowski might try to assassinate him. "It would be just like him to do such a thing," Lincoln mused. See Lamon, *Recollections*, p. 274; and "Gurowski," in Heidler and Heidler, eds., *Encyclopedia of the American Civil War*, pp. 902–3.

40. Plumb to Thomas Corwin, Jan. 29, 1862, Plumb Papers, LOC; Pike to William Pitt Fessenden, Sept. 3, 1863, Pike Papers, LOC. In a letter to Pike in a separate collection of the diplomat's personal papers, Adam Gurowski

gripes about "pighead Lincoln"—
another example of such intra-
department grumbling. See Gurowski
to Pike, Aug. 30, 1861, Pike Papers, University of Maine. Thomas Schoonover,
in *Dollars Over Dominion* (Baton
Rouge, 1978), makes good use of much
of the Plumb and Pike correspondence,
though he does not include Plumb's
account of the White House reception
or the Pike material from Maine.

41. See Magness and Page, *Colonization After Emancipation* (Columbia,
Mo., 2011), for intriguing new evidence
that Lincoln was more committed to
colonization than previously understood. Eric Foner's recent Pulitzer
Prize winner, *The Fiery Trial*, offers
much thoughtful discussion of Lincoln
and colonization. Gary Dillard Joiner
uses the Sherman quote in his study
*One Damn Blunder from Beginning to
End: The Red River Campaign of 1864*
(Lanham, Md., 2003). The quote about
"great blunders" is from Bigelow to
Edward L. Pierce, Oct. 6, 1892, in
Bigelow, *Retrospections*, v. 3, p. 628.
Lippmann is quoted in Robert A.
Divine, *Second Chance* (New York,
1967), p. 181; and McDougall, *Promised
Land, Crusader State*, p. 152. McDougall emphasizes the human element
throughout his 1997 study of U.S.
foreign policy. "Americans," he writes,
"are at once typically flawed human
beings, unique individualists obsessed
with both justice *and* money, and
citizens of the most powerful, hence
potentially the most corruptible,
country on earth. That observation
may be less than profound, but it is the
beginning of wisdom about American
behavior in the state of nature called
world politics. . . . Much of the time

we have simply been human, pursuing
our short-term self-interest more or
less skillfully, and the rest of the world
be damned" (McDougall, *Promised
Land, Crusader State*, pp. 1–2). When it
comes to Lincoln, the president's law
partner, William Herndon, was one of
the earliest Lincoln biographers to
challenge the apotheosis. "No man is
absolutely perfect," Herndon told a
lecture audience in Dec. 1865. "We are
not gods—nor goddesses, just yet"
(Herndon, "Analysis of the Character
of Abraham Lincoln," p. 347). More
recently, Jon Meacham has admired
this quality in the best Lincoln
biographies. See Meacham, " 'The
Lincoln Anthology' edited by Harold
Holzer, 'The Best American History
Essays on Lincoln' edited by Sean
Wilentz, Ronald C. White's biography
'A. Lincoln' and others," *The Los
Angeles Times*, Feb. 1, 2009.

42. Johannsen, *To the Halls of the
Montezumas*, preface (first foreign
war); David Davis to his wife, June 7,
1847, Davis Papers, ALPLM; Davis
to his wife, June 25, 1847, ibid; *Sangamo Journal*, July 8, 1847. Robert W.
Johannsen's study of the war contends that "[i]t was the first American
war to rest on a truly popular base"
(Johannsen, *To the Halls of the Montezumas*, p. 16). For the final quote see
Melville to Gansevoort Melville, May
29, 1846, in Davis and Gilman, eds.,
The Letters of Herman Melville,
p. 28; and Johannsen, *To the Halls of
the Montezumas*, p. 10.

43. White, *A. Lincoln*, p. 139. On Lincoln lobbying for the congressional
nomination, see, for example, Lincoln to Henry E. Dummer, Nov. 18,
1845, *CWL*, vol 1., p. 350; Lincoln

to Benjamin F. James, Dec. 6, 1845, *CWL*, v. 1, pp. 351–52; Lincoln to N. J. Rockwell, Jan. 21, 1846, *CWL*, v. 1, p. 359. On the Lincolns' aspirations for Washington, see also David Davis to his wife, Aug. 8, 1847, Davis Papers, ALPLM; and Burlingame, *Inner World*, p. 309 ("loom largely" etc.).

44. Mary Lincoln biographer Ruth Randall, too, found this episode easy to visualize. She notes that her "imagination likes to play upon the Lincoln family" as they traveled on a riverboat during a leg of this trip (Randall, *Mary Lincoln*, p. 105). See also White, *A. Lincoln*, p. 139 (foliage etc.). The final quote is from Lincoln to William Henry Herndon, Dec. 13, 1847, *CWL*, v. 1, p. 420.

CHAPTER ONE: LINCOLN VS. HERNDON

1. Richard W. Thompson, "Abraham Lincoln," Richard W. Thompson Papers, ALPLM, pp. 10, 14–15; Whitney, *Life on the Circuit with Lincoln*, 37 (nervous). For a description of the House chamber, see the *Rockford Forum*, May 2, 1848, in Riddle, *Congressman Lincoln*, p. 74; Watterston, *A New Guide to Washington*, pp. 24–26; Dickens, *American Notes*, pp. 293–95; Maria Horsford to her children, quoted in Findley, *A. Lincoln: The Crucible of Congress*, p. 97; John J. Hardin to [David Allen Smith], Jan. 23, 1844, Hardin Family Papers, Chicago History Museum, quoted in *ALAL*, v. 1, p. 262; John J. Hardin to Eliza Caldwell Browning, Dec. 26, 1843, Orville H. Browning Papers, ALPLM, quoted in *ALAL*, v. 1, p. 264. Michael Burlingame, in *ALAL*, v. 1, pp. 261–64 and 266–68, offers a particularly complete and vivid description of the House and Lincoln's speech.

2. On Lincoln's public speaking anxieties, see Henry C. Whitney, *Life on the Circuit with Lincoln* (Boston, 1892), p. 37, cited in *RW*, p. 492; Lincoln to Herndon, Jan. 8, 1848, *CWL*, v. 1, p. 430; and *ALAL*, v. 1, pp. 267–68. For an excellent physical description

of Lincoln, see Herndon, "Analysis of the Character of Abraham Lincoln," pp. 356–59. See also Sandburg, *Abraham Lincoln*, p. 91; and Oates, *With Malice Toward None*, loc. 437 (pants).

3. Lincoln, " 'Spot' Resolutions," Dec. 22, 1847, *CWL*, v. 1, p. 421.

4. Watterston, *A New Guide to Washington*, pp. 25–26; Baker, p. 140 (red-and-gold). On Lincoln's voice see Herndon, *Herndon's Lincoln*, p. 248; and Thomas, *Portrait for Posterity*, p. 107. For Lincoln's Mexican War remarks, see "Speech in the United States House of Representatives: The War with Mexico," Jan. 12, 1848, in *CWL*, v. 1, pp. 431–42.

5. *Hudson River Chronicle* (Sing-Sing, N.Y.), Aug. 15, 1848, quoted in Foner, *Fiery Trial*, p. 53 ("abundance of gesture"); Omaha *Daily Bee*, Feb. 9, 1896, cited in *ALAL*, v. 1, p. 166 (hold him in place); William Henry Herndon to Truman Bartlett, July 19, 1887, in Hertz, *The Hidden Lincoln*, p. 191 ("bony forefinger"); Lincoln to Herndon, Feb. 1, 1848, in *CWL*, v. 1, p. 448 (rushed through).

6. Merry, p. 27 ("silent contempt"); Beveridge, v. 2, p. 131 (lengthy diary); Boritt, "Lincoln's Opposition to the

Mexican War," p. 91 (sending copies home); Lincoln to Herndon, Jan. 19, 1848, in *CWL*, v. 1, p. 445 ("I have made a speech").

7. Howe, *What Hath God Wrought*, pp. 738–39 (acted provocatively); *Baltimore Patriot*, n.d., copied in the *Rockford Forum*, Jan. 19, 1848; *Illinois State Register*, Jan. 14, 1848; Jan. 28, 1848; Mar. 10, 1848; *Missouri Republican* quoted in Greenberg, *A Wicked War*, p. 253.

8. Merk, *Manifest Destiny and Mission in American History*, p. 184; Bauer, p. 384 (terms); Foote, *Civil War*, v. 1, locs. 258–70 (territory gained).

9. *HL*, p. 177 ("very heart"); Herndon to Theodore Parker, Nov. 27, 1858, quoted in Newton, *Lincoln and Herndon*, pp. 245–46 ("mud instinct"); Herndon to Jesse Weik, Feb. 11, 1887, HW, LOC.

10. Lincoln to Herndon, Feb. 1, 1848, *CWL*, v. 1, pp. 446–48. For the point about the signoff, see Donald, *"We Are Lincoln Men,"* pp. 78, 99–100.

11. Donald, *Lincoln's Herndon*, p. 185 (romantic era). On the rationales for expansionism, see Weinberg, *Manifest Destiny*, pp. 13–16, 101. For the first Whitman quote, see *Brooklyn Daily Eagle*, Sept. 23, 1847, quoted in McDougall, *Promised Land, Crusader State*, p. 95 ("best kind"). See ch. 4, "Expansionism, or Manifest Destiny (so called)," for an insightful discussion of the topic. See also Howe, *What Hath God Wrought*, p. 769 ("miserable, inefficient").

12. Joseph Fort Newton, however, contends that Herndon was "essentially religious." (Newton, *Lincoln and Herndon*, p. 154.) On Lincoln's unorthodox religious beliefs see Guelzo,

Abraham Lincoln: Redeemer President (Grand Rapids, 1999); White, *Lincoln's Greatest Speech* (New York, 2002); and Winger, *Lincoln, Religion, and Romantic Cultural Politics* (DeKalb, 2003). On Herndon the reformer, see Donald, *Lincoln's Herndon*, p. 60. Prof. Donald's work represents the most thorough examination of the Lincoln-Herndon relationship. See *Lincoln's Herndon* (New York, 1948); *Lincoln* (New York, 1995); and *"We Are Lincoln Men": Abraham Lincoln and His Friends* (New York, 2003). Joseph Fort Newton's study, *Lincoln and Herndon* (Cedar Rapids, 1910), also includes much useful material.

13. Richard Carwardine has observed that Lincoln was "no provincial hick," adding that his "horizons stretched across the 19th-century world." Carwardine's essay in *The Global Lincoln* collects much evidence to support this thesis. He also notes that "Lincoln's reading gave him a keen sense of the United States' escape from the autocratic forces of the Old World. In this he was essentially a creature of his time: in the young Republic the experience of the revolutionary generation shaped a persisting, if fading, collective American memory of the war of independence from tyrannical rule." (Carwardine, "Lincoln's Horizons," *Global Lincoln*, pp. 32–37.) Cf. the traditional view, affirmed recently by George Herring, who observes that Lincoln "had traveled only to Canada, knew no foreign languages, and even by nineteenth-century-American standards would be considered provincial." (Herring, p. 228.) See also Dennis F. Hanks interview with Herndon, June 13, 1865, in *HI*, p. 36 ("strings of them"); *ALAL*, v. 1, p. 18 (with respect); Lincoln, "Address to the New Jersey State Senate," Feb. 21, 1861, in *CWL*, v. 4, p. 235 ("something more than common"); Washington's farewell address is quoted in Ramsay, *Life of George Washington*, p. 298. Lincoln's cousin Dennis Hanks recalls Lincoln borrowing Ramsay's *Washington*. (Dennis F. Hanks interview with Herndon, June 13, 1865, in *HI*, p. 41.)

14. Dennis F. Hanks to William Henry Herndon, Dec. 24, 1865, in *HI*, p. 146; *HL*, p. 49 ("field songs"); Lair, *Songs Lincoln Loved*, p. 19 ("None Can Love"); David Turnham to Herndon, Sept. 16, 1865, in *HI*, p. 129. For the *Sinbad* quote, I have used Sir Richard Burton's 1885 translation, despite the fact that it was not yet available in Lincoln's day. Burton's translation is the most widely quoted, and no record exists of which edition Lincoln may have read. (Burton, trans., *The Seven Voyages of Sinbad the Sailor* [Lawrence, Kan., 1999], p. 15.) See also Oates, *With Malice Toward None*, loc. 226 ("spider").

15. Carpenter, *Inner Life*, pp. 97–98.

16. Campanella's *Lincoln in New Orleans* (Lafayette, 2010) is a terrific recent study. See pp. 1, 12–13, 70, 123, 156–57, and 235. See also Donald, *Lincoln*, p. 34–35; Howe, *What Hath God Wrought*, p. 10; Thomas, *Abraham Lincoln*, pp. 17–18; Tocqueville quoted in Foner, *The Fiery Trial*, p. 10.

17. Lincoln, "Communication to the People of Sangamo County," Mar. 9, 1832, *CWL*, v. 1, pp. 5–8 ; and "Campaign Circular from the Whig Committee," Mar. 4, 1843, *CWL*, v. 1, pp. 311–12. Lincoln scholar Michael Burlingame has collected examples of anonymous newspaper articles,

probably by Lincoln, that also make this point.

18. This and the following paragraphs are drawn primarily from Herndon and Weik, *Herndon's Lincoln*, pp. 66–67 and 125–26; Donald, *Lincoln's Herndon*, pp. 4–5; Beveridge, v. 1, p. 118, and v. 2, p. 2; and Newton, *Lincoln and Herndon*, pp. 4–10. The editors of the best edition of Herndon's Lincoln biography, Douglas L. Wilson and Rodney O. Davis, point out that in later years Herndon himself was not completely confident in his memory of the details of this incident. In 1888 he wrote to his collaborator, Jesse Weik: "Try and get me right—If L came up to Bogues mill I saw Lincoln, & if he did not then I did not see him at Bogues mill." (Herndon to Weik, Nov. 10, 1888, HW, LOC.) See also Newton, *Herndon and Lincoln*, pp. 4–5; *HL*, p. 66 ("lost in boyish wonder").

19. *ALAL*, v. 1, p. 67 ("British Band"); Howe, *What Hath God Wrought*, pp. 418–19 (Black Hawk); Lincoln, "Speech in the U.S. House of Representatives on the Presidential Question," July 27, 1848, *CWL*, v. 1, pp. 501–16 (mosquitoes); "Conversation with Hon. J. T. Stuart, June 23, 1875," Hay Papers, Brown University, in Burlingame, ed., *An Oral History of Abraham Lincoln*, p. 8.

20. Royal Clary interview with Herndon, [Oct. 1866?,] in *HI*, pp. 370–73; *ALAL*, v. 1, p. 68; Browne, *The Every-Day Life of Abraham Lincoln*, p. 107, quoted in ibid.

21. In one 1836 article, published under the name "Johnny Blubberhead," a writer who was likely Lincoln sarcastically "bemoaned the failure of the country to go to war with England in order to enhance Martin Van Buren's electoral prospects." In another ironic letter, Lincoln, pretending to be a Democratic congressman, lamented the fact that America would not gin up a war against France (*ALAL*, v. 1, pp. 107–8). The Lyceum speech is in *CWL*, v. 1, pp. 108–15. There is much debate among Lincoln scholars over the identity of the "towering genius" Lincoln sees as a threat in this speech. Edmund Wilson, the novelist Gore Vidal, and others have suggested that Lincoln may have been subconsciously referring to himself (Wilson, *Patriotic Gore*, pp. 106–8). Allen Guelzo suggests the genius is Martin Van Buren (Guelzo, *Abraham Lincoln: Redeemer President*, p. 91). Michael Burlingame nominates Stephen Douglas. (*ALAL*, v. 1, pp. 140–41.)

22. Lincoln, "Address Before the Young Men's Lyceum of Springfield, Illinois," Jan. 27, 1838, in *CWL*, v. 1, pp. 108–15. See McPherson, *Battle Cry of Freedom*, p. 9; and Merry, p. 132, for the growth statistics.

23. Beveridge, v. 2, p. 2; Newton, *Lincoln and Herndon*, pp. 4, 8 (nearby college); Donald, *Lincoln's Herndon*, pp. 11–15. David Donald casts some doubt on whether Herndon was actually enrolled at the college during this period, suggesting that Herndon may have exaggerated the incident.

24. *HL*, p. 125; Donald, *Lincoln's Herndon*, pp. 14–15; *HI*, p. 470; Newton, *Lincoln and Herndon*, pp. 9–10; Beveridge, v. 2, p. 2 (sit on a keg); Herndon to the Massachusetts Historical Society, Mar. 29, 1842, quoted in Donald, *Lincoln's Herndon*, p. 14 ("staring us all in the face").

25. Baker, pp. 89 (greeting in French), 104; Brown, "Springfield Society before the Civil War," p. 479 ("spirited horses"); Hay, "Edward D. Baker," in Burlingame, ed., *At Lincoln's Side*, p. 153 ("Old School"); Clinton, *Mrs. Lincoln*, p. 44 (two-story brick); Sandburg, *Prairie Years*, v. 1, p. 251 (not making it to Mexico).

26. Beveridge, v. 1, pp. 207–8; Brown, "Springfield Society before the Civil War," pp. 478–80 ("hops"), 493 (lighting); *HL*, p. 121 ("priests, dogs, and servants").

27. Lincoln to Mary S. Owens, May 7, 1837, in *CWL*, v. 1, p. 78 ("but one woman"); Ninian W. Edwards interview with Herndon, [1865–1866], in *HI*, p. 446; Elizabeth and Ninian W. Edwards interview with William Henry Herndon, July 27, 1887, in *HI*, p. 623 (shade trees); Donald, *Lincoln*, p. 101 ("silk-stocking" Whigs); Lincoln to Mary S. Owens, May 7, 1837, in *CWL*, v. 1, p. 78 ("flourishing about").

28. Baker, pp. 32–33, 45–46 (Belgian rugs), 51 (Lexington banker and physical description); Elizabeth L. Norris to Emilie Todd Helm, September 28, 1895, Norris Papers, ALPLM; Townsend, *Lincoln and the Bluegrass*, pp. 58, 59; *Kentucky Statesman*, Sept. 14, 1860, clipping in Mentelle Papers, Transylvania University; Townsend, *The Boarding School of Mary Todd Lincoln*, p. 10 (corpse); *HL*, p. 134 ("merry dance").

29. Elizabeth Todd Edwards interview with Herndon, [1865–66,] in *HI*, pp. 443–44 ("irresistibly so" and "position, fame, and power"); Elizabeth and Ninian W. Edwards interview with Herndon, July 27, 1887, in *HI*, p. 623 (poor breeding and "most

ambitious woman"); Baker, p. 29
("seven years"); Lamon, *Recollections*,
p. 21 ("not pretty").

30. *CWL*, v. 1, p. 303 (wedding date);
Herndon to Jesse Weik, Jan. 16, 1886,
HW, LOC; Donald, *Lincoln*, p. 84 ("fine
conversationalist" and "haughty");
Jesse Weik interview with Herndon,
Weik Papers, box 2, memo book 2,
ALPLM ("family power"); John T.
Stuart interview with Herndon, [late
June 1865,] in *HI*, p. 64 ("policy match).
Michael Burlingame believes that "[i]t
is possible that Lincoln thought he
could enhance his political career
through a marriage alliance with the
more aristocratic Whig element, but
such a calculating approach to wedlock
seems out of character for Lincoln"
(*ALAL*, v. 2, p. 197). See also Guelzo,
Abraham Lincoln: Redeemer President,
p. 57, cited in Howe, *What Hath God
Wrought*, p. 597 ("larger world of
trade"). Guelzo's *Abraham Lincoln:
Redeemer President* is an impressive
"intellectual biography" that presents
Lincoln as a steady Whig. On Lincoln
and the Whig party see also Boritt,
*Lincoln and the Economics of the Amer-
ican Dream* (Memphis, 1978); Donald,
"A Whig in the White House," in
Lincoln Reconsidered, p. 133; Daniel
Walker Howe, "Why Abraham Lincoln Was a Whig," *Journal of the Abraham Lincoln Association*, v. 16, no. 1,
pp. 27–39; Joel H. Silbey, "Always a
Whig in Politics: The Partisan Life of
Abraham Lincoln," *Journal of the Abraham Lincoln Association*, v. 8, no. 1,
pp. 21–43. For the Gibbon gift see
CWL, v. 8, p. 436. A leather-bound history of Europe and the Roman Empire
that also bears Ninian Edwards's sig-

nature and is said to have once resided
in the Lincoln-Herndon law office is
now housed in the Lincoln Collection
at the Abraham Lincoln Presidential
Library and Museum in Springfield,
Ill. My thanks to curator James
Cornelius of the Lincoln Collection for
allowing me to examine these books.
For the final quote, see Lincoln to
Samuel D. Marshall, Nov. 11, 1842, in
CWL, v. 1, p. 305 ("profound wonder").

31. Beveridge, v. 2, pp. 67–68; Donald,
"We Are Lincoln Men," p. 91; Donald,
Lincoln's Herndon, p. 21 (popularity
dropped off, influence of the aristo-
crats); Lincoln to Martin S. Morris,
Mar. 26, 1843, in *CWL*, v. 1, p. 320
("family distinction"); Berry, *House of
Abraham*, p. xi; Foner, *Fiery Trial*, p. 13
("good enough for God"); White,
A. Lincoln, p. 128 (age); *HL*, p. 168
("I can trust you").

32. For a description of the office,
see "Lincoln's Law Offices in the
Tinsley Building, 1843–1852," *Lincoln
Lore*, No. 1579, Sept. 1969, pp. 1–4;
Newton, *Lincoln and Herndon*, p. 42;
Donald, *Lincoln's Herndon*, pp. 22, 33;
Donald, *Lincoln*, p. 103; Statement of
Gibson W. Harris, quoted in Weik,
The Real Lincoln, pp. 106–7, cited in
Donald, *Lincoln's Herndon*, p. 22 (office
description quote); *HL*, p. 207 (read
aloud and shirked his work); Herndon
to Jesse Weik, Oct. 21, 1885, HW,
LOC (fled the office).

33. Albert Beveridge notes that
"expansion . . . became the over-
shadowing issue of the campaign."
(Beveridge, v. 2, p. 69.) See also
McDougall, *Throes of Democracy*,
p. 260 ("foreign policy"); Lincoln
to Williamson Durley, Oct. 3, 1845,

CWL, v. 1, pp. 347–48 ("never much interested"); McDougall, *Throes of Democracy*, p. 79 (GTT); Merry, p. 76 ("unquenchable thirst"); Lincoln, "Speech on the Annexation of Texas," May 22, 1844, *CWL*, v. 1, p. 337 ("altogether inexpedient"); Boritt, *Lincoln and the Economics of the American Dream*, p. 105 ("nothing but Texas"). My thanks to George C. Herring for reminding me of the important role foreign policy played in the 1796 and 1812 campaigns.

34. Bauer, pp. 8, 24; and Merry, pp. 10, 188, 194 (Polk's inaugural, orders Taylor to Rio Grande, terms of offer).

35. Howe, *What Hath God Wrought*, p. 24 (*vaqueros*); Bauer, p. 19 ("prudence"); Merry, pp. 188, 192, 240 ("actual state of war" and "Star Spangled Banner").

36. Bauer, pp. 34–35 (brawls and *Moor of Venice*), 40 (watched the gringos and leaped nude).

37. Pedro de Ampudia to Don Z. Taylor, April 12, 1846, in *House Exec. Doc. No. 60*, p. 140; Taylor to the Adjutant General, April 26, 1846, in ibid., pp. 140–41; Eisenhower, *So Far from God*, pp. 63, 65; Merry, pp. 240–45; Howe, *What Hath God Wrought*, p. 732.

38. Merry, pp. 243–45. I have drawn heavily on Merry's account of the raid for the preceding section.

39. *HL*, p. 231 ("little engine"); Lincoln to Benjamin F. James, Nov. 17, 1845, *CWL*, v. 1, p. 349 ("operate against me"); Lincoln to Henry Dummer, Nov. 18, 1845, *CWL*, v. 1, p. 350 ("set a few stakes" and "turn about"); Mitgang, *Abraham Lincoln: A Press Portrait*, pp. 40–41 (avert a duel); Hardin quoted in Riddle,

Congressman Lincoln, p. 56 ("aggression and insult"); Lincoln to Hardin, Feb. 7, 1846, *CWL*, v. 1, p. 360–365 (strained relationship).

40. Beveridge, v. 2, pp. 78–80 ("blazed"). Donald Riddle writes that "[i]mmediately the prairies were afire." (Riddle, *Lincoln Runs for Congress*, p. 160.) See also Merk, *Manifest Destiny*, p. 37 ("most hawkish states"); Beveridge, v. 1, pp. 78–80 (Hardin); *HL*, p. 173 ("best legal talent"); Foner, *Fiery Trial*, p. 53 (most volunteers).

41. *Illinois State Register*, May 8, 1846, quoted in Beveridge, v. 2, p. 78.

42. *Sangamo Journal*, June 4, 1846, quoted in Riddle, *Congressman Lincoln*, p. 11 ("warm, thrilling"); *HL*, p. 173.

43. Johannsen, *To the Halls of the Montezumas*, p. 16 (penny press); Mott, *American Journalism*, pp. 248–49 (war correspondents); Howe, *What Hath God Wrought*, p. 697 ("major facilitator"). Howe's monumental history of this era emphasizes the critical role played by the nineteenth-century communications revolution.

44. Howe, *What Hath God Wrought*, p. 3 (millennialism); Merk, *Manifest Destiny*, p. 122; and McDougall, *Promised Land, Crusader State*, p. 95 ("regenerate the world"); Johannsen, *To the Halls of the Montezumas*, p. 296 ("air of decay"); McDougall, *Throes of Democracy*, p. 299 ("duty of neighbors").

45. Frederick Merk argues that the Mexican War enthusiasm was largely a product of the Northeastern penny press and its Midwestern counterparts like the *Illinois State Register*. (Merk, *Manifest Destiny*, pp. 35–37 and passim.) Robert W. Johannsen makes a compelling case that the excitement was a national phenomenon. (Johannsen, *To the Halls of the Montezumas*, passim.)

46. Johannsen, *To the Halls of the Montezumas*, pp. 26–27 ("all Whigs" and teenage boys), 169 ("little clothing"), 186–91 ("cast as redeemers"). The final quote is on p. 191. I have drawn heavily on Johannsen's research and interpretations in the preceding paragraph.

47. Beveridge, v. 2, p. 80; Baker, p. 104 (British-born Baker).

48. W. C. P. Breckinridge reminiscences, *Morning Herald*, July 24, 1903 ("physical manhood"); *Sangamo Journal*, July 23, 1846 ("ignoble death"); *Sangamo Journal*, June 25, 1846 ("Foreign nations"). Transcriptions of all three articles in William H. Townsend Papers, University of Kentucky.

49. Riddle, *Lincoln Runs for Congress*, pp. 167–68 (neutralizing it); *The Illinois Gazette* (Lacon), July 25, 1846, in *CWL*, v. 1, p. 381–82 (spoke on Oregon and Mexico); White, *A. Lincoln*, pp. 134–35 (by a wide margin).

50. White, *A. Lincoln*, p. 136 (another sixteen months); *ALAL*, v. 1, p. 241; Lincoln to Joshua Speed, Oct. 22, 1846, in *CWL*, v. 1, pp. 389–91.

51. Herndon to Jesse Weik, Dec. 29, 1885, HW, LOC.

52. This account of the Battle of Buena Vista is drawn primarily from Bauer, pp. 209–18. See also McDougall, *Throes of Democracy*, p. 294 ("A little more grape"); *ALAL*, v. 1, p. 277 (slogan); and Johannsen, *To the Halls of the Montezumas*, pp. 106–107.

53. Bauer, p. 216 (Hardin had fought heroically).

54. *Illinois State Register*, Apr. 2, 1847, quoted in Beveridge, v. 2, p. 92n4 ("beloved by all"); Lincoln, "Resolutions Adopted at John J. Hardin Memorial Meeting," in *Sangamo Journal*, Apr. 8, 1847, in *CWL*, v. 1, pp. 392–93.

55. J. G. Buckingham, private letter, quoted in Findley, *A. Lincoln: Crucible of Congress*, p. 60 ("curvetting and galloping"); Beveridge, v. 2, p. 93.

56. Bauer, pp. 220–21 ("robberies, murders, and rapes"), 225 ("missing daughters"), 268 (wooden leg); Beveridge, v. 2, pp. 93–94.

57. McPherson, *Battle Cry of Freedom*, pp. 3–4 ("bursting into applause"); Bauer, pp. 318 and 322 ("victorious commander").

58. Findley, *A. Lincoln: The Crucible of Congress*, p. 32 (know everyone); Illinois *Weekly Journal*, Oct. 28, 1847, quoted in Townsend, *Lincoln and His Wife's Hometown*, p. 140 ("twice the good looks").

59. Helm, *True Story of Mary, Wife of Lincoln*, pp. 99–100.

60. Townsend, *Lincoln and His Wife's Hometown*, p. 146 ("away fighting in Mexico"); *Papers of Henry Clay*, v. 10, p. 320, quoted in Heidler and Heidler, *Henry Clay*, pp. 414–15 ("outrages committed").

61. Townsend, *Lincoln in His Wife's Hometown*, pp. 144, 156 (Cromwell and Napoleon); Wilson, ed., *Intimate Memories of Lincoln*, p. 243 ("almost worshipped"); Davis and Wilson, eds., *The Lincoln-Douglas Debates*, p. 34 ("beau ideal"); *ALAL*, v. 1, pp. 92, 224; Heidler and Heidler, *Henry Clay*,

p. 71 (denim suit); Townsend, *Lincoln in His Wife's Hometown*, p. 152 (Lexington courthouse).

62. *New Orleans Daily Picayune*, Dec. 23, 1846, quoted in Heidler and Heidler, *Henry Clay*, p. 412 ("slay a Mexican"); Remini, *Henry Clay*, pp. 680–81 (pistols); *Papers of Henry Clay*, v. 10, p. 274, cited in Heidler and Heidler, *Henry Clay*, p. 410 ("dictates of conscience"); *Papers of Henry Clay*, v. 10, p. 316, cited in Heidler and Heidler, *Henry Clay*, p. 416 ("calamitous").

63. Merry, p. 394 (Clay's age); Clay, "Speech in Lexington, Ky., Nov. 13, 1847, in *Papers of Henry Clay*, v. 10, p. 362 ("frost of age"); Greenberg, *A Wicked War*, p. 228 ("trumpet"); Townsend, *Lincoln in His Wife's Hometown*, pp. 152–53. The scene of Clay's speech draws heavily on Townsend's account of the event.

64. Clay, "Speech in Lexington, Ky.," Nov. 13, 1847, in *Papers of Henry Clay*, v. 10, pp. 361–77 ("direful and fatal").

65. Townsend, *Lincoln in His Wife's Hometown*, p. 155 (length of speech); Howe, *What Hath God Wrought*, p. 828 (beamed it); Palmerston quoted in Greenberg, *A Wicked War*, p. 236; Anson G. Henry to Lincoln, Dec. 29, 1847, ALP, LOC ("Old Zac").

66. Usher F. Linder statement for J. G. Holland, in *HI*, p. 569 (shared a meal and "Mr. Lincoln's expectations"); Heidler and Heidler, *Henry Clay*, p. xx, n. 24 (no corroborating evidence).

67. Gouverneur, *As I Remember*, p. 170; Beveridge, v. 2, p. 102 ("scrambling village"); Busey, *Personal Reminiscences*, p. 65 (pigs and geese); Green,

Washington, v. 1, pp. 164 (muddy streets), 156 ("English woolens"), 173 ("city of Washington").

68. Findley, *A. Lincoln: Crucible of Congress*, p. 85; Randall, *Mary Lincoln*, pp. 107–8 (Lincolns arrived); Beveridge, v. 2, p. 101 (unpleasant welcome); Riddle, *Congressman Lincoln*, pp. 8, 13 (laconic record).

69. Watterston, *New Guide to Washington*, pp. 24–25; Riddle, *Congressman Lincoln*, p. 31; Beveridge, v. 2, pp. 108–109; Browne, *Every-Day Life of Abraham Lincoln*, p. 191 ("roar of laughter").

70. LaFeber, *The American Age*, p. 88; Bemis, *John Quincy Adams and the Foundations of American Foreign Policy*, pp. 8, 182, 253.

71. Adams's "monsters" speech, it is worth noting, was intended as a challenge to those Americans who wished to aid foreign revolutionaries in the early 1820s; it was written long before the Mexican War. My thanks to George C. Herring for stressing this point. See also Howe, *What Hath God Wrought*, p. 742 ("irreconcilables"); Carpenter, *Inner Life*, p. 212; Schroeder, *Mr. Polk's War* (Madison, 1973).

72. Polk, "Third Annual Message," Dec. 7, 1847, in Richardson, ed., *A Compilation of the Messages and Papers of the Presidents, 1789–1897*, v. 4 (Washington, 1897), pp. 532–64.

73. Fuller, *Movement for the Acquisition of All Mexico*, p. 61 (All-Mexico); *New York Herald*, Oct. 8, 1847, quoted in ibid., p. 82. See also Merk, *Manifest Destiny*, p. 123 ("Sabine virgins"); *Illinois State Register*, Nov. 12, 1847, quoted in Merk, p. 148 ("philanthropy and benevolence").

74. Howe, *What Hath God Wrought*, p. 807 ("sensationalism"); Merk, *Manifest Destiny*, p. 120n29; Johannsen, *To the Halls of the Montezumas*, p. 243; *CG*, 30th Cong., 1st Sess., p. 79, quoted in Fuller, *Movement for the Acquisition of All Mexico*, p. 103.

75. Weinberg, *Manifest Destiny*, p. 161 ("American democracy"); Fuller, *Movement for the Acquisition of All Mexico*, p. 81; and Weinberg, *Manifest Destiny*, p. 161 (evangelical revival); New York *Herald*, Jan. 30, 1848, quoted in Fuller, *Movement for the Acquisition of All Mexico*, pp. 107–8 ("evidence of civilization"). See also Weinberg, *Manifest Destiny*, p. 175.

76. Polk, *Diary of James K. Polk*, v. 2, Dec. 22, 1846, p. 288, quoted in Merry, p. 331 (Polk's diary); *Appendix to CG*, 29th Cong., 2nd Sess., p. 217; Beveridge, v. 1, pp. 107n4, 120–21; and Merk, *Manifest Destiny*, p. 96 (Giddings). See also Monaghan, p. 64, and Boritt, "Lincoln's Opposition to the Mexican War," p. 89.

77. Lincoln, "Autobiography Written for John L. Scripps," c. June 1860, in *CWL*, v. 4, pp. 61–66 ("in the president"); and "Speech at Wilmington, Del.," June 10, 1848, in ibid., v. 1, p. 476.

78. Lincoln, " 'Spot' Resolutions in the United States House of Representatives," in ibid., v. 1, pp. 421–22.

79. Lincoln to Herndon, Jan. 8, 1848, in ibid., v. 1, p. 430.

80. Lincoln to Herndon, Feb. 1, 1848, in ibid., v. 1, p. 448.

81. Lincoln to Herndon, Feb. 15, 1848, in ibid., v. 1, pp. 451–52.

82. Ibid. ("constitutional argument"). Mark E. Neely Jr. emphasizes this point. See Neely, "Lincoln and the Mexican War," pp. 6–7. See also Lincoln to Herndon, July 11, 1848, in *CWL*, v. 1, p. 499 ("while you're young!").

83. Herndon to Parker, Nov. 27, 1858, quoted in Newton, *Lincoln and Herndon*, pp. 245–46 ("young, undisciplined"); Herndon, "Big Me," reel 11, HW, LOC ("somewhat of a radical"); *HL*, p. 228 (lead to abolition); Herndon, "Analysis of the Character of Abraham Lincoln," pp. 349, 351 ("Godward"). Herndon made these observations after the Civil War. He presumably was referring to the latter conflict, but it seems safe to assume that Lincoln's law partner felt the same way about the Mexican War.

84. Herndon to Weik, Jan. 9, 1886, HW, LOC ("glittering generalities"); Donald, *Lincoln's Herndon*, p. 41 ("tears on the jury"); Herndon to Weik, Dec. 12, 1889, July 25, 1890, HW, LOC ("bones philosophy"). See also Donald, *"We Are Lincoln Men,"* pp. 73–75.

85. *HL*, pp. 175–176, 179 ("sealed Lincoln's doom," "made a mistake," and "political suicide"). See also Boritt, "Lincoln's Opposition to the Mexican War," pp. 81–82 (little evidence); Neely, "Lincoln and the Mexican War," pp. 23–24; and Findley, *A. Lincoln: Crucible of Congress*, p. x.

86. Neely, "Lincoln and the Mexican War," pp. 16–17, 23. See also Boritt, "Lincoln's Opposition to the Mexican War," p. 89.

87. Lincoln, "What General Taylor Ought to Say," [March?] 1848, in *CWL*, v. 1, p. 454; Lincoln to Greeley, June 27, 1848, in *CWL*, v. 1, p. 493–94

("revolution extended"). See also Neely, "Lincoln and the Mexican War," p. 15 ("distracting question").
88. Merk, *Manifest Destiny*, p. 184 (ending the war); Fuller, *The Movement for the Acquisition of All Mexico*, pp. 115–16 (senators voted against treaty); Merk, *Manifest Destiny*, pp. 189–90 (supported Polk); Bauer, p. 388 ("Girl I Left Behind").
89. Lincoln to Mary, Apr. 16, 1848, in *CWL*, v. 1, p. 465 ("say nothing"); Lincoln to Mary, June 12, 1848, in ibid., v. 1, p. 477.
90. Lincoln to Rev. John M. Peck, May 21, 1848, in ibid., v. 1, p. 473.
91. Lincoln to Archibald Williams, Apr. 30, 1848, in ibid., v. 1, p. 467–68 (smarter choice); McPherson, *Battle Cry of Freedom*, p. 58 ("perpetual frown" and no political record).
92. Lincoln to Herndon, June 22, 1848, in *CWL*, v. 1, p. 491 ("wild boys"); Lincoln to Herndon, June 12, 1848, in ibid., v. 1, pp. 476–77 ("war thunder"); *HL*, p. 179 ("warmed up"); *Illinois State Register*, June 30, 1848, cited in *HL*, p. 438n77 (tepid support).
93. Lincoln, "Speech in the U.S. House on the Presidential Question," July 27, 1848, in *CWL*, v. 1, pp. 505–15; *Baltimore American*, quoted in *ALAL-DC*, ch. 8, p. 815 ("roar of merriment").
94. Neely, "Lincoln and the Mexican War," pp. 14–15 (tempered his expansionism); Lincoln, "Speech at Worcester, Massachusetts," Sept. 12, 1848, in *CWL*, v. 2, pp. 1–5; "Governor Henry J. Gardner (statement for Edward L. Pierce)," [Feb.–May 1890,] in *HI*, pp. 698–99. See also *ALAL*, v. 1, pp. 280–81.

95. Beveridge, v. 2, p. 190 ("rain and snow"); Findley, *A. Lincoln: Crucible of Congress*, p. 93; Clark, *Abraham Lincoln in the National Capital*, p. 8; Oates, *With Malice Toward None*, loc. 1695 (stepping aside for Logan).
96. Hay, *Diary*, entry for Aug. 13, 1863, p. 73.
97. See, for example, Neely Jr., "Lincoln and the Mexican War," p. 23 and passim.
98. Paul Findley correctly observes that in Congress Lincoln "learned to temper his idealism with pragmatism, to reject unrealistic objectives and settle for steps that were within reach" (Findley, *A. Lincoln: Crucible of Congress*, p. 261; see also p. 216). For an example of a British statesman who was a master "of that same mysterious art," see Bell, v. 2, p. 428.
99. See, for example, Guelzo, *Abraham Lincoln: Redeemer President*, p. 57, cited in Howe, *What Hath God Wrought*, p. 597 (Midwestern drudgery); Lincoln to Williamson Durley, Oct. 3, 1845, in *CWL*, v. 1, p. 347; Boritt, *Lincoln and the Economics of the American Dream*, p. 140 (inevitable).
100. Abner Y. Ellis to Herndon, Dec. 6, 1866, in *HI*, p. 500 (off-color stories and "star gazing"); H. E. Dummer interview with Herndon, [1865–1866,] in *HI*, pp. 442–43 ("smutty stories").
101. This account of the Ottawa debate draws on Tarbell, *Life of Abraham Lincoln*, v. 1, pp. 312–13; *ALAL*, v. 1, pp. 487–88; *Chicago Press and Tribune*, Aug. 23, 1858, and *New York Evening Post*, Aug. 27, 1858, quoted in Davis and Wilson, eds., *The Lincoln-Douglas Debates*, pp. 1–2;

Beveridge, v. 4, pp. 283–85; and Guelzo, *Lincoln and Douglas* (New York, 2008), pp. 113–16.

102. The physical description of Douglas is from Donald, *Lincoln's Herndon*, p. 72. See also *Ottawa (Ill.) Republican*, Aug. 28, 1858, quoted in *ALAL*, v. 1, p. 488 ("demonized howl").

103. Davis and Wilson, eds., *The Lincoln-Douglas Debates*, pp. 11, 16–17 (opening volley).

104. Ibid., p. 21.

105. Ibid., pp. xi–xii (expansionist measures), 61 (boy in hoops).

106. Ibid., p. 47 ("not generally opposed"); *Illinois State Register*, Oct. 22, 1858, quoted in *ALAL*, v. 1, p. 527.

107. The debate scrapbooks are in HW, LOC; the clippings I cite are on pp. 75 and 80 of the microfilm version. See also Herndon to Theodore Parker, Oct. 3, 1858, cited in *ALAL*, v. 1, p. 541 (small-town churches); *HL*, p. 251; and Donald, *Lincoln's Herndon*, p. 122 (scrapbooks).

108. Donald, *Lincoln's Herndon*, p. 110 ("undeveloped feeling"). Lincoln

biographer Albert J. Beveridge once told Herndon's associate Jesse Weik that he believed Herndon greatly admired Douglas's "power, ability and masterfulness." (Beveridge to Weik, Aug. 18, 1926, Albert J. Beveridge Papers, folder 4, ALPLM.) David Donald observes, "If it was a choice between being a contented moneybags or a wild-eyed crusader, Herndon felt he had no discretion" (Donald, *Lincoln's Herndon*, p. 65; see also p. 64). Herndon to Lyman Trumbull, Feb. 19, 1858, Trumbull Papers, LOC ("I hate power").

109. Lincoln, "Speech in the United States House of Representatives on Internal Improvements," June 20, 1848, in *CWL*, v. 1, p. 484.

110. For a recent reassessment of the Lincoln-Herndon friendship, from one of the leading authorities on Herndon, see Donald, *"We Are Lincoln Men,"* pp. 67–100.

111. Henry C. Whitney to Herndon, July 18, 1887, in *HI*, pp. 621–22; *RW*, p. 492 ("bitter and despairing").

CHAPTER TWO: LINCOLN VS. SEWARD

1. *Cincinnati Daily Commercial*, Nov. 21, 1860, and Nov. 24, 1860 ("disagreeably intense"); *New York Tribune*, Nov. 14, 1860 ("hearty Western welcomes" and "heaps and hills"), and Nov. 10, 1860 ("as many nationalities"). See also White, *A. Lincoln*, pp. 351–52; and Holzer, *Lincoln President-Elect*, pp. 21, 61, 142.

2. See, for example, Boritt, *Lincoln and the Economics of the American Dream*, passim.

3. "Republican Party," *New Encyclopaedia Britannica (Micropaedia)*, v. 9, p. 1035; "Whig Party," *New Encyclopaedia Britannica (Micropaedia)*, v. 12, p. 621.

4. "Republican Party," *New Encyclopaedia Britannica (Micropaedia)*, v. 9, p. 1035; Foote, *Civil War*, v. 1, locs. 31 (seceding states) and 724 (New Jersey); *Philadelphia Bulletin*, Dec. 14, 1860, copied in *New York Times*, Dec. 20, 1860, in *RW*, p. 6 ("drive me insane"). See also Holzer, *Lincoln President-Elect*, pp. 153 (worn and pale), 197.

5. Hay, *New York World*, Mar. 4, 1861, in Burlingame, ed., *Lincoln's Journalist*, p. 50 ("hydraulic pressure"); McClintock to Lincoln, Feb. 5, 1861, ALP, LOC.

6. For physical descriptions of Seward, see Bancroft, v. 1, p. 190; Van Deusen, p. 10; Laugel, *United States During the Civil War*, p. 312; Goodwin, p. 30. Goodwin's *Team of Rivals* is an extraordinary recent account of the Lincoln-Seward friendship and rivalry.

7. Carpenter, *Inner Life*, p. 69 ("man soliloquizing aloud"); Seward, *Reminiscences of a War-Time Statesman and Diplomat*, p. 147 ("depend upon you"); Lincoln to Seward, Mar. 11, 1861, in *CWL*, v. 4, p. 281.

8. Seward, *Seward at Washington, 1846–1861*, pp. 487 ("my country"), 491 ("dictatorship"), 497 ("conciliatory person").

9. Seward quoted in *ALAL*, v. 2, p. 98 ("hereditary principality"); George Fogg to Lincoln, Feb. 5, 1861, ALP, LOC. See also *ALAL*, v. 1, p. 737.

10. Robert L. Wilson to Herndon, Feb. 10, 1866, in *HI*, p. 207 (hang himself); Villard, *Memoirs*, v. 1, p. 156; New York *Evening Post*, Mar. 16, 1861, cited in Burlingame, ed., *Abraham Lincoln: The Observations of John G. Nicolay and John Hay*, p. 40 (bed after lunch); Nicolay, *Lincoln's Secretary*, p. 101 ("Satan himself"); Lincoln to Joshua Speed, [Jan. 3?] 1842, *CWL*, v. 1, p. 265 ("defective nerves"). See also Holzer, *Lincoln President-Elect*, p. 436; White, *A. Lincoln*, p. 403; and Shenk, *Lincoln's Melan-*

choly, p. 21. On the weather, see, for example, Herman Melville to his wife, Mar. 25, 1861, in Davis and Gilman, eds., *Letters of Herman Melville*, pp. 209–10; and Hay, *New York World*, Mar. 4, 1861, in Burlingame, ed., *Lincoln's Journalist*, p. 48. For Lincoln's migraine, see Sam Ward to S. L. M. Barlow, Mar. 30, 1861, quoted in Nevins, *War for the Union*, v. 1, p. 58. See also Donald, *Lincoln*, p. 289; and *ALAL*, v. 2, pp. 108–9.

11. Herring, p. 3 (Jefferson quote).

12. Ibid., pp. 132–33 (War of 1812), 155–57 ("ringing affirmation"). For the description of Americans as an "absurdly self-confident folk," see Perkins, *History of the Monroe Doctrine*, p. 111.

13. Kissinger, *Diplomacy*, pp. 94 (Crimean War shatters Concert of Europe), 95, 102–3 (post-Crimean order), 106 ("days of principles"), 127 (Darwin, etc.). See also Herring, p. 267.

14. Cortada, "A Case of International Rivalry," pp. 53–69; "Dominican Republic," *New Encyclopaedia Britannica (Micropaedia)*, v. 4, pp. 167–68 (Dominican landscape); William Moss Wilson, "The 'Foreign War Panacea,' " *New York Times*, Mar. 17, 2011. Dexter Perkins observes that "there are few more unqualified faiths than the faith of the American people in the Monroe Doctrine." See Perkins, *History of the Monroe Doctrine*, "Foreword."

15. *New York Times*, Apr. 1, 1861, and *New York Herald*, Apr. 2, 1861, cited in *ALAL*, v. 2, p. 115 (still ill); White, *A. Lincoln*, p. 404, notes that the missive arrived in the morning. For background on the Santo Domingo maneuver, see Crook, *Diplomacy During the American Civil War*, pp. 21–22. See also Lincoln to Seward, Apr. 1, 1861, ALP, LOC, note 2.

16. Seward, "Some Thoughts for the President's Consideration," Apr. 1, 1861, Seward Papers, University of Rochester; Seward, *Reminiscences*, p. 149; Frederick W. Seward, "After Thirty Years," Seward Papers, University of Rochester. See also Goodwin, pp. 341–43.

17. Brauer, "Seward's 'Foreign War Panacea,' " p. 148 (rumors flew); *New York Times*, "Foreign Intervention in American Affairs," Apr. 1, 1861.

18. The holograph version of Lincoln's response is in the ALP, LOC. See Lincoln to Seward, Apr. 1, 1861, ALP, LOC.

19. Sandburg, *Abraham Lincoln*, p. 433; Burlingame, *Inner World*, p. 190 (tore up letters); *CWL*, v. 4, p. 317, note 1 (orally). The memo was ultimately published by John Nicolay and John Hay in their 10-volume 1890 biography, *Abraham Lincoln: A History*. Much of their material had also been published in the preceding few years in *The Century* magazine. For more on the historiography, see Ferris, "Lincoln and Seward in Civil War Diplomacy" (*Journal of the Abraham Lincoln Association* 12 [1991], no. 1).

20. Brauer, "Seward's 'Foreign War Panacea,' " p. 133; Donald, *Charles Sumner and the Rights of Man*, p. 22. Seward biographer Glyndon Van Deusen acknowledged that it was "possible" that Seward "simply lost his head" in April 1861—but that the evidence argues against it (Van Deusen, p. 301). See also Bancroft, v. 2, pp. 151, 471–72; Welles quoted in Paolino, *Foundations of the American Empire*, p. 13; Nicolay and Hay, *Abraham Lincoln: A History*, v. 3, p. 445. See also Ferris, "Lincoln and Seward in Civil War Diplomacy," for a discussion of the role Welles and Hay played in shaping the Lincolnian foreign-affairs legacy.

21. This is the implication of Ferris, *Desperate Diplomacy*, passim. See also Herring, p. 227; and Jones, *Blue and Gray Diplomacy*, p. 24.

22. Herring, p. 255. "If ever an American political leader had a record of consistently working for territorial and commercial expansion entirely by peaceful means," notes Norman Ferris, "that man was Seward." (Ferris, "Lincoln and Seward in Civil War Diplomacy," p. 21.)

23. Doris Kearns Goodwin notes the similar contexts in which the men grew up. Both men were Whigs and beneficiaries of the market revolution. See Goodwin, pp. 28–29.

24. Mead, *Special Providence*, pp. 99–131. The quote is on p. 105. The classic study of the intersection of finance and commerce with international relations is Kennedy, *Rise and Fall of the Great Powers* (London, 1988). Allen Guelzo, in his study *Abraham Lincoln: Redeemer President*, emphasizes Lincoln's Hamiltonian roots.

25. Guelzo, *Abraham Lincoln: Redeemer President*, pp. 63, 71; Botts, *The Great Rebellion* (New York, 1866), p. 196 ("Henry-Clay Whig"). See also Donald, "A Whig in the White House," in *Lincoln Reconsidered*, p. 133.

26. This point is the central thrust of Gabor Boritt's groundbreaking study, *Lincoln and the Economics* *of the American Dream* (Memphis, 1978).

27. *RW*, p. 150. See also Boritt, *Lincoln and the Economics of the American Dream*, p. 93 ("old woman's dance"); Guelzo, *Abraham Lincoln: Redeemer President*, p. 131 ("eventual triumph").

28. Baker, ed., *Works of Seward*, v. 3, p. 188 ("force the fruit"); Bancroft, v. 1, p. 469 ("empire of the world"); Crook, *Diplomacy During the American Civil War*, p. 18 (trade entrepots); Bancroft, v. 1, p. 469 ("power of the earth"); Paolino, *Foundations of the American Empire*, p. 40; and McDougall, *Promised Land, Crusader State*, p. 106 ("god of boundaries"). Paolino's study, in particular, emphasizes Seward's central focus on economic expansion. Jay Sexton, in his recent work *Debtor Diplomacy* (Oxford, 2005), makes the case for examining the financial factors in addition to the commercial.

29. Baker, ed., *Works of Seward*, v. 4, pp. 454–55, 461.

30. Herndon to Seward, Mar. 21, 1854, Seward Papers, University of Rochester. See also Bancroft, v. 1, p. 362.

31. Bancroft, v. 1, pp. 2, 6–8; Van Deusen, p. 3 (Seward's father); Seward, *Autobiography*, p. 104 (voyage).

32. Seward, *Autobiography*, pp. 116 ("What a romance"), 123 (*Childe Harold*), 105 (swimming etc.).

33. Ibid., pp. 105 ("slips and quays"), 115 ("coal-smoke"), 113 ("listless"), 109.

34. Ibid., pp. 111 ("continually disturbed"), 116 ("still less"), 105–6 ("destitute of principle").

35. Ibid., pp. 125–26 (countryside), 127 (unpaved streets etc.), 127 ("political changes"), 131 (guillotine). See also Bancroft, v. 1, p. 49.

36. Seward, *Autobiography*, p. 135 (bust of himself etc.).

37. Van Deusen, pp. 23 (returns to law), and 29 ("galley slave"); Bancroft, v. 1, pp. 171 (treadmill), and 56 ("fondness"); Seward to Albert H. Tracy, June 23, 1831, quoted in Goodwin, p. 77 ("banish care").

38. Seward, *Autobiography*, pp. 205–6 ("with affection"); Bancroft, v. 1, p. 546 ("every sentiment"); Herring, p. 255 ("logical successor").

39. Van Deusen, p. 549; Adams quoted in Bemis, *John Quincy Adams and the Foundations of American Foreign Policy*, pp. 60 ("connections in Europe"), and 64 ("much perseverance"). The brackets on the word "System" are Bemis's.

40. LaFeber, *American Age*, p. 134 (reciprocity); Sexton, *Debtor Diplomacy*, p. 7; Sexton, *Monroe Doctrine*, pp. 113–14.

41. Monaghan, p. 73 ("double game"); Bancroft, v. 2, pp. 68 ("influence and predjudice"), 151 ("half a century"), 60 ("increases them").

42. This account of the McLeod Affair is drawn primarily from Bancroft, v. 1, pp. 111–16; and Van Deusen, pp. 76–79. See also Howard Jones, *To the Webster-Ashburton Treaty* (Chapel Hill, 1977); and Jones and Donald A. Rakestraw, *Prologue to Manifest Destiny: Anglo-American Relations in the 1840s* (Lanham, Md., 1997).

43. Van Deusen, p. 77 (pounding drums); Sexton, *Debtor Diplomacy*, p. 30 ("immediate and frightful"); Palmerston to Lord John Russell, Jan. 19, 1841, Russell Papers, BNA ("perseveringly pressed").

44. Sexton, *Debtor Diplomacy*, pp. 31–33 (Webster and Britain); Van

Deusen, p. 78 (envoys to New York);
Bancroft, v. 1, p. 115 ("smother").
45. Seward quoted in Bancroft,
v. 2, p. 473 (" 'masterly inactivity' ");
Van Deusen, p. 105 ("bastard war");
Seward, *Autobiography*, p. 809; Goodwin, p. 123 ("national adversaries").
46. Edward L. Pierce statement
for Herndon, [1887?,] in *HI*, p. 690
("echo"); Francis B. Carpenter,
"A Day with Governor Seward at
Auburn," July 1870, Seward Papers,
University of Rochester ("slavery
question"); Seward, *Seward at Washington, 1846–1861*, p. 80 ("have been
doing"). See also Goodwin, p. 127.
47. William H. Seward Jr., "Kossuth's Visit to Auburn, May 29, 1852,"
Seward Papers, University of Rochester; Bancroft, v. 1, pp. 312–14 (Kossuth); Van Deusen, pp. 139–40.
48. Lincoln, "Resolutions on Behalf
of Hungarian Freedom," Jan. 9, 1852,
in *CWL*, v. 2, p. 115.
49. Adams quoted in Lippmann,
U.S. Foreign Policy, p. 17 ("cockboat");
Lincoln, "Resolutions on Behalf of
Hungarian Freedom," Jan. 9, 1852, in
CWL, v. 2, p. 116 ("yoke of despotism").
50. For a discussion of their similar
backgrounds, see Goodwin, p. 28.
51. Frances Seward to William H.
Seward, July 20, 1856, Seward Papers,
University of Rochester; Van Deusen,
p. 178.
52. Van Deusen, p. 212; Goodwin,
p. 213; Foreman, *World on Fire*, p. 40
(meeting next president); Seward,
Seward at Washington, 1846–1861,
p. 369 (smaller than ever).
53. Seward, *Seward at Washington,
1846–1861*, pp. 370–71.
54. Ibid., p. 382.
55. Ibid., pp. 385–90.

56. Ibid., pp. 391 ("egotism"), 431
(Waterloo); "Interview with Napoleon III," Seward Papers, University
of Rochester.
57. Herring, p. 225 (intersection
of nationalism and globalization);
Seward, *Seward at Washington,
1846–1861*, pp. 363–64 ("I ween").
58. Bancroft, v. 2, pp. 46–49.
59. Lincoln, "Campaign Circular
from the Whig Committee," Mar. 4,
1843, in *CWL*, v. 1, pp. 311–13.
60. Lincoln to Lyman Trumbull,
Apr. 29, 1860, in *CWL*, v. 4, pp. 45–46.
On the nineteenth-century norms
regarding the president's interaction
with the public, see Donald, *Lincoln*,
p. 440; and Carwardine, *Lincoln*,
p. 261.
61. *ALAL*, v. 1, pp. 443–44; Stephen
Douglas quoted in Davis and Wilson,
eds., *Lincoln-Douglas Debates*, p. 241;
Winger, *Lincoln, Religion, and Romantic Cultural Politics*, pp. 22–26.
62. Herndon to Jesse Weik, Feb. 21,
1891, HW, LOC ("cold flat thing");
Corneau, "A Girl in the Sixties,"
p. 407 (Hay in audience). See also
ALAL, v. 1, pp. 444–45; and Donald,
Lincoln's Herndon, p. 63.
63. Lincoln, "Second Lecture on Discoveries and Inventions," *CWL*, v. 3,
pp. 356–57. For two thoughtful analy-
ses of the speech, see Winger, *Lincoln, Religion, and Romantic Cultural
Politics*, pp. 15–48; and Foner, *Fiery
Trial*, p. 115. Winger contrasts Lincoln's "ironic Protestant perspective"
with Stephen Douglas's unabashed,
self-righteous expansionism.
64. Weinberg, *Manifest Destiny*,
p. 202 (Senate report); Seward quoted
in ibid., p. 66 ("Gulf of Mexico");
LaFeber, *American Age*, p. 144

(opposed annexation); *Illinois State Journal*, Sept. 1860, cited in *ALAL*, v. 1, pp. 665–66. Scholar Michael Burlingame has identified a number of anonymous newspaper articles likely penned by Lincoln.

65. Oldroyd, *Lincoln Memorial*, pp. 474–76, quoted in *RW*, p. 154 ("knows me"); Whitney, *Life on the Circuit with Lincoln*, p. 146 ("*run* you").

66. Baker, p. 158 ("Wigwam"); *ALAL*, v. 1, pp. 612 ("pennants and streamers" and expansionist planks), 603 (Weed nicknames and "rope-dancer's"); Donald, *Lincoln*, p. 248 ($100,000); Van Deusen, p. 222 (whisky swilling).

67. Nathan M. Knapp to Lincoln, May 14, 1860, ALP, LOC ("second choice"); Stanton, *Random Recollections*, pp. 215–16; Goodwin, pp. 10–11, 250; R. M. Blatchford to Seward, May 18, 1860, Seward Papers, University of Rochester; and Van Deusen, p. 224 ("today sure").

68. White, *A. Lincoln*, p. 326 (first-round tally); Stanton, *Random Recollections*, pp. 215–16; Goodwin, p. 250 (wild cheering); Halstead, *Caucuses of 1860*, p. 145; Nicolay and Hay, *Abraham Lincoln: A History*, v. 2, pp. 271–72. See also E. D. Morgan to Seward, May 18, 1860, Seward Papers, University of Rochester; and Van Deusen, p. 225 ("third ballot"); Stahr, *Seward*, pp. 188–89; Guelzo, *Abraham Lincoln: Redeemer President*, p. 245 ("back the tears"); Charles Francis Adams Jr., *Autobiography*, p. 69 ("cursing and swearing").

69. Halstead, *Caucuses of 1860*, p. 154; Nicolay and Hay, *Abraham Lincoln: A History*, v. 2, p. 278 (tar barrels, etc.); Charles Zane statement in *HI*, p. 491 ("than I am"); "Ecarte" [John Hay,]

Providence Journal, May 26, 1860, in Burlingame, ed., *Lincoln's Journalist*, pp. 1–3 (fireworks).

70. Schurz, *Reminiscences*, v. 2, pp. 221–22 ("Illinois lawyer!"); Charles Francis Adams Jr., *Autobiography*, pp. 62, 65–66. See also Van Deusen, pp. 233–34, 336.

71. Donald, *"We Are Lincoln Men,"* p. 148 ("of the other"); *New York Herald*, Oct. 2, 1860, quoted in *ALAL*, v. 1, p. 654 ("than by cordiality" and fifteen minutes); Charles Francis Adams Jr., *Autobiography*, pp. 64–65; Goodwin, p. 270 ("out of place").

72. Oates, *With Malice Toward None*, locs. 3744–56 ("Mr. Speaker!"); William H. Wilson to Lincoln, Oct. 29, 1860, ALP, LOC; Lincoln to William H. Wilson, Nov. 3, 1860, *CWL*, *Supplement 1832–1865*, p. 59. See also William Honselman to Lincoln, Oct. 21, 1860, ALP, LOC.

73. Luebke, ed., *Ethnic Voters and the Election of Lincoln*, pp. xvii, 215; Smith, "The Influence of the Foreign-Born of the Northwest in the Election of 1860," pp. 192–201.

74. Donald, *Lincoln's Herndon*, p. 125 ("Irish"); Mary Lincoln to Emilie Todd Helm, November 23, 1856, in Turner and Turner, *Mary Todd Lincoln*, p. 46; Lincoln to Joshua F. Speed, Aug. 24, 1855, *CWL*, v. 2, p. 323 ("hypocrasy"); Lincoln to Theodore Canisius, May 17, 1859, *CWL*, v. 3, p. 380. See also Smith, "The Influence of the Foreign-Born of the Northwest in the Election of 1860," pp. 197–98.

75. Smith, p. 195; White, *A. Lincoln*, p. 333 (divided Dems); Lincoln to Seward, Oct. 12, 1860, in *CWL*, v. 4, p. 125 ("into our hands"); White, *A. Lincoln*, p. 347 ("we are elected"); Baker, pp.

161–62 ("little lady"); Goodwin, p. 278 ("we are elected").

76. Lincoln told this to Canadian editor Josiah Blackburn in the summer of 1864; see *RW*, p. 31 ("this great event"); John Bigelow to William Hargreaves, July 30, 1860, John Bigelow Papers, New York Public Library ("Mastodon"). See also *ALAL*, v. 1, p. 647; and Clapp, *Forgotten First Citizen*, p. 136.

77. *Boston Herald*, Nov. 9, 1860, quoted in Holzer, *Lincoln President-Elect*, p. 51.

78. Foner, *Free Soil, Free Labor, Free Men*, p. 16, cites the observation of an "Iowa Republican" to illustrate the party line. Lincoln would almost certainly have concurred with this sentiment. See also Foner, *Fiery Trial*, p. 117.

79. *New York Herald*, Dec. 15, 1860, quoted in Holzer, *Lincoln President-Elect*, p. 148 ("eight days"); *New York Tribune*, Nov. 10, 1860, quoted in ibid., p. 21; Koerner, *Memoirs*, v. 2, pp. 108–9; *ALAL*, v. 1, p. 696 (Swiss example).

80. Lincoln to Lyman Trumbull, Dec. 10, 1860, in *CWL*, v. 4, pp. 149–50 ("time hereafter"); Lincoln to Elihu Washburne, Dec. 13, 1860, in ibid., v. 4, p. 151 ("chain of steel"); Lincoln to James Hale, Jan. 11, 1861, in ibid., v. 4, p. 172 ("more territory").

81. Lincoln to Seward, Dec. 8, 1860, in ibid., v. 4, pp. 148 and 149n1; Seward to Lincoln, Dec. 13, 1860, in Nicolay and Hay, *Abraham Lincoln: A History*, v. 3, p. 350.

82. Bancroft, v. 2, p. 5 (Northeastern businessmen). For a detailed description of the Crittenden Compromise, see *ALAL*, v. 1, pp. 694–98.

83. Foner, *Free Soil, Free Labor, Free Men*, pp. 222–23.

84. *New York Herald*, Dec. 27, 1860, quoted in Holzer, *Lincoln President-Elect*, p. 165 ("undisguised hostility"); Lincoln to Thurlow Weed, Dec. 17, 1860, in *CWL*, v. 4, p. 154 ("territorial question"); Holzer, *Lincoln President-Elect*, p. 166 (Seward should introduce, etc.).

85. *New York Times*, Dec. 24, 1860 ("evidence of delight"). See also Bancroft, v. 2, p. 8 (cigar-fueled); and Ferris, *The* Trent *Affair*, pp. 98–99.

86. Seward's speech is in *CG*, 36th Cong., 2nd Sess., pp. 341–44. See also *Chicago Tribune*, Jan. 17, 1861; Foner, *Fiery Trial*, p. 148; Holzer, *Lincoln President-Elect*, p. 213 (voted against Crittenden); Bensel, *Yankee Leviathan*, p. 18; and Bancroft, v. 2, p. 15.

87. George Fogg to Gideon Welles, Welles Papers, ALPLM ("not over-pleased"); Schurz to his wife, Feb. 9, 1861; and Schurz to his wife, Feb. 4, 1861, in Schafer, ed., *Intimate Letters of Carl Schurz*, pp. 247, 242; Seward to his family, Jan. 13, 1861, in *Seward at Washington, 1846–1861*, p. 496 ("good fruits"); Seward to his wife, Jan. 18, 1861, in ibid., p. 496 ("concessions"). See also Foner, *Fiery Trial*, p. 148; and Holzer, *Lincoln President-Elect*, pp. 214–15 (his input).

88. Seward to Lincoln, Dec. 28, 1860 ("reassuring and soothing"), and Seward to Lincoln, Dec. 29, 1860 ("by surprise"), both in ALP, LOC.

89. Black, "Circular," Feb. 28, 1861, *FRUS 1861*, pp. 31–32.

90. Blair to Lincoln, Jan. 25, 1861, ALP, LOC.

91. Romero dispatch, Jan. 23, 1861, in Segal, ed., *Conversations with Lincoln*, pp. 65–67. For a slightly different translation of this report, see Schoonover, ed., *Mexican Lobby*, pp. 2–3. See also Mahin, p. 110; and William Moss Wilson, "Lincoln's Mexican Visitor," *New York Times*, Jan. 17, 2011.

92. Lincoln to Seward, Feb. 1, 1861, in *CWL*, v. 4, p. 183.

93. Lutz, *Annual Report of the American Historical Association for the Year 1915*, p. 210.

94. *HL*, p. 287; Herndon, "Facts Illustrative of Mr. Lincoln's Patriotism and Statesmanship," p. 194; *ALAL-DC*, v. 1, p. 2061 (farewell address); Seward to Lincoln, Feb. 24, 1861, quoted in Nicolay and Hay, *Abraham Lincoln: A History*, v. 3, pp. 319–20 ("date from the inauguration"). See also Bancroft, v. 2, p. 24; and Holzer, *Lincoln President-Elect*, p. 441.

95. *ALAL*, v. 1, p. 758 ("ever saw him"); *HL*, pp. 289–90.

96. Mrs. James C. Conkling to Clinton L. Conkling, Feb. 12, 1861, in Pratt, *Concerning Mr. Lincoln*, pp. 48–49 (party color, "slap in the face"); *Daily Missouri Democrat* (St. Louis), Feb. 7, 1861, quoted in Holzer, *Lincoln President-Elect*, p. 286 ("lace collar").

97. Weik, *The Real Lincoln*, p. 307.

98. Lincoln to Lyman Trumbull, Dec. 10, 1860, in *CWL*, v. 4, p. 149. See also Foner, *Free Soil, Free Labor, Free Men*, p. 223.

99. Van Deusen, pp. 10 (shorter than his wife), 56 (gilt sword), 335 ("might recognize him"), 229 (Moses); *ALAL*, v. 1, p. 723 ("massive savior complex").

100. Rice, ed., *Reminiscences*, p. 39 (overslept); Holzer, *Lincoln President-Elect*, pp. 396 ("mild and cloudy"), 407; Van Deusen, p. 255 (ap-

pearance); Adams, *Education of Henry Adams*, p. 104 ("perpetual cigar"). See also *ALAL*, v. 2, pp. 37–38.

101. McDougall, *Throes of Democracy*, p. 409 ("virtually kidnapped"); *RW*, p. 43 ("churchwarden"); Van Deusen, p. 258; and Russell, *My Diary North and South*, p. 70, entry for Apr. 8, 1861 (dinners and whist); Remini, *Henry Clay*, p. 307 ("science of diplomacy"); Seward to his family, Feb. 23, 1861, in Seward, *Seward at Washington, 1846–1861*, p. 511 ("agreeable"); White, *A. Lincoln*, p. 383.

102. Tyrner-Tyrnauer, *Lincoln and the Emperors*, p. 105 ("crude"); Green, *Washington*, v. 1, p. 238 (key ministries, "mud," "fields").

103. [Hay], *New York World*, Mar. 4, 1861, in Burlingame, ed., *Lincoln's Journalist*, pp. 48–50.

104. *Baltimore Sun*, Mar. 7, 1861 ("national debt"); Nevins, *War for the Union*, v. 2, p. 196 ("temperance man"); Lutz, *Annual Report of the American Historical Association for the Year 1915*, pp. 210–11 ("make blunders"). See also *The Lincoln Log*, entry for Mar. 1, 1861.

105. Bigelow, *Retrospections*, v. 1, p. 367; Lincoln to Gideon Welles, May 14, 1861, *CWL*, v. 4, p. 370 (navy); Donald, *Lincoln*, p. 346 (finance). See also Boritt, *Lincoln and the Economics of the American Dream*, p. 199.

106. *RW*, p. 392 ("studying up"); Carroll, "Abraham Lincoln and the Minister of France," p. 145; Fanny Seward Diary, entry for Dec. 25, 1861, Seward Papers, University of Rochester.

107. Stoeckl dispatch no. 11, Feb. 26, 1861; and Stoeckl dispatch no. 15, Mar. 12, 1861. Both in Russian Foreign Ministry Archives, photostatic copies in LOC. The final quote is in

Graebner, "Northern Diplomacy and
European Neutrality," p. 61.

108. White, *A. Lincoln*, p. 387 (Seward's motivation); Green, *Washington*, v. 1, p. 239 (inaugural morning);
Nicolay and Hay, *Abraham Lincoln:
A History*, v. 3, pp. 324, 371 (sharpshooters and "first trick"); Foote, *Civil
War*, loc. 782 (Blood Tubs); Lincoln
to Seward, Mar. 4, 1861, in *CWL*, v. 4,
p. 273 ("countermand").

109. Grimsley, "Six Months in the
White House," p. 45; Benjamin H.
Hill quoted in Hubbard, *Burden of
Confederate Diplomacy* (Knoxville,
1998), p. 25; Mercier to Thouvenel,
Mar. 7, 1861, quoted in Carroll,
"Abraham Lincoln and the Minister
of France," pp. 145–46; Thomas W.
Evans to James Lesley Jr., Mar. 1, 1861,
Seward Papers, University of Rochester (*"amicable"*).

110. White, *A. Lincoln*, p. 387 ("long
and confidential"); *New York Times*,
Mar. 5, 1861, cited in Randall, *Mary
Lincoln*, pp. 209–10 ("Hail Columbia");
Barton, *Life of Abraham Lincoln*, p. 17
(quadrille and "ill at ease"); *New York
Herald*, Mar. 6, 1861, cited in *ALAL*,
v. 2, p. 62 ("queens of the earth");
Adams, *Education of Henry Adams*,
p. 107 ("not be enough"); Bigelow to
William Hargreaves, July 27, 1861, in
Clapp, *Forgotten First Citizen*, p. 147;
Rev. Benjamin E. Millard reminiscence, in *New York Times*, Mar. 15,
1885.

111. Foner, *Free Soil, Free Labor, Free
Men*, p. 123.

112. Raymond, *Life and Public
Services of Abraham Lincoln*, p. 720
("burning the other") in *RW*, p. 375;
Lincoln quoted in Peterson, *Lincoln in
American Memory*, p. 101 ("pigs for the

tits"); Seward to his family, Mar. 16,
1861, in Seward, *Seward at Washington,
1846–1861*, p. 530 ("closets"); Viele,
"A Trip with Lincoln, Chase and
Stanton," p. 818, in *RW*, p. 453 (can't
say no).

113. Rice, ed., *Reminiscences*, pp. 239–
40 ("your man"); O'Toole, *Five of
Hearts*, p. 341 ("light duties"); Melville
to his wife, Mar. 24–25, 1861, in Davis
and Gilman, eds., *Letters of Herman
Melville*, pp. 209–10 ("full band" etc);
Parker, *Herman Melville*, v. 2, pp.
460–64 (failed to win plum).

114. Lincoln to Seward, Mar. 18, 1861,
CWL, v. 4, pp. 292–93; Koerner to
Lincoln, Mar. 28, 1861, ALP, LOC.
I have inserted the two dashes in the
Koerner quote for readability. See also
ALAL, v. 2, pp. 91–92; Schurz, *Reminiscences*, v. 2, pp. 221, 223; *New York
Herald*, Mar. 19, 1861, quoted in Donner, "Carl Schurz as Office Seeker,"
p. 129; Schurz to his wife, Mar. 28,
1861, in Schafer, ed., *Intimate Letters*,
p. 253; Brauer, "Appointment of Carl
Schurz," p. 77. An exhibit in the
National Museum of American History in Washington, D.C., makes the
point that foreign policy is uniquely
important for American presidents
because of the diverse composition of
its citizenry.

115. For Mary Lincoln's relationship
with Seward, see George B. Lincoln to
Gideon Welles, Apr. 25, 1874, in "New
Light on the Seward-Welles-Lincoln
Controversy?" *Lincoln Lore*, No. 1718,
Apr. 1981, p. 3 ("Never!"); Keckley,
Behind the Scenes, p. 131 ("skein of
thread" and "can trust him"); Rice,
ed., *Reminiscences*, p. 481 ("abolition
sneak"). For a thorough discussion
of Mary Lincoln's interference in

appointments, see *ALAL*, v. 2, pp. 262–73, especially pp. 264 and 266. See also Burlingame, *Inner World*, pp. 283–85; *RW*, pp. 68–69 ("disgrace"); Randall, *Mary Lincoln*, p. 193 ("very reluctantly"); Monaghan, p. 15; Holzer, *Lincoln President-Elect*, pp. 198, 332 (hard to control); Donald, *"We Are Lincoln Men,"* p. 155.

116. Mary Lincoln to Seward, Mar. 22, [1861,] in Turner and Turner, *Mary Todd Lincoln*, p. 81 (Honolulu); Grimsley, "Six Months in the White House," p. 64; Herndon, "Lincoln's Religion," *Illinois State Journal*, Dec. 13, 1873, cited in Randall, *Mary Lincoln*, p. 426; Post, "Lincoln and the Reverend Dr. James Smith," pp. 397–99. Smith was ultimately appointed consul on Feb. 18, 1863, and remained in office for the next eight years.

117. Clay, *Memoirs*, pp. 284, 321; Richmond *Southern Opinion* quoted in Randall, *Mary Lincoln*, p. 412; *The Independent*, Aug. 10, 1882 ("blundering outspokenness"), and the *Illinois State Journal*, Sept. 1, 1883 ("distant concerns"), both clippings in Ruth Randall Papers, LOC. See also Burlingame, *Inner World*, pp. 315, 325; *ALAL-DC*, v. 1, p. 629; and Shenk, *Lincoln's Melancholy*, p. 96.

118. Elizabeth Todd Edwards interview with Herndon, [1865–66,] in *HI*, p. 445; Baker, pp. 198–99; Keckley, *Behind the Scenes*, p. 97 ("stupid state dinners").

119. Russell, *My Diary North and South*, p. 41, entry for Mar. 28, 1861; Baker, p. 199.

120. Lord Lyons to Lord John Russell, Mar. 26, 1861, Russell Papers, BNA, cited in Jones, *Blue and Gray Diplomacy*, pp. 26–27, and Jones, *Union*

in Peril, pp. 12–13. But see also Ferris, *Desperate Diplomacy*, pp. 213–14, for an account of the dinner that is more sympathetic to Seward.

121. Montgomery Blair to Lincoln, Mar. 15, 1861, ALP, LOC; McPherson, *Tried by War*, pp. 13, 16; Foote, *Civil War*, v. 1, locs. 943–1017.

122. Lincoln, "Message to Congress in Special Session," July 4, 1861, *CWL*, v. 4, p. 424; McPherson, *Tried by War*, p. 18.

123. Foote, *Civil War*, v. 1, locs. 1127–52; McPherson, *Tried by War*, p. 9 (seizing arsenals); Samuel James to Seward, Mar. 20, 1861, Seward Papers, University of Rochester ("do something").

124. Nicolay, "Memorandum," July 3, 1861, in Burlingame, ed., *With Lincoln in the White House*, pp. 46–47.

125. Seward to his wife, Mar. 29, 1861, in Seward, *Seward at Washington, 1846–1861*, p. 534 ("before us"); Donald, *"We Are Lincoln Men,"* p. 152 (firing offense); Nicolay and Hay, *Abraham Lincoln: A History*, v. 3, p. 449 ("dismissed the incident").

126. Schurz to Lincoln, Apr. 5, 1861, ALP, LOC; Schurz, "Abraham Lincoln," p. 739.

127. Brauer, "Gabriel García y Tassara," pp. 9, 12–13. For a smart analysis of the colonization issue, see Eric Foner's essay, "Lincoln and Colonization," in Foner, ed., *Our Lincoln* (New York, 2008). The quote about colonization as a "middle ground" is on p. 145. See also Foner's recent Pulizer Prize–winning history, *The Fiery Trial* (New York, 2010).

128. Foner, "Lincoln and Colonization," in Foner, ed., *Our Lincoln*, p. 148. See also, pp. 150–51 (meeting with

Thompson, Crosby in Guatemala), 158 (just as racist); and *ALAL*, v. 2, p. 394.
129. Anderson, "1861: Blockade vs. Closing the Confederate Ports," pp. 190–93. The quote is on p. 190. On the blockade debate, see also *ALAL-DC*, v. 2, ch. 23, pp. 2459–60; and Jones, *Blue and Gray Diplomacy*, pp. 56–57.
130. *New York Herald*, July 8, 1867, in *RW*, p. 423 ("we can"). Fehrenbacher grades this reminiscence a D, but he doesn't seem to take into account the fact that Honest Abe may simply have been dissembling.
131. Corwin, *The President*, p. 264 (blockade during recess); Lincoln, "Inscription in Album of Mary Rebecca Darby Smith," Apr. 19, 1861, *CWL*, v. 4, p. 339.
132. My thanks to Howard Jones for walking me through the nuances of the neutrality decision. See also Edward Everett diary, Aug. 23, 1861, Everett Papers ("give them hell!" and "suggestions of Mr. Seward"); Donald, *Charles Sumner and the Rights of Man*, p. 21; *ALAL*, v. 2, pp. 160–62 (could buy weapons etc.); Carwardine, *Lincoln*, p. 181 ("caged tiger"); Conway, *Autobiography*, v. 1, p. 350 ("corvine"); Seward, *Seward at Washington, 1846–1861*, p. 584 ("degree"); Lincoln, "Revision of William H. Seward to Charles Francis Adams," May. 21, 1861, *CWL*, v. 4, pp. 376–80 (Seward dispatch); Adams quoted in Ferris, *Desperate Diplomacy*, p. 51 ("shallow madness").
133. Lincoln, "Revision of William H. Seward to Charles Francis Adams," May 21, 1861, *CWL*, v. 4, pp. 376–80; Donald, *"We Are Lincoln Men,"* p. 154.
134. Goodwin, *passim*; Donald, *"We Are Lincoln Men,"* p. 160.

135. Carpenter, *Inner Life*, pp. 128–29 (signed without reading); O. J. Hollister, *Life of Schuyler Colfax* (New York, 1886), p. 200 ("Uncle Abe's nose"); Nicolay and Hay, *Abraham Lincoln: A History*, v. 6, p. 265 ("unperceived"); Eaton, *Grant, Lincoln and the Freedmen*, p. 178 ("I am his master"); *ALAL*, v. 2, p. 456.
136. Bancroft, v. 2, pp. 173–74.
137. D. P. Crook notes that both Lincoln and Seward shared "the mediating approach of the old Whig party" on slavery. The same is largely true of their foreign policy strategies, with the exceptions outlined above. (Crook, *Diplomacy During the American Civil War*, p. 18.) Howard Jones notes that "even though their styles were as different as night and day, they worked in close harmony" after April 1, 1861. (Jones, *Blue and Gray Diplomacy*, p. 38.)
138. Seward dispatch cited in Ferris, *Desperate Diplomacy*, p. 14.
139. Donald, *Charles Sumner and the Rights of Man*, p. 25 ("mild and gentle"); Seward to his wife, June 5, 1861, *Seward at Washington, 1846–1861*, p. 590 ("cooperation").
140. Cortada, "A Case of International Rivalry," pp. 66–76, esp. 66, 68 (annexation date), 73 (revolts), 76 (Lincoln's response); Welles, *Lincoln and Seward*, pp. 183–84. See also Mahin, p. 204. In practice, it should be noted, European powers often challenged the principles of the Monroe Doctrine during the mid-nineteenth century, and it was not until long after the Civil War that the doctrine achieved its modern-day stature. My thanks to George C. Herring for emphasizing this point.

141. Nicolay and Hay, *Abraham Lincoln: A History*, v. 3, p. 379 ("virtue of patience").
142. Grimsley, "Six Months in the White House," pp. 61–63; Charles Sumner to James A. Hamilton, June 8, 1861, in Hamilton, *Reminiscences*, p. 483; *RW*, p. 433 ("all things right").
143. Lincoln to Albert G. Hodges, Apr. 4, 1864, *CWL*, v. 7, p. 281.
144. On Lincoln and presidential "war power," see McPherson, *Tried by War*, pp. 23–25, 30 (incl. quote to Hodges); Rossiter, *American Presidency*, pp. 98–99; Schlesinger, Jr., *Imperial Presidency*, pp. 58–64; and Corwin, *The President*, pp. 264–267 (expanding the navy and "significant precedents").
145. McDougall, *Throes of Democracy*, pp. 251–52, 350–53; and Remini, *Henry Clay*, pp. 137, 643 (Whigs and navy); Henderson, *Hidden Coasts*, p. 238.

CHAPTER THREE: LINCOLN VS. PALMERSTON

1. Pease and Randall, eds., *Diary of Orville Hickman Browning*, v. 1, pp. 488–89 (entry for July 28, 1861); McPherson, *Battle Cry of Freedom*, p. 347 (casualties); Russell, *My Diary North and South*, p. 467, entry for July 22, 1861 (weather); Robert L. Wilson to Herndon, Feb. 10, 1866, in *HI*, p. 207 ("*damned bad*").
2. Oates, *With Malice Toward None*, loc. 4959; Foote, *Civil War*, v. 1, locs. 1544–56; and *ALAL-DC*, v. 2, ch. 23, p. 2538 ("green alike").
3. Schurz to Lincoln, Aug. 6, 1861, and Aug. 13, 1861. Both letters in ALP, LOC.
4. Foote, *Civil War*, v. 1, loc. 2402 ("Anaconda").
5. Pease and Randall, eds., *Diary of Orville Hickman Browning*, v. 1, pp. 488–89 (entry for July 28, 1861); McPherson, *Battle Cry of Freedom*, p. 313 (naval stats). McPherson notes that fewer than a dozen of these were actually available for the blockade. See also McPherson, *Tried by War*, p. 41 (sleepless night).
6. McPherson, *Battle Cry of Freedom*, p. 370 (Hatteras); Butler, *Autobiography and Personal Reminiscences*, p. 288 (night shirt); John Appleton to Cassius Marcellus Clay, Sept. 22, 1861, Clay Papers, Lincoln Memorial University ("pretty well over"). See also *ALAL*, v. 2, p. 212.
7. Donald, *Lincoln*, p. 346; Boritt, *Lincoln and the Economics of the American Dream*, p. 199 (pretending ignorance); Lincoln to Gideon Welles, May 14, 1861, *CWL*, v. 4, p. 370 ("little about ships"); Lincoln, "Application for Patent on an Improved Method of Lifting Vessels over Shoals," Mar. 10, 1849, in ibid., v. 2, p. 32 (patent); Seward, *Seward at Washington, 1846–1861*, p. 623 (approaching Seward); French, *Witness to the Young Republic*, p. 412; Samuel C. Bushnell to Gideon Welles, 1877, in *Battles and Leaders of the Civil War*, v. 1, p. 748 ("something in it").
8. Lincoln to Gideon Welles, [c. Dec. 1861?,] *CWL*, v. 5, p. 33 (frustrated); Burlingame, ed., *Dispatches from Lincoln's White House*, p. 32, cited in *ALAL*, v. 2, p. 200 ("pale and careworn"); Ferris, *The* Trent *Affair*, p. 18 (Wilkes's age, mission, etc.);

Henderson, *Hidden Coasts*, p. 230 (Wilkes's background, Welles quote, type of ship); Nevins, *War for the Union*, v. 1, p. 388 ("a superabundance"); Warren, pp. 11–12 (Fijian village and "not as obedient"); Welles, *Diary*, v. 1, p. 73, entry for Aug. 10, 1862.

9. The following account of the capture of Mason and Slidell draws heavily on Ferris, *The* Trent *Affair*, pp. 18–28.

10. Jenkins, v. 1, p. 197 ("one of the most important"); *New York Times*, Dec. 11, 1861 ("embodiment of dispatches").

11. Russell, *My Diary North and South*, p. 575, entry for Nov. 18, 1861 ("storm of exultation"); *New York Times*, Nov. 17, 1861 ("rings with applause"); Ridley, *Palmerston*, p. 553 (theater audiences); Barnum to Wilkes, Dec. 11, 1861, Wilkes Papers, LOC, cited in Jenkins, pp. 197–98 (Barnum); *Boston Daily Evening Transcript*, Nov. 18, 1861, quoted in Ferris, *The* Trent *Affair*, p. 32 ("heavy blow"); Van Deusen, p. 309 ("brave, adroit"); Warren, p. 27 (blisters). See also Bancroft, v. 2, pp. 227–28; and *ALAL*, v. 2, p. 222.

12. *New York Herald*, Nov. 18, 1861; Welles, *Lincoln and Seward*, p. 185; *Richmond Inquirer*, copied in *New York Times*, Nov. 26, 1861; Rice, ed., *Reminiscences*, p. 245 ("prize court"); Lossing, *Pictorial History of the Civil War*, v. 2, pp. 156–57 ("white elephants"); Gurowski, *Diary, Mar. 4, 1861–Nov. 12, 1862*, p. 135 ("giving the traitors up"). See also *ALAL*, v. 2, pp. 222–23; and Ferris, *The* Trent *Affair*, pp. 128–29, 231–32n.

13. For the account of the *Trent* Affair in this chapter I have drawn on two fine monographs: Ferris, *The* Trent *Affair* (Knoxville, 1977); and Warren, *Fountain of Discontent* (Boston, 1981). I also learned much from Jones, *Union in Peril* (Lincoln and London, 1992); and Jones, *Blue and Gray Diplomacy* (Chapel Hill, 2010). Michael Burlingame, in *ALAL*, v. 2, pp. 221–29, also offers a comprehensive account of Lincoln's role in the crisis. For the quotations and information in the preceding paragraph, see also Charles Mackay to Seward, Nov. 29, 1861, in *War of the Rebellion*, ser. 2, v. 2, pp. 1106–8; Rumbold, *Recollections of a Diplomatist*, v. 2, p. 83; Crook, *Diplomacy During the American Civil War*, p. 47 (channel fleet); Palmerston to George Lewis, Nov. 27, 1861, quoted in Ferris, *The* Trent *Affair*, p. 44 ("Relations with Seward & Lincoln"); Jenkins, v. 1, pp. 213–14 (gunpowder etc.), 215 (10,500 troops); Palmerston to Queen Victoria, Dec. 5, 1861, in Connell, *Regina vs. Palmerston*, p. 347.

14. Abner Y. Ellis statement to Herndon, Jan. 1866, in *HI*, p. 174; Ida M. Tarbell interview with Byron Sunderland, Tarbell Papers, Allegheny College, in *RW*, p. 436.

15. Tocqueville quoted in McDougall, *Promised Land, Crusader State*, p. 55; Foreman, *World on Fire*, pp. xxiv, 27–28 ($444 million and Tocqueville); Sexton, *Debtor Diplomacy*, p. 12 (largest creditor and "true lords of Europe"); Zakaria, *From Wealth to Power*, p. 61 (debt not oppressive).

16. Riddle, *Congressman Lincoln*, p. 95, and Paludan, p. 110 ("national blessing"); Howe, *What Hath God*

Wrought, p. 596 (out the window); Boritt, *Lincoln and the Economics of the American Dream*, p. 58 ("national debt"); Joshua F. Speed interview with Herndon, Jan. 5, 1889, in *HI*, p. 719 (prostitute).

17. Sexton, *Debtor Diplomacy*, p. 7.

18. Herndon, "Analysis of the Character of Abraham Lincoln," pp. 371–72 (ridiculed Herndon); *RW*, p. 241 ("snaky tongue"); Guelzo, *Abraham Lincoln: Redeemer President*, p. 174 ("fuel of interest").

19. Lincoln, "Address Before the Young Men's Lyceum," *CWL*, v. 1, pp. 114–15 ("reason, cold, calculating"); Guelzo, *Abraham Lincoln: Redeemer President*, pp. 6, 91, 106, 117–19 (Bentham, Mill and Lincoln's fatalism), 370; John T. Stuart interview with Herndon, Dec. 20, 1866, in *HI*, p. 519 (Euclid); Herndon statement, undated, in *RW*, p. 243 ("reason of wise men"); *HL*, pp. 193–94, 357 (Euclid and "he was always just").

20. Bell, v. 1, p. 7, and Bourne, *Palmerston: The Early Years*, p. 27 (Adam Smith); Bourne, *Palmerston: The Early Years*, p. 453 (Euclid); Palmerston to Lord John Russell, Apr. 25, 1862, Russell Papers, BNA. See also Jenkins, v. 1, pp. 83–84.

21. Bell, v. 2, p. 275, and v. 1, p. 148; Bourne, *Palmerston*, p. 380 (ties to constitutional governments); Ridley, *Palmerston*, pp. 145, 334 ("chivalrous enterprises," "Quixote," and "shibboleth"); Bourne, *Palmerston*, p. 627 ("conflicting interests" and "no eternal allies").

22. Bell, v. 2, p. 275 ("bloody nose"); Palmerston to Lord John Russell, Apr. 25, 1862, Russell Papers, BNA

("Passion than Interest"); Palmerston to Somerset, Dec. 29, 1860, Palmerston Papers, British Library ("Disunited"); Crook, *Diplomacy During the American Civil War*, p. 189 ("emotional crisis").

23. Bell, v. 1, p. vii, and Ferris, *Desperate Diplomacy*, p. 15 (born before Constitution); Ridley, *Palmerston*, pp. 6–7 (trip to Paris); Bourne, *Palmerston*, pp. 13, 20 ("charming" and "zest"); Bell, v. 1, p. 5 ("frame of iron"); Bourne, *Palmerston*, pp. 3, 5, 28–29 (sickly, blisters, etc.). The quote is on pp. 28–29.

24. Bourne, *Palmerston*, pp. 80 ("very pedantic" and "so priggish"), 82, 44 (stammering and cold), 156–60 (assassination attempt); Bell, v. 1, p. 21 ("pepper the faces").

25. Bell, v. 1, pp. 96–97, and Ridley, *Palmerston*, pp. 2, 277 ("Lord Cupid"); Bourne, *Palmerston*, p. 191, and Ridley, *Palmerston*, pp. 41–42 (Almack's); Ridley, *Palmerston*, p. 118, and Bourne, *Palmerston*, p. 213 ("Ha, ha"); Bourne, *Palmerston*, pp. 201–2, 211 (illegitimate children), 255 ("subscriptions") and 212–14 (sex euphemisms).

26. Ridley, *Palmerston*, p. 105 (in 1830); Bell, v. 1, p. 191 (drowning etc.); Bourne, *Palmerston*, pp. 221 ("windmill") and 116 ("night and chaos").

27. Bell, v. 1, pp. 73, 105–6, and Ridley, *Palmerston*, p. 189 (conservatism, form of government); Ridley, *Palmerston*, p. 166 ("motives of generous sympathy"); Bourne, *Palmerston*, p. 314 ("reign of Metternich"). On Palmerston's Quadruple Alliance, see also Ridley, *Palmerston*, pp. 171–72, and Bourne, *Palmerston*, pp. 380–87.

28. Ridley, *Palmerston*, p. 109, and

Bourne, *Palmerston*, p. 422 (smoking and "paleness"); Bell, v. 1, p. 261, and Bourne, *Palmerston*, p. 424 ("Sugar Canes"); Bourne, *Palmerston*, p. 422 ("Penknives"); Bell, v. 1, p. 262 (church), and v. 1, p. 201 (windows).

29. Bourne, *Palmerston*, p. 185 ("tall, dark"); Bell, v. 1, p. 227, and Bourne, *Palmerston*, pp. 435–37 (tutoring, carriage rides, quote); Ridley, *Palmerston*, pp. 228 (Pam's marriage), 392 (Victoria's marriage), and 392–93 (grew apart); Bourne, *Palmerston*, p. 191 (thirty-year affair); Victoria quoted in Warren, p. 101 (old man).

30. Bell, v. 1, pp. 99, 259; Ridley, *Palmerston*, pp. 116 (Belgian envoy), 117 ("miss the soup" and "old Turk").

31. Ridley, *Palmerston*, p. 394 ("worthless private character").

32. Bell, v. 2, pp. 29 (Immoral One) and 75–76; Ridley, *Palmerston*, pp. 519 (Immoral One), 556 ("Christian nations"), and 583 ("Oh, surely").

33. Donald Southgate takes this nickname as the title of his Palmerston biography. See Southgate, *Most English Minister* (New York, 1966). See also Bourne, *Palmerston*, p. 349 ("wish to be"); Ridley, *Palmerston*, p. 387 ("watchful eye"); Crook, *The North, the South, and the Powers*, p. 12 ("three deckers"); Bell, v. 2, p. 45 ("Jupiter Anglicanus").

34. Bell, v. 2, p. 117 (Disraeli); Ridley, *Palmerston*, p. 120 (Talleyrand).

35. Sexton, *Debtor Diplomacy*, p. 30, and Ridley, *Palmerston*, p. 273 ("bunting"); Jones, *Blue and Gray Diplomacy*, p. 34 ("essentially and inherently"); *London Press*, Mar. 23, 1861, quoted in Adams, *Great Britain and the American Civil War*, v. 1, pp. 54–55 ("horse race"); Palmerston to Victoria, Jan. 1, 1861, in *Letters of Queen Victoria*, v. 3, pp. 538–39; Ridley, *Palmerston*, p. 548; Jones, *Abraham Lincoln*, p. 43.

36. Porter, ed., *Oxford History of the British Empire*, v. 3, pp. vii, ix (imperial century and dominance after Napoleonic Wars); "British Empire," *New Encyclopaedia Britannica (Micropaedia)*, v. 2, pp. 528–30 (territories included); Warren, p. 135 (856 ships); Ferguson, *Empire*, pp. 165–66 (fresco, largest in world, quote).

37. Porter, ed., *Oxford History of the British Empire*, p. 13 (Great Game); Palmerston to Somerset, May 26, 1861, Palmerston Papers, British Library ("morsel"); LaFeber, *New Empire*, p. 28 ("excellent states"); Bancroft, v. 2, p. 330 ("we want cotton"); Nevins, *War for the Union*, v. 2, pp. 251–52; Palmerston to Newcastle, May 24, 1861, Palmerston Papers, British Library. See also Jenkins, v. 1, pp. 85 (PM in control), 98–99, and 163–64; and Ferris, *Desperate Diplomacy*, pp. 17 ("irregular army" and "useful hint"), 27 ("strong in Canada" and little over a week), and 94–95.

38. Clay to Lincoln, July 25, 1861; and Clay to Seward, May 22, 1861. Both letters in ALP, LOC.

39. Palmerston to Russell, Oct. 18, 1861, Russell Papers, BNA.

40. Palmerston to Newcastle, Nov. 12, 1861, Palmerston Papers, British Library.

41. This account of the Nov. 12 Palmerston-Adams meeting is drawn from Charles Francis Adams to Seward, Nov. 15, 1861, "Confidential," Despatches from U.S. Ministers (Great Britain), NARA; Ferris, *The Trent Affair*, pp. 14–17; Jenkins, v. 1,

pp. 209–10; Mahin, p. 65; and Foreman, *World on Fire*, pp. 168–69.
42. Jenkins, v. 1, p. 210 ("tart");
Palmerston to Newcastle, Nov. 7,
1861, quoted in ibid., v. 1, pp. 207–8;
Lord John Russell to Palmerston,
Nov. 12, 1861, quoted in ibid., v. 1,
p. 207.
43. Henry Adams later described
Palmerston's "characteristic" chuckle:
"The laugh was singular, mechanical,
wooden, and did not seem to disturb
his features. 'Ha! . . . Ha! . . . Ha!'
Each was a slow, deliberate ejac-
ulation, and all were in the same
tone, as though he meant to say:
'Yes! . . . Yes! . . . Yes!' by way of
assurance. It was a laugh of 1810 and
the Congress of Vienna" (Adams,
Education of Henry Adams, p. 135).
44. Charles Francis Adams to Seward,
Nov. 15, 1861, "Confidential," Des-
patches from U.S. Ministers (Great
Britain), NARA; Palmerston to
Russell, Nov. 13, 1861, Russell Papers,
BNA; Ferris, *The* Trent *Affair*,
pp. 14–15; Palmerston to Victoria,
Nov. 13, 1861, in Connell, *Regina vs.
Palmerston*, p. 345.
45. Ferris, *The* Trent *Affair*, p. 44
(news arrives); Marx article in *Die
Presse*, Dec. 2, 1861 (filed Nov. 28), in
MAC, pp. 113–14; Marx to Engels,
Dec. 9, 1861, in ibid., p. 253.
46. London *Times*, Nov. 28, 1861,
quoted in Ferris, *The* Trent *Affair*,
p. 47 ("outburst of passion"). Ferris
argues convincingly that the American press reaction was also basically
"placatory" (Ferris, *The* Trent *Affair*,
p. 35). Cardiff *Mercury*, Nov. 30, 1861,
quoted in Blackett, *Divided Hearts*,
pp. 21–22 ("Yankee bluster"). The
brackets are Blackett's.

47. Ferris, *The* Trent *Affair*, p. 45
(cabinet meeting); Palmerston to
Russell, Nov. 29, 1861, Russell Papers,
BNA ("deliberately insulted");
Palmerston to Lord Granville, Nov.
29, 1861, Granville Papers, BNA (halt
arms exports); Palmerston to Russell, Nov. 29, 1861, Russell Papers,
BNA; Palmerston to Queen Victoria,
Nov. 29, 1861, in *Letters of Queen Victoria*, v. 3, pp. 595–96 ("gross outrage"
and "reparation and redress").
48. Ibid. (Scott rumors); Weed to
Seward, Nov. 28, 1861, ALP, LOC;
Palmerston to Granville, Dec. 26,
1861, Granville Papers, BNA ("thun-
derclap"). See also Warren, p. 139;
and Ferris, *The* Trent *Affair*, pp. 83,
150.
49. Martin, *Life of His Royal Highness the Prince Consort*, v. 5, pp.
421–27 (Albert illness and "somewhat
meager"); Warren, p. 116 ("scarcely
hold").
50. Revisions of Prince Albert,
quoted in Martin, *Life of His Royal
Highness the Prince Consort*, v. 5, pp.
422–23.
51. Martin, *Life of His Royal Highness the Prince Consort*, v. 5, pp. 422–25
("excellent" and heartening indications); Russell to Lyons, Nov. 30, 1861,
quoted in Jones, *Blue and Gray Diplomacy*, p. 98; Russell to Lyons, Dec. 1,
1861, Russell Papers, BNA ("a rational
man"); Palmerston to Russell, Dec. 6,
1861, Russell Papers, BNA ("fighting
for it").
52. Rogers, ed., *Speeches on Questions
of Public Policy by the Right Honourable John Bright*, pp. 85–99. The
quotes are on pp. 97 and 99.
53. James Lesley Jr. to Frederick
Seward, Dec. 4, 1861, Seward Papers,

University of Rochester; Jenkins, v. 1, pp. 215–16; Connell, *Regina vs. Palmerston*, p. 347; May, *The Union, the Confederacy, and the Atlantic Rim*, p. 8.
54. Trumbull quoted in McPherson, *Battle Cry of Freedom*, p. 362 ("Action, action" and Ball's Bluff description); Rice, ed., *Reminiscences*, pp. 172–73; *ALAL*, v. 2, pp. 199–200.
55. *New York Herald*, Nov. 18, 1861; Ferris, *The* Trent *Affair*, p. 128; Lincoln to Edward Everett, Nov. 18, 1861, *CWL*, v. 5, p. 26 ("Slidell!"); Francis B. Carpenter, "A Day with Governor Seward at Auburn," July 1870, p. 56, Seward Papers, University of Rochester.
56. Welles, *Lincoln and Seward*, p. 185 ("doubts" etc.); *New York Tribune*, Dec. 31, 1861; R. M. Mason to Amos Lawrence, Jan. 14, 1861 [1862], quoted in Randall, *Lincoln the President*, v. 2, p. 41 ("two wars"). On Lincoln's reaction, see also Crook, *The North, the South, and the Powers*, pp. 115–16; Warren, pp. 30, 37–38; and *ALAL*, v. 2, pp. 222–23.
57. Welles, "Capture and Release of Mason and Slidell," p. 647; Stoeckl dispatch no. 68, Nov. 18, 1861, Russian Foreign Ministry Archives, photostatic copies in LOC. See also *ALAL*, v. 2, pp. 222–23; Ferris, Trent *Affair*, p. 120; and Donald, *"We Are Lincoln Men,"* p. 161.
58. Warren, pp. 35 (soldiers at Willard's), 37 (Welles's approval), 28–29 (Everett); *New York Times*, Nov. 19, 1861.
59. "From the outset," notes historian Gordon Warren, "it was clear to Lincoln that if he publicly repudiated the capture, he might damage the war. Conversely, if he bestowed his blessing on it he would destroy any possibility of maneuver if the British government were to demand the prisoners' release. The United States could not afford to alienate the world's greatest maritime power, thereby offering the Confederacy an ally. Somehow Lincoln had to extract the country from its predicament without demoralizing public opinion and jeopardizing national honor; yet, he had to avoid insulting Britain. Popular feeling was running so high that the slightest miscalculation could have precipitated an international showdown. Lincoln decided on a policy of delay, leaving the next move up to the British" (Warren, p. 38). See also p. 137 for British preparations to "fight the American Revolution and the War of 1812 again."
60. Opdyke to Lincoln, Dec. 25, 1861, ALP, LOC.
61. Gasparin to Lincoln, Dec. 2, 1861. This French-language letter resides in the ALP, LOC. Yet unlike most other Gasparin missives, there is no official English transcription online. I have been assisted in my translation from the French by an English transcription of the letter on Library of Congress stationery in the Barbee Papers at Georgetown University.
62. Galt memo, Dec. 5, 1861, quoted in Skelton, *Life and Times of Sir Alexander Tilloch Galt*, pp. 315–16; Warren, pp. 170–71.
63. Crook, *The North, the South, and the Powers*, pp. 154 (no military buildup), 158 ("pacific"); Cartland, *Southern Heroes*, pp. 8–9; Warren, p. 171.
64. Pease and Randall, eds., *Diary of Orville Hickman Browning*, v. 1,

pp. 513–14 (entry for Dec. 10, 1861); Lincoln quoted in Paludan, p. 92; Hay, *Missouri Republican*, Dec. 18, 1861, in Burlingame, ed., *Lincoln's Journalist*, pp. 164–65.

65. Lincoln, "Annual Message to Congress," *CWL*, v. 5, pp. 40–41; Warren, p. 170 ("show the world"); Paludan, p. 92 (tamp down); *Baltimore Sun*, Dec. 23, 1861, copied in the *New York Times*, Dec. 26, 1861; Randall, *Lincoln the President*, v. 2, pp. 44–45.

66. Dean Mahin, too, notes that Lincoln and Seward tended to keep Congress in the dark regarding foreign policy, with the exception of Sumner. (Mahin, pp. 10–11.) See also Pierce, ed., *Memoir and Letters of Charles Sumner*, v. 4, p. 121 ("too many secretaries"); Donald, *Lincoln*, pp. 321–22; Rice, ed., *Reminiscences*, p. 223; Edward Everett diary, Aug. 23, 1861, Everett Papers ("watch him"); Donald, *Charles Sumner and the Rights of Man*, p. 21; Oates, *With Malice Toward None*, loc. 4763; *ALAL*, v. 2, p. 162; Holzer, *Lincoln President-Elect*, p. 417.

67. *Missouri Republican*, Dec. 18, 1861, in Burlingame, ed., *Lincoln's Journalist*, p. 166.

68. Seward to his family, Oct. 31, 1861, in Seward, *Seward at Washington, 1846–1861*, p. 627; Welles, *Lincoln and Seward*, p. 185.

69. Pease and Randall, eds., *Diary of Orville Hickman Browning*, v. 1, p. 515 (entry for Dec. 15, 1861); Warren, pp. 142–43 (Mrs. Slidell); Lincoln quoted in Monaghan, p. 187; Goodwin, p. 398 ("bulldog").

70. Russell, *My Diary North and South*, p. 587, entry for Dec. 16, 1861; Jones, *Union in Peril*, p. 88 ("haggard and worn"); Howe, *Life and Letters of George Bancroft*, v. 2, pp. 147–48; Everett to Clay, Jan. 5, 1862, Clay Papers, Lincoln Memorial University. See also Warren, pp. 174–75. Norman Ferris reminds his readers that Bancroft "was an old political opponent of Seward's" (Ferris, *The* Trent *Affair*, p. 244n25).

71. John W. Forney reminiscence, in *Progress*, *A Mirror for Men and Women*, September 4, 1880. Michael Burlingame, in *ALAL*, v. 2, pp. 224–25, cites a slightly different version of this recollection from a transcribed copy in the Barbee Papers, Georgetown University.

72. Burlingame points out that Lincoln "sought to influence public opinion through journalism written by his personal secretaries" (Burlingame, "Lincoln Spins the Press," p. 65); Hay, *Missouri Republican*, Dec. 21, 1861, in Burlingame, ed., *Lincoln's Journalist*, pp. 171–74; Hay, *Missouri Republican*, Dec. 20, 1861, in ibid., p. 167. See also ibid., p. xi.

73. Weed to Seward, Dec. 7, 1861, Seward Papers, University of Rochester ("war footing"); Jenkins, v. 1, p. 222 (other letters); Weed to Seward, Dec. 10, 1861, Seward Papers, University of Rochester ("inevitable").

74. Weed to Seward, Dec. 10, 1861, Seward Papers, University of Rochester ("wholly misunderstood"); Weed to Seward, Dec. 25, 1861, in *Seward at Washington, 1861–1872*, p. 37 ("ransacking"); Weed to Seward, Dec. 7, 1861, Seward Papers, University of Rochester (dismissal). See also Donald, *"We Are Lincoln Men,"* p. 161 (Newcastle).

75. Bright quoted in Ridley, *Palmerston*, p. 437 ("what a hoax!"); Cobden quoted in Jenkins, v. 1, p. 236 ("old dodger"); Bright quoted in Ausubel, *John Bright*, p. 125 ("hoary imposter"); Crook, *The North, the South, and the Powers*, p. 8 (bound Britain tightly); Palmerston to Cobden, Jan. 8, 1862, Palmerston Papers, British Library ("human nature"). See also Ridley, *Palmerston*, pp. 286, 495, 590.

76. Cobden to Bright, Dec. 6, 1861, quoted in Jenkins, v. 1, p. 220 ("veto" and "courteous and conceding"); Bright to Sumner, quoted in Randall, *Lincoln the Liberal Statesman*, p. 143 ("At all hazards"); Donald, *Charles Sumner and the Rights of Man*, pp. 36–37 (met almost daily); Fillmore to Lincoln, Dec. 16, 1861, ALP, LOC; Sumner to Bright, Dec. 23, 1861, in *RW*, p. 433 ("no war").

77. Ferris, *The* Trent *Affair*, pp. 144–45 ("without instructions"), 148 ("We shall not have war"), 149 ("As to any Despatch").

78. Jones, *Blue and Gray Diplomacy*, pp. 34, 103 (physical description and CFA quote); Jenkins, v. 1, p. 82 (shocked some visitors); Fitzmaurice, *Life of Granville*, v. 1, p. 407 *("croupier")*; Warren, p. 216 (rumors of death); Martin, *Life of His Royal Highness the Prince Consort*, v. 5, pp. 440–41 (Albert's death), and 437 ("too awful"); Palmerston to [R.?]osas, Jan. 5, 1862, Palmerston Papers, British Library ("deepest affliction"). See also Bell, v. 2, p. 281.

79. Bell, v. 1, p. 325 ("exercise a religion"); Ridley, *Palmerston*, p. 529 ("ate like a vulture"); Clarendon to the Duchess of Manchester, Dec. 17, 1861, quoted in Maxwell, *Life and Letters of George William Frederick*, v. 2, pp. 253–54 ("*very* far"); Granville

to Canning, Dec. 16, 1861, quoted in Fitzmaurice, *Life of Granville*, v. 1, pp. 404–5 ("a little anxious"). See also Ferris, *The* Trent *Affair*, pp. 150–51.

80. Wallace and Gillespie, eds., *Journal of Benjamin Moran*, v. 2, pp. 926–29, entries for Dec. 16, 19, 23, and 24, 1861 (London atmospherics); Adams, *Education of Henry Adams*, p. 119 ("glutton of gloom").

81. Wallace and Gillespie, eds., *Journal of Benjamin Moran*, v. 2, p. 930, entry for Dec. 26, 1861 ("unfit for his place"); Henry Adams to Charles Francis Adams Jr., Nov. 30, 1861 ("greatest criminal"), and Henry Adams to Charles Francis Adams Jr., Dec. 13, 1861, both in Ford, ed., *Cycle of Adams Letters*, v. 1, pp. 76 ("criminal"), 83 ("boots").

82. Marx to Engels, Dec. 19, 1861, in *MAC*, pp. 254–55.

83. Palmerston to Granville, Dec. 26, 1861, Granville Papers, BNA ("Fool's Paradise"); *Morning Post* (London), Dec. 30, 1861, quoted in Adams, *Great Britain and the American Civil War*, v. 1, p. 229; Russell to Palmerston, Jan. 7, 1862, quoted in Adams, *Great Britain and the American Civil War*, v. 1, p. 230 ("59 minutes"); Palmerston to Westbury, Dec. 31, 1861, Palmerston Papers, British Library. See also Ferris, *The* Trent *Affair*, pp. 150, 159–60.

84. Pease and Randall, eds., *Diary of Orville Hickman Browning*, entry for Dec. 21, 1861, v. 1, pp. 516–17; Lincoln, "Draft of a Dispatch in Reply to Lord John Russell," [Dec. 10? 1861,] in *CWL*, v. 5, pp. 62–64. See also *ALAL*, v. 2, p. 225; Ferris, *The* Trent *Affair*, pp. 175–77 (Bright's influence, perils of arbitration), 242n19; and Crook, *The*

North, the South, and the Powers, p. 158 (dangers of "procrastination").

85. Norman Ferris makes a compelling case for "the changed tone of certain newspapers," and cites several of the examples I have noted in this paragraph. It seems unlikely, however, that Ferris would attribute this "changed tone" to Lincoln's media savvy. See Ferris, *The* Trent *Affair*, p. 136.

86. Ibid., p. 131 ("mere emotion"); Hay, *Missouri Republican*, Dec. 28, 1861, in Burlingame, ed., *Lincoln's Journalist*, p. 178 ("bewildering flight"); Russell, *My Diary North and South*, p. 589, entry for Dec. 23, 1861 ("tremendous storm").

87. *New York Tribune*, Dec. 24, 1861; Crook, *The North, the South, and the Powers*, pp. 158–59.

88. Pease and Randall, eds., *Diary of Orville Hickman Browning*, v. 1, p. 518 (weather and French minister's letter); Beale, ed., *Diary of Edward Bates, 1859–1866*, pp. 213–16, entries for Dec. 25, 1861, and Jan. 1, 1862; Bright quoted in Adams, *Great Britain and the American Civil War*, v. 1, p. 232 ("make every concession"); Jenkins, v. 1, p. 227 (Chase's view); Carroll, "Abraham Lincoln and the Minister of France," pp. 148–49 (French letter). See also Goodwin, p. 399.

89. Jones, *Union in Peril*, pp. 91–92; Goodwin, passim (a clever manager); Seward, *Reminiscences*, p. 189 ("compare the points"). David Donald suggests that in his handling of the *Trent* crisis, Lincoln "had maneuvered the Secretary of State into adopting the position that he had favored all along" (Donald, *"We Are Lincoln Men,"* p. 162).

90. Pease and Randall, eds., *Diary of Orville Hickman Browning*, v. 1, p. 518 ("no war"); Porter, *Campaigning with Grant*, p. 408 ("loaded to the muzzle"); Seward, *Reminiscences*, p. 190 ("my own mind"); *New York Times*, Dec. 26, 1861; Ferris, *The* Trent *Affair*, p. 186.

91. Pease and Randall, eds., *Diary of Orville Hickman Browning*, entry for Dec. 27, 1861, v. 1, p. 519; Fanny Seward Diary, entry for Dec. 27, 1861, Seward Papers, University of Rochester; Donald, *Charles Sumner and the Rights of Man*, pp. 38–39; Jones, *Union in Peril*, p. 92; Bancroft, v. 2, pp. 241–42 ("cheerfully liberated").

92. *CG*, 37th Cong., 2nd Sess., p. 177; Bancroft, v. 2, pp. 236 ("surrender"), 243–44 (*New York Tribune*, Dec. 30, 1861), 252 ("contraband"); Warren, p. 184 ("monument"). See also Jones, *Abraham Lincoln*, p. 62, and Jones, *Union in Peril*, p. 93.

93. Porter, *Campaigning with Grant*, p. 408; *ALAL*, v. 2, p. 227. Gabor Boritt, analyzing Lincoln's views on territorial expansion, notes that "[e]conomic development demanded peace. It also required England's friendship, which was sorely threatened by America's expansionist penchant." (Boritt, *Lincoln and the Economics of the American Dream*, p. 141.)

94. Porter, *Campaigning with Grant*, pp. 408–9; *ALAL*, v. 2, p. 227.

95. Francis B. Carpenter, "A Day with Governor Seward at Auburn," July 1870, p. 55, Seward Papers, University of Rochester; Randall, *Lincoln the President*, v. 2, p. 50; Seward, *Reminiscences*, p. 190; Goodwin, pp. 400–401.

96. Wallace and Gillespie, *Journal of Benjamin Moran*, v. 2, pp. 937–40 (entries for Jan. 2, 8, and 9, 1862).

97. Warren, p. 216 (medicated); Granville to Canning, Dec. 19, 1861, in Fitzmaurice, *Life of Granville*, v. 1, p. 405 ("gout coming out"); Connell, *Regina vs. Palmerston*, pp. 359–60; *Morning Post* (London) quoted in Jenkins, v. 1, p. 239.

98. Palmerston quoted in Ferris, *The* Trent *Affair*, p. 193 ("wary of the Yankees"); Palmerston to Russell, Jan. 19, 1862, Russell Papers, BNA; Bright quoted in Bigelow, *Retrospections*, v. 1, pp. 441–42, cited in Ferris, *The* Trent *Affair*, p. 153. See also Crook, *Diplomacy*, p. 157.

99. *ALAL*, v. 2, p. 228 (New Year's reception); Lincoln quoted in McPherson, *Battle Cry of Freedom*, p. 368 ("out of the tub").

100. Blue, *Salmon P. Chase*, pp. 147–49 (Chase's efforts, Belmont quote); Paludan, p. 109 (treasury broke, hoarding gold, etc).

101. Paludan, p. 110; Boritt, *Lincoln and the Economics of the American Dream*, pp. 206–7; Lamon, *Recollections of Lincoln*, pp. 215–19.

102. Paludan, pp. 109–12. See also Bensel, *Yankee Leviathan*, pp. 2, 14, 18, 68–69, 152–53, 162–63, 236–37.

103. For the Springfield tradition about Herndon seeking a diplomatic post, see Clinton Levering Conkling to A. P. Higley, Dec. 7, 1917; Clinton L. Conkling memo, Dec. 1917; Jesse W. Weik to Conkling, Feb. 11, 1917; all in Conkling Papers, ALPLM. For more on Herndon's trip to Washington see Donald, *Lincoln's Herndon*, pp. 152–56, and Donald, *"We Are Lincoln Men,"* pp. 89–90. Donald

dismisses the Springfield tradition and believes that Herndon's trip was likely made on behalf of an acquaintance and "not in his own interest" (Donald, *Lincoln's Herndon*, p. 155). See also *New York Evening Post*, Jan. 21, 1862, typed copy in Barbee Papers, Georgetown University ("considerably careworn"); Milton Hay interview in the *Illinois State Journal*, Sept. 1, 1883, clipping in Ruth Randall Papers, LOC ("very sour"). Hay, for his part, later complained that he was misquoted by the reporter, acknowledging that Lincoln had offered his law partner a post that the younger man "had declined as unsuitable" but insisting that Herndon "felt no grievance" about the offer. (Milton Hay to the editor of the *State Journal*, in Wilson, *Intimate Memories of Lincoln*, p. 49.) For the joke about the old pair of pants, see Porter, *Incidents and Anecdotes*, pp. 294–95.

104. Edward Lee Plumb to Thomas Corwin, Jan. 29, 1862, copy, Plumb Papers, LOC; *Baltimore Sun*, Jan. 30, 1862; *Washington Evening Star*, Jan. 29, 1862. See also *The Lincoln Log*, entry for Jan. 28, 1862.

105. McPherson, *Battle Cry of Freedom*, pp. 375–77 (date of launch, *Times* quote); Adams, *Great Britain and the American Civil War*, v. 1, p. 276 (Adams quote); Jones, *Blue and Gray Diplomacy*, p. 125; Charles Francis Adams diary, entry for Mar. 29, 1862, Adams Family Papers (Lady Palmerston's reception).

106. Clay to Seward, no. 17, Jan. 24, 1862; and Clay to Seward, no. 15, Jan. 7, 1862. Both dispatches in *FRUS 1862*, pp. 443–46.

107. Lincoln to Queen Victoria, Feb. 1, 1862, in *CWL*, v. 5, p. 117.

108. Baker, pp. 205–7; and Donald, *Lincoln*, pp. 335–36 (levee color); Clinton, *Mrs. Lincoln*, pp. 130 and 163–65 (chandeliers); Poore, *Perley's Reminiscences*, v. 2, pp. 116–20.
109. Monaghan, p. 219 (date); Keckley, *Behind the Scenes*, p. 103 ("hard, hard"); Nicolay, *Lincoln's Secretary*, pp. 132–33 ("my boy is gone"); Donald, *Lincoln*, pp. 336–38; *ALAL*, v. 2, p. 298; Baker, pp. 182 (Strickland), 216 (aping Victoria, bonnet, etc.); Mary Lincoln to Ruth Harris, [May 17, 1862,] in Turner and Turner, *Mary Todd Lincoln*, pp. 125–26.
110. *RW*, p. 78 ("sweet communion" etc.); Baker, pp. 211, 219–20 (both Vic and Eugénie; Colchester and Brooks quote); Clinton, *Mrs. Lincoln*, pp. 186–87.

111. Clay to Seward, Apr. 13, 1862, quoted in Monaghan, p. 214.
112. Foner, *Free Soil, Free Labor, Free Men*, p. 117; Burlingame, *Inner World*, p. 23; Rice, ed., *Reminiscences*, p. 583. The most recent account of the Gordon episode is Soodalter, *Hanging Captain Gordon* (New York, 2006). See also Rowley, "Captain Nathaniel Gordon," pp. 216–24.
113. Milne, "Lyons-Seward Treaty of 1862," pp. 511–14, 520. See also Crook, *Diplomacy*, pp. 68–69; Jones, *Union in Peril*, p. 118; Foreman, *World on Fire*, pp. 237–38.
114. [Karl Marx,] "English Public Opinion," *New York Tribune*, Feb. 1, 1862, in Marx, *Dispatches for the "New York Tribune,"* p. 305.

Chapter Four: Lincoln vs. Marx

1. Franklin, *Emancipation Proclamation*, p. 94 (sunny, cool); Brooks, "How We Went a-Calling on New Year's Day," Jan. 3, 1863, in Burlingame, ed., *Lincoln Observed*, p. 15 ("gold lace, feathers"); Fanny Seward diary, entry for Jan. 1, 1863, Seward Papers, University of Rochester ("full court dress" and lozenge trimming). See also Donald, *Lincoln*, p. 407; Goodwin, p. 498; Guelzo, *Emancipation Proclamation*, pp. 181–84; Foreman, *World on Fire*, p. 355.
2. Scovel, "Personal Recollections of Abraham Lincoln," p. 506 (exhausted); Brooks, "How the President Looks," Dec. 4, 1862, in Burlingame, ed., *Lincoln Observed*, p. 13 ("hair is grizzled"); "Fredericksburg, Va., First Battle of," in Faust, ed., *Historical Times Illustrated Encyclopedia of the Civil War*,

p. 287; Pease and Randall, eds., *Diary of Orville Hickman Browning*, entry for Dec. 18, 1862, v. 1, p. 600 ("brink of destruction"). See also Goodwin, p. 498; Guelzo, *Emancipation Proclamation*, p. 181; *ALAL*, v. 2, pp. 468–69 (hadn't slept); and Foreman, *World on Fire*, p. 355.
3. Seward, *Seward at Washington, 1861–1872*, p. 151; Arnold, *Life of Abraham Lincoln* (Chicago, 1885), p. 266; *ALAL*, v. 2, pp. 468–69.
4. Lincoln, "Protest in the Illinois Legislature on Slavery," Mar. 3, 1837, in *CWL*, v. 1, p. 74 ("injustice and bad policy"); Lincoln, "Reply to Chicago Christians," Sept. 13, 1862, in *CWL*, v. 5, p. 423 ("help us in Europe"); Guelzo, *Emancipation Proclamation*, p. 185 (copies shipped abroad).
5. Holzer, *Lincoln President-Elect*,

p. 33; Lincoln, "Speech at a Republican Banquet, Chicago," Dec. 10, 1856, in *CWL*, v. 2, p. 385 ("Our government"); Lincoln, "Fragment: Notes for Speeches [Aug. 21, 1858]," in *CWL*, v. 2, pp. 552–53 ("In this age"); Herndon to Weik, Feb. 26, 1891, HW, LOC; Carwardine, *Lincoln*, p. 44 (Herndon quote); Nye, *Soft Power*, passim ("soft power"). See also Carwardine, *Lincoln*, pp. 47–48, 136, 184.
6. Wheen, *Karl Marx*, p. 166 (British Museum); McLellan, *Marx*, p. 141 (Feuerbach); Marx quoted in Christman, ed., *The American Journalism of Marx and Engels*, p. xi ("The philosophers"); Marx, "A Criticism of American Affairs," *Die Presse* (Vienna), Aug. 9, 1862, in *MAC*, p. 211; and Foner, *British Labor and the American Civil War*, pp. 11, 91 ("pressure from without"); Marx, *Dispatches for the "New York Tribune,"* p. xviii (largest in the world).
7. McLellan, *Karl Marx*, p. 288 ("highly valued"); Mott, *American Journalism*, p. 271 (Great Moral Organ); Lincoln to Greeley, June 27, 1848, in *CWL*, v. 1, p. 493; Lincoln to Lyman Trumbull, Dec. 28, 1857, in *CWL*, v. 2, p. 430 (pored over the *Tribune*); Guelzo, *Emancipation Proclamation*, pp. 132–33 (mail slot); Harper, *Lincoln and the Press*, p. 101 (readers); Nevins, *American Press Opinion*, v. 1, pp. 112–13 ("great as any statesman's"); Croffut, "Lincoln's Washington," p. 58, in *RW*, p. 123 ("about a ton").
8. Marx to Frederick Engels, Aug. 14, 1851, in *MAC*, p. xvi ("impudent"); Christman, ed., *The American Journalism of Marx and Engels*, p. xviii ("industrial bourgeoisie"); *MAC*, p. xv ("foremost"); Carpenter, *Inner Life*, p. 152; Marx quoted in Jones,

Union in Peril, p. 156 ("As the American War of Independence").
9. Kissinger, *Diplomacy*, pp. 94 (Crimean War shatters Concert of Europe), 95, 102–3 (post-Crimean order), 106 ("days of principles"), 127 (Darwin, etc.). See also Herring, pp. 266–67, 271; Gabriel, locs. 2902, 6202; and Carwardine, *Lincoln*, pp. 190, 228.
10. Gabriel is good on the creative spirit of the Romantic era; see locs. 1187–90, 1198. See also "Genius," *Oxford English Dictionary*, 2nd ed., Simpson and Weiner, eds., v. 6 (Oxford: Clarendon Press, 1989), p. 444.
11. Blackburn, *Unfinished Revolution*, pp. 1–2; Marx, *Capital*, v. 1, part 3, ch. 10, sec. 7, in *MAC*, p. 20; Foner, *Free Soil, Free Labor, Free Men*, p. 16, cites the observation of an "Iowa Republican" to illustrate the party line. Lincoln would almost certainly have concurred with this sentiment. See also Foner, *Fiery Trial*, p. 117. Gabor Boritt's study of Lincoln's economic vision skillfully analyzes the sixteenth president's views on money and markets (Boritt, *Lincoln and the Economics of the American Dream*, passim).
12. Marx, "A Criticism of American Affairs," *Die Presse*, Aug. 9, 1862, in *MAC*, pp. 210–12; Whitney, *Life on the Circuit with Lincoln*, p. 374.
13. Marx, "On Events in North America," *Die Presse*, Oct. 12, 1862, in *MAC*, p. 222 ("without intellectual brilliance"); Marx, "The Dismissal of Fremont," *Die Presse*, Nov. 26, 1861, in ibid., pp. 109–10 ("mediocrities" and "aversion for all originality"); Marx, "A Criticism of American Affairs," *Die Presse*, Aug. 9, 1862, in ibid., p. 211.
14. "Shiloh, Battle of," *Encyclopaedia Britannica (Micropaedia)*, v. 10, pp.

739–40; John McClintock sermon, Apr. 16, 1865, in *RW*, p. 314 ("educated up to it"); McDougall, *Throes of Democracy*, pp. 429–30 (seven times Bull Run, "Romanticism expired"). The literature on Lincoln, public opinion, and slavery is vast, but especially insightful is Richard Carwardine's *Lincoln* (New York, 2006), pp. 45–90, 190, 313. Lincoln's "attentive but not subservient engagement with public sentiment," Carwardine writes, provided "the essential basis . . . of his power" (Carwardine, *Lincoln*, p. 136). In a separate essay on Lincoln and the press, Carwardine points out that "[t]he Civil War marked a new phase in the history of American journalism" (Carwardine, "Abraham Lincoln and the Fourth Estate," p. 2). Eric Foner's *Fiery Trial* (New York, 2010) also includes a fascinating discussion of Lincoln and slavery in the context of evolving popular views. See Foner, *Fiery Trial*, p. xix. On Lincoln and public opinion, see also Holzer, "If I Had Another Face, Do You Think I'd Wear This One?" p. 57; Burlingame, "Lincoln Spins the Press," p. 65; and Donald, *Lincoln*, p. 416. Richard Carwardine and Jay Sexton, in an engaging recent collection of essays, note how the nineteenth-century information age helped to shape Lincoln's image abroad (Carwardine and Sexton, eds., *The Global Lincoln*, pp. 16–17, 21).

15. Bailey, "America's Emergence as a World Power," p. 9; Carwardine, *Lincoln*, pp. 228, 250. Howard Jones's studies of Lincoln and slavery in the diplomacy of the Civil War highlight the president's success in infusing the Union effort with moral purpose at home while simultaneously removing "the major obstacle to a realistic foreign policy on both sides of the Atlantic." (See Jones, *Abraham Lincoln*, pp. 87, 188.) See also Jones's introduction to the Bison Books edition of Monaghan, p. xi. Gabor Boritt points out that Lincoln's economic vision was intricately related to his moral sense: "For Lincoln these two grounds had always been the same: his political economy was an intensely moral science" (Boritt, *Lincoln and the Economics of the American Dream*, p. 193). Stewart Winger observes that "Marx's historical theory was clearly an urgent millennialist vision of world history, difficult to comprehend without the moral outrage that informed it" (Winger, *Lincoln, Religion, and Romantic Cultural Politics*, p. 52). For more on Lincoln and Marx, see Robin Blackburn's recent book *An Unfinished Revolution*, a collection of primary-source materials that also includes a 100-page introductory essay. Blackburn argues that "the Civil War and its sequel had a larger impact on Marx than is often realized—and, likewise, that the ideas of Marx and Engels had a greater impact on the United States . . . than is usually allowed" (Blackburn, *Unfinished Revolution*, pp. 1–100; the quote is on p. 5).

16. For this sketch of Marx's early life, I have drawn primarily on McLellan, *Karl Marx: His Life and Thought* (New York, 1973); McLellan, *Karl Marx: Interviews and Recollections* (Totowa, N.J., 1981); Gabriel, *Love and Capital* (New York, 2011); and Wheen, *Karl Marx* (New York, 1999). In this paragraph, see McLellan, *Marx*, pp. 1–2 (Mosel, vineyards),

17 ("disturbing the peace" and duel); and Gabriel, locs. 1143, 1383, 1402 (pistol and saber duels), 1443. The final quotation is from a letter to Marx from his father, Dec. 9, 1837, *MECW*, v. 1, p. 688.

17. On Marx's marriage, Gabriel's *Love and Capital* is particularly insightful. McLellan, *Marx*, pp. 2–5 (Marx genealogy, father's conversion), 15 (Earls of Argyll), 18 (physical description of Jenny). Karl Marx to Jenny Marx, Dec. 15, 1863, *MECW*, v. 41, p. 499; Jenny Marx to Karl Marx, [Aug. 1844,] *MECW*, v. 3, p. 584. See also *KMIR*, p. 1; and Wheen, pp. 16–17, 49.

18. Lenore O'Boyle, "The Democratic Left in Germany, 1848," p. 379, quoted in Gabriel, loc. 1649; McLellan, *Marx*, p. 46 (newspaper funding); *KMIR*, p. 3 ("powerful man of twenty-four").

19. McLellan, *Marx*, pp. 58, 59–61; Wheen, p. 44. See also Wheen's forward in Marx, *Dispatches for the "New York Tribune,"* x–xi.

20. Wheen, pp. 75–76, 119; McLellan, *Marx*, p. 130; Gabriel, locs. 2489–2504.

21. Marx and Engels, "Manifesto of the Communist Party," in Tucker, ed., *Marx-Engels Reader*, pp. 473–83. See also Wheen, pp. 4–5.

22. Gabriel, locs. 3421–58 (Switzerland to Sicily), and 3675 (171 newspapers); *KMIR*, p. 20 (daggers, revolvers); McLellan, *Marx*, p. 134.

23. Gabriel, locs. 3857–70 (pistol, bayonets, etc.); Engels, "Marx and the *Neue Rheinische Zeitung*," *MECW*, v. 26, p. 127; *KMIR*, p. 16 ("no journalist"). See also Wheen, pp. 130–46. The quotes are on pp. 131–32.

24. On the sympathies of the *Tribune* see Howe, *What Hath God*

Wrought, p. 793. For Dana in Europe see Wilson, *Life of Charles A. Dana*, pp. 62–92. The first quote is on p. 74 ("vain for barbarism"). The second quote, from the *New-York Daily Tribune*, Aug. 29, 1848, is in *MAC*, p. xv. For the first Marx-Dana meeting, see also Marx, *Dispatches for the "New York Tribune,"* p. xvii.

25. McLellan, *Marx*, pp. 226 ("Second Coming") and 228 ("hellishly expensive"); *KMIR*, pp. xiv ("it's a pity"), and 34–36 (Prussian intel report).

26. McLellan, *Karl Marx*, pp. 232 ("secret propaganda society"), 236 (forming a newspaper); Engels to Marx, Feb. 13, 1851, *MECW*, v. 38, p. 289; Blitzer, "Introduction," *American Journalism of Marx and Engels*, p. xvi ("ourselves alone"); Wheen, pp. 155 (teaching refugees), 180 (two pounds each); Blackburn, *Unfinished Revolution*, p. 3; *KMIR*, p. 43 ("electric spark"); Gabriel, locs. 4666–67 (scarf and monocle).

27. Wheen, pp. 159 (sold their beds), 171 (nanny); *KMIR*, p. 25 ("less anxious" and "nagging daily worries"); Gabriel, loc. 5447.

28. Howe, *What Hath God Wrought*, p. 305 (Hegel); McLellan, *Marx*, pp. 240–41 ("fulcrum of world commerce"); *Neue Rheinische Zeitung*, Jan. 7, 1849, in *MAC*, p. 12 ("money-bag republicans"); Marx to Engels, Oct. 13, 1851, in *MAC*, p. 37 (exhibition and "gold ore"); *Neue Rheinische Zeitung*, Jan.–Feb., 1850, in *MAC*, pp. 14–15 ("center of gravity").

29. Marx, *Dispatches for the "New York Tribune,"* p. xx ("blotting-paper vendor"); Marx to Engels, Dec. 2, 1854, in *MAC*, pp. 40–41 (second-rate thinker); Blitzer, "Introduction,"

American Journalism of Marx and Engels, p. xvii (18 foreign correspondents).

30. Marx, *Dispatches for the "New York Tribune,"* pp. 24–27 (China), 51–53 (Greek insurrection), 72–84 (Spanish revolution), 234–37 (Indian revolt); Lincoln to Charles Wilson, June 1, 1858, *CWL*, v. 2, pp. 456–57 ("extensively read"); Lincoln to Greeley, June 27, 1848, *CWL*, v. 1, p. 493 (wrote Greeley); Blitzer, "Introduction," *American Journalism of Marx and Engels*, p. xx (more than 350); Herndon to Theodore Parker, Sept. 25, 1858, and Oct. 4, 1858, in Newton, *Lincoln and Herndon*, pp. 220–22 (on the Trib); Gabriel, loc. 5896 (byline on "front news page"). Robin Blackburn concludes that "it is likely that [Lincoln] read quite a few of the articles Marx wrote for the *Tribune*" (Blackburn, *Unfinished Revolution*, p. 4).

31. McLellan, *Marx*, p. 284 ("newspaper muck"); Wheen, p. 170 (sleeping during day); *KMIR*, p. 35; *MAC*, pp. xvii (illegible scrawl and "letters"), and xviii ("decided opinions of his own" and "appropriated all my articles").

32. "By the outbreak of the [American Civil War]," writes R. J. M. Blackett, "the mechanisms for molding public opinion [in Britain] had long been established. The movement against West Indian slavery, for instance, had employed a combination of meetings, lectures, pamphlets, newspapers, agents, and petitions in its effort to frame public opinion and pressure Parliament to free the slaves. The agitation around the Civil War drew on this tradition, but it was complicated by the fact that, in this instance, the issues involved matters over which the British government had no direct control." (Blackett, *Divided Hearts*, p. 123. See also p. 169.) See also Monaghan, p. 47.

33. Tucker, ed., *Marx-Engels Reader*, pp. 579–85 ("planless, knotted chaos"); McLellan, *Marx*, p. 263 (convenient location); Wheen, p. 265 (stole); Gabriel, loc. 5216 ("great cotton lord"); Jenny Marx to Engels, Dec. 2, [1850,] *MECW*, v. 38, p. 250; *KMIR*, pp. xv–xvi ("There's Frederick!").

34. McLellan, *Marx*, pp. 281 ("bubbling and boiling"), 262 ("hotting up"), 260 (Chartists), and 360 (withdrawn from politics). See also Marx, *Dispatches for the "New York Tribune,"* pp. 49–50 (on the lookout).

35. Wheen, pp. 219–22 (windfall, Moor, and pawnshop); *KMIR*, pp. 37 ("princely dwelling"), 99 (horse); Gabriel, loc. 6365 (St. Paul's view); *MAC*, pp. xviii ("out of the muck"), and xix (*"gebothert"* and "lousy Yankees").

36. Marx, *New York Daily Tribune*, Oct. 19, 1853, quoted in Wheen, pp. 187–88 ("What he aims at"); Marx, *Dispatches for the "New York Tribune,"* pp. 150 ("idol"), 191 ("vampyres"), 192 ("industrial slaveholders"), 196 (irresponsible).

37. Marx to Engels, Jan. 11, 1860, in *MAC*, p. 247.

38. Marx to Engels, July 11, 1861, in ibid., pp. 249–50; Marx to Lion Philips, May 6, 1861, in ibid., pp. 247–48 ("last card"). See also ibid., pp. xxii–xxiii.

39. Marx to Engels, Jan. 1, 1860, in ibid., p. 247; Franklin, *Emancipation Proclamation*, pp. 1–8 (behind the times); "British Empire," *New*

Encyclopaedia Britannica (Micropaedia), v. 2, p. 529 (Britain bans).
40. Jones and Rakestraw, eds., "Diplomacy of the Civil War," in *American Foreign Relations since 1600: A Guide to the Literature*, p. 372 (property rights); Trefousse, *Lincoln's Decision for Emancipation*, pp. 4–5 (racism and first quote); Lincoln to Orville Browning, Sept. 22, 1861, *CWL*, v. 4, p. 532.
41. Lincoln, "Speech at Hartford, Conn.," Mar. 5, 1860, *CWL*, v. 4, pp. 5–6, 10; Lincoln, "Remarks to Committee of Reformed Presbyterian Synod," July 17, 1862, *CWL*, v. 5, pp. 327; Forney, *Anecdotes of Public Men*, v. 1, p. 265, in *RW*, p. 161.
42. Franklin, *Emancipation Proclamation*, p. 14 (first inaugural); Foreman, *World on Fire*, p. 106 (Seward to his diplomats); Trefousse, *Lincoln's Decision for Emancipation*, p. 17; Marx, "The American Question in England," Oct. 11, 1861, in *Dispatches for the "New York Tribune,"* pp. 266–76.
43. Marx and Engels, *Civil War in the United States*, pp. 27–31; Runkle, "Karl Marx and the American Civil War," p. 122; Kempton, "K. Marx, Reporter," p. 2; Mott, *American Journalism*, p. 216 (number of newspapers).
44. See, for example, Holzer, " 'If I Had Another Face, Do You Think I'd Wear This One?' " p. 57; Burlingame, "Lincoln Spins the Press," p. 65; and Carwardine, "Abraham Lincoln and the Fourth Estate," p. 9.
45. *HL*, pp. 231–32, 389; and Harper, *Lincoln and the Press*, pp. 18, 20, 45–46 (composing rooms); Monaghan, p. 16; and Thomas, *Abraham Lincoln*, p. 196 (bought a printing press); *RW*,

pp. 483 ("Greeley is so rotten") and 498 (pumped visiting correspondents); Welles, *Diary*, v. 2, pp. 111–12, entry for Aug. 19, 1864; *ALAL*, v. 2, p. 144 (lost sleep); Carpenter, *Inner Life*, p. 156 ("they *'lie'* ").
46. Carpenter, *Inner Life*, p. 77 (pear).
47. Trefousse, *Lincoln's Decision for Emancipation*, p. 8; Jessie Benton Fremont, "The Lincoln Interview: Excerpt from 'Great Events,' " in Herr and Spence, eds., *Letters of Jessie Benton Fremont*, pp. 264–69; Hay, *Diary*, p. 123, entry for [Dec. 9, 1863]. See also Donald, *Lincoln*, pp. 314–15; Goodwin, pp. 389–92; Oates, *With Malice Toward None*, loc. 5154; *ALAL*, v. 2, pp. 205–6.
48. W. McCaully to Lincoln, Sept. 20, 1861, ALP, LOC; Herndon to Lyman Trumbull, Nov. 20, 1861, Trumbull Papers, LOC; Herndon, "Facts Illustrative of Mr. Lincoln's Patriotism and Statesmanship," p. 180; Herndon to unknown recipient, Jan. 15, 1874, in Hertz, *Hidden Lincoln*, p. 82 ("never ran"). See also Foner, *Fiery Trial*, p. 178; Donald, *"We Are Lincoln Men,"* pp. 87–88; *RW*, p. 254. The brackets in the "iron rings" quote are Fehrenbacher's.
49. Lester, *Life and Public Services of Charles Sumner* (New York, 1874), pp. 359–60, cited in *RW*, p. 295 ("This thunderbolt"); Statement of Emil Preetorius to J. McCan Davis, Dec. 2, 1898, Tarbell Papers, Allegheny College, cited in ibid., p. 370 ("rather be a follower"); Sumner to Lieber, Sept. 17, 1861, in Pierce, ed., *Memoir and Letters of Charles Sumner*, v. 4, p. 42 ("vain"); Sumner to Elizabeth, Duchess of Argyll, Aug. 11, 1862, Sumner Papers,

Harvard University, cited in *RW*, p. 435 ("time is essential").

50. Marx, "The Dismissal of Fremont," *Die Presse*, Nov. 26, 1861, in *MAC*, pp. 109–11. See also Marx, "Civil War in the United States," *Die Presse*, Nov. 7, 1861, in ibid., pp. 87–94.

51. Schurz, *Reminiscences*, v. 2, pp. 309–10; Hay, *Diary*, p. 23, entry for May 11, 1861; Thayer, *Life of John Hay*, v. 1, pp. 101–3.

52. Schurz, *Reminiscences*, v. 1, pp. 139–40.

53. *KMIR*, p. 28 ("pigmy-struggles" and teenage girls); Marx to Lion Philips, May 6, 1861, in *MAC*, pp. 247–48; McLellan, *Marx*, pp. 287–88; Blitzer, "Introduction," *American Journalism of Marx and Engels*, p. xxiii; *MAC*, p. xix ("jackass"). See also Dana, *Recollections*, pp. 1–2.

54. Marx to Engels, Feb. 13, 1860, *MECW*, v. 41, p. 47 ("stone-broke"); Marx to Engels, Jan. 18, [1861], ibid., v. 41, p. 247 ("Job"); Marx to Engels, June 18, 1862, in ibid., v. 41, p. 380 ("indescribable"); Marx to Engels, Aug. 20, [1862,] in ibid., v. 41, p. 411 ("green"). See also Wheen, pp. 241 ("stone-broke"), 245 (lemonade and castor oil), and 254 ("start some sort of business"); Gabriel, locs. 7092 and 7309; *MAC*, p. xx ("Hemmorrhoidarius"); *KMIR*, p. 40 (smallpox); McLellan, *Marx*, p. 321 ("pawnbrokers").

55. Gabriel, locs. 7364, 7106; *KMIR*, p. 102; *MAC*, p. xxii (Tussy recollection); Marx to Engels, May 6, 1862, in ibid., p. 258 ("painfully miss"); Marx to Engels, Apr. 28, 1862, in ibid., p. 257 ("correct views"). See also ibid., p. xx (conservative *Die Presse*).

56. Sanford to Seward, May 12, 1861,

"Private," Despatches from U.S. Ministers (Belgium), NARA; Schurz to Seward, Sept. 14, 1861, no. 18, Despatches from U.S. Ministers (Spain), NARA; Donald, *Charles Sumner and the Rights of Man*, pp. 16–17 (war powers); Wilson, ed., *Intimate Memories of Lincoln*, p. 12. See also Ferris, *Desperate Diplomacy*, p. 184; Adams, *Great Britain and the American Civil War*, v. 2, p. 91; *ALAL*, v. 2, pp. 333–34; and Burlingame, *Inner World*, p. 175.

57. Hale, *Memories of a Hundred Years*, v. 2, p. 191; Guelzo, *Emancipation Proclamation*, p. 69.

58. Adams, *Great Britain and the American Civil War*, v. 2, pp. 80–82 (could spook aristocrats); Guelzo, *Emancipation Proclamation*, p. 225 (Indian Mutiny); "Indian Mutiny," *New Encylopaedia Britannica (Micropaedia)*, v. 6, pp. 288–89; McClellan to Lincoln, July 7, 1862, ALP, LOC; and *ALAL*, v. 2, p. 320 ("conservative policy"); Lincoln, "Annual Message to Congress," Dec. 3, 1861, *CWL*, v. 5, p. 49 ("violent and remorseless").

59. Hale, *Memories of a Hundred Years*, v. 2, pp. 193–95; Donald, *Charles Sumner and the Rights of Man*, p. 51; Guelzo, *Emancipation Proclamation*, p. 94; Donald, *Lincoln*, p. 346 (didn't consult Seward).

60. See, for example, *New York World*, Mar. 8, 1862, and *Providence Journal*, Mar. 8, 1862, both in *ALAL*, v. 2, p. 339; Lincoln to Greeley, Mar. 24, 1862, *CWL*, v. 5, p. 169; Foner, *Fiery Trial*, p. 196 (*New York Tribune* and "thunderbolt").

61. Trefousse, *Lincoln's Decision for Emancipation*, p. 32; Lincoln,

"Proclamation Revoking General Hunter's Order of Military Emancipation," May 19, 1862, *CWL*, v. 5, pp. 222–23.

62. [Hay,] *Missouri Republican*, Apr. 27, 1862, in Burlingame, ed., *Lincoln's Journalist*, pp. 253–54; and [Hay,] *Missouri Republican*, May 23, 1862, in ibid., p. 265; Trefousse, *Lincoln's Decision for Emancipation*, p. 33 (Sumner); Franklin, *Emancipation Proclamation*, p. 23; and *CWL*, v. 5, p. 325n1 (Congress adjourns).

63. Lincoln, "Appeal to Border State Representatives to Favor Compensated Emancipation," July 12, 1862, *CWL*, v. 5, p. 318.

64. Welles, *Diary*, v. 1, pp. 70–71.

65. Trefousse, *Lincoln's Decision for Emancipation*, p. 35; Jones, *Lincoln*, p. 109.

66. Hay to Mary Jay, July 20, 1862, in Burlingame, ed., *At Lincoln's Side*, p. 23; Carpenter, *Inner Life*, pp. 21–22; Welles, "History of Emancipation," pp. 844–45. See also Guelzo, *Emancipation Proclamation*, pp. 117–18; Franklin, *Emancipation Proclamation*, pp. 39–43; *ALAL*, v. 2, pp. 362–64.

67. Meeting notes, July 22, 1862, Stanton Papers, LOC ("break up our relations"); Carpenter, *Inner Life*, pp. 21–22; Guelzo, *Emancipation Proclamation*, p. 123; Wert, Jeffry D., "Seven Days' Campaign, Va.," *Historical Times Illustrated Encyclopedia of the Civil War*, Faust, ed., pp. 667–68. See also "Peninsula Campaign," in ibid., p. 571 (size of McClellan's force, etc.).

68. Seward, *Seward at Washington, 1861–1872*, p. 118.

69. Gasparin to Lincoln, July 18, 1862,

ALP, LOC; Lincoln to Gasparin, Aug. 4, 1862, *CWL*, v. 5, pp. 355–56.

70. Tappan to Lincoln, Nov. 22, 1862; Dahlgren to Lincoln, Jun. 12, 1862. Both letters in ALP, LOC. I have slightly altered the punctuation in the Dahlgren letter for clarity.

71. Hale, *Horace Greeley*, p. 260 ("Hell"); Phillips, *Speeches, Lectures, and Letters*, pp. 450, 457; Laugel, *Diary*, entry for Sept. 13, 1864, reprinted in *The Nation*, v. 75, no. 1933, p. 48; Hofstadter, *American Political Tradition*, p. 165. See also *ALAL*, v. 2, pp. 397, 400, 638.

72. Marx, "A Criticism of American Affairs," *Die Presse*, Aug. 9, 1862, in *MAC*, pp. 210–12; Marx to Engels, Aug. 7, 1862, and Marx to Engels, Sept. 10, 1862, both in ibid., pp. 260–61.

73. Undated clipping, Nicolay Papers, LOC, quoted in *RW*, p. 269.

74. Lincoln to Greeley, Aug. 22, 1862, *CWL*, v. 5, pp. 388–89. The excerpts from Greeley's original letter are included in the annotation to this entry.

75. My thinking about Lincoln's response to Greeley's "Prayer" was influenced by a conversation over dinner in Springfield with the current dean of Lincoln scholars, Michael Burlingame. I am indebted to Professor Burlingame for generously sharing his thoughts on the subject. See also Trefousse, *Lincoln's Decision for Emancipation*, pp. 41–43; *ALAL*, v. 2, p. 403; and Foner, *Fiery Trial*, p. 229.

76. McPherson, *Battle Cry of Freedom*, pp. 528–33 (2nd Bull Run); Rice, ed., *Reminiscences*, p. 124.

77. [Hay,] *Missouri Republican*, Sept. 5,

1862, in Burlingame, ed., *Lincoln's Journalist*, pp. 299–302 ("gloomier city"); Hay, *Diary*, p. 38, entry for Sept. 1, 1862 ("whipped again"); Bates postscript on Edwin M. Stanton, Salmon P. Chase, Caleb B. Smith, and Edward Bates to Lincoln, Sept. 2, 1862, ALP, LOC.

78. The best figures on French and British cotton supplies are in Jones, *Blue and Gray Diplomacy*, pp. 77 (two hundred thousand Frenchmen etc.), 163 (crisis levels), and 208 (three quarters). See also Foner, *British Labor and the American Civil War*, pp. 5 (three quarters), 8, and 47 (*New York Times*, Sept. 12, 1862); Adams to Seward, no. 221, Sept. 12, 1862, *FRUS 1862*, pp. 189–90; Adams to Seward, no. 225, Sept. 25, 1862, ibid., pp. 198–99.

79. Palmerston to Russell, Sept. 14, 1862, and Sept. 23, 1862, Russell Papers, BNA; Walpole, *Life of Lord John Russell*, v. 2, pp. 360–61; Bancroft, v. 2, p. 304.

80. [Hay,] *Missouri Republican*, Sept. 11, 1862, in Burlingame, *Lincoln's Journalist*, pp. 305–7.

81. Lincoln, "Reply to Emancipation Memorial Presented by Chicago Christians of All Denominations," Sept. 13, 1862, *CWL*, v. 5, pp. 419–25.

82. Franklin, *Emancipation Proclamation*, p. 46 (fourteen-hour, etc.); Lamon, *Recollections*, p. 289; McClellan quoted in McPherson, *Battle Cry of Freedom*, p. 545 ("masterpiece"); Seward to Adams, [Circular,] Sept. 22, 1862, *FRUS 1862*, p. 195.

83. Jones, *Abraham Lincoln*, p. 109; Adams, *Great Britain and the American Civil War*, v. 2, p. 41 (carefully awaiting); Palmerston to Russell,

Sept. 30, 1862, Russell Papers, BNA ("like bulldogs"); Palmerston to Russell, Oct. 2, 1862, Russell Papers, BNA ("full of difficulty"); Palmerston to Russell, Oct. 8, 1862, Russell Papers, BNA ("fresh wind"); Palmerston to Russell, Oct. 22, 1862, Russell Papers, BNA ("decided turn"). Allen Guelzo argues that as a tool of foreign relations, emancipation was the "worst method . . . at the worst time." (Guelzo, *Emancipation Proclamation*, p. 9.)

84. Marx to Engels, Oct. 29, 1962, in *MAC*, pp. 262–63 ("decisive"); Marx, "On Events in North America," Oct. 12, 1862, *Die Presse*, in ibid., pp. 220–23 ("campaign in Maryland" and "reason does conquer"); Marx and Engels, "The Situation in the American Theater of War," May 30, 1862, *Die Presse*, in ibid., p. 200; Marx to Engels, Aug. 7, 1862, and Marx to Engels, Sept. 10, 1862, in ibid., pp. 260–61 (assures Engels). See also ibid., p. xxv.

85. Chase, *Diary*, Donald, ed., entry for Sept. 22, 1862, pp. 149–53; Welles, *Diary*, v. 1, entry for Sept. 22, 1862, pp. 142–45. See also Franklin, *Emancipation Proclamation*, pp. ix–x.

86. Hay, *Diary*, pp. 40–41, entries for [mid-Sept. 1862?] and [Sept. 24, 1862]; Franklin, *Emancipation Proclamation*, p. 58 (Seward sent copies); Seward to Charles Francis Adams, Sept. 26, 1862, no. 359, Diplomatic Instructions (Great Britain), NARA ("The interests of humanity"); Seward, *Seward at Washington, 1861–1872*, p. 135; Bancroft, v. 2, p. 338; Hay, *Diary*, p. 40 ("confused"); McClintock sermon, in *Voices from the Pulpit*, p. 136, cited in

RW, p. 314 (serious doubts). See also Adams, *Great Britain and the American Civil War*, v. 2, p. 100.

87. *New York Tribune*, Sept. 23 and 24, 1862, quoted in Franklin, *Emancipation Proclamation*, p. 62; *Missouri Republican*, Sept. 29, 1862, in Burlingame, ed., *Lincoln's Journalist*, p. 312; Lincoln, "Reply to a Serenade in Honor of the Emancipation Proclamation," Sept. 24, 1862, *CWL*, v. 5, p. 438.

88. Everett diary, entries for Sept. 21–25, 1862, Everett Papers; Everett to Adams, Sept. 30, 1862, in Frothingham, *Edward Everett*, pp. 445–48.

89. London *Post*, Oct. 8, 1862, quoted in Franklin, *Emancipation Proclamation*, p. 71 ("trash"); London *Times*, Oct. 7, 1862, in Mitgang, *Abraham Lincoln: A Press Portrait*, pp. 320–22 ("a Chinaman"); Adams, *Great Britain and the American Civil War*, v. 2, p. 103 (*Blackwood's*). See also Jones, *Abraham Lincoln*, p. 116.

90. Newman Hall, "An Interview with Robert T. Lincoln," *The Broadway: A London Magazine*, [Sept. 1867,] copy in Ruth Randall Papers, LOC.

91. Dana to Seward, Sept. 23, 1862, ALP, LOC; Carpenter, *Inner Life*, p. 84; *ALAL*, v. 2, pp. 417, 462–63.

92. Marx to Engels, Oct. 29, 1862, in *MAC*, pp. 262–63.

93. Lincoln, "Address on Colonization to a Deputation of Negroes," Aug. 14, 1862, *CWL*, v. 5, pp. 370–72 ("better for us both"); Ninian W. Edwards to Lincoln, Aug. 9, 1861, ALP, LOC (Edwards report); Foner, "Lincoln and Colonization," in Foner, ed., *Our Lincoln*, p. 151 (shelved after Welles's opposition and modern-day Colombia).

94. Chase, *Diary*, Donald, ed., entry for Sept. 24, 1862, p. 156; Seward, *Seward at Washington, 1861–1872*, p. 227 ("taking any out"); Lincoln, "Annual Message to Congress," Dec. 1, 1862, *CWL*, v. 5, p. 534 ("favor colonization"). See also Foner, "Lincoln and Colonization," in Foner, ed., *Our Lincoln*, pp. 136, 158–59 (Baker comment, canvassing the powers, constitutional amendment).

95. Sumner to Lincoln, Oct. 11, 1862, ALP, LOC; R. C. Wyllie to Thomas J. Dryer, July 27, 1861, *FRUS 1861*, p. 434; David L. Gregg to Lincoln, Jan. 24, 1863, ALP, LOC; Lincoln, "Memorandum Concerning Sandwich Islands," Jan. 9, 1863, *CWL*, v. 6, p. 5111; Seward to Lincoln, Jan. 21, 1863, ALP, LOC.

96. Hay, *Diary*, entry for Nov. 13, 1861, p. 32 (barely protested); McClellan to his wife, Nov. 17, 1861, in Sears, ed., *The Civil War Papers of George B. McClellan*, p. 135, cited in Burlingame, *Inner World*, p. 182 ("original gorilla"); Welles, *Diary*, v. 1, p. 118, entry for Sept. 8, 1862 ("slows"); McClellan to his wife, Sept. 25, 1862, McClellan Papers, LOC, cited in McPherson, *Battle Cry of Freedom*, p. 559 (complained to his wife); McClellan to Lincoln, July 7, 1862, ALP, LOC (alienate European decision makers); Guelzo, *Emancipation Proclamation*, pp. 168–69 (dismissed McClellan day after election); Marx, "The Removal of McClellan," *Die Presse*, Nov. 29, 1862, in *MAC*, p. 233 ("mediocrity"); Marx, "A Criticism of American Affairs," *Die Presse*, Aug. 9, 1862, in ibid., p. 212 ("waging of war").

97. Palmerston to Russell, Oct. 22, 1862, Russell Papers, BNA ("decided turn"). The most distinguished treatment of the autumn 1862 intervention crisis is in Jones, *Abraham Lincoln and a New Birth of Freedom* (Lincoln, 1999). For the Gladstone and Palmerston quotes see also pp. 122 ("made a nation"), 124 ("not far wrong"), 130 ("lookers-on").

98. William Henry Wadsworth to S. L. M. Barlow, Dec. 16, 1862, Barlow Papers, Huntington Library, San Marino, Calif., quoted in McPherson, *Tried by War*, p. 145; Donald, *Lincoln*, p. 425 (emboldened).

99. Sumner quoted in Donald, *Charles Sumner and the Rights of Man*, p. 97 ("argument, persuasion"; the brackets are Donald's); *New York Tribune*, Dec. 12, 1862, quoted in Crook, *Diplomacy During the American Civil War*, p. 107.

100. Seward to Dayton, Dec. 1, 1862, *FRUS 1863*, v. 1, pp. 638–39; and Seward to James Shepherd Pike, Dec. 23, 1862, *FRUS 1863*, v. 2, p. 802. See also Mahin, p. 139.

101. Guelzo, *Emancipation Proclamation*, pp. 179–80 ("judgment of mankind"); Sumner to Livermore, Jan. 9, 1863, in Livermore, "Emancipation Pen," *Proceedings of the Massachusetts Historical Society* (Apr. 1911), p. 597. Howard Jones, in his introduction to the Bison Books edition of Jay Monaghan's classic volume on Lincoln and foreign relations, *A Diplomat in Carpet Slippers*, notes that Lincoln "kept the administration's focus on the national interest while covering foreign policy with a veneer of idealism and morality." Elsewhere Jones notes that Lincoln "personified a balanced combination of idealist and realist who recognized the preeminence of slavery in the war but exercised great caution in making it the central issue." (Jones, "Introduction," in Monaghan, pp. ix–x.) See also Jones, *Blue and Gray Diplomacy*, p. 189: "Ideal and reality had meshed in shaping Lincoln's decision, combining his longtime animosity toward slavery with the Union's misfortunes on the battlefield to formulate a new policy that initially drew little support."

102. Lincoln, "Annual Message to Congress," Dec. 1, 1862, *CWL*, v. 5, pp. 518, 537.

103. On the intersection of Lincoln and public opinion, see, for example, Foner, *The Fiery Trial*, pp. xix and 189; and Carwardine, *Lincoln*, pp. 45–90.

104. Wheen, "Forward," *Dispatches for the "New York Tribune,"* p. x (first editorial); Marx, "The London *Times* on the Orleans Princes in America," Nov. 7, 1861, in ibid., p. 293 ("public opinion-mongers").

105. *Bee-Hive* quoted in Foner, *British Labor and the American Civil War*, p. 29 ("mindless man" and even after the preliminary).

106. Foner, *British Labor and the American Civil War*, pp. 56–57; Blackett, *Divided Hearts*, p. 143; Marx to Engels, Jan. 2, 1863, in *MAC*, p. 266 ("cost nothing").

107. Blackett, *Divided Hearts*, p. 196 (100 gatherings); Nevins, *War for the Union*, v. 2, p. 271 ("nobodies" and "paroxysms of euphoria"); Charles Francis Adams to Seward, Jan. 23, 1863, no. 307, Despatches from U.S. Ministers (Great Britain), NARA; Adams, *Great Britain and the American Civil War*, v. 2, p. 108; Oates, *With Malice Toward None*, locs. 6689–6702 ("rallied"); Ausubel, *John Bright*, p. 130 (Bright quote).

108. Marx, "A London Workers' Meeting," *Die Presse*, Feb. 2, 1862, in *MAC*, pp. 157–58.

109. Adams, *Great Britain and the American Civil War*, v. 2, p. 113 (resolution text); Donald, *Charles Sumner and the Rights of Man*, pp. 111–12; Blackett, *Divided Hearts*, pp. 209–11 (more on resolutions); Donald, *Lincoln*, p. 415; Jones, *Abraham Lincoln and a New Birth of Freedom*, p. 155 (secret payments); Lincoln to the Workingmen of Manchester, England, Jan. 19, 1863, *CWL*, v. 6, p. 64 (public letters).

110. Pease and Randall, eds., *Diary of Orville Hickman Browning*, v. 1, pp. 618–19, entry for Jan. 22, 1863.

111. Henry Adams later told historian Ephraim Douglass Adams that he assumed Marx had been involved, although the latter Adams could find little supporting evidence for the claim. See Adams, *Great Britain and the American Civil War*, v. 2, pp. 291–93; and Foner, *British Labor and the American Civil War*, p. 57. Historian Royden Harrison discounts the possibility that Marx helped organize the meeting, and speculates that Marx may have left before the end. See Harrison, *Before the Socialists*, pp. 41–42. For the quotes see Marx to Engels, Apr. 9, 1863, in *MAC*, p. 268 ("spoke *excellently*"); and Marx to Joseph Weydemeyer, Nov. 29, 1864, quoted in Foner, *British Labor and the American Civil War*, pp. 12–13.

112. On this point I am indebted to the analysis of diplomatic scholar Howard Jones, who has written persuasively on the subtleties of European reactions to Lincoln's proclamation. "Lincoln had been only partly correct in believing that emancipation would kill the idea of foreign intervention," Jones writes. "In the immediate sense, his Proclamation encouraged interventionists in both England and France to fear a racial war. . . . [B]ut over the long term the document convinced the British to drop the cause of intervention." Jones, *Blue and Gray Diplomacy*, p. 290. See also Jones, *Abraham Lincoln and a New Birth of Freedom*, p. 104. D. P. Crook agrees: "Much evidence still stands to the effect that the northern image improved, especially in the long run, after Lincoln adopted a war aim more intelligible to European opinion." Crook, *Diplomacy During the American Civil War*, p. 96. For Palmerston's wish to see the United States divided, see Palmerston to Russell, Jan 19, 1862, quoted in Bell, v. 2, p. 315.

113. Henry Adams to Charles Francis Adams Jr., Jan. 23, 1863, in Ford, ed., *Cycle of Adams Letters*, v. 1, p. 243.

114. Harrison, *Before the Socialists*, pp. 68–69.

115. Blackett, *Divided Hearts*, pp. 142–43; Ellison, *Support for Secession*, pp. 189–92. "Most studies of British views on the war," writes R. J. M. Blackett, citing, among other sources, Martin Crawford's *The Anglo-American Crisis*, "ignore this exchange between readers and editors, so vital to an understanding of the nature of public opinion, and by concentrating almost exclusively on editorials, conclude erroneously that most newspapers favored the Confederacy." (Blackett, *Divided Hearts*, p. 143.)

116. On the *Bee-Hive*, see Logan, "The Bee-Hive Newspaper," pp. 343 ("effete aristocrats"), 344–45, 348 ("wage slaves"). See also Marx to Engels, Dec. 2, 1864, quoted in Foner, *British Labor and the American Civil War*, p. 82 ("It is impossible"); and Harrison, "E.S. Beesly and Karl Marx," p. 34.

117. Marx, "Inaugural Address of the Working Men's International Association," in Tucker, ed., *Marx-Engels Reader*, p. 519 ("mysteries"); McLellan, Marx, p. 368 ("haunts me"); Marx to Engels, Dec. 27, 1863, *MECW*, v. 41, p. 503 ("Frankenstein"). See also Wheen, pp. 72, 294; *KMIR*, p. xviii (perennial sores, and opium and arsenic); Gabriel, loc. 5951 (Spanish fly).

118. Marx to Engels, Sept. 10, 1862, in *MAC*, p. 261 ("bourgeois republic"); Moore, *European Socialists and the American Promised Land*, p. 24 ("multiplied its vices"); Greeley, quoted in Crook, *The North, the South, and the Powers*, p. 372 ("unprincipled egotism"); Marx, "Manifesto of the Communist Party," in Tucker, ed., *Marx-Engels Reader*, p. 475 ("egotistical calculation").

119. Lincoln, "Address Before the Young Men's Lyceum," *CWL*, v. 1, pp. 114–15 ("reason, cold, calculating").

120. Lincoln to Isaac M. Schermerhorn, Sept. 12, 1864, *CWL*, v. 8, p. 2 ("Steam-power"). I am indebted to Howard Jones for helping me to understand the nuances of Lincoln's evolving antislavery position in the context of international diplomacy. For a succinct encapsulation of this argument, see Jones and Rakestraw, eds., "Diplomacy of the Civil War," in *American Foreign Relations Since 1600: A Guide to the Literature*, p. 372.

121. Carwardine, *Lincoln*, p. 250; Donald, *Lincoln*, p. 416.

122. French, *Witness to the Young Republic*, pp. 416–17; Jones, *Abraham Lincoln*, pp. 1, 146–47; Jones, *Blue and Gray Diplomacy*, p. 290.

123. Marx quoted in Wheen, p. 157 ("clumsily cunning"); Marx, "A Historic Parallel," Mar. 31, 1859, in *Dispatches for the "New York Tribune*," p. 92 ("reckless gambler").

CHAPTER FIVE: LINCOLN VS. NAPOLEON

1. Mary Lincoln quoted in Keckley, *Behind the Scenes*, p. 157 ("worn out"); Rice, ed., *Reminiscences*, pp. 249–50. See also Goodwin, p. 702.

2. Bradford Wood to Salmon P. Chase, May 19, 1863, Chase Papers, LOC, cited in *ALAL*, v. 2, p. 611 (diplomat in Denmark wants to come home); Grant to Stanton, Nov. 10, 1864, *Papers of Ulysses S. Grant*, v. 12, p. 398; Adams to Seward, Nov. 25, 1864, *FRUS 1865*, v. 1, p. 1. See also *ALAL*, v. 2, p. 729.

3. Jones, *Blue and Gray Diplomacy*, p. 293 (Polish revolt); Ridley, *Palmerston*, pp. 571–74; Crook, *Diplomacy*, p. 162 (date of invasion); Crook, *The North, the South, and the Powers*, p. 353; Foreman, *World on Fire*, p. 627 (looks weak).

4. Dayton to Seward, no. 129, Mar. 25, 1862, cited in Case and Spencer, *United States and France*, p. 288; Perkins, *History of the Monroe Doctrine*, p. 118. See also Mead, *Special Providence*, p. 23.

5. Mahin, p. 196 (Lincoln recognized); Josephine Shaw Lowell diary, entry for May 20, 1863, copy in Allan Nevins Papers, Columbia University, cited in *ALAL*, v. 2, pp. 478–79. The brackets in this quote were presumably inserted by Prof. Burlingame. Lincoln in this quote is referring specifically to a French mediation proposal in early 1863.

6. Donald, *Lincoln*, p. 553; *New York Herald*, Jan. 21, 1864, quoted in Mahin, pp. 234–35 ("grand army"); Stoeckl to Foreign Office, Jan. 24, 1865, No. 187, cited in Adams, *Great Britain and the American Civil War*, v. 2, p. 251 ("sure source"); Geofroy to Drouyn, Jan. 24, 1865, quoted in Crook, *The North, the South, and the Powers*, p. 358 ("pivot of reconciliation").

7. Important accounts of the Hampton Roads Conference include Campbell, *Reminiscences and Documents Relating to the Civil War during the Year 1865*, pp. 11–17; *Daily Chronicle and Sentinel* (August, Ga.), June 7, 1865; Hunter, "The Peace Commission of 1865," *Southern Historical Society Papers 1876*, Apr. 1877, pp. 168–76. I have also consulted secondary accounts, including Nicolay and Hay, "The Hampton Roads Conference," *Century*, v. 38, issue 6 (Oct. 1889), pp. 846–52; *ALAL*, v. 2, pp. 755–59; Donald, *Lincoln*, pp. 556–60; Goodwin, pp. 690–95; Bancroft, v. 2, pp. 410–15. See also Donald, *Lincoln*, pp. 556–57; *New York Herald*, Feb. 3, 1865, cited in Goodwin, p. 692 (small bag); Van Deusen, p. 383 (champagne and whisky); *New York Times*, Feb. 6, 1865, quoted in Goodwin, pp. 692–93 (bunting).

8. Lincoln to Herndon, Feb. 2, 1848, in *CWL*, v. 1, p. 448.

9. Ibid. ("consumptive man"); Campbell, *Reminiscences*, pp. 11–12.

10. Campbell, *Reminiscences*, pp. 12–13, 16. On the similarities between Seward's "foreign war panacea" and Stephens's Mexico scheme, see Jones, *Lincoln*, p. 185 and *ALAL*, v. 2, p. 751.

11. Nicolay and Hay, "Hampton Roads Conference," *Century*, v. 38, issue 6 (Oct. 1889), p. 851; Campbell, *Reminiscences*, p. 17 ("maturely considered"); Angle, *Lincoln Reader*, p. 504 ("keep the champagne"). See also Donald, *"We Are Lincoln Men,"* pp. 174–75; and Taylor, *Seward*, p. 236.

12. Lincoln scholar David Donald uses the above quote as the epigraph for his biography, which emphasizes Lincoln's fatalism. Other scholars, such as Doris Kearns Goodwin, have argued against the notion that Lincoln was a fatalist. See Goodwin, p. 236. Richard Carwardine observes that Lincoln "may have been fatalistic, but he was also ambitious, enterprising, and determined. . . . The fatalist and activist were thus fused in Lincoln" (Carwardine, *Lincoln*, pp. 43–44). Michael Burlingame, while he notes the president's "characteristic fatalism," compares Lincoln's attitude to the message in Reinhold Niebuhr's "Serenity Prayer": "God grant me the serenity to accept the things I cannot change; the courage to change the things I can; and the wisdom to know the difference." Lincoln, Burlingame argues, believed he could "shape events up to a point" (*ALAL*, v. 2, p. 711).

13. Lincoln, "Second Inaugural

Address," Mar. 4, 1865, *CWL*, v. 8, p. 332; Boritt, *Lincoln and the Economics of the American Dream*, p. 267 ("progress" quote); McPherson, *Tried by War*, pp. xiv ("progress" quote), 3 (Hay's recollection). Howard Jones, in his studies of Civil War diplomacy, emphasizes how Lincoln had come to consider "[d]omestic policy . . . inseparable from foreign affairs" (Jones, *Abraham Lincoln*, pp. 15, 191).

14. Boritt, *Lincoln and the Economics of the American Dream*, p. 270.

15. Schlesinger Jr., *Imperial Presidency*, pp. 68–69; Perkins, *History of the Monroe Doctrine*, p. 122. James McPherson finds "Isaiah Berlin's distinction between negative and positive liberty . . . useful to explain the transformation wrought by the Civil War in the relationship between power and liberty. Negative liberty is freedom *from* interference by outside authority with individual thought or behavior. Positive liberty is freedom *to* achieve a status of freedom previously denied by disability or law. Negative liberty is vulnerable to power; positive liberty is a form of power." See McPherson, *Abraham Lincoln and the Second American Revolution*, p. 137. Jay Sexton argues that "within [the Monroe Doctrine] lurked the imperial ambitions of the expansionist United States." Sexton, *Monroe Doctrine*, p. 3.

16. Crook, *The North, the South, and the Powers, 1861–1865*, p. 358 (deeply troubled); Maximilian to Napoleon, Jan. 27, 1865, in Corti, v. 2, p. 871 ("barely sufficient"); Ridley, *Napoleon III*, p. 97 (burglars); Ridley, *Palmerston*, p. 413 ("my dear friend");

Kissinger, *Diplomacy*, p. 106 ("the worm").

17. Jerrold, v. 1, p. 71; Ridley, *Napoleon III*, p. 23.

18. Jerrold, v. 1, pp. 84 (quiet and introverted), 75 ("Oui-Oui"), 93 (dressmaker), 123 (vineyards and pines); Ridley, *Napoleon III*, pp. 24 (Oui-Oui), 39–40 (hosiery shop etc).

19. Ridley, *Napoleon III*, p. 51 (bird), 91 (local girls); Bierman, *Napoleon III*, p. 15 ("not attractive enough").

20. Ridley, *Napoleon III*, pp. 55 (Rubicon), 61–67 (expelled); Bierman, *Napoleon III*, pp. 18–19 (mom rescues).

21. Simpson, *Rise of Louis Napoleon*, pp. 101, 104–5, 107–19; Ridley, *Napoleon III*, pp. 101–4; Jerrold, v. 1, pp. 332 (visit a cousin), 349 (cocked hat etc.), 354 ("Long Live Napoleon!").

22. Louis Napoleon to M. Vieillard, Apr. 30, 1837, in Jerrold, v. 2, pp. 6, 8–9; Ridley, *Napoleon III*, pp. 109–11 (three hundred thousand).

23. The Disraeli recollection is in Monypenny, *Life of Benjamin Disraeli*, v. 2, pp. 93–94. On Louis Napoleon in Britain, see also Ridley, *Napoleon III*, pp. 114, 119–120; Planché, *Recollections and Reflections*, v. 2, pp. 45–46; *Courier*, Feb. 4, 1839, in Jerrold, v. 2, p. 86; Bierman, *Napoleon III*, p. 34 (Savile Row).

24. For the Boulogne coup, see Jerrold, v. 2, pp. 123–31; Ridley, *Napoleon III*, pp. 128–32; Guérard, *Reflections on the Napoleonic Legend*, p. 148; Whitridge, *Men in Crisis*, p. 88; Gabriel, locs. 4428–40 (bacon).

25. Hanna and Hanna, p. 5 (Joan of Arc); Louis Napoleon to Hortense Cornu, Feb. 14, 1845, in Jerrold, v. 2, pp. 305, 446 ("death in life"); Simpson,

Rise of Louis Napoleon, p. 207; "Vergeot (*Éléonore*)," in *Dictionnaire du Second Empire*, pp. 1304–5; Smith, *Bonapartes*, p. 116; Ridley, *Napoleon III*, p. 176.

26. For the escape from Ham, see Jerrold, v. 2, pp. 343–54; Simpson, *Rise of Louis Napoleon*, pp. 246–54; Ridley, *Napoleon III*, pp. 186–92; Bierman, *Napoleon III*, pp. 49–50.

27. Jerrold, v. 2, pp. 388, 397–99; Bierman, *Napoleon III*, pp. 60 ("Him!"), 67 (bathwater).

28. Ridley, *Napoleon III*, p. 203; Rosebault, *When Dana Was the Sun*, p. 44.

29. Ridley, *Napoleon III*, pp. 283, 312; Marx, "Eighteenth Brumaire of Louis Bonaparte," in Tucker, ed., *Marx-Engels Reader*, p. 607; Bierman, *Napoleon III*, p. 86 (chicken and champagne); Gabriel, locs. 4428–40; Clay to J. R. Johnston, Jan. 11, 1853, copy and transcription in William H. Townsend Papers, University of Kentucky.

30. Kissinger, *Diplomacy*, pp. 106–7; Ridley, *Napoleon III*, p. 348.

31. The anecdote about the chamberlain's instructions is in the journals of Edmond and Jules de Goncourt, entry for Mar. 15, 1862 (Baldick, ed., *Pages from the Goncourt Journal*, p. 70). See also Bierman, *Napoleon III*, pp. 75, 129, 169, 241; Barker, *Distaff Diplomacy*, pp. 28–29; Ridley, *Napoleon III*, pp. 402–3; Tyrner-Tyrnauer, *Lincoln and the Emperors*, p. 55 ("what rascals").

32. Bierman, *Napoleon III*, p. 136 (fifteen thousand candles); Corti, v. 1, pp. 37 (blue eyes etc.), 39 (marriage date), 48–52 (description of court, etc.); Disraeli to Mrs. Brydges Willyams, May 1, 1855, in Buckle, *Life of Disraeli*,

v. 4, pp. 4–5; Russell to Cowley, Jan. 21, 1853, Cowley Papers, BNA (*"intrigante"*). See also Barker, *Distaff Diplomacy*, pp. 3, 5; and Ridley, *Napoleon III*, p. 331 (stock exchange).

33. Ridley, *Napoleon III*, pp. 147 (talkative), 161 ("short tempered and bossy"), 166 (dagger), 411 (bullfights); Tyrner-Tyrnauer, *Lincoln and the Emperors*, p. 60 ("war on America").

34. For Hidalgo's account of the scheme's origins, see Hidalgo to Maximilian and Charlotte, Apr. 15, 1865, "Secret Notes," AKM, photostatic copies in LOC. Nancy Barker Nichols points out that Hidalgo's account must be used with care, since he "always exaggerated his own role." She notes, however, that although Maximilian had already been "sounded through regular diplomatic channels" earlier that summer, the project indeed took on new urgency that autumn with Eugénie playing "the key role in reopening the negotiation with the Archduke." See Barker, *Distaff Diplomacy*, pp. 89–92. See also Corti, v. 1, pp. 33, 37. I have generally followed Catherine A. Phillips's translations of the documents from the AKM in Count Corti's book, but have occasionally altered a word here and there to more accurately reflect the text of the original documents.

35. Hidalgo to Maximilian and Charlotte, Apr. 15, 1865, "Secret Notes," AKM, photostatic copies in LOC. See also Corti, v. 1, pp. 78–79, 94, 98–99.

36. Hidalgo to Maximilian and Charlotte, Apr. 15, 1865, "Secret Notes," AKM, photostatic copies in LOC. See also Corti, v. 1, p. 101; Barker, *Distaff Diplomacy*, p. 12 (superstitions).

37. Napoleon to Comte de Flahault, Oct. 1861, in Corti, v. 1, p. 361–62; Hanna and Hanna, p. 28 (raiding convoys).

38. Hanna and Hanna, pp. 96–97, 126 ("29 and jobless" etc.); Corti, v. 2, p. 438 (Featherhead); Charlotte to Eugénie, Jan. 22, 1862, in Corti, v. 1, p. 322 ("holy one" etc.).

39. Hanna and Hanna, p. 40 (troops arrive); Kennedy, *Rise and Fall of the Great Powers*, p. 169; Bell, v. 2, p. 195 (celebratory gunfire).

40. Crook, *Diplomacy*, p. 7 (critical counterweight); Napoleon III to Forey, July 3, 1862, quoted in Perkins, *History of the Monroe Doctrine*, p. 117.

41. Marx, "An International *Affaire Mirés*," *Die Presse*, May 2, 1862, in *MAC*, p. 193 ("overseas adventures"); Cowley to Russell, Dec. 7, 1862, Cowley Papers, BNA ("mistresses"); Jones, *Blue and Gray Diplomacy*, p. 72; Palmerston to Somerset, Dec. 29, 1860, Palmerston Papers, British Library.

42. Marx, "The Intervention in Mexico (II)," *New York Daily Tribune*, Nov. 23, 1861, in *MAC*, pp. 102, 107.

43. Seward to Dayton, Mar. 31, 1862, no. 135, Diplomatic Instructions (France), NARA; French dispatch, n.d., reprinted in the *New York Times*, Nov. 18, 1861; Seward dispatch quoted in Perkins, *History of the Monroe Doctrine*, p. 126. The quote about the "language of the Monroe Doctrine" is Perkins's.

44. Romero's note on the Monroe Doctrine is in Perkins, *History of the Monroe Doctrine*, p. 127; Romero dispatch, Aug. 31, 1861, in Schoonover, ed., *Mexican Lobby*, pp. 7–9; Seward to Corwin, no. 2, Apr. 6, 1861, *FRUS 1861*, p. 65.

45. Marx, "The Intervention in Mexico (II)," *New York Daily Tribune*, Nov. 23, 1861, in *MAC*, p. 107; *New York Times*, Nov. 17, 1861.

46. Seward to Dayton, Mar. 31, 1862, no. 135, Diplomatic Instructions (France), NARA; Lincoln to the Senate, Dec. 17, 1861, in *CWL*, v. 5, pp. 73–74; Lincoln to the Senate, Jan. 24, 1862, *CWL*, v. 5, p. 109; Findley, *A. Lincoln*, p. 247 (loan to Mexico); Jones, *Union in Peril*, p. 76 ("foreclosing"); Corwin to Robert W. Shufeldt, June 27, 1862, Shufeldt Papers, LOC; Thomas Corwin to A. C. Allen, May 18, 1862, ALP, LOC; Hanna and Hanna, pp. 53–54; Matías Romero dispatch, July 3, 1862, in Schoonover, *Mexican Lobby*, p. 26; Crook, *Diplomacy*, p. 159; Mahin, pp. 110–21. Dean Mahin suggests that "[t]here are several reasons for doubting that Lincoln and Seward" genuinely "hoped for the implementation" of the loan treaty (Mahin, p. 113).

47. Monaghan, p. 222; Haslip, *Crown of Mexico*, pp. 179–80 (baroque churches etc.).

48. McPherson, *Battle Cry of Freedom*, p. 683 (thirty-five thousand); [Hay,] *Missouri Republican*, July 18, 1862, in Burlingame, ed., *Lincoln's Journalist*, pp. 278–81.

49. Hanna and Hanna, p. 9 ("great unfathomed"); Mathilde quoted in Hector Fleischmann, *Napoleon III and the Women He Loved* (London: Holden and Hardingham), pp. 12–13; Kissinger, *Diplomacy*, p. 108 ("like rabbits"); [Hay,] *Missouri Republican*, Nov. 8, 1861, in Burlingame, ed., *Lincoln's Journalist*, p. 132 ("plots and schemes").

50. Lincoln, "Speech at Cooper

Union," Feb. 27, 1860, *CWL*, v. 3,
p. 541.

51. Bigelow to Seward, Aug. 22, 1862,
Despatches from U.S. Consuls (Paris),
NARA ("carrion crow").

52. Lamon Papers, Huntington
Library, San Marino, Calif., Drafts
and Anecdotes, folder 6, in *RW*, p. 288
(Richelieu); Spencer, "The Jewett-
Greeley Affair," pp. 239 (stop the
bleeding), 258 ("most friendly feelings"). See also Jones, *Blue and Gray
Diplomacy*, pp. 288–89; Jones, *Lincoln*,
p. 160; *ALAL*, v. 2, p. 479.

53. Thomas, *Lincoln*, p. 377; Russell,
My Diary North and South, pp. 399–
400, entry for July 10, 1861 (Vallandigham description); Donald, *Lincoln*,
p. 420 ("King Lincoln").

54. Vallandigham, "The Great Civil
War in America (Speech in the House
of Representatives, Jan. 14, 1863)," in
Freidel, *Union Pamphlets of the Civil
War*, v. 2, pp. 713 ("union is empire"),
734 ("accept it"). See also Jones, *Blue
and Gray Diplomacy*, p. 288 ("accept
it at once"); Jones, *Lincoln*, p. 159;
McPherson, *Tried by War*, p. 171.

55. *Boston Daily Journal*, Feb. 14, 1863
("careworn and dejected"); Henry Sanford to Seward, Jan. 20, 1863, Seward
Papers, University of Rochester (Latin
rivalry); *New York Times*, Feb. 20, 1863,
cited in Crook, *Diplomacy During the
American Civil War*, pp. 160–61
("larger Texas"); Dayton to Seward,
Jan. 15, 1863, no. 255, Despatches from
U.S. Ministers (France), NARA;
Hamilton to Lincoln, Feb. 16, 1863,
ALP, LOC. See also *ALAL-DC*, v. 2,
ch. 30, pp. 3287–88; Hanna and Hanna,
p. 81; Jones, *Blue and Gray Diplomacy*,
p. 294; and Spencer, "Jewett-Greeley
Affair," p. 245.

56. Nicolay and Hay, *Abraham
Lincoln: A History*, v. 6, p. 359 (Kock
letter); Foner, "Lincoln and Colonization," in Foner, ed., *Our Lincoln*,
pp. 160, 163–64; *ALAL*, v. 2, pp. 395–
96; Magness and Page, *Colonization
After Emancipation*, pp. 8, 10, 37, 55,
118, 125, 126.

57. Seward quoted in Harrison,
Before the Socialists, pp. 42–43 ("Our
armies"); Brooks, *Washington in
Lincoln's Time* (New York, 1895), pp.
57–58; Henry Adams to Charles Francis Adams Jr., June 25, 1863, in Ford,
ed., *Cycle of Adams Letters*, v. 2, pp.
40–41; Romero dispatch, May 16, 1862,
in Schoonover, ed., *Mexican Lobby*,
p. 25. On Chancellorsville and its
aftermath see also McPherson, *Battle
Cry of Freedom*, pp. 638–45, 651; and
McPherson, *Tried by War*, p. 177.

58. Corti, v. 1, pp. 211 (entry date), 212
(emperor wept), 220 (posters); Hanna
and Hanna, p. 87 (Te Deum); Haslip,
Crown of Mexico, pp. 185–86 (flowers).

59. Gurowski, *Diary*, v. 2, pp. 241–
42; Burt, "Lincoln on His Own
Story-Telling," *Century*, v. 73, Feb.
1907, pp. 500–501; Keckley, *Behind
the Scenes*, pp. 118–20; Helm, *Mary,
Wife of Lincoln*, p. 226. See also
Monaghan, p. 311; Shenk, *Lincoln's
Melancholy*, p. 193; Donald, *Lincoln*,
p. 446; Baker, p. 227.

60. *New York Tribune*, Sept. 26, 1861
(French lessons); Baker, pp. 192–93,
196, 200; Carroll, "Abraham Lincoln
and the Minister of France," p. 147;
Keckley, *Behind the Scenes*, p. 101
("long tail").

61. Hay to John G. Nicolay, Sept. 11,
1863, in Burlingame, ed., *At Lincoln's
Side*, pp. 53–54. See also Boritt, *Lincoln
and the Economics of the American*

Dream, p. 267. Boritt uses this quote in his chapter 18, titled "The Backwoods Jupiter," to introduce an insightful discussion of Lincoln's military strategy. See also Jones, *Abraham Lincoln*, pp. 15, 191.

62. Nicolay and Hay, *Abraham Lincoln: A Life*, v. 5, pp. 155–56; McPherson, *Tried by War*, p. 3.

63. Hay, *Diary*, p. 80, entry for Sept. 9, 1863 (Hooker description); Smith, "The Destruction of Fighting Joe Hooker," *American Heritage*, v. 44, issue 6, Oct. 1993 ("Handsome Captain"); Brooks, *Washington in Lincoln's Time* (New York, 1895), pp. 59–60; Welles, *Diary*, v. 1, p. 229, entry for Jan. 24, 1863 (I have removed a dash from the Welles quote for readability); Lincoln to Hooker, Jan. 26, 1863, *CWL*, v. 6, p. 79 ("beware of rashness"). See also Monaghan, p. 285; Burlingame, *Inner Life*, p. 81; *RW*, p. 472.

64. Lincoln to Hooker, June 10, 1863, *CWL*, v. 6, p. 257; Lincoln to Halleck, Sept. 19, 1863, *CWL*, v. 6, p. 467. The Hooker quotation is from a footnote in *CWL*, v. 6, p. 257. See also Boritt's analysis of this missive in *Lincoln and the Economics of the American Dream*, p. 270. See also McPherson, *Tried by War*, p. 200.

65. McPherson, *Battle Cry of Freedom*, p. 664 (deflated the Copperheads); Henry Adams to Charles Francis Adams Jr., July 23, 1863, in Ford, ed., *Cycle of Adams Letters*, v. 2, p. 58. See also Foreman, *World on Fire*, p. 495.

66. Welles, *Diary*, v. 1, p. 385, entry for July 27, 1863. Welles's original manuscript diary actually reads, "But I *do* expect an improvement" in the condition of Mexicans under French tute-lage [my italics]; he later replaced the "do" with a "don't." Yet it seems likely from the context of this passage that this was an oversight—not a change of perspective—on Welles's part, since he also describes the French scheme as a "calamity." The possibility exists, however, that Welles believed Mexicans themselves might benefit from French rule even as the project threatened American interests.

67. Hay, *Diary*, p. 70, entry for Aug. 6, 1863; Hay to John G. Nicolay, Aug. 7, 1863, in Burlingame, ed., *At Lincoln's Side*, pp. 48–50; Hay to John G. Nicolay, Sept. 11, 1863, in ibid., p. 54; Hay to Charles G. Halpine, Aug. 14, 1863, in ibid., p. 50. See also Monaghan, p. 321.

68. Maximilian to Napoleon III, Aug. 10, 1863, in Corti, v. 1, pp. 227–28.

69. Francis P. Blair Sr. to Lincoln, Aug. 1, 1863, ALP, LOC; Lincoln to Stanton, July 29, 1863, *CWL*, v. 6, pp. 354–55; Lincoln to Banks, Aug. 5, 1863, *CWL*, v. 6, p. 364; Lincoln to Grant, Aug. 9, 1863, *CWL*, v. 6, p. 374.

70. Lincoln to Mary, Aug. 8, 1863, *CWL*, v. 6, p. 372.

71. Goodwin, p. 545; Dennett, *John Hay*, p. 39. See also Burlingame, "Surrogate Father Abraham," in *Inner World*, pp. 73–91.

72. Hay, *Diary*, pp. 70–71, entry for Aug. 9, 1863.

73. Nichols, *Life of Abraham Lincoln*, p. 317; Mahin, p. 233–34.

74. Hay, *Diary*, pp. 78–80, entry for Sept. 9, 1863.

75. Hay, *Diary*, pp. 81–82, entry for Sept. 10, 1863; O'Toole, *Five of Hearts*, 61 (wine cellar). See also Hay, *Diary*, p. 314n.

76. Hay, *Diary*, pp. 81–84, entry for

Sept. 10, 1863; Hay, *Diary*, p. 87, entry for Sept. 27, 1863.

77. Seward to Bigelow, Sept. 9, 1863, in Bancroft, v. 2, pp. 426–27; Mercier to Drouyn de Lhuys, Sept. 14, 1863, quoted in Carroll, "Abraham Lincoln and the Minister of France," p. 150. See also Nicolay and Hay, *Abraham Lincoln: A History*, v. 7, pp. 403–4 ("strict neutrality").

78. Stephen A. Hurlbut to Lincoln, Aug. 18, 1863, ALP, LOC; Francis P. Blair Jr. to Montgomery Blair, Sept. 24, 1863, ALP, LOC; Seward to Dayton, Sept. 26, 1863, "Confidential," no. 406, Diplomatic Instructions (France), NARA. See also Nicolay and Hay, *Abraham Lincoln: A History*, v. 7, pp. 402–3.

79. Plumb to Romero, Dec. 2, 1863, "Confidential," Plumb Papers, LOC. On Plumb's relationship with Romero see also Schoonover, ed., *Mexican Lobby*, pp. xiv, 13, and 16.

80. Napoleon III to Maximilian, Sept. 19, 1863; Napoleon III to Maximilian, Oct. 2, 1863, in Corti, v. 1, pp. 256 and 260.

81. Lincoln to Banks, Sept. 19, 1863, *CWL*, v. 6, p. 465; McPherson, *Battle Cry of Freedom*, p. 683; Foote, *Civil War: Fredericksburg to Meridian*, pp. 774–75; Hanna and Hanna, p. 162 (seven thousand); Banks to Lincoln, Feb. 12, 1864, ALP, LOC.

82. Crook, *The North, the South, and the Powers*, pp. 317–18 (for its own protection); Hanna and Hanna, p. 8 (Tocqueville); Ridley, *Napoleon III*, p. 356 (shared that view).

83. *Harper's Weekly*, Oct. 17, 1863, and Nov. 21, 1863; *New York Herald*, Sept. 17, 1863; Clay to Seward, Jan. 25, 1864, *FRUS 1864*, v. 3, p. 283. See also

Monaghan, p. 331; and Clinton, *Mrs. Lincoln*, p. 205.

84. *New York Herald*, Nov. 12, 1863, quoted in Crook, *Diplomacy*, p. 145; Welles, *Diary*, v. 1, p. 443, entry for Sept. 25, 1863; Hay, *Diary*, pp. 124, 126–27, entries for Dec. 9, Dec. 10, and Dec. 12, 1863.

85. Wyke to Herzfeld, Nov. 27, 1863, carton 5, AKM, photostat in LOC; Herzfeld to Depont, Dec. 12, 1863, in Corti, v. 1, p. 287; Crook, *The North, the South and the Powers*, p. 353 (Mexicanization).

86. Corti, v. 1, p. 289 ("no possible object"); Hay, *Diary*, p. 116, entry for Nov. 22, 1863 ("Lord knows who").

87. Green, *Washington*, v. 1, p. 268; Scovel to Lincoln, Dec. 18, 1863, ALP, LOC.

88. Lincoln, "Annual Message to Congress," Dec. 8, 1863, *CWL*, v. 7, pp. 36–49; Welles, *Diary*, v. 1, p. 445.

89. Welles, *Diary*, v. 1, pp. 494–95, entry for Dec. 25, 1863.

90. Gurowski, *Diary: 1863–'64–'65*, entry for Jan. 20, 1864, p. 81; Monaghan, p. 349.

91. McDougall resolution quoted in Nicolay and Hay, *Abraham Lincoln: A History*, v. 7, p. 407.

92. Pease and Randall, eds., *Diary of Orville Hickman Browning*, v. 1, p. 493, entry for Aug. 5, 1861 ("quite drunk"); Buchanan, "James A. McDougall," pp. 203, 208–9. McDougall's speech to the Senate is in *CG*, 37th Cong., 3rd Sess., Appendix, pp. 94–100.

93. Buchanan, "James A. McDougall," p. 210 ("drunken clown"); Seward to Dayton, Jan. 12, 1864, "Confidential," no. 456, Diplomatic Instructions (France), NARA. See also Bancroft, v. 2, pp. 428–29.

94. Pike to William Pitt Fessenden, Sept. 3, 1863, Pike Papers, LOC; Plumb to Sumner, Jan. 26, 1864, Plumb Papers, LOC.

95. Donald, *Charles Sumner and the Rights of Man*, p. 102 (Sumner quote); Nicolay and Hay, *Abraham Lincoln: A History*, v. 7, p. 407 (Sumner kills); Romero dispatch, Mar. 23, 1864, in Schoonover, ed., *Mexican Lobby*, pp. 38–39.

96. Brooks, "Personal Recollections of Abraham Lincoln," *Harper's New Monthly Magazine*, v. 31, issue 182 (July 1865), pp. 226–27.

97. Foner, "Lincoln and Colonization," in Foner, *Our Lincoln*, p. 164; *ALAL*, v. 2, pp. 395–96. Magness and Page, in *Colonization After Emancipation*, argue that colonization's "demise was largely born of the budgetary fight raging around the Emigration Office"—not simply the Haiti debacle. See p. 93.

98. *Philadelphia Sunday Dispatch*, May 1, 1864.

99. Leopold I to Maximilian, Feb. 4, 1864, in Corti, v. 1, pp. 316–17.

100. Tyrner-Tyrnauer, *Lincoln and the Emperors*, p. 110 ("Archdupe"); Napoleon III to Maximilian, Mar. 28, 1864, in Corti, v. 1, p. 340; Haslip, *Crown of Mexico*, pp. 231–32 (departure color); Bierman, *Napoleon III*, p. 239 (Austrian vessel). See also Corti, v. 1, pp. 351, 358, 359 (quote); and Hanna and Hanna, p. 129 *(Novara)*.

101. Foote, *Civil War: Red River to Appomattox*, pp. 33 (river color), 39 (red slime), 40 ("Napoleon P. Banks"), 45 (quote). See also Foreman, *World on Fire*, p. 366 (red clay); *ALAL*, v. 2, p. 741; McPherson, *Battle Cry of*

Freedom, p. 722; McPherson, *Tried by War*, pp. 209–10.

102. Welles, *Diary*, v. 2, pp. 25–27, entry for May 9, 1864. See also *ALAL*, v. 2, p. 647.

103. Davis's resolution is in *CG*, 38th Cong., 1st Sess., Apr. 4, 1864, pp. 1408–9. See also Seward to Bigelow, "Private and Unofficial," no. 141, copy in Records of the Foreign Service Posts of the Department of State (Paris), v. 457, NARA; Nicolay and Hay, *Abraham Lincoln: A History*, v. 7, pp. 407–8 (Davis committee chair and Sumner kills); Henig, *Henry Winter Davis*, pp. 203–4; *ALAL*, v. 2, p. 741; and Monaghan, p. 359. *New York Herald* quoted in Milton Lyman Henry, Jr., "Henry Winter Davis," p. 7, Hyman Papers.

104. Seward to Bigelow, May 5, 1864, "Confidential," no. 128, copy in Records of the Foreign Service Posts of the Dept. of State (Paris), v. 457, NARA; Bancroft, v. 2, p. 429n.

105. Steere, *Wilderness Campaign*, p. 1 (tangled vines); McPherson, *Battle Cry of Freedom*, pp. 724 (pine trees etc.), 742 (casualties).

106. Carpenter, *Inner Life*, pp. 30–31 (rings under eyes etc.), 217 ("tired spot," dinner upstairs); Oates, *With Malice Toward None*, locs. 7608–20 ("kill me").

107. Welles, *Diary*, v. 2, p. 35, entry for May 20, 1864; Seward to Bigelow, May 21, 1864, John Bigelow Papers, New York Public Library.

108. Lincoln to Salmon P. Chase and Edwin M. Stanton, May 5, 1864, *CWL*, v. 7, p. 331 (order re: horses); Ridley, *Napoleon III*, p. 238 (on horseback).

109. *Philadelphia Sunday Dispatch*, May 29, 1864 ("Parisian attire");

Springfield Republican, Jun. 7, 1875, clipping in Ruth Randall Papers, LOC; *Boston Transcript*, n.d., in Moore, ed., *Rebellion Record*, v. 11, p. 22; Jane G. Swisshelm letter, n.d., *Chicago Journal*, copied in "Mrs. Lincoln and Foreign Goods," *New York World*, May 3, 1864.

110. Haslip, *Crown of Mexico*, pp. 242–44.

111. Ibid., p. 245 (beauty, roads); Corti, v. 2, pp. 417–20, 422. See especially Charlotte to Eugénie, June 18, 1864, v. 2, p. 422.

112. Haslip, *Crown of Mexico*, pp. 251 (flowers, sombreros, etc.), 262 (west of Mexico City); Corti, v. 2, pp. 429 (views, trees, birds, scents), 431 ("basalt crag"), 435 (beautiful women), 437 (gardens), 836 ("as in Europe").

113. Rice, ed., *Reminiscences*, p. 390 ("gnawing"); Nicolay and Hay, *Abraham Lincoln: A History*, v. 7, p. 421 (GOP resolution). See also Mahin, p. 233.

114. Lincoln to William Dennison and Others, June 27, 1864, *CWL*, v. 7, p. 411. See also Monaghan, p. 370.

115. Sandburg, *The Prairie Years and the War Years*, p. 518 (rationale for Johnson); Savage, *Life and Public Services of Andrew Johnson*, p. 297 (speech). See also Mahin, p. 234.

116. Lincoln, "Speech at Great Central Sanitary Fair," June 16, 1864, *CWL*, v. 7, pp. 395–96.

117. Milton Lyman Henry Jr., "Henry Winter Davis and the Radical Republican Use of Foreign Policy," unpublished paper in Harold Hyman Collection, Prairie View, Texas; Schoonover, *Dollars Over Dominion*, pp. 122–23; Hay, *Diary*, p. 211, entry for June 24, 1864.

118. Foreman, *World on Fire*, p. 645

("mental overwork"); Hay, *Diary*, p. 247, entry for Nov. 11, 1864.

119. Romero dispatch, July 31, 1864, in Schoonover, ed., *Mexican Lobby*, pp. 46–47.

120. James Shepherd Pike to Seward, Nov. 2, 1864, *FRUS 1864*, v. 3, p. 326.

121. McPherson, *Battle Cry of Freedom*, p. 775 (comparisons to Napoleon); Goodwin, p. 655 (Seward in Auburn).

122. Seward to Maj. Gen. E. R. S. Canby, Sept. 30, 1864, *FRUS 1864*, v. 3, p. 155. See also Mahin, p. 227; and Lincoln to Napoleon III, Sept. 12, 1864, *CWL*, v. 7, p. 550 ("Your Good Friend").

123. Hay, *Diary*, pp. 243–46, entry for Nov. 8, 1864; White, *Lincoln's Greatest Speech*, p. 47.

124. Brooks, *Washington, D.C., in Lincoln's Time*, pp. 200–201; Brooks, in Burlingame, ed., *Lincoln Observed*, p. 145; Lincoln, "Response to a Serenade by the OH Del.," June 9, 1864, *CWL*, v. 7, p. 384; Lincoln to Andrew McCallen, June 19, 1858, *CWL*, v. 2, p. 469 (dreaded serenades); Lincoln, "Response to a Serenade," Nov. 10, 1864, ALP, LOC.

125. Lincoln, "Response to a Serenade," Nov. 10, 1864, ALP, LOC; *ALAL*, v. 2, p. 724–25; Nicolay and Hay, *Abraham Lincoln: A History*, v. 9, pp. 379–80 ("weightiest and wisest").

126. Marx, "Address of the International Working Men's Association to President Lincoln," in *MAC*, pp. 236–37; Marx to Lion Philips, Nov. 29, 1864, in *MAC*, p. 272 ("gigantic transformation"); Motley to Lincoln, Nov. 28, 1864, ALP, LOC.

127. Sherman to Grant, Nov. 6, 1864, in Hart, *Sherman*, p. 328; Lincoln to

Sherman, Dec. 28, 1864, *CWL*, v. 8, p. 181 ("anxious, if not fearful").

128. Thomas, *Abraham Lincoln*, p. 488 (red clay, "John Brown's Body"); Sandburg, *The Prairie Years and the War Years*, pp. 623–24; Henry Adams to Charles Francis Adams Jr., Dec. 16, 1864, in Ford, ed., *Cycle of Adams Letters*, v. 2, pp. 232–33.

129. Napoleon III to Maximilian, Nov. 16, 1864, in Corti, v. 2, p. 449; Charlotte to Eugénie, Jan. 26, 1865, in ibid., pp. 873–74 ("grave crisis" and "big battalions"); Charlotte to Eugénie, Dec. 27, 1864, in ibid., p. 865 ("much hampered").

130. *ALAL*, v. 2, p. 752.

131. Laugel, *The United States During the Civil War*, pp. xi–xii, 311–14.

132. Ibid., pp. 321–23.

133. Napoleon quoted in Perkins, *History of the Monroe Doctrine*, p. 137 ("What I really want"); Napoleon III, *Oeuvres*, V, pp. 227–28, quoted in Smith, *Napoleon III*, p. 180.

134. Napoleon III to Maximilian, Mar. 1, 1865, in Corti, v. 2, p. 887.

135. Maximilian to Karl Ludwig, Feb. 24, 1865, in Corti, v. 2, p. 465.

136. Joshua F. Speed to Herndon, Jan. 12, 1866, in *HI*, pp. 156–57 ("very unwell"); Paludan, p. 295.

137. White, *Lincoln's Greatest Speech*, pp. 31 (weather), 34 (Capitol dome), 41 (glasses), 42 (sun), 48 (703 words), 50 (foolscap); *Chicago Tribune*, Mar. 22, 1865 ("skeleton-like"); Goodwin, p. 697 ("gold lace"); Donald, *Lincoln*, p. 565 ("gewgaws").

138. Lincoln, "Second Inaugural Address," Mar. 4, 1865, *CWL*, v. 8, p. 333.

139. Niebuhr, *The Christian Century*, quoted in White, *Lincoln's Greatest Speech*, pp. 118–19.

140. White, *Lincoln's Greatest Speech*, p. 196 (*Tribune* quote); Bigelow to Seward, Mar. 21, 1865, in Bigelow, *Retrospections*, v. 2, p. 427.

141. White, *Lincoln's Greatest Speech*, p. 190 (*Herald* quote); Lincoln to Thurlow Weed, Mar. 15, 1865, *CWL*, v. 8, p. 356.

142. "Mme. Demorest's Mirror of Fashions," Apr. 1865; Mary Lincoln to Abram Wakeman, Mar. 20, 1865, copied in the *Washington Star*, Jan. 19, 1930. Both clippings in the Ruth Randall Papers, LOC.

143. Charlotte to Eugénie, Mar. 29, 1865, in Corti, v. 2, pp. 894–95; Wydenbruck correspondence, Mar. 31, 1865, in ibid., pp. 496–97.

144. Lincoln to Stanton, Mar. 30, 1865, *CWL*, v. 8, p. 377; Porter, *Incidents and Anecdotes*, p. 294. See also McPherson, *Battle Cry of Freedom*, pp. 845–47; and *ALAL*, v. 2, pp. 788–92.

145. In later years Mary would turn on the French. In 1880, when she was living in exile in France, she complained to one correspondent that the French were "[t]he *most unprincipled, heartless, avaricious* people, on the face of the earth. With the exception of a *very few*, I detest them all" (Mary to Edward Lewis Baker Jr., June 12, 1880, in Turner and Turner, *Mary Todd Lincoln*, pp. 698–99).

146. Chambrun, "Personal Recollections," pp. 27, 31, 32, 34; Mary Lincoln to Charles Sumner, Apr. 10, 1865, and Apr. 11, 1865, in Turner and Turner, eds., *Mary Todd Lincoln*, pp. 216–17. See also *ALAL*, v. 2, pp. 795, 797–98.

147. Fanny Seward Diary, entry for Apr. 5, 1865, Seward Papers,

University of Rochester; Seward, *Seward at Washington, 1861–1872*, pp. 270–71. See also Bancroft, v. 2, p. 415; Van Deusen, p. 411; and Goodwin, pp. 720–21.

148. Seward, *Seward at Washington, 1861–1872*, pp. 271. See also Goodwin, pp. 724–25.

149. For two excellent recent studies of the Lincoln-Seward relationship, see Goodwin, *Team of Rivals* (New York, 2005) and Donald, *"We Are Lincoln Men"* (New York, 2003).

150. Fanny Seward Diary, entries for Apr. 10, 1865, and Apr. 13, 1865, Seward Papers, University of Rochester (euphoric revelers); Mary Lincoln interview with Herndon, Sept. 1866, in *HI*, p. 357; Noyes W. Miner, "Personal Reminiscences of Abraham Lincoln," p. 54, Miner Papers, ALPLM. See also Guelzo, *Abraham Lincoln: Redeemer President*, p. 434; and Donald, *Lincoln*, p. 570.

151. Goodwin, pp. 609–10; Oates, *With Malice Toward None*, loc. 4909; Monaghan, p. 189. Allen Guelzo, in his brilliant Lincoln biography, *Abraham Lincoln: Redeemer President* (1999), notes that some of Lincoln's supporters disapproved of this type of escapism. "Both evangelical Protestants and even many secular Whigs were deeply suspicious of the theater," Guelzo writes, "since they understood all too well that actors in nineteenth-century America were the principal rivals of preachers in setting out and legitimizing culture" (Guelzo, *Abraham Lincoln: Redeemer President*, p. 315).

152. Ward Hill Lamon to Lincoln, Dec. 10, 1864, in Lamon, *Recollections*, p. 275; A. H. Flanders to John G.

Nicolay, Jan. 27, 1861, ALP, LOC (special coat). See also Donald, *Lincoln*, p. 569 (on Shakespeare); Nicolay, *Lincoln's Secretary*, pp. 59–60; and Holzer, *Lincoln President-Elect*, p. 285.

153. There is controversy about who actually bored the hole. Some historians insist Booth carved it himself. Others cite the recollection of Frank Ford, son of theater owner Harry Clay Ford; in the 1960s, Frank insisted that his father had always maintained that he had ordered the hole carved himself. (Frank Ford to Dr. George J. Olszewski, Apr. 13, 1962, in Reck, *A. Lincoln: His Last 24 Hours* [Columbia, 1987], pp. 73–75.)

154. Bryan, *Great American Myth*, p. 167; Donald, *Lincoln*, p. 596; *ALAL*, v. 2, p. 817; Goodwin, p. 738.

155. Pendel, *Thirty-Six Years in the White House*, pp. 41–43; Dennett, *John Hay*, p. 36 (Spanish). See also Goodwin, p. 741; Donald, *"We Are Lincoln Men,"* p. 211; Donald, *Charles Sumner and the Rights of Man*, pp. 215–16; O'Toole, *Five of Hearts*, p. 40.

156. Hay, *Diary*, p. 195, entry for May 13, 1864 (dismissed); *ALAL*, v. 2, pp. 817–18; Donald, *Lincoln*, pp. 598–99 (Stanton quote).

157. This account of the attempted assassination of Seward draws primarily on Seward, *Seward at Washington, 1861–1872*, pp. 276–77.

158. Seward, *Seward at Washington, 1861–1872*, pp. 278–81; Francis Carpenter reminiscence in Perkins, *The Picture and the Men*, pp. 131–32; Monaghan, p. 422; Bancroft, v. 2, p. 417; Goodwin, pp. 737, 744–45.

159. Hay to Charles Edward Hay, Mar. 31, 1865, in Burlingame, ed., *At Lincoln's Side*, p. 103.

160. Hay to Robert Lincoln, Aug. 26, 1865, Hay Papers, Brown University.
161. Grace Bigelow Diary, entry for July 4, 1865, Bigelow Family Papers, New York Public Library.
162. Hay to Francis Carpenter, Jan. 22, [1866,] Hay Papers, Brown University; Hay to Robert Lincoln, Aug. 26, [1865,] Hay Papers, Brown University.
163. Hay to his brother, Aug. 4, [1865,] Hay Papers, Brown University ("not in a state"); Ridley, *Napoleon III*, p. 520 (demobilization, eight times, senior generals, quote); Bancroft, v. 2, pp. 433 (soldiers joining republicans, Grant quote), 436n (Seward to Bigelow, July 14, 1865); Hanna and Hanna, pp. 238–39 (fifty thousand troops, smuggling muskets); Sheridan, *Personal Memoirs*, v. 2, pp. 219–28; Welles, *Diary*, v. 2, p. 317, entry for June 16, 1865; Nicolay and Hay, *Abraham Lincoln: A History*, v. 7, p. 423 (Hay on Seward).
164. Napoleon III to Maximilian, Aug. 29, 1865, in Corti, v. 2, p. 541; Eugénie to Charlotte, Sept. 28, 1865, in ibid., p. 920 ("discourteous" etc).
165. Palmerston to Maximilian, July 17, 1865, Palmerston Papers, British Library; Mahin, p. 270; Corti, v. 2, p. 552. See also Ridley, *Palmerston*, pp. 547, 584 ("gone!" and Bright); Bell, v. 2, p. 418; Kennedy, *Rise and Fall of the Great Powers*, p. xxiii (relative economic decline).
166. Bigelow to Seward, Dec. 26, 1865, in Bigelow, *Retrospections*, v. 3, pp. 298–301.
167. Hay to his mother, Jan. 16, 1866, Hay Papers, Brown University; O'Toole, *Five of Hearts*, p. 69 (Hay's height).
168. Eugénie to Anna Murat, Aug. 10, 1866, quoted in Barker, *Distaff Diplomacy*, p. 158 ("bolt"); Charlotte to Maximilian, Aug. 1866, in Corti, v. 2, pp. 671–72.
169. Hay to "My Dear Sir," Aug. 17, 1866, Hay Papers, Brown University (French assurances); Hay to "My Dear Sir," Aug. 28, 1866, Hay Papers, Brown University (other confidants).
170. Napoleon III to Maximilian, Aug. 29, 1866, in Corti, v. 2, p. 945.
171. Corti, v. 2, pp. 780 (leaves for Queretaro), 794 (dead bodies), 808 (convent), 820–21 (execution); Ridley, *Maximilian and Juarez*, pp. 276–77 (execution detail, six bullets, etc.). See also Hanna and Hanna, p. 300.

CHAPTER SIX: LINCOLN VS. LINCOLN

1. Hay to Seward, Jan. 18, 1868, in Hay, ed., *Letters of John Hay*, v. 1, pp. 347–48.
2. Hay Diary No. 7, July 1867, Hay Papers, Brown University; McPherson, " 'The Whole Family of Man': Lincoln and the Last Best Hope Abroad," in May, ed., *The Union, the Confederacy, and the Atlantic Rim*, p. 147. McPherson does note, however, that "[i]t is an oversimplification to attribute [the success of the Reform Bill] mainly to Union victory in the Civil War."
3. Washington quoted in McPherson, " 'The Whole Family of Man': Lincoln and the Last Best Hope Abroad," in May, ed., *The Union, the Confederacy, and the Atlantic Rim*, p. 133; Lincoln, "Message to Congress

in Special Session," July 4, 1861, *CWL*, v. 4, p. 426.

4. Historian Anne Hummel Sherrill, who has compared Lincoln's republicanism to a kind of religious faith, argues that the triumph of democratic principles "was not a lesson deducible from the facts" during the Civil War, "for the facts proved the point either way." (Sherrill, *John Hay: Shield of Union*, p. 25). See also Clymer, *John Hay*, pp. 92–93, 96; and Carwardine and Sexton, eds., *Global Lincoln*, p. 31. The final quote is from Hay to Herndon, Sept. 5, 1866, in Hertz, *Hidden Lincoln*, p. 307.

5. Herring, p. 250. For the growth figures, see LaFeber, *American Age*, pp. 160–61, and Kennedy, *Rise and Fall of the Great Powers*, p. 242. See also Hay to Roosevelt, July 27, 1898, in Thayer, *John Hay*, vol. 2, p. 337 ("splendid little war").

6. See, for example, the insightful discussion of the tension between "Lincoln the unifier and Lincoln the liberator" in "Interchange: The Global Lincoln," *Journal of American History*, v. 96, no. 2, pp. 493–95. Adam I. P. Smith, however, adds in the same discussion that "supporters of Lincoln the nationalist would not . . . [necessarily] have seen any contradiction between Lincoln the spokesman for democracy and Lincoln the embodiment of national integration—the one justified the other in their minds." The debate about Lincoln's contradictory nature could fill a book of its own. Some historians and commentators, imagining Lincoln's reaction to the Gilded Age, have portrayed the sixteenth president as a tragic figure. "Had he

lived to seventy," Richard Hofstadter wrote in 1948, "he would have seen the generation brought up on self-help come into its own, build oppressive business corporations, and begin to close off those treasured opportunities for the little man." Hofstadter pitted the president's expansionist economic policies against his moral sense. "He himself presided over the social revolution that destroyed the simple equalitarian order of the 1840's, corrupted what remained of its values, and caricatured its ideals," Hofstadter concluded. "Booth's bullet, indeed, saved him from something worse than embroilment with the radicals over Reconstruction. It confined his life to the happier age that Lincoln understood—which unwittingly he helped to destroy" (Hofstadter, *American Political Tradition*, pp. 137–38). The iconoclast Edmund Wilson took a version of this notion one step further in 1962, limning Lincoln as a kind of masochist. He suggested that the president had figuratively "foreseen and accepted his doom; he knew it was part of the drama." Wilson considered it "morally and dramatically inevitable that this prophet who had crushed opposition and sent thousands of men to their deaths should finally attest his good faith by laying down his own life with theirs." In recent years the writer and essayist Gore Vidal has dramatically—and controversially—reimagined the Lincoln of Hofstadter and Wilson. The final act of Vidal's 1984 novel, *Lincoln*, is a scene of John Hay after the assassination musing about whether Lincoln had somehow willed his own murder. More recent scholars have questioned whether Lincoln would have really been so appalled by the Gilded Age. Gabor Boritt, who made "the development of the double image of Lincoln" between "man and god" a central theme of an eloquent historiographical essay, takes a more benign view of Lincoln's nationalism. In contrast to European state builders like Cavour and Bismarck, Boritt notes, "Lincoln's Dream helped lead America to the nationalism of Theodore Roosevelt, Woodrow Wilson, and Franklin Delano Roosevelt." (Boritt, *Lincoln and the Economics of the American Dream*, pp. 275–311. Quote is on p. 281.) Allen Guelzo has observed that "the tension between his Calvinistic 'melancholy' and bourgeois assertiveness" had actually acted as a kind of "mutual restraint." In Guelzo's view, this dynamic spawned a "depth and resiliency" that became Lincoln's "most valuable character assets" (Guelzo, *Abraham Lincoln: Redeemer President*, p. 463).

7. Lincoln, "Speech at Springfield, Illinois," Oct. 4, 1854, *CWL*, v. 2, p. 255. See also Jones, *Abraham Lincoln and a New Birth of Freedom*, passim; and McPherson, *Tried by War*, p. 132 (re: new birth).

8. Wilson, *Patriotic Gore*, pp. xxxi–xxxii; McDougall, *Throes of Democracy*, p. 400.

9. Fulbright quoted in McDougall, *Promised Land, Crusader State*, p. 206. McDougall's survey of the American foreign-policy tradition is an eloquent analysis of the battle between the competing visions of America as beacon and crusader. Reinhold Niebuhr has also trenchantly described the tension between love and justice in foreign affairs: "A rational ethic aims at justice," Niebuhr explains, "and a religious ethic makes love the ideal." (Niebuhr, *Moral Man and Immoral Society*, p. 57).

10. Herndon, "Analysis of the Character of Abraham Lincoln," p. 347 (Herndon quote).

11. Donald, "A Whig in the White House," in *Lincoln Reconsidered*, p. 133 ("peculiar paradox").

12. Thayer, *John Hay*, v. 1, p. 57.

13. O'Toole, *Five of Hearts*, pp. 155–56 (house description, size of dining room); Gilder and Gilder, eds., *Authors at Home*, pp. 140–44. See also Dennett, *John Hay*, p. 146.

14. Gilder and Gilder, eds., *Authors at Home*, p. 141 (Seward's house); Adams, *Education of Henry Adams*, pp. 325–26 ("would suddenly break off"); O'Toole, *Five of Hearts*, p. 216 (lullabies).

15. Burlingame, ed., *Abraham Lincoln: The Observations of John G. Nicolay and John Hay*, p. 1 (1886 excerpts).

16. Nicolay and Hay, *Abraham Lincoln: A History*, v. 1, pp. 216 ("young, bright"), 232–33 (Texas), 273 ("obstinately obtuse").

17. Norman Ferris has analyzed the effects of Nicolay and Hay's biography on Seward's reputation in his essay "Lincoln and Seward in Civil War Diplomacy," *Journal of the Abraham Lincoln Association*, v. 12, no. 1 (1991).

18. Nicolay and Hay, *Abraham Lincoln: A History*, v. 3, pp. 445 ("extraordinary state paper" and "continental crusade") and 449 ("how serious a fault"). For Hay's respect for Seward, see Dennett, *John Hay*, pp. 52 and 266; and Donald, *"We Are Lincoln Men,"* p. 201.

19. [Lincoln,] "Meditation on the Divine Will," [Sept. 2, 1862?,] *CWL*, v. 5, pp. 403–4. See also *CWL*, v. 8, p. 333 (second inaugural to Hay).

20. Herndon to Jesse Weik, Dec. 5, 1886, HW, LOC ("unimportant trash"); Herndon to Weik, Feb. 11, 1887, HW, LOC; *HL*, p. 347 ("march of time").

21. Herndon to Horace White, n.d., in Newton, *Lincoln and Herndon*, p. 308 ("Job's turkey"); Clymer, "John Milton Hay," in Garraty and Carnes, eds., *American National Biography*, v. 10 (New York, 1999), p. 368 (Hay's donations etc.).

22. *Missouri Republican*, Dec. 30, 1861, in Burlingame, ed., *Lincoln's Journalist*, p. 181 ("met and tamed"); O'Toole, *Five of Hearts*, p. 128 (country house); Clymer, *John Hay: The Gentleman as Diplomat*, p. 104 ("more English"). On Hay's Anglophilia see also Clymer, "John Milton Hay," *American National Biography*, p. 368.

23. Clymer, *John Hay: The Gentleman as Diplomat*, p. 102 (Hawaii); Dennett, *John Hay*, p. 220 ("Pax Britannica"); Hay, "A Partnership in Beneficence," *Addresses of John Hay*, pp. 78–79; Thayer, *John Hay*, v. 2, p. 181 (Victoria quote).

24. O'Toole, *Five of Hearts*, pp. 294 (Cairo), 296 ("cowboy regiment"), 295 ("chocolate éclair" and "take Cuba"). See also Clymer, *John Hay: The Gentleman as Diplomat*, pp. 114–15, 119 (not pushing like TR); and Clymer, "John Milton Hay," *American National Biography*, p. 369 (drawing closer).

25. Hay to Roosevelt, July 27, 1898, in Thayer, *John Hay*, v. 2, p. 337 ("splendid" etc.); Clymer, "John Milton Hay," *American National Biography*,

p. 369 (favored annexation of Philippines etc.); Clymer, *John Hay: The Gentleman as Diplomat*, p. 139 ("I cannot"). Evan Thomas offers a slightly different interpretation of Hay's "splendid little war" letter. Thomas finds "a wonderfully smug assumption" in Hay's appeal to the "American character," pointing out that Hay implies "that the essential American character is better—somehow more decent—than that of other nations." (Thomas, *War Lovers*, p. 364.)

26. Hay to Adams, July 8, 1900, quoted in Dennett, *John Hay*, p. 298 ("Absolute"); Lincoln, "Emancipation Proclamation," Jan. 1, 1863, *CWL*, vol. 6, p. 30 ("considerate judgment"). This line, which echoes Thomas Jefferson's appeal to the "opinions of mankind," was added at the suggestion of treasury secretary Salmon P. Chase. See Guelzo, *Emancipation Proclamation*, p. 179.

27. O'Toole, *Five of Hearts*, p. 304 (view); Lincoln quoted in Hofstadter, *American Political Tradition*, p. 173 ("ashes and blood"); Hay to Sir John Clark, Sept. 18, 1900, in Dennett, *John Hay*, pp. 324–25 ("dust and ashes").

28. On the Open Door notes, see "Open Door policy," *Encyclopaedia Britannica (Micropaedia)*, v. 8, p. 962; Clymer, "John Milton Hay," p. 369; Herring, pp. 331–35; and Mead, *Special Providence*, p. 108. See also LaFeber, *American Age*, p. 219 ("key to world politics"); Bemis, *John Quincy Adams and the Foundations of American Foreign Policy*, p. 567; and Paolino, *Foundations*, p. 212; (reciprocity becomes Open Door).

29. Thomas, *The War Lovers*, pp. 140–41 (sandwich cart, devout, etc.);

McKinley quoted in O'Toole, *Five of Hearts*, p. 345; Dennett, *John Hay*, p. 335 ("stabilization"); Adams, *Education of Henry Adams*, p. 503 ("combine").

30. Dennett, *John Hay*, pp. 335 (Dennett quote), 401 ("crusading"); Adams, *Education of Henry Adams*, p. 392 ("broke in halves"). See also Weinberg, *Manifest Destiny*, p. 462.

31. Hay to Roosevelt, July 27, 1898, in Thayer, *John Hay*, v. 2, p. 337 (right after all); Peterson, *Lincoln in American Memory*, p. 164 (telling TR Lincoln stories); Roosevelt to Henry Cabot Lodge, Jan. 28, 1909, quoted in Burlingame, ed., *At Lincoln's Side*, p. xii ("delightful man"); Hay to Roosevelt, Mar. 3, 1905, in Thayer, *John Hay*, v. 2, p. 363 (ring).

32. Clymer, "John Milton Hay," *American National Biography*, p. 370 (Panama Canal); Clymer, *John Hay: The Gentleman as Diplomat*, p. 210 (preferred McKinley). Clymer adds, however, that the two men "agreed . . . more than they disagreed." See also Dennett, *John Hay*, p. 419 (TR and reciprocity); O'Toole, *Five of Hearts*, p. 371 (Canadian boundary); Hay to his wife, July 4, 1903, in Dennett, *John Hay*, p. 347 ("no comfort"); Roosevelt to Henry Cabot Lodge, Jan. 28, 1909, in O'Toole, *Five of Hearts*, p. 389.

33. Hay, "The Press and Modern Progress," May 19, 1904, in *Addresses of John Hay*, pp. 243 ("irresistible power"), 250 ("cosmic tendency").

34. Marx, "The Eighteenth Brumaire of Louis Bonaparte," in Tucker, ed., *Marx-Engels Reader*, p. 595. My thinking about this dynamic was also informed by Arthur Schlesinger Jr.'s brilliant book *The Cycles of American History* (Franklin Center, Pa., 1986), especially chapter one, "The Theory of America: Experiment or Destiny?" Schlesinger writes in the book's foreword, "Science and technology revolutionize our lives, but memory, tradition, and myth frame our response. Expelled from individual consciousness by the rush of change, history finds its revenge by stamping the collective unconscious with habits, values, expectations, dreams. The dialectic between past and future will continue to form our lives." (Schlesinger, p. xviii.)

35. Thayer, *John Hay*, v. 2, pp. 399, 405–7. See also Goodwin, p. 753; and O'Toole, *Five of Hearts*, p. 384. For a fictional rendering of this scene, see Vidal, "Those Whom the Gods Would Disappoint They First Make Charming," *Books at Brown* (Providence, 1990), pp. 8–10.

Selected Bibliography

Manuscript Collections

Adams Family Papers, Massachusetts Historical Society, microfilm at Library of Congress, Washington, D.C.

Albert J. Beveridge Papers, Abraham Lincoln Presidential Library, Springfield, Illinois.

Albert J. Beveridge Papers, Library of Congress, Washington, D.C.

Archiv Kaiser Maximilians von Mexiko, Haus-, Hof- und Staatsarchiv (Vienna, Austria), photostatic copies in Library of Congress, Washington, D.C.

David Rankin Barbee Papers, Lauinger Library, Georgetown University, Washington, D.C.

John Bigelow Papers, New York Public Library, New York, New York.

Bigelow Family Papers, New York Public Library, New York, New York.

Salmon P. Chase Papers, Library of Congress, Washington, D.C.

Cassius Marcellus Clay Papers, Abraham Lincoln Library and Museum, Lincoln Memorial University, Harrogate, Tennessee.

Conkling Family Papers, Abraham Lincoln Presidential Library, Springfield, Illinois.

Lord Cowley Papers, British National Archives, Kew, England.

David Davis Papers, Abraham Lincoln Presidential Library, Springfield, Illinois.

Tyler Dennett Papers, Library of Congress, Washington, D.C.

Despatches from U.S. Consuls in Paris, 1790–1906, National Archives and Records Administration, College Park, Maryland.

Despatches from U.S. Ministers to Belgium, 1832–1906, National Archives and Records Administration, College Park, Maryland.

Despatches from U.S. Ministers to France, 1789–1869, National Archives and Records Administration, College Park, Maryland.

Despatches from U.S. Ministers to Great Britain, 1791-1906, National Archives and Records Administration, College Park, Maryland.

Despatches from U.S. Ministers to Spain, 1792–1906, National Archives and Records Administration, College Park, Maryland.

Diplomatic Instructions of the Department of State, 1801–1906 (France), National Archives and Records Administration, College Park, Maryland.

Diplomatic Instructions of the Department of State, 1801–1906 (Great Britain), National Archives and Records Administration, College Park, Maryland.

Edward Everett Papers, Massachusetts Historical Society, microfilm at Library of Congress, Washington, D.C.

Lord Granville Papers, British National Archives, Kew, England.

Artemus Hale Diary, Library of Congress, Washington, D.C.

John Hay Collection, Brown University, Providence, Rhode Island.

John Hay Papers, Library of Congress, Washington, D.C.

Herndon-Weik Collection, Library of Congress, Washington, D.C.

Harold Hyman Collection, Coleman Library, Prairie View A&M University, Prairie View, Texas.

Lincoln Centennial Association Records, Abraham Lincoln Presidential Library, Springfield, Illinois.

Lincoln Collection, Abraham Lincoln Presidential Library, Springfield, Illinois.

Abraham Lincoln Papers, Library of Congress, Washington, D.C.

McLellan Lincoln Collection, Brown University, Providence, Rhode Island.

Manton Marble Papers, Library of Congress, Washington, D.C.

John A. McClernand Papers, Abraham Lincoln Presidential Library, Springfield, Illinois.

Mentelle Family Papers, Transylvania University, Lexington, Kentucky.

Elizabeth L. Norris Papers, Abraham Lincoln Presidential Library, Springfield, Illinois.

Noyes W. Miner Papers, Abraham Lincoln Presidential Library, Springfield, Illinois.

Benjamin Moran Diary, Library of Congress, Washington, D.C.

Nicolay-Hay Papers, Abraham Lincoln Presidential Library, Springfield, Illinois.

Palmerston Papers, British Library, London, England.

James Shepherd Pike Papers, Library of Congress, Washington, D.C.

James Shepherd Pike Papers, Fogler Library, University of Maine, Orono.

Edward Lee Plumb Papers, Library of Congress, Washington, D.C.

Ruth Painter Randall Papers, Library of Congress, Washington, D.C.

Records of the Foreign Service Posts of the Department of State (Paris), National Archives and Records Administration, College Park, Maryland.

Lord John Russell Papers, British National Archives, Kew, England.

Carl Schurz Papers, Library of Congress, Washington, D.C.

William Henry Seward Papers, Rush Rhees Library, University of Rochester, Rochester, New York.

Robert W. Shufeldt Papers, Library of Congress, Washington, D.C.

Edwin M. Stanton Papers, Library of Congress, Washington, D.C.

Eduard de Stoeckl Correspondence, Russian Ministry of Foreign Affairs, Principle Archive, photostatic copies in the Library of Congress, Washington, D.C.

Horatio Nelson Taft Diary, Library of Congress, Washington, D.C.

Richard W. Thompson Papers, Abraham Lincoln Presidential Library, Springfield, Illinois.

William H. Townsend Papers, University of Kentucky, Lexington.

Lyman Trumbull Papers, Library of Congress, Washington, D.C.

Jesse Weik Papers, Abraham Lincoln Presidential Library, Springfield, Illinois.

Gideon Welles Papers, Abraham Lincoln Presidential Library, Springfield, Illinois.

Gideon Welles Papers, Library of Congress, Washington, D.C.

BOOKS, ARTICLES, AND PUBLISHED PRIMARY SOURCES

Adams, Ephraim Douglass. *Great Britain and the American Civil War*, 2 vols. New York: Russell & Russell, 1924.

Adams, Charles Francis, Jr. *Charles Francis Adams, 1835–1915: An Autobiography*. Boston: Houghton Mifflin, 1916.

Adams, Henry. *The Education of Henry Adams: An Autobiography*. New York: Modern Library, 1996.

Adams, Henry. *Mont-Saint-Michel and Chartres*. Boston: Houghton Mifflin, 1905.

Anderson, Stuart. "1861: Blockade vs. Closing the Confederate Ports." *Military Affairs* 41, no. 4 (Dec. 1977): 190–94.

Angle, Paul M. *The Lincoln Reader.* Kingsport, Tenn.: Kingsport Press, 1947.

Ausubel, Herman. *John Bright: Victorian Reformer*. New York: Wiley, 1966.

Avary, Myrta Lockett, ed. *Recollections of Alexander H. Stephens: His Diary Kept When a Prisoner at Fort Warren, Boston Harbor, 1865*. New York: Doubleday, Page, 1910; Da Capo reprint, 1971.

Bailey, Thomas A. "America's Emergence as a World Power: The Myth and the Verity." *Pacific Historical Review* 30, no. 1 (Feb. 1961): 1–16.

Baker, George E., ed. *The Works of William H. Seward*, 5 vols. Boston: Houghton Mifflin, 1884.

Baker, Jean. *Mary Todd Lincoln*. New York: Norton, 1987.

Bancroft, Frederic. *The Life of William H. Seward*, 2 vols. New York: Harper & Brothers, 1900.

Barker, Nancy Nichols. *Distaff Diplomacy: The Empress Eugénie and the Foreign Policy of the Second Empire*. Austin: University of Texas Press, 1967.

Barker, Nancy Nichols. "France, Austria, and the Mexican Venture, 1861–1864." *French Historical Studies* 3, no. 2 (1963): 224–45.

Barton, William E. *The Life of Abraham Lincoln*, vol. 2. Indianapolis: Bobbs-Merrill, 1925.

Basler, Roy P., ed. *The Collected Works of Abraham Lincoln*, 8 vols. New Brunswick, N.J.: Rutgers University Press, 1953.

Basler, Roy P., ed. *The Collected Works of Abraham Lincoln, Supplement 1832–1865*. Westport, Conn.: Greenwood, 1974.

Bauer, Karl Jack. *The Mexican War, 1846–1848*. New York: Macmillan, 1974.

Bayne, Julia Taft. *Tad Lincoln's Father*. Boston: Little, Brown, 1931.

Beale, Howard K., ed. *The Diary of Edward Bates, 1859–1866*. Washington D.C.: Government Printing Office, 1933.

Beisner, Robert L., ed. *American Foreign Relations Since 1600: A Guide to the Literature*. 2nd edition. Santa Barbara, Calif.: ABC-CLIO, 2003.

Bell, Herbert C. F. *Lord Palmerston*, 2 vols. London: Frank Cass, 1966.

Bemis, Samuel Flagg. *John Quincy Adams and the Foundations of American Foreign Policy*. Westport, Conn.: Greenwood, 1949.

Bensel, Richard Franklin. *Yankee*

Leviathan: The Origins of Central State Authority in America, 1859–1877. Cambridge, U.K.: Cambridge University Press, 1990.

Benson, Arthur Christopher, and Viscount Esher. *The Letters of Queen Victoria: A Selection from Her Majesty's Correspondence Between the Years 1837 and 1861*, vol. 3. New York: Longmans, Green, 1907.

Beveridge, Albert J. *Abraham Lincoln, 1809–1858*, 4 vols. Boston: Houghton Mifflin, 1928.

Bierman, John. *Napoleon III and His Carnival Empire*. New York: St. Martin's, 1988.

Bigelow, John. *Retrospections of an Active Life*, vols. 1, 2, 3, and 4. New York: Baker & Taylor, 1909.

Billings, Roger, and Frank J. Williams, eds. *Abraham Lincoln, Esq.: The Legal Career of America's Greatest President*. Lexington: University Press of Kentucky, 2010.

Blackburn, Robin. *An Unfinished Revolution: Karl Marx and Abraham Lincoln*. London: Verso, 2011.

Blackett, R. J. M. *Divided Hearts: Britain and the American Civil War*. Baton Rouge: Louisiana State University Press, 2001.

Blue, Frederick J. *Salmon P. Chase: A Life in Politics*. Kent, Ohio: Kent State University Press, 1987.

Booker, Richard, ed. *Abraham Lincoln in Periodical Literature, 1860–1940*. Chicago: Fawley Brost, 1941.

Boritt, Gabor. *Lincoln and the Economics of the American Dream*. Memphis: Memphis State University Press, 1978.

Boritt, Gabor. "Lincoln's Opposition to the Mexican War." *Journal of the Illinois State Historical Society* 67, no. 1 (Feb. 1974): 79–100.

Bourne, Kenneth. *Palmerston: The Early Years, 1784–1841*. London: Allen Lane, 1982.

Bradford, Gamaliel. "The Wife of Abraham Lincoln." *Harper's Monthly Magazine*, vol. 151 (Sept. 1925): 489–98.

Brauer, Kinley J. "The Appointment of Carl Schurz as Minister to Spain." *Mid-America* 56, no. 2 (April 1974): 75–84.

Brauer, Kinley J. "Gabriel García y Tassara and the American Civil War: a Spanish Perspective." *Civil War History* 21 (March 1975): 5–27.

Brauer, Kinley J. "Seward's 'Foreign War Panacea': An Interpretation." *New York History* 55 (Apr. 1974): 133–57.

Bray, Robert. "What Abraham Lincoln Read—an Evaluative and Annotated List." *Journal of the Abraham Lincoln Association* 28, no 2 (Summer 2007), http://hdl.handle.net/2027/spo.2629860.0028.204 (accessed Apr. 4, 2011).

Brooks, Noah. *Washington, D.C., in Lincoln's Time: A Memoir of the Civil War Era by the Newspaperman Who Knew Lincoln Best*. Herbert Mitgang, ed. Athens: University of Georgia Press, 1989.

Brooks, Noah. "Personal Recollections of Abraham Lincoln," *Harper's New Monthly Magazine* 31, no. 182 (July 1865): 226–27.

Brown, Caroline Owsley. "Springfield Society Before the War." *Journal of the Illinois State Historical Society* 15, no. 1–2 (Apr.–Jul. 1922): 477–500.

Browne, Francis Fisher. *The*

Every-Day Life of Abraham Lincoln. Lincoln: University of Nebraska Press, 1995.

Bryan, George S. *The Great American Myth.* New York: Carrick and Evans, 1940.

Bryan, Wilhelmus Bogart. *A History of the National Capital*, vol. 2, 1815–1878. New York: Macmillan, 1916.

Buchanan, Russell. "James A. McDougall: A Forgotten Senator." *California Historical Society Quarterly* 15, no. 3 (Sept. 1936): 199–212.

Buckingham, J. E., Sr. *Reminiscences and Souvenirs of the Assassination of Abraham Lincoln.* Washington, D.C.: Darby, 1894.

Buckle, George Earl. *The Life of Benjamin Disraeli, Earl of Beaconsfield.* New York: Macmillan, 1916.

Bullard, F. Lauriston. "When John F. Stuart Sought to Send Lincoln to South America." *Lincoln Herald* 47, nos. 3–4 (Oct.–Dec. 1945): 21, 29.

Burlingame, Michael. *Abraham Lincoln: A Life*, 2 vols. Baltimore: Johns Hopkins University Press, 2008.

Burlingame, Michael. *The Inner World of Abraham Lincoln.* Urbana: University of Illinois Press, 1994.

Burlingame, Michael, ed. *Abraham Lincoln: The Observations of John G. Nicolay and John Hay.* Carbondale: Southern Illinois University Press, 2007.

Burlingame, Michael, ed. *At Lincoln's Side: John Hay's Civil War Correspondence and Selected Writings.* Carbondale: Southern Illinois University Press, 2000.

Burlingame, Michael, and John R. Turner Ettlinger, eds. *Inside Lincoln's White House: The Complete Civil War Diary of John Hay.* Carbondale: Southern Illinois University Press, 1999.

Burlingame, Michael, ed. *Lincoln Observed: Civil War Dispatches of Noah Brooks.* Baltimore: Johns Hopkins University Press, 1998.

Burlingame, Michael. "Lincoln Spins the Press." In *Lincoln Reshapes the Presidency*, ed. Charles M. Hubbard, 65–78. Macon, Ga.: Mercer University Press, 2003.

Burlingame, Michael, ed. *Lincoln's Journalist: John Hay's Anonymous Writings for the Press, 1860–1864.* Carbondale: Southern Illinois University Press, 1998.

Burlingame, Michael. "Nicolay and Hay: Court Historians." *Journal of the Abraham Lincoln Association* 19, no. 1 (1998): 1–20.

Burlingame, Michael, ed. *An Oral History of Abraham Lincoln: John G. Nicolay's Interviews and Essays.* Carbondale: Southern Illinois University Press, 1996.

Burlingame, Michael, ed. *With Lincoln in the White House: Letters, Memoranda, and Other Writings of John G. Nicolay, 1860–1865.* Carbondale and Edwardsville: Southern Illinois University Press, 2000.

Burt, Silas W. "Lincoln on His Own Story-Telling." *Century Magazine* 73 (Feb. 1907): 499–502.

Busey, Samuel C. *Personal Reminiscences and Recollections of Forty-Six Years' Membership in the Medical Society of the District of Columbia, and Residence in This City.* Washington, D.C., 1895.

Butler, Benjamin F. *Butler's Book: Autobiography and Personal Reminiscences of Major-General Benjamin Butler.* Boston: A. M. Thayer, 1892.

Campanella, Richard. *Lincoln in New Orleans: The 1828–1831 Flatboat Voyages and Their Place in History.* Lafayette: University of Louisana at Lafayette Press, 2010.

Campbell, John A. *Reminiscences and Documents Relating to the Civil War During the Year 1865.* Baltimore: John Murphy, 1887.

Carroll, Daniel B. "Abraham Lincoln and the Minister of France, 1860–1863." *Lincoln Herald* 70, no. 3 (Fall 1968): 142–53.

Cartland, Fernando G. *Southern Heroes, or, the Friends in War Time.* Cambridge: Riverside Press, 1895.

Carwardine, Richard. *Lincoln: A Life of Purpose and Power.* New York: Vintage, 2007.

Carwardine, Richard. "Abraham Lincoln and the Fourth Estate: The White House and the Press During the American Civil War." *American Nineteenth Century History* 7, no. 1 (March 2006): 1–27.

Carwardine, Richard, and Jay Sexton, eds. *The Global Lincoln.* Oxford, U.K.: Oxford University Press, 2011.

Case, Lynn M., and Warren F. Spencer. *The United States and France: Civil War Diplomacy.* Philadelphia: University of Pennsylvania Press, 1970.

Chambrun, Marquis de. "Personal Recollections of Mr. Lincoln." *Scribner's* 13, no. 1 (Jan. 1893): 26–38.

Chapman, A. S. "The Boyhood of John Hay." *Century Magazine* 78 (July 1909): 444–54.

Chernow, Ron. *Alexander Hamilton.* New York: Penguin, 2004.

Christman, Henry M., ed. *The American Journalism of Marx and Engels: A Selection from the New York Daily Tribune.* New York: New American Library, 1966.

Clapp, Margaret. *Forgotten First Citizen: John Bigelow.* New York: Greenwood Press, 1968. Originally published in 1947.

Clark, Allen C. *Abraham Lincoln in the National Capital.* Washington, D.C.: W. F. Roberts, 1925.

Clay, Cassius Marcellus. *The Life of Cassius Marcellus Clay: Memoirs, Writings, and Speeches.* Cincinnati, Ohio: J. Fletcher Brennan, 1886.

Clinton, Catherine. *Mrs. Lincoln: A Life.* New York: HarperCollins, 2009.

Clymer, Kenton J. *John Hay: The Gentleman as Diplomat.* Ann Arbor: University of Michigan Press, 1975.

Connell, Brian. *Regina vs. Palmerston: The Correspondence Between Queen Victoria and Her Foreign and Prime Minister, 1837–1865.* Garden City, N.Y.: Doubleday, 1961.

Conway, Moncure Daniel. *Autobiography of Moncure Daniel Conway,* vol. 1. Boston: Houghton Mifflin, 1904.

Corneau, Octavia Roberts, ed. "A Girl in the Sixties: Excerpts from the Journal of Anna Ridgely (Mrs. James L. Hudson)." *Journal of the Illinois State Historical Society* 22, no. 3 (Oct. 1929): 401–46.

Cortada, James W. "A Case of

International Rivalry in Latin America: Spain's Occupation of Santo Domingo, 1853–1865." *Revista de Historia de América*, no. 82 (Jul.–Dec. 1976): 53–82.

Corti, Count Egon Caesar. *Maximilian and Charlotte of Mexico*. Catherine A. Phillips, trans. Hamden, Conn.: Archon Books, 1968.

Corwin, Edward S. *The President: Office and Powers*, 1787–1984, 5th rev. ed. New York: New York University Press, 1984.

Crook, D. P. *Diplomacy During the American Civil War*. New York: Wiley, 1975.

Crook, D. P. *The North, the South, and the Powers 1861–1865*. New York: Wiley, 1974.

Current, Richard N. "Comment." *Journal of the Abraham Lincoln Association* 12, no. 1 (1991): 17, http://hdl.handle.net/2027/spo.2629860.0012.106 (accessed Feb. 12, 2011).

Current, Richard N. "Fiction as History: A Review Essay." *Journal of Southern History* 52, no. 1 (Feb. 1986): 77–90.

Curtis, George William, ed. *The Correspondence of John Lothrop Motley*, 2 vols. New York: Harper & Brothers, 1889.

Dall, Caroline H. "Pioneering." *Atlantic Monthly* 19 (Apr. 1867): 403–17.

Dana, Charles A. *Recollections of the Civil War: With the Leaders at Washington and in the Field in the Sixties*. New York: Appleton, 1902.

Davis, Henry Winter. *Speeches and Addresses Delivered in the Congress of the United States, and on Several Public Occasions*. New York: Harper & Brothers, 1867.

Davis, Merrell R., and William H. Gilman, eds. *The Letters of Herman Melville*. New Haven, Conn.: Yale University Press, 1960.

Davis, Rodney O., and Douglas L. Wilson. *The Lincoln-Douglas Debates*. Urbana: Knox College Lincoln Studies Center and University of Illinois Press, 2008.

Dennett, Tyler. *John Hay: From Poetry to Politics*. New York: Dodd, Mead, 1933.

Dennett, Tyler, ed. *Lincoln and the Civil War in the Diaries and Letters of John Hay*. New York: Dodd, Mead, 1939.

Dickens, Charles. *American Notes for General Circulation*, vol. 1. London: Chapman & Hall, 1842.

Donald, David, ed. *Inside Lincoln's Cabinet: The Civil War Diaries of Salmon P. Chase*. New York: Longmans, Green, 1954.

Donald, David Herbert. *Charles Sumner and the Rights of Man*. New York: Knopf, 1970.

Donald, David Herbert. *Lincoln*. New York: Simon & Schuster, 1995.

Donald, David Herbert. *Lincoln Reconsidered: Essays on the Civil War Era*, 3rd ed. New York: Vintage, 2001.

Donald, David Herbert. *Lincoln's Herndon*. New York: Knopf, 1948.

Donald, David Herbert. *"We Are Lincoln Men": Abraham Lincoln and His Friends*. New York: Simon & Schuster, 2003.

Donner, Barbara. "Carl Schurz as Office Seeker." *Wisconsin Magazine of History* 20, no. 2 (Dec. 1936): 127–42.

Donner, Barbara. "Carl Schurz the Diplomat." *The Wisconsin Magazine of History* 20, no. 3 (March 1937): 291–309.

Eaton, John. *Grant, Lincoln and the Freedmen: Reminiscences of the Civil War.* 1907. Reprint, New York: Negro Universities Press, 1969.

Eisenhower, John S. D. *So Far from God: The U.S. War with Mexico, 1846–1848.* New York: Doubleday, 1989.

Ellison, Mary L. *Support for Secession: Lancashire and the American Civil War.* Chicago: University of Chicago Press, 1972.

Erickson, Gary Lee. "The Last Years of William Henry Herndon." *Journal of the Illinois State Historical Society* 67, no. 1 (Feb. 1974): 101–19.

Faust, Drew Gilpin. *This Republic of Suffering: Death and the American Civil War.* New York: Vintage, 2008.

Faust, Patricia L. *Historical Times Illustrated Encyclopedia of the Civil War.* New York: Harper & Row, 1986.

Fehrenbacher, Don E., and Virginia Fehrenbacher, eds. *Recollected Words of Abraham Lincoln.* Stanford, Calif.: Stanford University Press, 1996.

Ferguson, Niall. *Empire: The Rise and Demise of the British World Order and the Lessons for Global Power.* New York: Basic Books, 2003.

Ferris, Norman. "Abraham Lincoln and the *Trent* Affair." *Lincoln Herald* 69 (1967): 131–35.

Ferris, Norman. *Desperate Diplomacy: William H. Seward's Foreign Policy, 1861.* Knoxville: University of Tennessee Press, 1976.

Ferris, Norman B. "Lincoln and Seward in Civil War Diplomacy: Their Relationship at the Outset Reexamined." *Journal of the Abraham Lincoln Association*, vol. 12, no. 1 (1991): 61, http://hdl.handle.net/2027/spo.2629860.0012.105 (accessed Feb. 12, 2011).

Ferris, Norman B. *The* Trent *Affair: A Diplomatic Crisis.* Knoxville: University of Tennessee Press, 1977.

Filon, Augustin. *Recollections of the Empress Eugénie.* London: Cassell and Company, 1920.

Findley, Paul. *A. Lincoln: The Crucible of Congress.* Jacksonville, Ill.: Findley Books, 1979.

Fischer, LeRoy H. *Lincoln's Gadfly, Adam Gurowski.* Norman, Oklahoma: University of Oklahoma Press, 1964.

Fitzmaurice, Lord Edmond. *The Life of Granville George Leveson Gower, Second Earl Granville, 1815–1891,* vol. 1. New York: Longmans, Green, 1905.

Foner, Eric. *The Fiery Trial: Abraham Lincoln and American Slavery.* New York: Norton, 2010.

Foner, Eric. *Free Soil, Free Labor, Free Men: The Ideology of the Republican Party Before the Civil War.* New York: Oxford University Press, 1970.

Foner, Eric, ed. *Our Lincoln: New Perspectives on Lincoln and His World.* New York: Norton, 2008.

Foner, Philip S. *British Labor and the American Civil War.* New York: Holmes & Meier, 1981.

Foote, Shelby. *The Civil War*, vol. 1, *Fort Sumter to Perryville*. New York: Vintage, 1986.

Ford, Worthington Chauncy, ed. *A Cycle of Adams Letters, 1861–1865*, 2 vols. Boston: Houghton Mifflin, 1920.

Foreman, Amanda. *A World on Fire: An Epic History of Two Nations Divided*. London: Allen Lane, 2010.

Franklin, John Hope. *The Emancipation Proclamation*. Garden City, N.Y.: Doubleday, 1963.

Freidel, Frank, ed. *Union Pamphlets of the Civil War, 1861–1865*, vol. 2. Cambridge, Mass.: Belknap Press, 1967.

French, Benjamin Brown. *Witness to the Young Republic: A Yankee's Journal, 1828–1870*, eds. Donald B. Cole and John J. McDonough. Hanover, N.H.: University Press of New England, 1989.

Frothingham, Paul Revere. *Edward Everett: Orator and Statesman*. Boston: Houghton Mifflin, 1925.

Fuller, John Douglas Pitts. *The Movement for the Acquisition of All Mexico, 1846–1848*. Baltimore: Johns Hopkins Press, 1936.

Gabriel, Mary. *Love and Capital: Karl and Jenny Marx and the Birth of a Revolution*. New York: Little, Brown, 2011.

Gilder, J. L., and J. B. Gilder, eds. *Authors at Home: Personal and Biographical Sketches of Well-Known American Writers*. New York: Cassell, 1889.

Glicksberg, Charles I. "Henry Adams Reports on a Trades-Union Meeting." *New England Quarterly* 15, no. 4 (Dec. 1942): 724–28.

Goldwert, Marvin. "Matías Romero and Congressional Opposition to Seward's Policy Toward the French Intervention in Mexico." *The Americas* 22, no. 1 (July 1965): 22–40.

Goncourt, Edmond and Jules de. *Pages from the Goncourt Journals*, ed. Robert Baldick. New York: New York Review, 2006.

Good, Timothy S., ed. *We Saw Lincoln Shot: One Hundred Eyewitness Accounts*. Jackson: University Press of Mississippi, 1997.

Goodwin, Doris Kearns. *Team of Rivals: The Political Genius of Abraham Lincoln*. New York: Simon & Schuster, 2005.

Gouverneur, Marian. *As I Remember: Recollections of American Society during the Nineteenth Century*. New York: Appleton, 1911.

Graebner, Norman A. "Northern Diplomacy and European Neutrality." In *Why the North Won the Civil War*. David Herbert Donald, ed. New York: Simon & Schuster, 1996.

Green, Constance McLaughlin. *Washington: A History of the Capital, 1800–1950*. Princeton, N.J.: Princeton University Press, 1962.

Greenberg, Amy S. *A Wicked War: Polk, Clay, Lincoln, and the 1846 U.S. Invasion of Mexico*. New York: Knopf, 2012.

Greenleaf, Richard. "British Labor Against American Slavery." *Science and Society* 17, no. 1 (Winter 1953): 42–58.

Greenleaf, Richard, and Royden Harrison. "Marx and the St. James Hall Meeting." *Science and Society* 28, no. 3 (Summer 1964): 323–25.

Greeley, Horace. *Recollections of a Busy Life.* New York: J. B. Ford, 1868.

Greenblatt, Stephen, ed. *The Norton Anthology of English Literature.* New York: Norton, 2006.

Grimsley, Elizabeth Todd. "Six Months in the White House." *Journal of the Illinois State Historical Society* 19, no. 3–4 (Oct. 1926–Jan. 1927): 43–73.

Guelzo, Allen. *Abraham Lincoln: Redeemer President.* Grand Rapids, Mich.: Eerdmans, 1999.

Guelzo, Allen C. *The Emancipation Proclamation: The End of Slavery in America.* New York: Simon & Schuster, 2004.

Guérard, Albert Léon. *Reflections on the Napoleonic Legend.* New York: Charles Scribner's Sons, 1924.

Gurowski, Adam. *Diary,* vols. 1 and 2. New York: Carleton, 1864.

Gurowski, Adam. *Diary: 1863–'64–'65.* Washington, D.C.: Morrison, 1866.

Hale, Edward Everett. *Memories of a Hundred Years,* vol. 2. New York: Macmillan, 1903.

Hale, William Harlan. *Horace Greeley: Voice of the People.* New York: Harper & Brothers, 1950.

Halstead, Murat. *Caucuses of 1860: A History of the National Political Conventions of the Current Presidential Campaign.* Columbus: Follett, Foster and Co., 1860.

Hanna, Alfred J., and Kathryn A. Hanna. *Napoleon III and Mexico: American Triumph over Monarchy.* Chapel Hill: University of North Carolina Press, 1971.

Harper, Robert S. *Lincoln and the Press.* New York: McGraw Hill, 1951.

Harris, William C. "The Hampton Roads Peace Conference: A Final Test of Lincoln's Presidential Leadership." *Journal of the Abraham Lincoln Association* 21, issue 1 (Winter 2000).

Harrison, Royden. *Before the Socialists: Studies in Labor and Politics, 1861–1881.* London: Routledge and Kegan Paul, 1965.

Harrison, Royden. "E. S. Beesly and Karl Marx." *International Review of Social History* 4 (1959): 22–58.

Hart, Basil H. Liddell. *Sherman: Soldier, Realist, American.* Westport, Conn.: Greenwood, 1958.

Haslip, Joan. *The Crown of Mexico: Maximilian and His Empress Carlota.* New York: Holt, Rinehart & Winston, 1971.

Hay, John. *Addresses of John Hay.* New York: Century/DeVinne Press, 1906.

Hay, John. "Ellsworth." *Atlantic Monthly* 8, no. 65 (July 1861): 119–25.

Hay, John. *Letters of John Hay and Extracts from Diary,* 3 vols. Washington, D.C.: printed but not published, 1908.

Hay, Melba Porter, ed. *The Papers of Henry Clay,* vol. 10. Lexington: University Press of Kentucky, 1991.

Heidler, David S., and Jeanne T. Heidler, eds. *Encyclopedia of the American Civil War: A Political, Social, and Military History.* New York: Norton, 2002.

Heidler, David S., and Jeanne T. Heidler. *Henry Clay: The Essential American.* New York: Random House, 2010.

Helm, Katherine. *The True Story of Mary, Wife of Lincoln.* New York: Harper & Brothers, 1928.

Henderson, Daniel. *The Hidden Coasts: A Biography of Admiral Charles Wilkes*. Westport, Conn.: Greenwood, 1953.

Henig, Gerald S. *Henry Winter Davis: Antebellum and Civil War Congressman from Maryland*. New York: Twayne, 1973.

Herndon, William H. *Address on Free Trade vs. Protection*. Springfield, Ill. January 28, 1870. Pamphlet.

Herndon, William H. "Analysis of the Character of Abraham Lincoln: A Lecture by William H. Herndon." *Abraham Lincoln Quarterly* 1, no. 7 (Sept. 1941): 343–83.

Herndon, William H. "Facts Illustrative of Mr. Lincoln's Patriotism and Statesmanship: A Lecture by William H. Herndon." *Abraham Lincoln Quarterly* 3 (Mar. 1944–Dec. 1945): 178–203.

Herndon, William Henry, and Jesse W. Weik. *Herndon's Life of Lincoln*. Cleveland: World, 1949.

Herr, Pamela, and Mary Lee Spence, eds. *The Letters of Jessie Benton Frémont*. Urbana and Chicago: University of Illinois Press, 1993.

Herring, George. *From Colony to Superpower: U.S. Foreign Relations Since 1776*. Oxford, U.K.: Oxford University Press, 2008.

Hertz, Emanuel. *The Hidden Lincoln: From the Letters and Papers of William H. Herndon*. New York: Blue Ribbon Books, 1940.

Hoar, George Frisbie, ed. *Charles Sumner: His Complete Works*, vol. 8. Boston: Lee and Shepard, 1900.

Hofstadter, Richard. *The American Political Tradition*. New York: Vintage, 1989.

Holzer, Harold. "If I Had Another Face, Do You Think I'd Wear This One?" *American Heritage* 34, no. 2 (Feb.–Mar. 1983): 57–63.

Holzer, Harold. *Lincoln President-Elect: Abraham Lincoln and the Great Secession Winter 1860–1861*. New York: Simon & Schuster, 2008.

Howe, Daniel Walker. *What Hath God Wrought: The Transformation of America, 1815–1848*. New York: Oxford University Press, 2007.

Howe, Daniel Walker. "Why Abraham Lincoln Was a Whig." *Journal of the Abraham Lincoln Association* 16, no. 1 (Winter 1995): 26, http://hdl.handle.net/2027/spo.2629860.0016.105 (accessed Apr. 4, 2011).

Howe, M. A. DeWolfe. *The Life and Letters of George Bancroft*, vol. 2. New York: Scribner's, 1908.

"Interchange: The Global Lincoln." *Journal of American History* 96, no. 2 (Sept. 2009): 462–99.

Jenkins, Brian. *Britain and the War for the Union*, vol. 1. Montreal: McGill-Queen's University Press, 1974.

Jerrold, Blanchard. *Life of Napoleon III*, 4 vols. London: Longmans, Green, 1874.

Johannsen, Robert. *To the Halls of the Montezumas: The Mexican War in the American Imagination*. New York: Oxford University Press, 1985.

Johnson, Patricia. "Sensitivity and Civil War: The Selected Diaries and Papers, 1858–1866, of Frances Adeline [Fanny] Seward." Ph.D. diss., University of Rochester, 1964.

Jones, Howard. *Abraham Lincoln and a New Birth of Freedom: The Union and Slavery in the Diplomacy of the Civil War.* Lincoln: University of Nebraska Press, 1999.

Jones, Howard. *Blue and Gray Diplomacy: A History of Union and Confederate Foreign Relations.* Chapel Hill: University of North Carolina Press, 2010.

Jones, Howard. *Union in Peril: The Crisis over British Intervention in the Civil War.* Lincoln: University of Nebraska Press, 1992.

Keckley, Elizabeth. *Behind the Scenes: Thirty Years a Slave, and Four Years in the White House.* New York: G. W. Carleton, 1868.

Kempton, Murray. "K. Marx, Reporter." *New York Review of Books.* June 15, 1967.

Kennan, George F. "On American Principles." *Foreign Affairs*, Mar.–Apr. 1995: 116–26.

Kennedy, Paul. *The Rise and Fall of the Great Powers.* London: Unwin Hyman, 1988.

Kissinger, Henry. *Diplomacy.* New York: Simon & Schuster, 1994.

LaFeber, Walter. *The American Age: United States Foreign Policy at Home and Abroad Since 1763.* New York: Norton, 1994.

LaFeber, Walter. *The New Empire: An Interpretation of American Expansion, 1860–1898.* Ithaca, N.Y.: Cornell University Press, 1963.

Lair, John. *Songs Lincoln Loved.* New York: Duell, Sloan & Pearce, 1954.

Lamon, Ward Hill. *Recollections of Abraham Lincoln, 1847–1865.* Chicago: A. C. McClurg, 1895.

Laugel, Auguste. *The United States During the Civil War.* Bloomington: Indiana University Press, 1961.

Lehrman, Lewis E. *Lincoln at Peoria: The Turning Point.* Mechanicsburg, Pa.: Stackpole Books, 2008.

The Lincoln Log: A Daily Chronology of the Life of Abraham Lincoln. The Lincoln Sesquicentennial Commission and the Papers of Abraham Lincoln, http://www.thelincolnlog.org (accessed Aug. 14, 2012).

Lippmann, Walter. *U.S. Foreign Policy: Shield of the Republic.* Boston: Little, Brown, 1943.

Logan, Kevin L. "The *Bee-Hive* Newspaper and British Working Class Attitudes Toward the American Civil War." *Civil War History* 22 (Dec. 1976): 337-48.

Luebke, Frederick C., ed. *Ethnic Voters and the Election of Lincoln.* Lincoln, Nebraska: University of Nebraska Press, 1971.

Luthin, Reinhard H. "Lincoln and the Tariff." *American Historical Review* 49, no. 4 (July 1944): 609–29.

Lutz, Ralph Haswell. "Rudolph Schleiden and the Visit to Richmond, April 25, 1861." *Annual Report of the American Historical Association for the Year 1915.* Washington, D.C.: Smithsonian Institution Press, 1917.

Macartney, Clarence Edward. *Lincoln and His Cabinet.* New York: Scribner's, 1931.

Magness, Phillip W., and Sebastian N. Page. *Colonization After Emancipation: Lincoln and the Movement for Black Resettlement.* Columbia: University of Missouri Press, 2011.

Mahin, Dean B. *One War at a Time: The International Dimensions of the American Civil War.* Washington, D.C.: Brassey's, 1999.

Martin, Theodore. *The Life of His Royal Highness the Prince Consort,* vol. 5. London: Smith, Elder, 1880.

Marx, Karl, and Frederick Engels. *The Civil War in the U.S.* London: Lawrence, 1937.

Marx, Karl. *Dispatches for the "New York Tribune": Selected Journalism of Karl Marx.* London: Penguin, 2007.

Marx, Karl, and Frederick Engels. *Karl Marx, Frederick Engels: Collected Works,* vols. 1, 3, 26, 31, 38-42. New York: International Publishers, 1975.

Maxwell, Sir Herbert. *The Life and Letters of George William Frederick, Fourth Earl of Clarendon,* vol. 2. London: Edward Arnold, 1913.

May, Robert E., ed. *The Union, the Confederacy, and the Atlantic Rim.* West Lafayette, Ind.: Purdue University Press, 1995.

McCormack, Thomas J., ed. *Memoirs of Gustave Koerner, 1809–1896,* vol. 2. Cedar Rapids, Iowa: Torch Press, 1909.

McDougall, Walter. *Promised Land, Crusader State.* Boston: Houghton Mifflin, 1997.

McDougall, Walter. *Throes of Democracy: The American Civil War Era, 1829–1877.* New York: HarperCollins, 2008.

McGann, Jerome J., ed. *Lord Byron: The Complete Poetical Works,* vol. 2. Oxford, U.K.: Clarendon Press, 1980.

McLellan, David. *Karl Marx: His Life and Thought.* New York: Harper & Row, 1973.

McLellan, David, ed. *Karl Marx: Interviews and Recollections.* Totowa, N.J.: Barnes & Noble Books, 1981.

McPherson, Edward. *The Political History of the United States of America During the Great Rebellion.* Washington, D.C.: Philp & Solomons, 1865.

McPherson, James M. *Abraham Lincoln and the Second American Revolution.* New York: Oxford University Press, 1990.

McPherson, James M. *Battle Cry of Freedom: The Civil War Era.* Oxford, U.K.: Oxford University Press, 1988.

McPherson, James M. *Tried by War: Abraham Lincoln as Commander in Chief.* New York: Penguin, 2008.

Mead, Walter Russell. *Special Providence: American Foreign Policy and How It Changed the World.* New York: Knopf, 2002.

Mearns, David Chambers. *Largely Lincoln.* New York: St. Martin's, 1961.

Menand, Louis. *The Metaphysical Club: A Story of Ideas in America.* New York: Farrar, Straus & Giroux, 2001.

Mencken, H. L. *Prejudices: Third Series.* New York: Knopf, 1922.

Merk, Frederick. *Manifest Destiny and Mission in American History.* New York: Vintage, 1963.

Merry, Robert W. *A Country of Vast Designs: James K. Polk, the Mexican War, and the Conquest of the American Continent.* New York: Simon & Schuster, 2009.

Messages of the President of the United States on the Subject of the Mexican War. Washington, D.C.: Wendell and Van Benthuysen, 1848.

Milne, A. Taylor. "The Lyons-Seward Treaty of 1862." *American Historical Review* 38, no. 3 (Apr. 1933): 511–25.

Mitgang, Herbert, ed. *Abraham Lincoln: A Press Portrait*. Chicago: Quadrangle Books, 1971.

Monaghan, Jay. *A Diplomat in Carpet Slippers: Abraham Lincoln Deals with Foreign Affairs*. Lincoln: University of Nebraska Press, 1997.

Monypenny, William Flavelle. *The Life of Benjamin Disraeli, Earl of Beaconsfield*, vol. 2. New York: Macmillan, 1913.

Moore, Frank, ed. *Rebellion Record: A Diary of American Events*, vol. 11. New York: Arno, 1977.

Moore, R. Laurence. *European Socialists and the American Promised Land*. New York: Oxford University Press, 1970.

Mott, Frank Luther. *American Journalism: A History of Newspapers in the United States Through 250 Years, 1690–1940*. New York: Macmillan, 1940.

Neely, Mark E., Jr. *The Last Best Hope of Earth: Abraham Lincoln and the Promise of America*. Cambridge, Mass.: Harvard University Press, 1993.

Neely, Mark E., Jr. "Lincoln and the Mexican War: An Argument by Analogy." *Civil War History* 24, no. 1 (Mar. 1978): 5–25.

Neely, Mark E., Jr. "War and Partisanship: What Lincoln Learned from James K. Polk." *Journal of the Illinois State Historical Society* 74, no. 3 (Autumn 1981): 199–216.

Nevins, Allan. *American Press Opinion: Washington to Coolidge*, vol. 1. Port Washington, N.Y.: Kennikat Press, 1928.

Nevins, Allan. *The War for the Union*, vols. 1 and 2. New York: Scribner's, 1960.

Newton, Joseph Fort. *Lincoln and Herndon*. Cedar Rapids, Iowa: Torch Press, 1910.

Nichols, Clifton M. *Life of Abraham Lincoln*. New York: Mast, Crowell & Kirkpatrick, 1896.

Nicolay, Helen. *Lincoln's Secretary: A Biography of John G. Nicolay*. New York: Longmans, Green, and Co., 1949.

Nicolay, Helen. *Personal Traits of Abraham Lincoln*. New York: Century, 1912.

Nicolay, John G., and John Hay. *Abraham Lincoln: A History*, 10 vols. New York: Century, 1917.

Niebuhr, Reinhold. *The Irony of American History*. Chicago: University of Chicago Press, 1952.

Niebuhr, Reinhold. *Moral Man and Immoral Society*. Louisville, Ky.: Westminster, 2001.

Nye, Joseph. *Soft Power: The Means to Success in World Politics*. New York: PublicAffairs, 2004.

Oates, Stephen B. *With Malice Toward None: The Life of Abraham Lincoln*. HarperCollins E-books, 2009.

Obama, Barack. *The Audacity of Hope: Thoughts on Reclaiming the American Dream*. New York: Three Rivers Press, 2006.

O'Toole, Patricia. *The Five of Hearts: An Intimate Portrait of Henry Adams and His Friends 1880–1918*. New York: Simon & Schuster, 1990.

Padover, Saul K., ed. *Karl Marx on America and the Civil War*. New York: McGraw-Hill, 1972.

Paléologue, Maurice. *The Tragic Empress: Intimate Conversations with the Empress Eugénie,*

1901–1911. London: Thornton Butterworth.

Paludan, Phillip Shaw. *The Presidency of Abraham Lincoln*. Lawrence: University Press of Kansas, 1994.

Paolino, Ernest. *The Foundations of the American Empire: William Henry Seward and U.S. Foreign Policy*. Ithaca, N.Y.: Cornell, 1973.

Papers Relating to Foreign Affairs, 1861, vol. 1. Washington, D.C.: Government Printing Office, 1861.

Papers Relating to Foreign Affairs, 1862. Washington, D.C.: Government Printing Office, 1862.

Papers Relating to Foreign Affairs, 1863, vols. 1 and 2. Washington, D.C.: Government Printing Office, 1864.

Papers Relating to Foreign Affairs, 1864, vol. 3. Washington, D.C.: Government Printing Office, 1865.

Papers Relating to Foreign Affairs, 1865, vol. 1. Washington, D.C.: Government Printing Office, 1866.

Parker, Hershel. *Herman Melville: A Biography*, vol. 2, 1851–1891. Baltimore: Johns Hopkins University Press, 2002.

Parton, James. *The Life of Horace Greeley, Editor of the New York Tribune, from His Birth to Present Time*. Boston: Houghton Mifflin, 1885.

Pease, Theodore Calvin, and James G. Randall, eds. *The Diary of Orville Hickman Browning*, vol. 1, 1850–1864. Springfield: Illinois State Historical Library, 1925.

Pendel, Thomas F. *Thirty-Six Years in the White House*. Washington, D.C.: Neale, 1902.

Perkins, Dexter. *A History of the Monroe Doctrine*. Boston: Little, Brown, 1955. Originally published in 1941.

Perkins, Dexter. *The Monroe Doctrine, 1826–1867*. Baltimore: Johns Hopkins, 1933.

Perkins, Fred B. *The Picture and the Men*. New York: A. J. Johnson, 1867.

Peterson, Merrill D. *Lincoln in American Memory*. New York: Oxford University Press, 1994.

Phillips, Wendell. *Speeches, Lectures, and Letters*. Boston: James Redpath, 1863.

Pierce, Edward L. *Memoir and Letters of Charles Sumner*, vol. 4. New York: Arno/New York Times, 1969.

Planché, J. R. *The Recollections and Reflections of J. R. Planché*, vol. 2. London: Tinsley Brothers, 1872.

Poore, Ben Perley. *Perley's Reminiscences of Sixty Years in the National Metropolis*, vol. 2. Philadelphia: Hubbard Brothers, 1886.

Porter, Andrew, ed. *The Oxford History of the British Empire: The Nineteenth Century*, vol. 3. Oxford, U.K.: Oxford University Press, 1999.

Porter, David Dixon. *Incidents and Anecdotes of the Civil War*. New York: Appleton, 1885.

Porter, Horace. *Campaigning with Grant*. New York: Century, 1897.

Post, Albert. "Lincoln and the Reverend Dr. James Smith." *Journal of the Illinois State Historical Society* 35, no. 4 (Dec. 1942): 397–99.

Pratt, Harry E., ed. *Concerning Mr. Lincoln: In Which Abraham Lincoln Is Pictured as He Appeared to Letter Writers of His Time*.

Springfield, Ill.: Abraham Lincoln Association, 1944.

Ramsay, David. *The Life of George Washington*. New York: Hopkins & Seymour, 1807.

Randall, J. G. *Lincoln the Liberal Statesman*. London: Eyre & Spottiswoode, 1947.

Randall, J. G. *Lincoln the President*, vol. 2. New York: Dodd, Mead, 1945.

Randall, Ruth Painter. *Mary Lincoln: Biography of a Marriage*. Boston: Little, Brown, 1953.

Raymond, Henry J. *The Life and Public Services of Abraham Lincoln*. New York: Derby & Miller, 1865.

Remini, Robert V. *Henry Clay: Statesman for the Union*. New York: Norton, 1991.

Rice, Allen Thorndike, ed. *Reminiscences of Abraham Lincoln by Distinguished Men of His Time*. New York: North American Pub. Co., 1886.

Richardson, Edward H. *Cassius Marcellus Clay: Firebrand of Freedom*. Lexington: University Press of Kentucky, 1976.

Riddle, Donald W. *Congressman Abraham Lincoln*. Urbana: University of Illinois Press, 1957.

Riddle, Donald W. *Lincoln Runs for Congress*. New Brunswick, N.J.: Rutgers University Press, 1948.

Ridley, Jasper. *Lord Palmerston*. New York: Dutton, 1970.

Ridley, Jasper. *Maximilian and Juarez*. New York: Ticknor & Fields, 1992.

Ridley, Jasper. *Napoleon III and Eugénie*. New York: Viking, 1980.

Robertson, James Rood. *A Kentuckian at the Court of the Tsars: The Ministry of Cassius Marcellus Clay to Russia, 1861–1862 and 1863–1869*. Berea College, Kentucky: Berea College Press, 1935.

Rogers, James Edwin Thorold, ed. *Speeches on Questions of Public Policy by the Right Honourable John Bright, M.P.* London: Macmillan, 1878.

Rosebault, Charles J. *When Dana Was the Sun: A Story of Personal Journalism*. Freeport, N.Y.: Books for Libraries Press, 1969.

Rowley, James A. "Captain Nathaniel Gordon, the Only American Executed for Violating the Slave Trade Laws." *Civil War History* 39, no. 3 (Sept. 1993): 216–24.

Rumbold, Sir Horace. *Recollections of a Diplomatist*, vol. 2. London: Edward Arnold, 1902.

Runkle, Gerald. "Marx and the American Civil War." *Comparative Studies in Society and History* 6 (1964): 117–41.

Russell, William Howard. *My Diary North and South*. Boston: Burnham, 1863.

Sandburg, Carl. *Abraham Lincoln: The Prairie Years and the War Years*. New York: Harcourt, 1954.

Sandburg, Carl, and Paul Angle. *Mary Lincoln: Wife and Widow*. New York: Harcourt, Brace, 1932.

Savage, John. *The Life and Public Services of Andrew Johnson*. New York: Derby & Miller, 1866.

Schafer, Joseph, ed. *Intimate Letters of Carl Schurz, 1841–1869*. Madison: State Historical Society of Wisconsin, 1928.

Schlesinger, Arthur M., Jr. *The Cycles*

of American History. Franklin Center, Pa.: Franklin Library, 1986.

Schlesinger, Arthur M., Jr. *The Imperial Presidency.* Boston: Houghton Mifflin, 1973.

Schofield, John M. *Forty-Six Years in the Army.* New York: Century, 1897.

Schoonover, Thomas David. *Dollars Over Dominion: The Triumph of Liberalism in Mexican–United States Relations, 1861–1867.* Baton Rouge and London: Louisiana State University Press, 1978.

Schoonover, Thomas D., ed. *Mexican Lobby: Matías Romero in Washington 1861–1867.* Lexington: University Press of Kentucky, 1986.

Schurz, Carl. "Abraham Lincoln." *The Atlantic Monthly* 67, no. 404 (June 1891): 721–50.

Schurz, Carl. *The Reminiscences of Carl Schurz,* vols. 1 and 2. New York: McClure, 1907.

Schurz, Carl. *Speeches, Correspondence and Political Papers of Carl Schurz.* Frederic Bancroft, ed. vol. 1, New York: G. P. Putnam's Sons, 1913.

Segal, Charles M., ed. *Conversations with Lincoln.* New York: Putnam's, 1961; New Brunswick, N.J.: Transaction, 2002.

Seitz, Don C. *Lincoln the Politician: How the Rail-Splitter and Flatboatman Played the Great American Game.* New York: Coward-McCann, 1931.

Seward, Frederick William. *Reminiscences of a War-Time Statesman and Diplomat.* New York: Putnam's, 1916.

Seward, Frederick W. *Seward at Washington, as Senator and Secretary of State: A Memoir of His Life, with Selections from His Letters, 1846–1861.* New York: Derby & Miller, 1891.

Seward, Frederick W. *Seward at Washington, as Senator and Secretary of State: A Memoir of His Life, with Selections from His Letters, 1861–1872.* New York: Derby & Miller, 1891.

Seward, Frederick W. *William H. Seward: An Autobiography, From 1801–1834.* New York: Derby & Miller, 1891.

Seward, William H. *Life and Public Services of John Quincy Adams.* Port Washington, N.Y.: Kennikat Press, 1971.

Sexton, Jay. *Debtor Diplomacy: Finance and American Foreign Relations in the Civil War Era, 1837–1873.* Oxford, U.K.: Clarendon Press, 2005.

Sexton, Jay. *The Monroe Doctrine: Empire and Nation in Nineteenth-Century America.* New York: Hill and Wang, 2011.

Shenk, Joshua Wolf. *Lincoln's Melancholy: How Depression Challenged a President and Fueled His Greatness.* Boston: Houghton Mifflin, 2005.

Sheridan, Philip H. *Personal Memoirs of P. H. Sheridan,* vol. 2. New York: Webster, 1888.

Sherrill, Anne Hummel. "John Hay: Shield of Union." Ph.D diss., University of California–Berkeley, 1966.

Sherrill, Anne Hummel, and Howard I. Kushner. *John Milton Hay: The Union of Poetry and Politics.* Boston: Twayne, 1977.

Silbey, Joel H. " 'Always a Whig in Politics': The Partisan Life of Abraham Lincoln." *Journal of the Abraham Lincoln Association* 8 no. 1 (1986): 43, http://hdl.handle.net/2027/spo.2629860.0008.105 (accessed Apr. 4, 2011).

Simon, John Y., ed. *The Papers of Ulysses S. Grant,* vol. 12. Carbondale: Southern Illinois University Press, 1984.

Simpson, F. A. *The Rise of Louis Napoleon.* London: John Murray, 1909.

Skelton, Oscar Douglas. *The Life and Times of Sir Alexander Tilloch Galt.* Toronto: Oxford University Press, 1920.

Smith, Donnal V. "The Influence of the Foreign-Born of the Northwest in the Election of 1860." *Mississippi Valley Historical Review* 19, no. 2 (Sept. 1932): 192–204.

Smith, Justin H. *The War with Mexico,* 2 vols. New York: Macmillan, 1919.

Smith, W. H. C. *Napoleon III.* New York: St. Martin's Press, 1972.

Smith, William H. C. *The Bonapartes: The History of a Dynasty.* Hambledon and London: Hambledon Continuum, 2005.

Southgate, Donald. *The Most English Minister: The Policies and Politics of Palmerston.* New York: St. Martin's Press, 1966.

Sowle, Patrick. "A Reappraisal of Seward's Memorandum of April 1, 1861, to Lincoln." *Journal of Southern History* 33, no. 2 (May 1967): 234–39.

Spargo, John. *Karl Marx: His Life and Work.* New York: Huebsch, 1910.

Spencer, Warren F. "The Jewett-Greeley Affair: A Private Scheme for French Mediation in the American Civil War." *New York History* 51, no. 3 (Apr. 1970): 238–68.

Stahr, Walter. *Seward: Lincoln's Indispensable Man.* New York: Simon & Schuster, 2012.

Stanton, Henry B. *Random Recollections.* New York: Harper & Brothers, 1887.

Steere, Edward. *The Wilderness Campaign.* Harrisburg, Pa.: Stackpole, 2001.

Stephens, Alexander H. *A Constitutional View of the Late War Between the States; Its Causes, Character, Conduct and Results,* vol. 2. Philadelphia: National Pub. Co., 1870.

Stoddard, William O. *Inside the White House in War Times: Memoirs and Reports of Lincoln's Secretary,* Michael Burlingame, ed. Lincoln: University of Nebraska Press, 2000.

Stryker, Lloyd Paul. *Andrew Johnson: A Study in Courage.* New York: Macmillan, 1930.

Taft, Charles Sabin. "Abraham Lincoln's Last Hours." *Century Magazine* 45, no. 4 (Feb. 1893): 634–36.

Tarbell, Ida M. *The Life of Abraham Lincoln,* vol. 1. New York: Lincoln Memorial Association, 1895.

Taylor, John M. *William Henry Seward: Lincoln's Right Hand.* New York: HarperCollins, 1991.

Temple, Wayne C. *Mary Todd Lincoln as a "Sailor."* Pamphlet, reprinted from the Fall 1959 *Lincoln Herald.*

Thayer, William Roscoe. *The Life of John Hay,* 2 vols. Boston: Houghton Mifflin, 1915.

Thomas, Benjamin P. *Abraham*

Lincoln: A Biography. New York: Knopf, 1953.

Thomas, Benjamin P. *Portrait for Posterity: Lincoln and His Biographers.* New Brunswick, N.J.: Rutgers University Press, 1947.

Thomas, Evan, and Richard Wolffe. "Obama's Lincoln." *Newsweek,* Nov. 15, 2008.

Thomas, Evan. *The War Lovers: Roosevelt, Lodge, Hearst, and the Rush to Empire,* 1898. New York: Little, Brown, 2010.

Thomas, John L., ed. *Abraham Lincoln and the American Political Tradition.* Amherst: University of Massachusetts Press, 1986.

Townsend, William H. *The Boarding School of Mary Todd Lincoln.* Lexington, Ky.: Privately printed, 1941.

Townsend, William H. *Lincoln and His Wife's Hometown.* Indianapolis: Bobbs-Merrill, 1929.

Townsend, William H. *Lincoln and the Bluegrass: Slavery and Civil War in Kentucky.* Lexington: University of Kentucky Press, 1955.

Traubel, Horace. *With Walt Whitman in Camden,* vols. 1–4. Boston: Small, Maynard, 1906.

Trefousse, Hans L. *Carl Schurz: A Biography.* Knoxville: University of Tennessee Press, 1982.

Trefousse, Hans L. *Lincoln's Decision for Emancipation.* Philadelphia: J. B. Lippincott, 1975.

Tucker, Robert, ed. *The Marx-Engels Reader.* New York: Norton, 1978.

Tulard, Jean, ed. *Dictionnaire du Second Empire.* Paris: Fayard, 1995.

Turner, Justin G., and Linda Levitt Turner. *Mary Todd Lincoln: Her Life and Letters.* New York: Knopf, 1972.

Tyrner-Tyrnauer, A. R. *Lincoln and the Emperors.* London: Rupert Hart-Davis, 1962.

Van Deusen, Glyndon. *William Henry Seward.* New York: Oxford University Press, 1967.

Vidal, Gore. *Empire: A Novel.* New York: Random House, 1987.

Vidal, Gore. *Lincoln: A Novel.* New York: Random House, 1984.

Vidal, Gore. "Those Whom the Gods Would Disappoint They First Make Charming." *Books at Brown,* vol. 35–36, pp. 1–10. Providence: Friends of the Brown University Library, 1988–1989.

Vidal, Gore. *United States: Essays, 1952–1992.* New York: Random House, 1993.

Villard, Henry. *Memoirs of Henry Villard, Journalist and Financier, 1835–1900,* 2 vols. Boston: Houghton Mifflin, 1904.

Wallace, Sarah Agnes, and Frances Elma Gillespie, eds. *The Journal of Benjamin Moran, 1857–1865,* vol. 2. Chicago: University of Chicago Press, 1949.

Waller, John O. "Charles Dickens and the American Civil War." *Studies in Philology* 57, no. 3 (July 1960): 535–48.

Walpole, Spencer. *The Life of Lord John Russell,* vol. 2. London: Longmans, Green, 1891.

Warren, Gordon H. *Fountain of Discontent: The* Trent *Affair and Freedom of the Seas.* Boston: Northeastern University Press, 1981.

Watterston, George. *A New Guide to Washington.* Washington, D.C.: Robert Farnham, 1842.

Weed, Harriet A., ed. *Autobiography*

of Thurlow Weed. Boston: Houghton Mifflin, 1883.

Weik, Jesse W. *The Real Lincoln: A Portrait*. Boston: Houghton Mifflin, 1922.

Weinberg, Albert K. *Manifest Destiny: A Study of Nationalist Expansion in American History*. Chicago: Quadrangle, 1963.

Welles, Gideon. "Capture and Release of Mason and Slidell." *The Galaxy* 15, no. 5 (May 1873): 640–51.

Welles, Gideon. *Diary of Gideon Welles*. Beale, Howard K., ed. 3 vols. New York: Norton, 1960.

Welles, Gideon. "The History of Emancipation." *The Galaxy* 14, no. 6 (Dec. 1872): 838–51.

Welles, Gideon. *Lincoln and Seward*. New York: Sheldon, 1874.

Wellesley, Sir Victor, and Robert Sencourt. *Conversations with Napoleon III: A Collection of Documents, Mostly Unpublished and Almost Entirely Diplomatic, Selected and Arranged with Introductions*. London: Ernest Benn, 1934.

Wheen, Francis. *Karl Marx*. London: Fourth Estate, 1999.

White, Ronald C., Jr. *A. Lincoln: A Biography*. New York: Random House, 2009.

White, Ronald C., Jr. *Abraham Lincoln's Greatest Speech*. New York: Simon & Schuster, 2002.

Whitney, Henry C. *Life on the Circuit with Lincoln*. Boston: Estes and Lauriat, 1892.

Whitridge, Arnold. *Men in Crisis: The Revolutions of 1848*. New York: Charles Scribner's Sons, 1949.

Williams, Frank. "John Hay and Abraham Lincoln: A Retrospective." *Books at Brown*, vol. 35–36,

pp. 11–22. Providence: Friends of the Brown University Library, 1988–1989.

Wilson, Douglas L. *Honor's Voice: The Transformation of Abraham Lincoln*. New York: Knopf, 1998.

Wilson, Douglas L., and Rodney O. Davis, eds. *Herndon's Informants: Letters, Interviews, and Statements About Abraham Lincoln*. Urbana: University of Illinois Press, 1998.

Wilson, Douglas L., and Rodney O. Davis, eds. *Herndon's Lincoln*. Urbana: University of Illinois Press, 2006.

Wilson, Edmund. *Patriotic Gore: Studies in the Literature of the American Civil War*. New York: Oxford University Press, 1962.

Wilson, James Grant. "Recollections of Lincoln." *Putnam's Magazine* 5, no. 5 (Feb. 1909): 515–29.

Wilson, James Harrison. *The Life of Charles A. Dana*. New York: Harper & Brothers, 1952.

Wilson, Rufus Rockwell, ed. *Intimate Memories of Lincoln*. Elmira, N.Y.: Primavera Press, 1945.

Wilson, Rufus Rockwell. *Washington: The Capital City and Its Part in the History of the Nation*, vol. 2. Philadelphia: Lippincott, 1901.

Winger, Stewart. *Lincoln, Religion, and Romantic Cultural Politics*. DeKalb: Northern Illinois University Press, 2003.

Zakaria, Fareed. *From Wealth to Power: The Unusual Origins of America's World Role*. Princeton, N.J.: Princeton University Press, 1998.

Zakaria, Fareed. *The Post-American World*. New York: Norton, 2008.